T
Great War at Home and Abroad

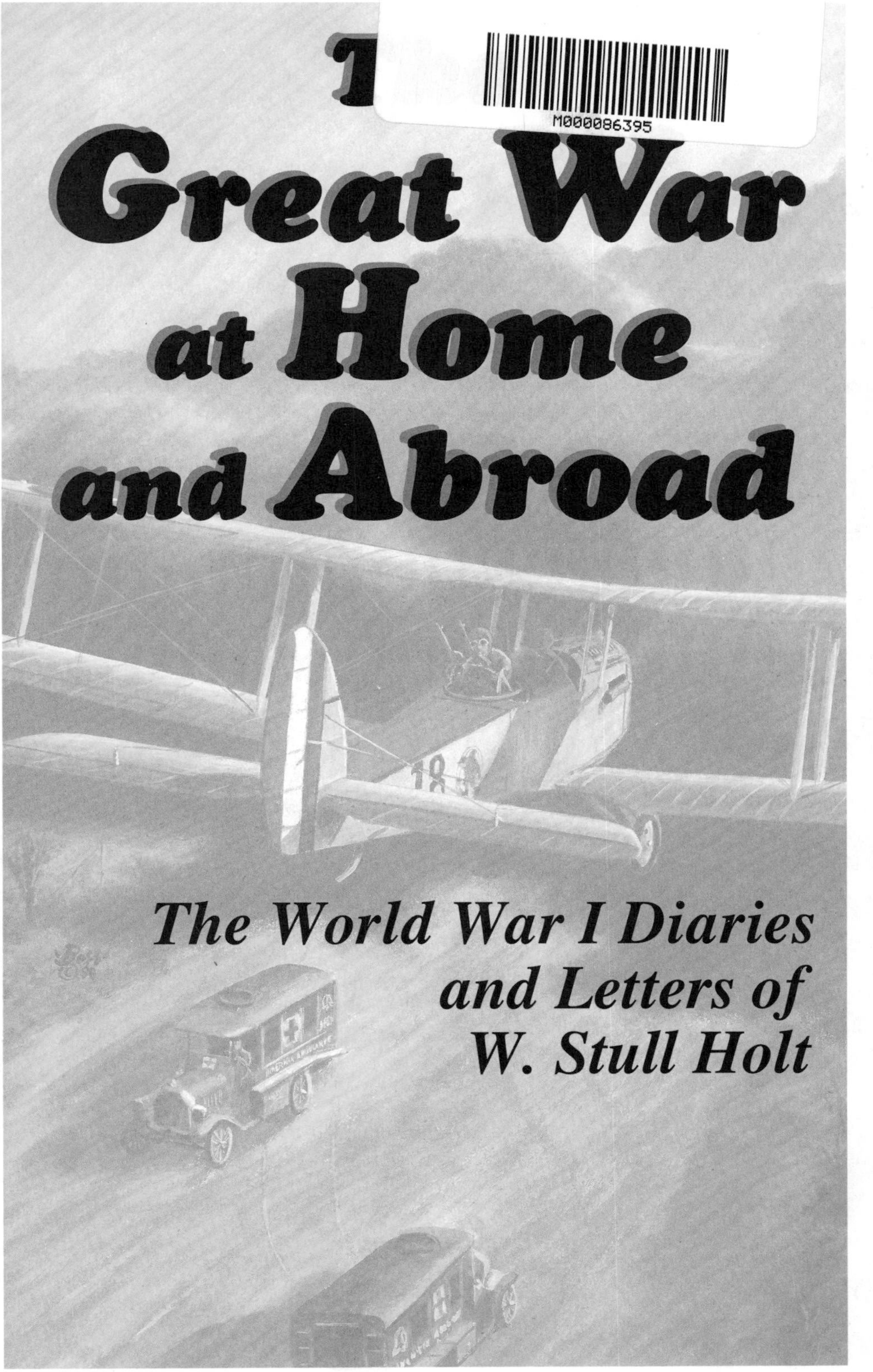

The World War I Diaries and Letters of W. Stull Holt

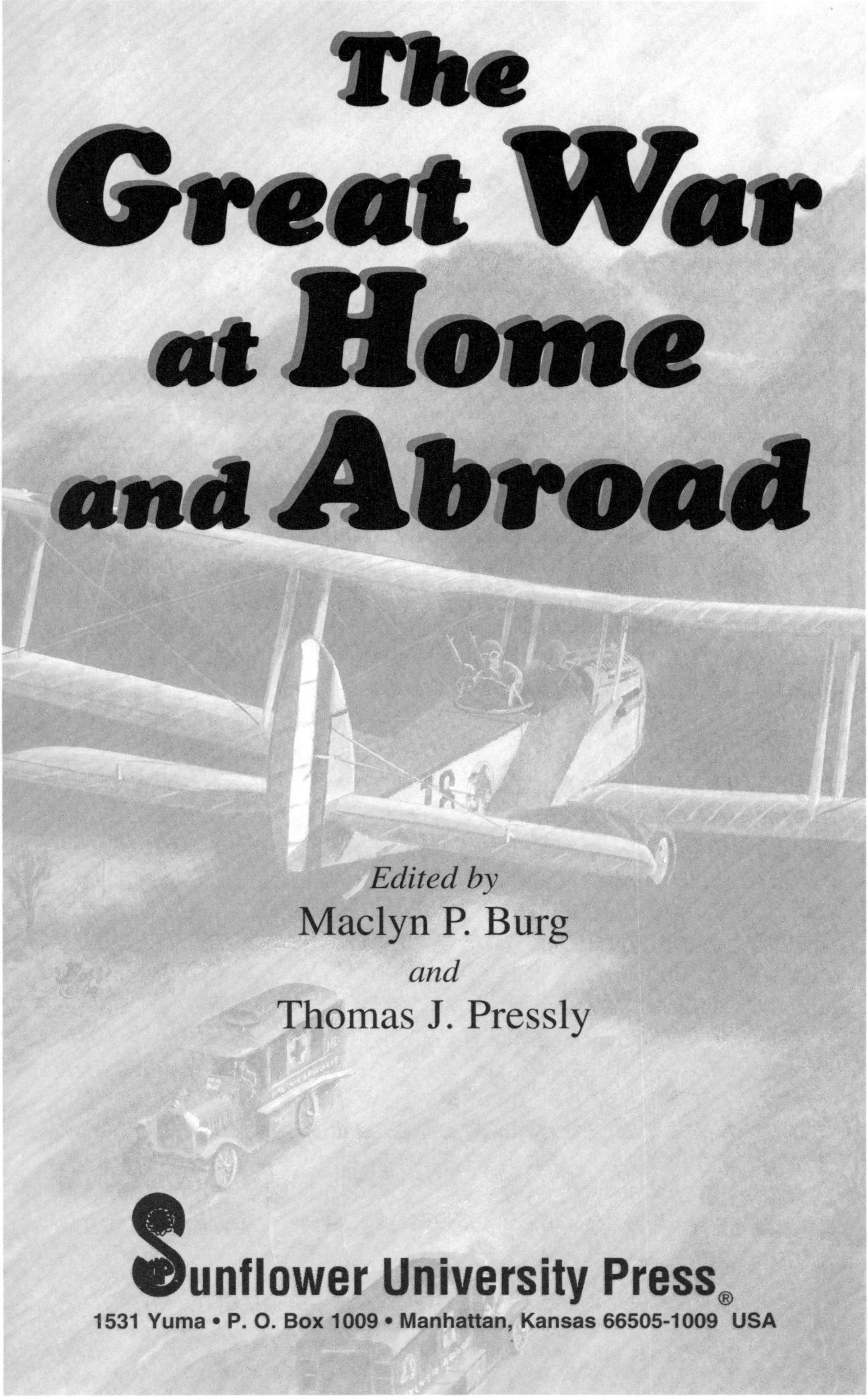

The Great War at Home and Abroad

Edited by

Maclyn P. Burg

and

Thomas J. Pressly

Sunflower University Press®

1531 Yuma • P. O. Box 1009 • Manhattan, Kansas 66505-1009 USA

Printed in the United States of America on acid-free paper.

Cover by Mike Boss, Hill City, Kansas.

Layout by Lori L. Daniel

ISBN 0-89745-222-4

Sunflower University Press is a wholly-owned subsidiary
of the non-profit 501(c)3 Journal of the West, Inc.

Dedicated to the Memory of Two Remarkable People:
Our Mother and Father, Lois and Stull Holt

Jocelyn Holt Marchisio
Enid Holt Dolstad

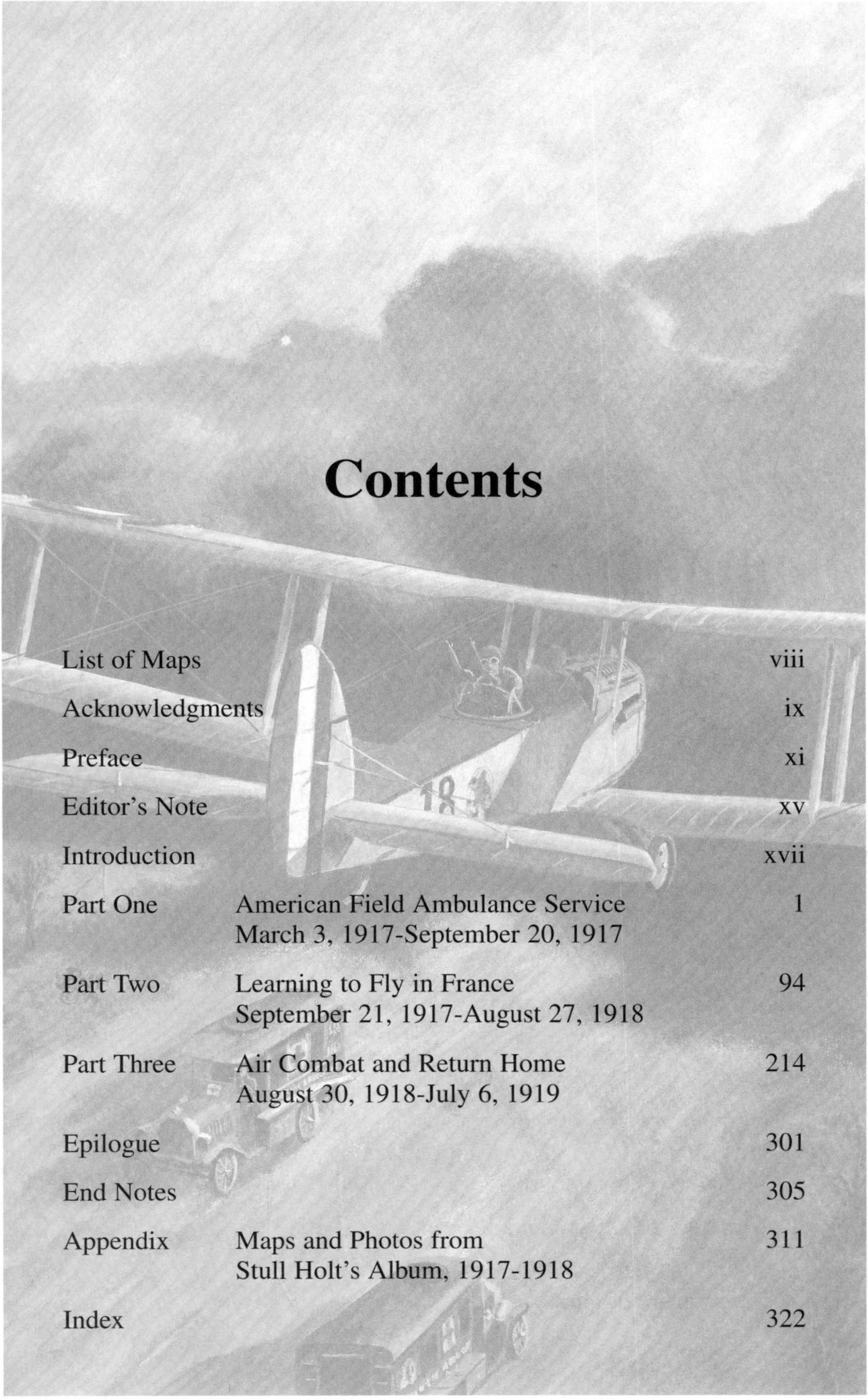

Contents

List of Maps		viii
Acknowledgments		ix
Preface		xi
Editor's Note		xv
Introduction		xvii
Part One	American Field Ambulance Service March 3, 1917-September 20, 1917	1
Part Two	Learning to Fly in France September 21, 1917-August 27, 1918	94
Part Three	Air Combat and Return Home August 30, 1918-July 6, 1919	214
Epilogue		301
End Notes		305
Appendix	Maps and Photos from Stull Holt's Album, 1917-1918	311
Index		322

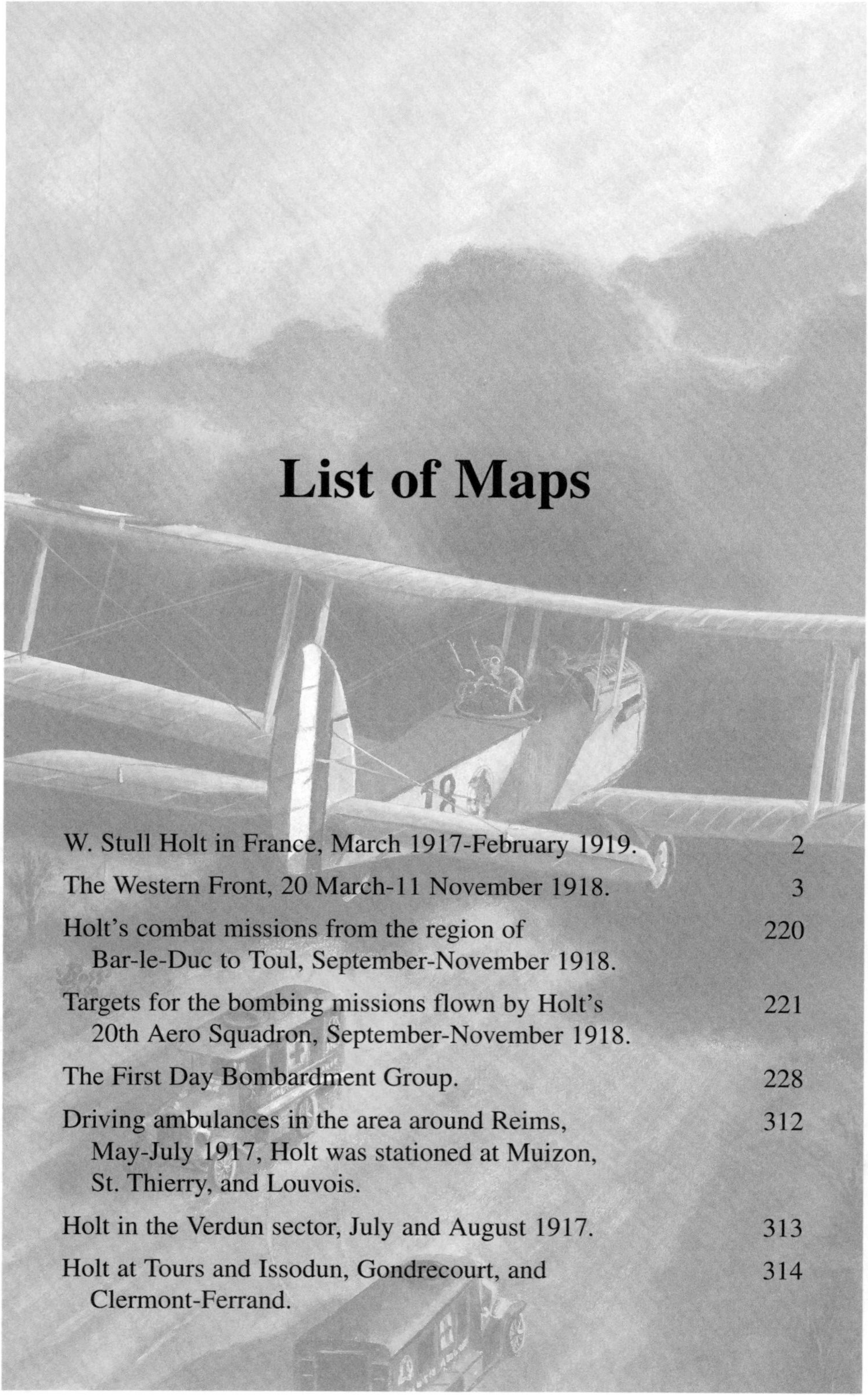

List of Maps

W. Stull Holt in France, March 1917-February 1919.	2
The Western Front, 20 March-11 November 1918.	3
Holt's combat missions from the region of Bar-le-Duc to Toul, September-November 1918.	220
Targets for the bombing missions flown by Holt's 20th Aero Squadron, September-November 1918.	221
The First Day Bombardment Group.	228
Driving ambulances in the area around Reims, May-July 1917, Holt was stationed at Muizon, St. Thierry, and Louvois.	312
Holt in the Verdun sector, July and August 1917.	313
Holt at Tours and Issodun, Gondrecourt, and Clermont-Ferrand.	314

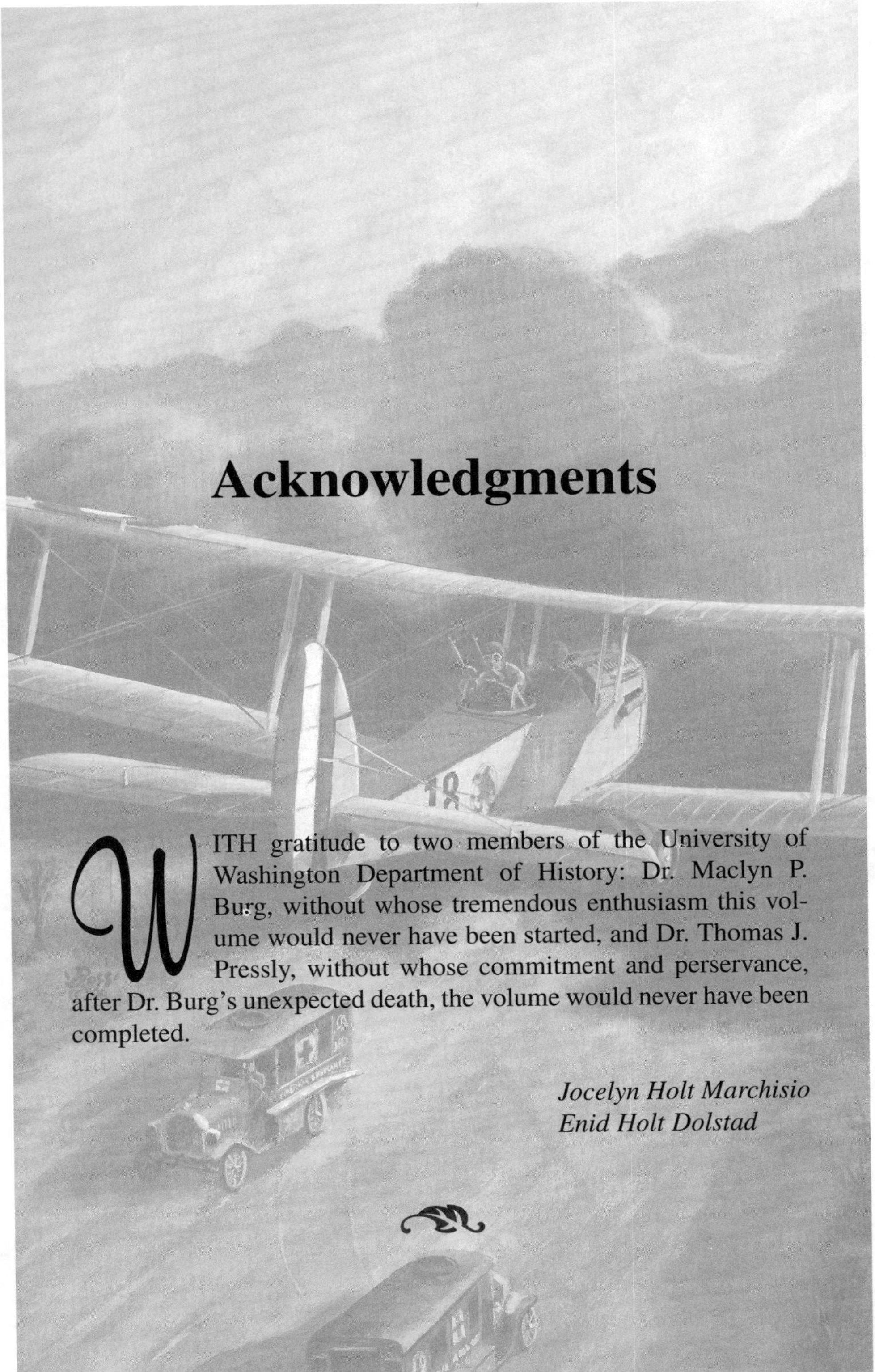

Acknowledgments

WITH gratitude to two members of the University of Washington Department of History: Dr. Maclyn P. Burg, without whose tremendous enthusiasm this volume would never have been started, and Dr. Thomas J. Pressly, without whose commitment and perservance, after Dr. Burg's unexpected death, the volume would never have been completed.

Jocelyn Holt Marchisio
Enid Holt Dolstad

Preface

THE idea for this book originated with the late Maclyn P. Burg, and he did most of the editing for publication. He transcribed all of the W. Stull Holt World War I papers, producing a typescript of approximately 1,000 pages which has been deposited, along with the papers themselves, in the University of Washington Library. Shortly after selecting the entries and completing the manuscript, Maclyn Burg unexpectedly died — before arrangements had been made for its publication. At that point, Dr. Burg's wife, Patricia, and W. Stull Holt's daughter, Jocelyn H. Marchisio, asked me to take charge of the text and see it through the publishing process.

At the time of Dr. Burg's death, I already had some familiarity with the manuscript. Dr. Burg and I had met W. Stull Holt, at approximately the same time, in the late 1940s and early 1950s — when Dr. Burg was an undergraduate at the University of Washington. In the autumn of 1949, I became a faculty member of the University of Washington Department of History, when Holt was the department chair.

Upon the recommendation of Dr. Robin Higham, president of Sunflower University Press, the manuscript was reduced by 20 percent. I have also added maps and photographs, which Dr. Burg and I had talked about, but which he did not have sufficient time to collect and prepare.

Thus, this book is primarily the work of Maclyn Burg, with the described additions and subtractions. My part in the project has been sustained by my longstanding friendship with both Stull Holt and Maclyn Burg, and I hope that the book will stand as a memorial to both of them.

I wish to thank a number of individuals for their assistance in the preparation of this volume, and I am certain that Maclyn Burg would have wanted to do the same. He would have wanted to thank first his wife, Patricia, and their children for their sympathy and support of his effort to document Stull Holt's World War I experiences. So, too, I wish to thank my wife, Cameron, and our children for their interest and cooperation in my task of completing the book. Both Dr. Burg and I received valuable aid from many persons associated with the University of Washington. Transcription of the Holt materials, advice, and other help came from members of the non-academic staff of the Department of History, especially from Suzanne Young and Edward Kamai; in addition, Stacy Waters of the University's Center for Advanced Research Technologies guided me in scanning the entire work. Both Dr. Burg and I relied upon, and benefitted from, the transcribing and typing skills of Judith Skow of Snohomish, Washington.

The colleagues of Dr. Burg and myself on the History faculty have provided encouragement and support throughout this project, and in particular, Jim Gregory, Jon Bridgman, and Ray Jonas responded helpfully to our various requests. Holt's former students who have provided aid of many sorts over several years include Jerry Clubb, Warren Cohen, Larry Gelfand, and Bob Skotheim. Alan D. Toelle, whose interview with Holt was published in 1980, shared with Dr. Burg and myself his impressions of Holt and of the aircraft of World War I; he also generously supplied some photographs of the airplane (#7 of the 20th Aero Squadron) in which Holt had flown combat missions. The editors at Sunflower University

Press, President Robin Higham, Publisher Carol A. Williams, and Editor Nancy Vesta have all been knowledgeable, patient, and efficient.

Finally, Dr. Burg and I were both aware that a primary debt of gratitude was due to the members of the Holt and Crump families who preserved letters, journals, photographs, and other materials from their lives during the First World War. Two present-day members of those families, Jocelyn Holt Marchisio and Enid Holt Dolstad, the daughters of Lois and Stull Holt, granted Dr. Burg and myself unrestricted access to the family papers and have supported this project from beginning to end. Without their enormous assistance, this book would not have been possible.

Thomas J. Pressly
February 1998

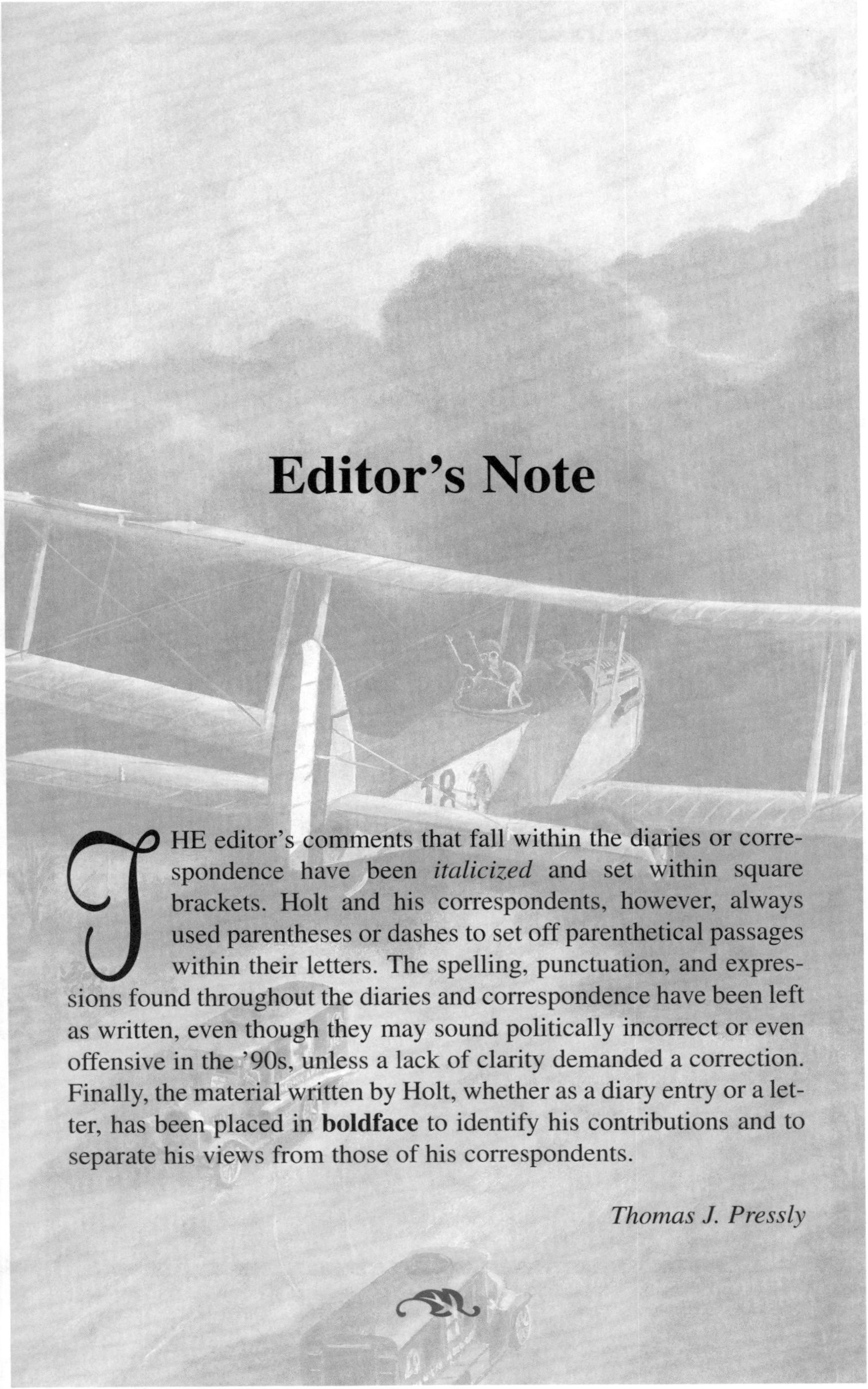

Editor's Note

THE editor's comments that fall within the diaries or correspondence have been *italicized* and set within square brackets. Holt and his correspondents, however, always used parentheses or dashes to set off parenthetical passages within their letters. The spelling, punctuation, and expressions found throughout the diaries and correspondence have been left as written, even though they may sound politically incorrect or even offensive in the '90s, unless a lack of clarity demanded a correction. Finally, the material written by Holt, whether as a diary entry or a letter, has been placed in **boldface** to identify his contributions and to separate his views from those of his correspondents.

Thomas J. Pressly

Stull Holt wrote on the back of his photograph, to his parents: "To the home folks from their little boy who looks grown up but isn't."

Introduction

W. STULL HOLT (1896-1981) sailed for France in late March 1917 to join the American Ambulance Field Service (AAFS). He had entered Cornell University shortly after the outbreak of World War I in August 1914. Why did this upper-middle-class, intelligent, Ivy League student leave college and volunteer for service in France before the United States entered the combat? Patriotism, idealism, and desire for adventure all played a part in his decision to go overseas. He ardently supported the Allied war effort, and he supported it in activities that involved danger to himself.

A considerable body of Holt's personal materials have survived: 144 letters that he wrote from France to his family and fiancée; 221 letters that he received in France from them and his friends; two diaries and four one-act plays that he composed in France; a thick stack of wartime picture postcards; numerous French theater, opera, and ballet programs; menus; several military technical manu-

The surviving 7 of the original 28 flying officers of the 20th Aero Squadron. The photo was taken at Maulan, November 11, 1918. From left to right: 1st Lieutenant J. Y. Stokes, Observer; 1st Lieutenant W. Stull Holt, Observer; 1st Lieutenant Sidney Howard, Pilot; Captain Cecil G. Sellers, Pilot and Commanding Officer; 1st Lieutenant Donald H. McWhirter, Pilot; 1st Lieutenant L. P. Keopfgen, Pilot; and 1st Lieutenant Gardner H. Fiske, Observer. Stokes and Sellers were awarded the Distinguished Service Cross for extraordinary herosim.

Holt Collection

als; and an album of photographs taken during his service in France.

From these varied materials we can trace Holt's wartime career, beginning with his departure for France on *La Touraine* to take up an assignment with Section One of the American Ambulance Field Service. His first driving experiences on Ford Model T ambulances — "flivvers" — came on the Champagne front; but his most significant work was carried out near Verdun during the French summer offensive in 1917, where he was gassed and awarded the French Croix de Guerre.

When his six-month contract with the AAFS was completed in early September, Holt enlisted in the American Air Service and was sent first to Tours for ground school and primary flying instruction and then to Issoudun for advanced flying training. He applied for observer training on March 9, 1918, although he had won his pilot's wings, and received further instruction in gunnery, photography, bombing, and communications.

After training, First Lieutenant Holt languished and fumed for months in several nonflying jobs, including the command of a battalion of Chinese laborers. Many American airmen experienced frustration as America tried to bring its military forces into action in the spring and summer of 1918. Finally, in September 1918, almost a year to the day after Holt left the Ambulance Service, he was assigned as an observer-bombardier-gunner to the 20th Aero Squadron of the American 1st Daylight Bombardment Group.

Because Holt saved the letters he received from his fiancée, friends, and family, we are given the opportunity to see the world of 1917-1918 through their eyes. We are privy to the wartime activities, attitudes, and perspectives of an extended American family on both sides of the Atlantic. As might be expected, the perceptions of the war by those on the homefront in the United States did not always match the outlook of Holt. Many of Holt's correspondents were women of various ages and backgrounds, including his mother, fiancée, and two sisters. The richness and diversity of the Holt wartime papers are reflected in the following brief sketches of the *dramatis personae* of Holt's extended family during his months in France in 1917 and 1918.

Lois Crump, his fiancée: Lois and Holt had met at Highland Lake in the summer of 1914. When Holt was admitted to Cornell the following autumn, the two began to correspond. Lois

Lois Crump, fiancée, and, after February 12, 1921, wife of W. Stull Holt. *Holt Collection*

enrolled as a student at New York University and was a student at Cornell later, after the war, but never graduated. During the war, she secured a job in the Bureau of Standards and moved to Washington.

Mr. and Mrs. Byron W. Holt, Stull Holt's parents: Mr. Holt was employed as manager of the investment department of Goodbody & Company, a post in which he carried the responsibility of writing the firm's monthly market letter. He also served as editor of Moody's Magazine. Born in Ohio in 1857, Byron Holt possessed a dry and caustic wit and was an enthusiastic, amateur tennis player of considerable skill. Mrs. Elizabeth Holt was born in 1859 in Dublin, Ireland, and married her husband in 1891.

Paula Holt, Stull's older sister: A graduate of Columbia University's Teachers' College, Paula taught public grade school in Brooklyn. When America entered the war in April, Paula was 23 years old. Her fiancée, Newton P. Selover was commissioned as a naval officer and assigned to an off-shore naval patrol craft based at Annapolis, Maryland. Paula went to Annapolis to join him. The young couple appear to have married, secretly, in March of 1918.

Elizabeth Holt, Stull's younger sister: She was 17 in 1918 and a bright and observant high school student. In the summer she was in love, or thought she was, with a freshman at Brown University whom she had met at Highland Lake in 1917. Her engagement to Kendrick Brown — a boy "of good American Farmer Connecticut Stock," her mother once said — was not viewed seriously by Mrs. Holt, but this relationship ultimately became the innocent foundation for a scandal in the summer of 1918.

William Dudley Smith, Holt's best friend at Cornell: He was several years older than Holt, but both were members of a Cornell fraternal association called "The Janus Club." Smith was a law student when the war broke out and constantly tried to get into the war, but his poor eyesight, his German ancestry, or some other circumstance, always prevented him from serving. We are the beneficiaries of his inability to find a military organization willing to take him, for his letters from the homefront are detailed, entertaining analyses of America's wartime opinion.

Marjorie Mallory, a YMCA staff member in Paris: She comes to our attention late in this collection of papers and diaries. Bill Smith mentions her to Holt on October 22, 1918. Holt seems to have told Smith that "loneliness, distance, [*and*] a pretty little radical" had conjoined to complicate Holt's life.

Lew Wallace Springer, an Air Service friend: Holt viewed the son of Dr. Frank Springer, a well-known New Mexico paleontologist, as one of his three best friends. He held "several different kinds of degrees . . . is a member of the bar . . . must be rich as he has a Pierce Arrow [*motorcar*] to play with . . . a wonderful aviator of the careful, exact, dependable type." Springer was five years older than Holt and held a law degree from George Washington University. Wallace Springer was an

The Holt Family: standing, from left, Byron W., Elizabeth, Paula, and W. Stull. Seated Elizabeth G. Kinsella. Photo taken in the spring of 1919.
Holt Collection

observer — like Holt — where being careful did not prevent him from stopping a bullet with his shoulder, just before the war's end. He survived the wound and the war.

Lesley Byrd Simpson, also an Air Service friend: The third of Holt's best friends, Simpson had been born in St. Louis, Missouri in 1891, one of six children. In 1905 the family moved to Pasadena, if Holt was correct in his understanding of Simpson's background. After graduating from grammar school, Simpson secured a high school education in between the jobs he took to help his family. Ultimately he entered the University of California, Berkeley, and became an air cadet for basic aviation ground school when America entered the war. He went overseas and completed his advanced flying training in France, where he met Holt and Springer. Springer and Simpson appear to be Holt's first contact with men from the Western United States. He found them to be impressive, saying to Lois that the Westerners always seemed to be "real men." "Simy," Springer, and Holt went to the western European front and into aerial combat at about the same time, but in different squadrons. Simpson also finished the war safely.

Since Holt's friends and family members wrote so many of the letters in the Holt Papers, the reader can savor the individual reactions of those homebodies to the war. Their reactions are not always similar to those of Holt, who thinks that rotogravure photos of New York's social elite "doing their bit for the War," were the epitome of bad taste. Of course, his family may have thought so, too, but they did not see their own homefront activities as being at all similar to the activities of New York's high society.

Perhaps because other papers from the soldiers and airmen of World War I have solely featured men's letters — leaving the women unheard — the words of the women who shared Stull Holt's life can be appreciated. It is interesting to note how Lois Crump handled Holt's moods and whims, his occasional insensitivities, and his long-delayed mention of marriage to her.

VOLUNTEER AMBULANCE DRIVERS WANTED

For the American Ambulance Field Service in France

QUALIFICATIONS. Volunteers must be American citizens, between 21 and 35 years old,*, able to drive and repair automobiles. Expert knowledge is not required, but some practical experience is essential. This can be obtained in a school, garage, or factory before sailing. Fords are used in the Field. Applicants must be able to refer to five or six persons of standing, such as physicians, lawyers, bankers, professors, or business men, who will vouch for their American citizenship, their reliability, sobriety, industry, and amenability to discipline. Only men who are in sympathy with the Allies and wish to help them are wanted. There is no place for sight-seers or adventurers.

* Age Qualification. The age limit given above is a suggestion and is not final. Men older than 35, if in excellent physical condition may be acceptable; men younger than 21 must have the written consent of their parents or guardians.

Term of Service. Minimum Enlistment in Field Service, 6 months. Preference will be given to candidates who are willing to enter the Service for more than six months, or for the duration of the war.

Nature of Service. Men are wanted for Ambulance Work in the Field.

The Field Ambulances serve Dressing Stations and Field Hospitals. There are 20 to 25 ambulances to each section. The sections serve with the French Army. Each Section is under the command of an American officer. All the drivers are Americans.

QUARTERS. Men of the Field Service are quartered together by sections of about twenty (men and cars) —attached to the French Armies at the front. When in Paris the Field Service has its headquarters in a fine old house donated for the duration of the war, at 21 rue Raynouard, to which address all mail for drivers should be sent. The cable address is "Amerifield, Paris."

EXPENSES. Roughly it costs about $300 to remain in the service six months; $500 to remain a year. The itemized expense is as follows:

Transportation from New York to Paris	$75.00
Return Transportation	75.00
Uniform and Equipment	50.00
Incidental Expenses ($15 a month)	90.00

Board and Lodging are furnished free of charge from the time of arrival in Paris.

Incidental Expenses include tobacco, laundry, etc., and may be regulated by the volunteer. The opportunity to spend money is small.

Uniforms are purchased in Paris at a cost for uniform, cap, and overcoat of about $50.

EQUIPMENT. Travel as light as you can. Take with you two pairs good leather driving mittens. Shoes, two pairs; they can't be too good. They ought to be water-tight and well-fitting. One medium weight sweater, waistcoat, or a T-shirt.

MONEY. If the amount is small, your money should be taken in cash (French gold or paper); if the amount is large, in a draft or letter of credit, preferably on Morgan, Harjes & Co., Paris, or Monroe, Paris.

PROCEDURE. 1—Write for application blank. 2—Send in this application form, properly filled out. 3—As soon as you are accepted you will be notified. 4—Be vaccinated. 5—*Be inoculated for typhoid.* Your physician will tell you how to proceed. Inoculation requires about three weeks. Accepted applicants should take with them to Paris the doctor's certificate showing that the regular prescribed inoculation has been given. 6—Get two dozen photographs 2½ x 2½ inches, unmounted and on a light background. These are for your passport and your military passes. 7—Get your birth certificate, or, if that is impossible, get an affidavit of your birth from some member of your family. 8—Apply for a passport. (See below.) 9—Report at the New York Headquarters one or two days before sailing to receive (*a*) a letter to the French Consul General, who will visé your passport free of charge; (*b*) a letter to the French Line, which will grant a reduction of 25 per cent in the price of your passage. *This office will reserve passage for you;* (*c*) a letter of [illegible] Committee in Paris; (*d*) letter in French accrediting you to the Service.

PASSPORTS. The State Department requires a letter from the Headquarters of the American Ambulance stating that the applicant is engaged in the service of the Ambulance. The letter will be sent after the preliminary correspondence. Application for a passport should be made to the clerk of the Federal Court of the District in which the applicant resides.

INQUIRIES AND CORRESPONDENCE should be addressed to Henry D. Sleeper, American Ambulance Field Service, Lee, Higginson & Co., 40 State Street, Boston, Mass., Telephone Main 5400; or to William R. Hereford, Headquarters American Ambulance, 14 Wall Street, New York, Telephone 3954 Rector.

This Service offers an opportunity to do a work of conservation well worth all the sacrifice it may involve. Since the beginning of the war we have carried over [illegible] wounded. The Americans engaged in it are of the highest type, and are gaining the gratitude of the Allies. These young men, representing the true spirit of the United States, are rendering a service to their own country. The international importance of the work of the American Ambulance is recognized not only here, but in Europe. The French Government, as tribute of their appreciation, have eighteen times cited our sections and section leaders for distinguished service, have conferred upon fifty-eight of our men the Croix de Guerre *for bravery, and upon two the [illegible]* Médaille Militaire, *the highest honor for military valor in France.*

An example of an American Ambulance Field Service (AAFS) poster is included here from the Holt papers. It may be the document that made solid his resolve to volunteer. Terms of service and costs the volunteer was expected to bear are noted, though Holt seems to have avoided some or all of these costs on the grounds of economic hardship.

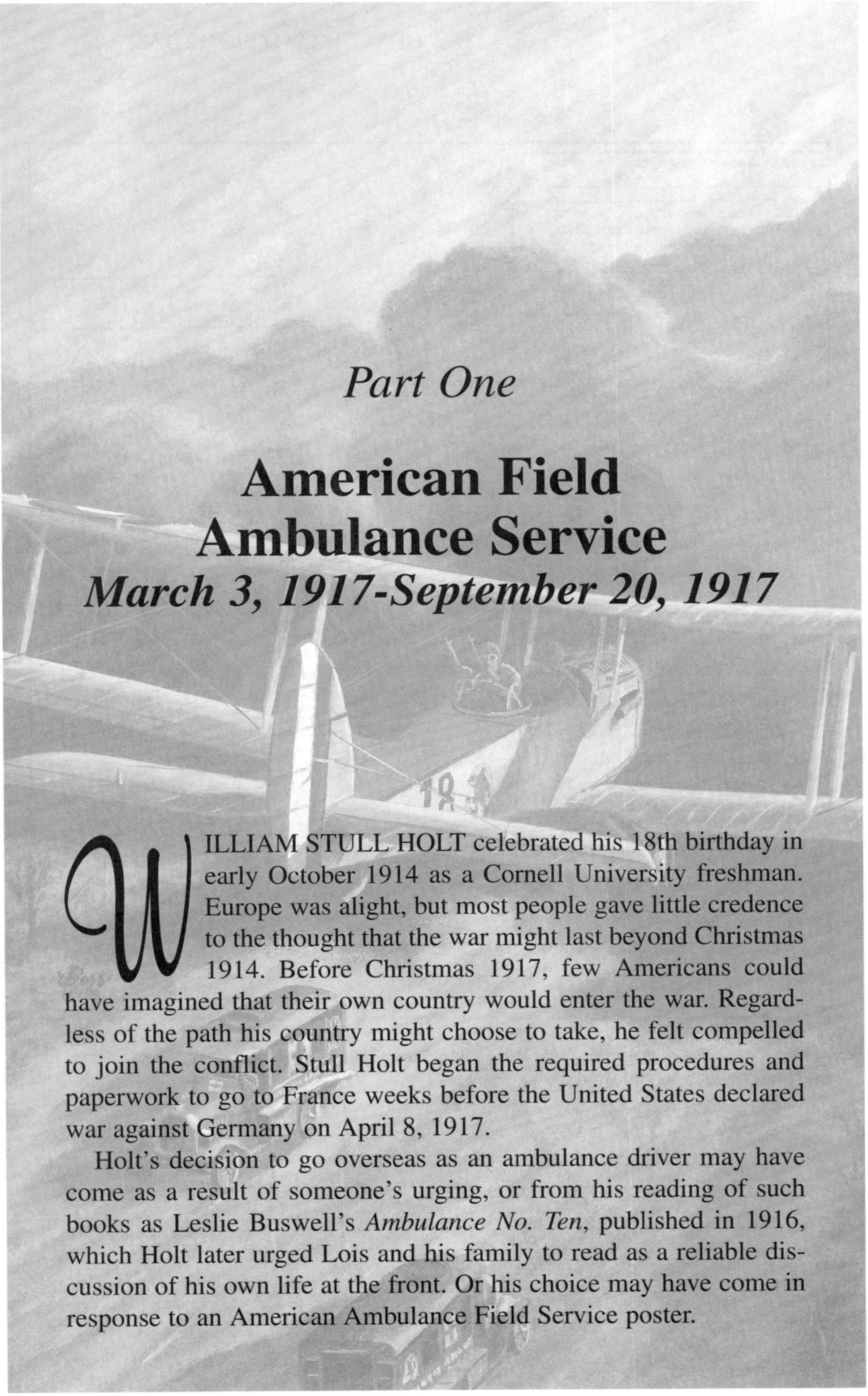

Part One

American Field Ambulance Service
March 3, 1917-September 20, 1917

WILLIAM STULL HOLT celebrated his 18th birthday in early October 1914 as a Cornell University freshman. Europe was alight, but most people gave little credence to the thought that the war might last beyond Christmas 1914. Before Christmas 1917, few Americans could have imagined that their own country would enter the war. Regardless of the path his country might choose to take, he felt compelled to join the conflict. Stull Holt began the required procedures and paperwork to go to France weeks before the United States declared war against Germany on April 8, 1917.

Holt's decision to go overseas as an ambulance driver may have come as a result of someone's urging, or from his reading of such books as Leslie Buswell's *Ambulance No. Ten*, published in 1916, which Holt later urged Lois and his family to read as a reliable discussion of his own life at the front. Or his choice may have come in response to an American Ambulance Field Service poster.

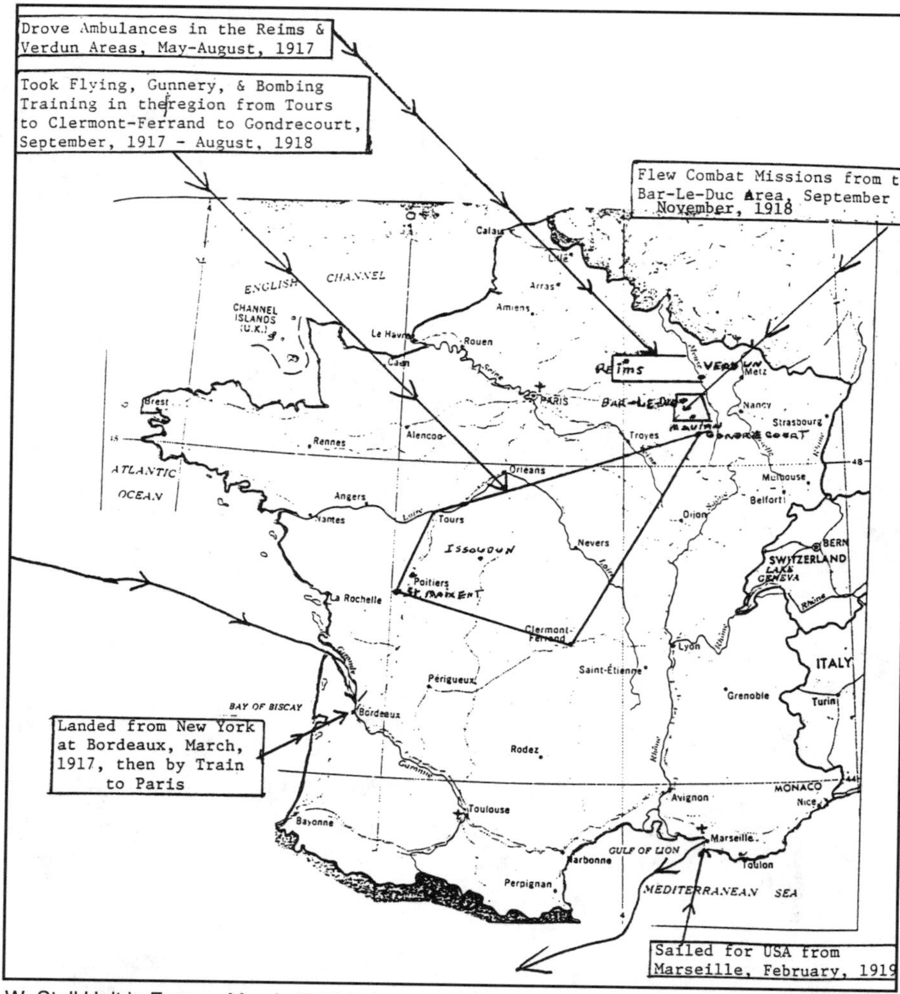

W. Stull Holt in France, March 1917-February, 1919. (Adapted from *Europe Today: An Atlas of Reproducible Pages* (Littleton, MA: World Eagle, Inc., 1985), 129, and used by the permission of the publisher.)

When Stull Holt reached France, a handful of Americans who were Foreign Legion or Ambulance Service "graduates" had already found their way into the Lafayette Escadrille[1] as pursuit, or *chasse*, pilots. Most of the Americans who learned to fly after serving time in the Ambulance Service or the Legion, were assigned thereafter to ordinary French squadrons, which did not possess the notoriety of the Lafayette Escadrille. Americans

From *American Military History*, Army Historical Series, Maurice Matloff, ed. (Washington, D.C.: Office of the Chief of Military History, U.S. Army, 1969), 386.

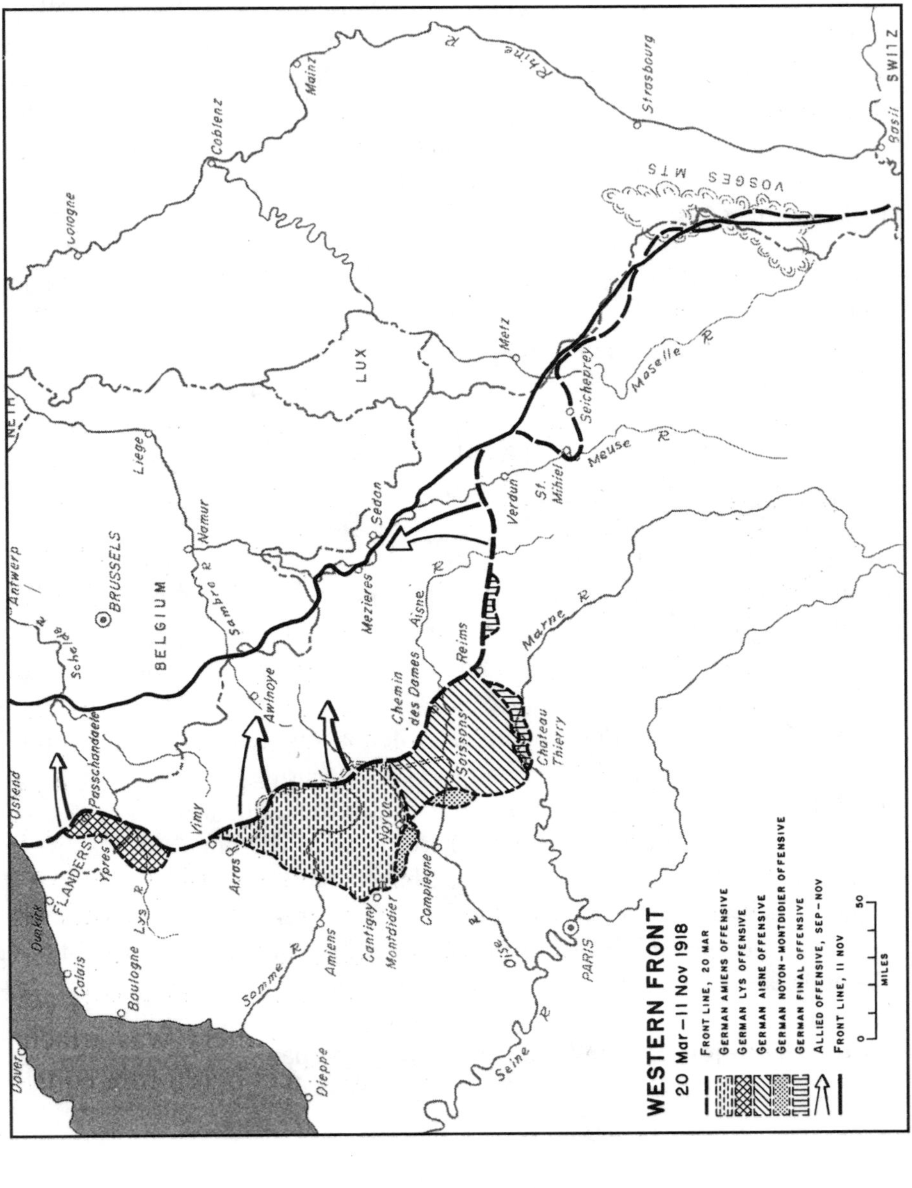

worked unheralded as *pilotes des chasse* or as observation and bombardment pilots.

In the Ambulance Service for six months, Holt drove at the Verdun front in the summer of 1917. The fighting fell short of the vast slaughter that had occurred there the year before, but it was ferocious and horrible. In August 1917, Holt wrote to his fiancée that he must remind himself: "I didn't wound him, nor build this road," in reference to transporting wounded men over execrable roads back to the dressing stations behind the lines.

As readers follow Holt's experiences, they will be introduced to a wartime lifestyle that was typical of the western front in the 1917 summer. Holt and his companions in the Ambulance Service moved in alternation from quiet, rear-area inactivity, which often left them bored and fretful, to the intense terror of negotiating wretched roads, at night, under constant artillery fire.

The wounded, the sad detritus of 20th century warfare, were slung into canvas stretchers, four to an ambulance, and other men, the so-called "walking wounded," clambered aboard wherever there was sufficient room to hold them. The Ford Model T ambulances were underpowered and poorly sprung for their task; the roads were macerated by the constant stream of horse-drawn artillery and the iron-shod wheels of supply wagons, and by the solid-rubber tires of massive, motor-driven *camions* (trucks). The roads, congestion, and shellfire combined to create nightmare journeys under the best of daytime circumstances. The trips at night were an almost unendurable hell for drivers and wounded alike.

Stull Holt's luck ran out in August when a fragment of a German poison gas shell struck his helmet and gas mask, tearing both from his head, leaving him stunned and choking in the gas cloud. His seatmate dragged Holt to a nearby dressing station where medical personnel took steps to neutralize the gas and save his life. Shaken badly, Holt returned to his vehicle hours later and continued to drive. The French government recognized his courage and determination by awarding him the Croix de Guerre. His fiancée and family were thrilled with his war cross, but Holt made light of it.

Now, let us join Holt in March 1917, as he prepares to leave for France.

March 5, 1917

W. Stull Holt, Esq.,
408 Stewart Ave.,
Ithaca, N.Y.

My dear Boy:

The Red Cross having asked for my consent for you to go to France for six months as an ambulance driver, I hereby give such consent. If, however, I thought that there was much risk of life, I would not of course wish you to go. I assume from your statements and from what I have read about the Red Cross service that the risk of life, once you are in France, is not great.

Your loving Father,

Thursday Morning [*March 8, 1917*]

Dear Lois,

You're not sore, [*are*] **you? I am. Because of the presence of 500,000,000 typhoid bacteria in my arm.**

Tomorrow I bid good-by to Ithaca and wend my way homeward. I had expected to leave here several days ago but couldn't break away. . . .

I expect to sail on March 17. Will give you the details when I see you which will be soon, but not too soon for

Stull

American Ambulance Field Service Fund
March twelfth, 1917.

My dear Mr. Holt:

. . . We will send to our New York office, money sufficient to pay your way from New York to Paris, buy your uniform, equipment in Paris, incidentals on board ship and leave you an allowance for almost five months. We will, before the end of that time, send you the remainder of your $300.00. . . .

Very sincerely yours,
E. E. Whalen

Saturday eve. [*March 16, 1917*]

Dear Stull,

The last you saw of us was in the pouring rain at the end of the pier. We stood until we could not see anything but the outline of the ships and then headed for home at least your mother, Paula, Eiz. & Newton Lela & I did. Mother and Enid went to see "A tale of Two Cities."

Mrs. Batcher went out after Lela & I got home so we had the house to ourselves. I wandered around for a while and then finally gave way to a grand old weep. Am not ashamed of myself either. Don't tell anybody this — will you? . . .

Wednesday -Thursday —

. . . Your service to France is now service to the U.S. also, Stull, so do your best. Good luck —

L. O. C. O.

DIARY: [*Approximately March 19, 1917*]

It is a strange world I am going to viz to-night the third night out. . . . I went down to the hold and saw them stoke coal. It was done by Senegalese, thin square shouldered and ragged. The heat wasn't so bad as the darkness and the cramped quarters. The steerage quarters are an awful hell-hole, dark so the eyes are strained, dirty, smelling of the slaughter house and garbage. The beds are double decked hammocks made of burlap in which the people sleep in their clothes with a dirty blanket on them.

We are now in the war zone. The only differences are the life boats are extended ready to drop, the rail is down back where our gun is and there are no deck lights and all portholes are covered up. Ocean traveling is not what it is cracked up to be. This is not a palace afloat. The constant jerking prevents easy reading or writing. The cabin is too small for comfortable arrangement of clothes and outfit. There is no place to lounge.

. . . Last night was the first night in the real war zone. All the rafts were untied and all lights out. We tried to make ourselves excited but didn't succeed very well altho some of the fellows slept in their clothes. I didn't. The early part of the evening Doc and I leaned over the railing and watched the phosphorus and the stars while we talked. Later

Miss Mingame, Bill Richards, Coulter and I sat in steamer chairs and chinned [*talked*].

Very windy and rough today. The waves swept all the front deck. We are told to sleep in our clothes or to stay up and everybody has to be up with lifebelts on at 5 o'clock. I can't seem to be properly excited the way the situation demands, altho I am laying my clothes out in readiness and have loaded my kodak. Dr. Ryan blossomed forth with a legion d'honor medal causing much eye-opening among the French officers and others. We got in without any trouble at all from submarines or custom officials, who looked like characters from "Treasure Island." The trip up the Gironde was great, especially when it got dark. The country lay peaceful and prosperous looking on both sides and the river was quiet like a Venician canal. We landed after much singing and enthusiasm by the Frenchmen, about 10 o'clock and all piled in one tram for our different hotels. Bordeaux looks just like what I associate with moving pictures of ancient time. All the houses are stone and come straight down to the narrow sidewalk. The streets were narrow and pitch dark. Jack Coulter, Bill Richards and I walked the streets for a while and then to bed. Next morning I lay in bed much to the disgust of the others who were fussing with military passes, baggage and what not and then had a full 20 minutes to spare. Nearly all the La Touraine passengers were on the train for Paris. The country is very well groomed and beautiful. The houses are all of stone and look at least 3 centuries old. Every once in a while we passed chateaus, prisoners working, cities (Tours, Poitiers, Orleans). I talked with Ryan, all the gang, and a lot with Miss Jocelyn and Miss Mingame. Finally got to Paris, was met and taken to 5 rue Likan as 21 R. Raynouard is full. The house was and is cold and damp as there is no coal or heat and it is the rainy season. The next morning we got our police papers, measured for our uniforms and found ourselves a little. Certain kinds of food are as scarce as students at college. We get no white bread, butter, milk, cake or pastry. The war bread is edible when eaten with salt. For breakfast oatmeal, hot milk, war bread. For lunch bread potatoes, vegetable, some kind of tough meat or hash, water. For supper vegetables, sometimes meat, some kind of pudding and coffee. We have been around in taxis, metro and walked a bit having some difficulty and fun in being understood. Paris looks more modern than Bordeaux but is full of old stone houses as well as uniformed

Holt with fellow volunteers for French service who had met enroute to France on board *La Touraine*, March 1917. Left to right: Bill Richards, John Coulter, Stull Holt, Dorothy Jocelyn.
Holt Collection

soldiers and all the women nearly wear mourning. Here at the ambulance headquarters things seem to be run badly. The fellows are mostly of the idle rich and not worth much except to parade the streets in fine uniforms. There are over a hundred here and we wont get out for over a month. If things were properly managed we would have been kept in America till the right time. Seventy fellows came on the Rochambeau and they are still standing around while the French carpenters, requisitioned, are building a rough floor for the overflow tent.

Everything is run on similar lines. The good work done by us, about which I am becoming a little skeptical, must be due to the wonderful opportunity and not to the efficiency or merit of the ambulance outfit. The place is overrun with rumors of the arrival of the new cars, the going to the front of certain individuals and of nearly every conceivable subject. One old reprobate woke up when three days out from N.Y. and asked where he was. Kind friends must have shanghaied him. He asked to be fired and was. There is a Princeton fellow whose family thought him still at college. He cabled home for money and was

Holt (right) with another ambulance driver from the United States (Patterson), in the railroad station at Muizon, France (near Reims). Muizon was the location of their first assignment at the front as drivers. (See p. 19.)
Holt Collection

told to "go to work." I am told you don't wear your uniform at the front but any kind of old clothes or else rob a *couche* [*a war casualty who is lying down*]**. I bought a pair of shoes for 58F** [*approximately $11.20*] **which Heywood says are better than you can get in the U.S. for that price. . . .**

Monday Night in My Bunk
[*March 26, 1917*]

Dear Lois,

I've been having a great time after a slight attack of sea sickness the first day out. There were only about thirty nine passengers and some are very interesting. I've heard tales of the war so horrible they can't be comprehended and others so strange they can't be believed. There are several French officers on board but vastly more interesting is Dr. Ryan (an American made colonel in several European armies). He is a Red Cross man, has been on every front since the war began, was

2 years in Mexico before that) and has, as a result seen and done a lot. The fellow I am with most is Jack Coulter. . . . The other night when it [*was*] so dark (it was after 12) no one could see and stop us he and I climbed a mast and pitched and tossed and rolled over 100 feet about the water. To-day has been frightfully rough, the waves swept the entire front part of the boat. I dressed in old clothes and stood out there over an hour. I also climbed the mast to take some pictures but an officer made me get down before I had many.

MOBILISATION. — (Camp retranché de

PERMIS DE SÉJOUR A UN ÉTRANG

M^r. Holt William Stull

né à New York le 2-10-1896

de nationalité américaine

s'est présenté le 31-3-1917

pour faire la déclaration de son domicile et de son identité.

Il a ——— enfants de ———

Il est autorisé à conserver sa résidence à Paris

rue Raynouard n° 21.

Il devra exhiber ce permis de séjour à toutes réquisitions des autorités.

Le Commissaire,

Signalement

Holt's registration with the French government, March 31, 1917, when he first arrived in Paris.
Holt Collection

To-night and to-morrow morning is the worst part of the trip for submarines. . . .

***Au revoir*, Stull.**

This is a real letter (in 3 reels). You'll have to write often to make up for it. I intend to write more news from now on. (I just counted 60 shells fired at a boche avion [*a German aircraft*].) **. . . But now there is so much of interest that even the little I can tell is worth while. (They are still firing at that fellow but none have gone near him)**

You ask me what I am going to do when my six months is up. Well its a long story but to make it short I'll tell you I don't know. But I'm certain of several things. One is that I am going to see the war over. I had made up my mind on that point before I ever set foot in Europe. Another is that I am not going back to the U.S. till *apres la guerre* [*after the war*]. **I have no desire to walk up and down Brooklyn Bridge all night. I expect that when my time is up in this service I will join the aviation corps re-enlist here or go in the Foreign legion. If any American troops do get over here I can be transferred to them then. My mind isn't made up yet. I will learn a lot about the different branches in the next few months and then will be in a better position to decide. <u>Please</u> say nothing at all about my plans for the future even though they are hazy as I have said nothing to the family yet.**

There are a lot of French *sauci* [*sausage*] **up all day. They are observation balloons shaped like a sausage. Last week some boche aeroplanes made a daring raid and set four on fire with shrapnel. The Frenchman in each *sauci* jumped with a parachute but one was burnt to death.**

I am going to save the rest of this sheet for a postscript. Till then *adieu*.

Stull.

P.S.

1. **My address is still the same.**
2. **Read "Ambulance No 10" and "Friends of France"**
3. **The trains and many of the autos have scenery painted on them.**

I have to get this off now if I want it to catch tonight's mail.

DIARY: **4/4/17-4/10/17**

. . . The U.S. has declared war thru Wilsons great message. The papers says there is great excitement home and here. There may be home but not here. It makes one proud to be an American and is a ray of hope to the French. They received it in the same quiet solemn way in which they have. They have plainly been thru a hard winter and are war weary. Sat April 7 we went down to the Olympia, a vaudeville house. The moral conditions are startling surpassing the wildest stories I have heard. Easter morning we went to Notre Dame. It is old and awe inspiring. Tall narrow and long inside. Dimly lighted, beautiful stain glass windows. The service jumped back a few centuries and only for the congregation I could have imagined it a service of the Knight Templars. There was a cardinal seated under a canopy like the ancient kings had before whom and before whose high hat they all kow-towed. In the afternoon Wurster joined us and we went to Versailles. Everything was shut up but we wandered about the gardens where Marie Antonette, du Barry [*Mistress of Louis XV who was executed during the French Revolution for treason*] **etc once trod. Yesterday, 9(th), we went to the hospital at Neiully. Everything is spic and span to the nth degree. They were very empty now but expect to be rushed soon. There are plaster casts there of men shot in the face before and after remodelling. There are hundreds of little experiences I can't put down or remember like the Frenchman who praised us so much at Versailles, the South American we met in the streets, the Austrailian in the Olympic theatre. In a restaurant where I got my first glass of milk and a bad one at that there was an American-French Jew head waiter. Very loquacious and interested in talking to us. He had been in the war at the beginning with the red pants** [*French Hussar unit*], **had been wounded, discharged and now had to go back much to his fear and regret. He was from Pagoda N.J. . . .**

4-6-1917

Dear Stull: —

. . . Things are going fairly smoothly at the office. Our profits were good last month tho I don't know how much yet. The market was strong until Apr 3 — The day after Wilson's war speech — which we will try to enclose. It then turned weak partly because the Administration is considering most drastic war taxation measures, such for instance, a tax of 60% on excess profits of corporations over the average of the last 2 or 3 yrs, greatly increased income taxes, inheritance taxes, increased internal revenue taxes etc. The idea being to favor conscription of wealth as well as of persons. Wall St. may lose some of its patriotism if it has to foot the war bills as they are presented instead of having them charged to posterity, "Its confiscation — outrageous, socialistic, and unheard of," etc. It will spoil our dream of bigger-than-ever war profits.

Please be sure to get proper sleep, diet and baths — when possible — and do not fail to practice deep breathing once or twice a day. Don't try for iron crosses. Your biggest duty is to live and return to your family.

Your loving father
Byron M. Holt

DIARY: **April 10** [*1917*]

It is snowing hard now.

Have been all over Olympia, Folies Bergere, Maxims, Rumplemayers. The morals of the French are on a decidedly different plane from those at home.

Tuesday, April 10, 1917

Dear Lois,

Happy Easter (2 days late but wished just as hard).

I suppose everyone in the U.S. is rushing about like lost souls volunteering for all sorts of things and creating a general disturbance. But they will soon, if they haven't already, settle down and things will be surprisingly normal. I am awfully glad I am over here. At home I would probably have to go in some training camp for 8 or more months and would never see Europe. If the U.S. is foolish enough (which I refuse to believe) to try and raise and send a large force over here soon, it would be criminal. What they need here is food, money and munitions. No considerable force of U.S. soldiers could be ready for over a year but money and food are ripe now.

Because of the declaration of war we will probably be worked much harder. There is a pretty general attitude that the others have sacri-

ficed enough and that the U.S. ought to bear a few burdens. That is where we come in. Some of the fellows are joining the aviation corps. I haven't as yet, the average life of an aviator being 3 months. Besides the state department has said it would much rather we would continue the work we are doing than do anything else.

. . . I go to the front within a week or 10 days. Where I neither know nor could tell if I did.

Regards to all from Stull

DIARY:

Today April 11 [*1917*] **the second day of real spring I am at the hospital printing books for the blind.** [*Before assigned to a unit, soldiers were often given the option of working at nonmilitary jobs while waiting.*]

Thursday-Apr. 12 [*1917*]

Dear Stull,

I was awfully glad to get your letter and to know that you are once again on solid ground. We were all glad in fact — glad that one more American was ready to do his best in upholding the light. I wish right now, more than ever before, that I were a man and could help my country fight. — but being a woman I shall have to stay here. I'll do my best tho — have enlisted my services in several different places and expect to be very busy this summer. . . .

Billy Sunday has started his campaign to stir up New York. I have heard him twice, so far, and he certainly is a wonderful man — I don't care what any one says or what Paula thinks of me for singing in the choir. He gave me a terrible shock at first but now I feel like singing my lungs out to help him. Last night he gave it to the men for the way most of them treat their wives. He said some of them took about as much care of their wives as they did of their mules and it's true — too true of a great many — That doesn't apply to all however.

[*William Ashley "Billy" Sunday (1862-1935), after a career as a professional baseball player, became an evangelist U.S. preacher in the early 20th century. He on one occasion conducted John Barleycorn's funeral (1920) to celebrate National Prohibition.*]

We have started a girls' training class down at school and will drill every Friday afternoon. . . .

The last time I visited Paula — last week . . . I listened to a private lecture by your honored father. It was the first time he ever deigned to engage in any sort of a conversation with me and I didn't breathe for the first five minutes for fear he'd stop — but he didn't — and I learned more in half an hour than I had in a month at school. I guess he thought I was a silly, shallow, thing like most girls are — but I don't want to be that and I don't want him to think that. . . .

Please write often and I'll do the same. Are you going to stay longer than six months? Please don't.

Je vous souhait mes bonnes amitiès [*I wish for you all the best*].

Au revoir, Lois

DIARY:

Today is April 18 [*1917*]**. Nothing much new. . . . have continued printing for the blind every afternoon. Took my driving test for chauffeur's license in the pouring rain. Francis ran over a woman and needed much cheering up and persuasion to stay in the service.**

Thursday April 19, 1917

Dear Lois.

So far I have received from all my countless friends in the States just one letter. But it more than makes up in quality for what I lack in quantity. You mailed it, I think, on Mar 23. The next boat with mail gets in early next week when I expect a whole library. . . .

. . . The traffic is awful in Paris, to drive thru. . . . Everybody does as they please here and some people have funny taste. They drive down and stop on the left side of the street as often as on the right, they pass other vehicles on either side or in the middle, they talk while driving and as all Frenchmen use their hands with their tongues you can imagine the results. . . . I have extinguished myself and gotten a chauffeurs license to drive at the front.

Which I expect to use in a very few days.

. . . My best to all, Stull

Brooklyn, Apr. 20-1917

Dear Boy: —

. . . A letter came to you from Cornell Un. to the effect that you had not either leave of absence or extension of scholarship, and that your scholarship would lapse unless they heard from you in a few days. — The note (type written) was dated — Apr. 6th but was not posted in Ithaca until Apr. 16th. Papa wrote immediately on Thursday, Apr. 19th, the day we got it — He said you had understood that your scholarship would be kept for you; and that he would be glad to defray the expense of cabling to you, if it were necessary to do so. . . .

. . . Dear Boy, — I must say over & over again; take good care of yourself, and keep as strong as possible and God bless you. and keep you in His care.

Your loving mother,

DIARY: **Sunday April 21** [*1917*]

Paris celebrated Americas entrance into the war. We paraded to Washinton's monument where before the assembled multitude who viewed us like we were animals at the zoo a band played songs and an announcement read. Ambassador Sharp was there. From there we paraded down thru the city to the Hotel de Ville. All the way a large crowd followed and down there the people were packed for blocks. . . .

April 26, 1917

Dear Boy: —

. . . We had, or rather, you had an answer from Cornell about the Scholarship. They have now extended it — have given you a leave of absence with extension until Sept. 1917. . . .

. . . These are troublous years before us. The war will end, and a new international life of brotherhood will come, & the world will leap forward into a new era; but we will pass through the growing pains and they may be very hard. — After the war, these millions of men have to be put back into another order of life — they will never live in the old conditions. Then the women, in the industries, what will become of them? — It looks to me as if we would have a time of trouble before we emerge. It is something, however, be be living at the time of one of the world's crises, and you are young enough to live into the reconstructed age, & to take your part in the shaping.

God bless you dear Boy. I ask Him to watch over you night & day.

Your loving mother

Monday April 30, 1917, At Paris

Dear Folks,

. . . A section was supposed to go to the front last week. It went to-day. I was supposed to go in another new section to-day but it won't go till the end of this week. . . . It is awfully hard to wait patiently but that is the biggest lesson the war can teach. Patience is needed more than courage. I was full of chomping energy at first and inclined to grumble when I didn't get a chance to use it. But I think I have learnt my lesson. The whole war is a test of patience. . . .

I'm becoming very "spread-eagle" since I've been over here — the French are small, disgustingly dirty physically and morally, and inefficient beyond all belief. Maybe thats because the war absorbs the best ones. I haven't been to see any of the people whose addresses I have because I haven't had the time nor much desire to.

. . . I read in the U.S. papers that came on the last boat, about how Billy Sunday opened his show. How intelligent people can stomache him is incomprehensible to me. He is playing on hurrah-patriotism now. Why didn't he give money to the Red Cross, wave the flag, and defy Prussian militarism during the last 3 years. Bah! (Crumps please copy)

I won't wait so long before I write again,

Love from Stull

DIARY: **May 1** [*1917*]

After much printing, hearing of tales, and adventures, I go to the front to Section 1 tomorrow. . . . Seventy five new men, 31 from Cornell arrived with much news and letters from home, Lois. . . . Now for the front.

From Muizon, Holt wrote early in May 1917 that the ambulance drivers were "quartered in a Chateau built in 1659. . . . It doesn't mean electric lights, running water or anything like that."
Holt Collection

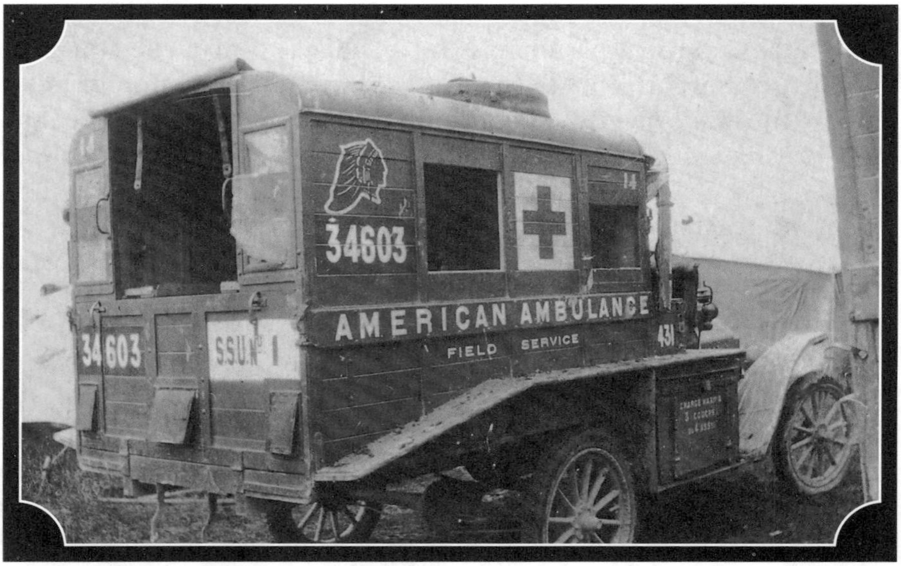

The ambulance Holt drove in France, #34603. *Holt Collection*

DIARY: [*May 2, 1917?*]

Went by railroad to Epernay. From there to Muizon where the section is. The road went thru Reims where I saw the famous cathedral, as well as shell holes in the houses. Passed thousands of auto-trucks and tons of supplies. About a mile from Reims was introduced to shell-fire when 6 or 8 big explosives went off about a block away. We ditched and watched them. I tore my pants getting into the *chameon* [*camion*]**. Arrived at Muizon in time for supper in the tent. Quartered in a chateau built in 1659 with French soldiers and officers: Right near a single-track railroad and station. Boche planes often bomb it and did so after supper when I saw the anti-aircraft guns (100 yards from the house) in action. None of the shots went near the boche but the casings nearly fell on us. There was an awful heavy cannon fire at night. It quieted today May 3 and I sat nearly all afternoon writing a letter under a tree watching the planes.**

The roads are hidden by a solid wall of brush tied in bundles as well as canvass. The autos and trains are painted.

At the Front, May 3, 1917

Dear Lois,

Your letter of Apr 12, the second I've received from you, was received with great joy. I'll write oftener from now on and think the news may prove interesting.

I am with Section 1 the older and best (by common reputation) of the 16 American Ambulance sections. We are situated in the Champagne sector not far from Reims (I saw the cathedral yesterday). The worse fighting of the war has been and is going on not far from here so we will be pretty busy. . . .[2]

We are quartered in a chateaux along with some French officers and soldiers. Some Russians moved out last week. The chateaux is a wonder, built in 1659, as you will agree when you see the picture of it some day. The word chateaux is misleading, it doesn't mean electric lights, running water or anything like that. Of course nobody expects it and nobody gets it. Our bathtub is a little creek that runs about 100 yds in back of the chateaux, and we don't use it very often. My hands are so dirty now that Curtis [*Lois's younger brother*] **would turn green with envy. I know one fellow who didn't change his underclothes for**

3 months and several who had to use gasoline to get clean. But now in the spring and summer things are better besides we are lucky enough to have our creek to go swimming in.

The most interesting, in fact nearly all the, fighting I've seen so far has been aeroplane. The first evening I got here 3 boche planes came over and the anti air craft guns got busy. They must have fired 150 shots in all but though it was spectacular none seemed to go near any of the boche. (Boche is the words always used to designate the Germans.) There is a single track railroad for supplies and a station very close by and nearly every night that's clear, the Boche planes come over on a little bombing expedition. Then the anti air craft guns, some of which are in 100 yds of the house, let loose and we all tumble out to see the fun. The boche fly very high, generally over 2 miles, and frequently you can see a boche way up with a Frenchman ½ a mile above the ground, under him. . . .

It is a wonderful spring day without a cloud in the sky and everything, myself included, throbbing with the joy of life. . . . I could easily imagine myself close to the Garden of Eden if it weren't for the constant thunder of the guns. They keep it up all day long but the real stuff comes at night all attacks are made then and the artillery works overtime. You can't conceive of the noise unless you've heard it, especially when the big boys in the batteries around us start in. Our section (20 cars, French lieut. and American lieut, in command) has done little work for a week or more but there is nothing to do but wait patiently for orders. . . .

[*Stull*]

DIARY: **May 4** [*1917*]

Started work. Went in no 3 (the oldest car going back to the rubbage heap) to Trigny and there got 3 *couchés* (wounded in the frightful cannonade last night and all morning) and took them to Prouilly without any trouble. Missed the hospital road twice but didn't go far (100 yds) either time, Back to Trigny where waited several hours then home to Muizon and supper. The *couchés* never made a moan but lay quiet with a dull uncomprehending stare. [See map, p. 312.]

DIARY: **May 6** [*1917*]

. . . There was activity last night and the paper reports 4000 pris-

oners a little north near Craonne but we had nothing to do all day. . . . The fellows frequently get lost which is not strange considering the darkness, strange roads, traffic, foreign language etc. Jim White on his first night out got lost with his *blessés* [*wounded soldiers*] **and finally landed in a mud ditch with his front wheels on a railroad track. He was afraid a train would come along and ran up and down whistling and shouting for help like a madman. Luckily he wasn't far from some of the other fellows who lifted him out.**

Saw a shell hole (420 [*420mm*]**) about 12 feet wide and tapering down to a depth of 6 feet. Another where the shell didn't explode was about 8 meters deep they say.**

I saw 16 *saucese* up at one time to-day.

Sunday-May 6- [*1917*]

Dear Stull,

. . . I have just been reading the paper which is full of pictures and articles on what women are doing on farms and otherwise. They seem to be working very hard and if the men work as hard we ought to be able to do something in this war —

. . . We have exactly one more week of school and then exams. On June 1st I start work at Eastman Gaines so that I may, as soon as possible, try for a government position —

. . . I have also heard a number of good sermons of "Billy" Sunday — Two were especially good, I have never heard their equal — He told the plain, simple truth in a plain straight-forward way, using very little slang — and acrobatics. I was wishing & am now, with all my heart that you could have heard those sermons — Billy is not half so black as people paint him and if some of the wretches who do all the talking against him would just take the time to go and hear him once — they might change their tune. . . .

Mother read in the paper the other day that women would be needed to take the places of men on the cars, subway etc — so if you hear that I have become a motorman or conductor don't be alarmed — I like to do that if I can't run an auto-

. . . God bless you, Stull, and keep you safe — that is my daily prayer —

Lois —

DIARY: **May 8** [*1917*]

. . . One of the fellows got a N.Y. Sunday Times 3 weeks old but eagerly read. Aparently the states have gone crazy with women's home defense leagues, junior naval recruits, and all sorts of such nonesense. After a few hospital ships return to America and the lists of killed are published they will stop such play and learn that war is a serious business. How serious it takes close contact to learn.

The Russians here were dirty beyond all conception. Their stink was unique. And when people appear dirty to fellows used to the filth and dirt of the *poilius* [*French soldiers*]**, they must be some dirt. They would sit and spit great pools on the floor, staring blankly at our fellows, who would have to kick them on the shins or push them out of the way. . . .**

Wed. May 9, 1917

Dear Lois,

Things have been extremely quiet so far as we are concerned and so I have plenty of time to write. Most of the real interesting pieces of news I can't tell they are *defendu* [*forbidden*]**; which is exasperating when there is anything exciting to tell. Things like names of places, movements of troops, results of attacks, effect of enemy shell fire etc are *defendu*.**

They sent over forty high explosive shells right in our vicinity the other night. None were very near the chateau but several shook it, and some of the eclat (pieces of shell that fly after the explosion like this [*drawing in original*]**) fell near the tent where we eat.**

We can generally tell when they are going to shell a place by the aeroplanes which come over to reconnoitre. When they did so the other day there was an exciting fight with some French planes. They were over 3 miles up and quite far away so they weren't very clear to us but we could follow every move. They would manuvere for position circling around each other and suddenly shoot out straight for the enemy plane with their machine guns popping. Finally one boche plane fell way down, righted for a moment and then dived straight for old Mother Earth. This ended the entertainment as the other boche headed back for their lives p.d.q.

In mentioning the big shells before I forgot to tell about their sound

which has a sinster fascination. It starts with a distant muffled boom sometimes impossible to hear, continues with a combination of whir and whistle that gets louder as the shell gets nearer to you. This part of it is quite terrifying as you can never tell from what direction it is coming and it always sounds as though it were headed straight for you. If it is very loud and near you the best thing to do is to throw yourself flat on the ground as then the *eclat* isn't so apt to get you. Several of the fellows slept on the ground the other night. The trip ends with an explosion or a dull thud if the shell falls in very soft ground and doesn't explode. I can see that it is a great nervous strain and can understand why so many men have nervous breakdowns and suffer from shell-shock. It hasn't bothered me at all yet probably because I haven't seen any men hit before my eyes. That makes a big difference.

I've carried some pretty badly wounded. They all lay still with an amazed, uncomprehending stare. They were fresh from the field, had only been wounded about four hours before. Things are managed this way. Up just behind the lines as close as the auto can go, is a *post de secour* [*poste de secour — wound dressing station near the frontline*] **where the *blessés* are brought by stretcher bearers. Here their wounds are temporarily dressed, which usually means just winding a bandage around. At the *post de secour* we get them and take them 5 to 10 miles back to a field hospital. These are long low wooden shacks with beds in them. Often they have no floor but old M.E.** [*Mother Earth*]**. Here they stay for a short time, part of a day to a week or more, and are then carried to another hospital near a railroad (which they later take to real hospitals far away). This later is called evacuation work. We do little of this as we nearly always have one or more *post de secours* and the large French ambulances do the evacuation work. Just at present we are waiting for a new *post de secour* that's why we are so idle. But, our idleness won't last long and when we work, believe me, <u>we work</u>. You have to find your own way around. Of course in a little while you know the roads and places but this territory is new to everyone of us. All they do is say go to town X — (some funny sounding name) and evacuate to Y — (equally weird). They generally give the general direction but that is all. Then you have to go to X. — Most of the work is done at night and you can use lights in only a few places. The roads are bad compared to anything we are used to in the states but better than I expected and very good in spots. On some roads the traffic,**

especially at night, is awful. There is a continual line of auto-trucks, horses, soldiers, touring cars with officers, and more auto-trucks, great big ones. So you see, with the strange, absolutely dark roads, full of holes and traffic driving isn't exactly easy. The only easy thing is to get lost which everybody does at sometime in his career. Some of the experiences are funny, So far I've not been really lost but drove past a hospital twice, only about 200 yds each time. Then I can't speak French enough to even ask my way anywhere intelligently. I forgot to mention that sometimes the road is being shelled but I haven't had to drive on one yet while it was being shelled.

One of the fellows received the N.Y. Times of Sunday Apr 15 and of previous weeks. We laughed for hours over the pictorial section. But it is not only laug[*h*]able, but disgusting. Aparently the very best society has taken up the war and it is all the rage now. . . . What do they think war is? A new form of summer diversion. It is alright for the women (plenty of the men are likewise depicted but the women are the worst) to have their fun. But it is not alright for the U.S. to dissipate its energy and waste time and money in such foolishness. I assure you they don't need all those brave girls to protect the U.S. from foreign invasion. But what is needed and what they should devote all their energy to is to send a well trained army of men as soon as possible. They could begin good work by sending 10,000 mechanics over here at once, and the next day they could send 10,000 men to drive the auto trucks over here. They are needed badly. So are men to work on repairing the roads, railroads etc.

After a few hospital ships unload in the states, and a great many more men don't return at all, people will forget such nonesense and get down to brass tacks. England had the same experience being troubled with amateur nurses and all sorts of committees at first.

Of course I realize the government isn't behind all this but is doing the right kind of work and as quickly as it can. But it does raise my ire to see how foolish and shallow most people are. If you could only look around here at the front for only 5 minutes you would understand my righteous indignation. . . .

It is now 5 hours later and on re-reading I think I shouldn't have said so much because if I remember correctly you said in one of your letters that you are drilling every week. Keep it up. It will probably do you good even tho it doesn't help in the war at all.

I had a great experience this afternoon. I walked about 4 miles to the highest hill nearby and in an *abri* (trench used as an observation post, really a cave to escape from shells) lay and watched the fight. I could see the French guns around and beneath me shoot and see the shrapnel explode over the German lines. The noise of the explosions was — well easy to be heard and at all times you could hear the whistle of shells, Everything was there — the front trenches far away and hidden by smoke and haze, the communicating trenches protected by barb wire entanglements. A little off to the right was what used to be a little village. We could see it clearly with glasses and it looked like a cemetery in the distance. I don't think a house was standing. The desolation was absolutely complete in large tracts of ground. Nothing or a little stump was formerly a patch of trees. There was no grass as the ground was all turned over by the explosions of shells. The hill on which we were, was a mass of trenches, batteries and observation posts you couldn't go 20 feet without seeing a shell hole.

I just got back in time for supper and this is right after that important function (we had horse meat tonight) so I am still a little dazed and have only jotted down incoherently a few things I saw. . . .

Regards to all from Stull

DIARY: **May 11** [*1917*]

A regiment of several thousand men went by real early in a long seemingly endless line of *chameons*. The boche, signalled probably by the aeroplane we saw earlier, threw some shells nearby trying to hit the road. None did but (another just scorched the air) they are too close to be enjoyed properly.

Played a little baseball, then took a wash down at the creek while a few shells screamed by. I saw one throw a geyser of black earth forty feet in the air.

Went and saw a big gun in action this afternoon. It was a 380[*mm*] **naval gun mounted on a railroad track. Along the track were several open graves to absorb the recoil. The shell was run on a little slide from the amunition car behind. With it in the gun were placed 3 bundles of powder. The gun was then locked, the muzzle raised, the car cranked forward and braced, the men left and an officer would look around to see nothing was too near in front, then raise his hand**

and the flame would leap out heating us 100 feet away, the gun would leap backward, smoke come out in clouds and the noise of the shell gradually lost itself over the hills. The shell went 20 km. So said a French officer who asked us when the war would end and when our soldiers were coming over. I took some pictures.

. . . Several boche planes came over the big gun while it was firing evidently to locate it. The 75s [*French 77mm*] **got busy and drove them away. There were over 25 men working on the gun.**

Played a little baseball after supper got up a good sweat then had a swim. It was great.

May 11, 1917.

Dear Stull, —

Papa is telling you most of the local news, so I will go into personalities. Lois was here two weeks ago. We didn't get much chance to talk — but the week or so before that, when I was at her house, we had everything out.

. . . I go to a motor engine class twice a week for three hours at a time and work hard. I have enrolled for motor service and will get a chauffer's in June, when I have taken my state examinations. Then I drive a government truck or something.

Your loving sister, Paula

May 12, 1917

Dear Lois,

. . . This is a birthday letter. . . .

You spoke in one of your letters of wishing to be neither shallow nor to appear to be. It is on that subject that I wouldst hold forth. You are now (I am too) at an age when you can go easily in either of two directions. You can become a student, a thinker, one who takes a vital interest in humanity and has its problems at heart; or equally easily you can fall, as does the vast majority of people, into one of the ruts of life and become a plain everyday citizen, neither thinking about nor understanding nor caring about society's troubles, hence becoming narrow and selfish. From all I know of you, you were meant to be the former and only lacked the stimulus which was sure to come in time. . . .

There are, as I see it, two requisites for a non-shallow person. These are intellectual honesty and intellectual activity. The first you can only get by yourself. In regard to the second I lay at your feet the results of my own slight efforts in that direction. I have found that I got (as is to be expected) a good deal of intellectual activity from my courses at college. But I got more from thinking and discussing with some of the fellows I knew there. I have gotten still more from the numerous people I have met thru my father and who are now my friends as well as his. But most of all was gotten from reading. From what I've seen of your typical day you haven't much time to read. That's the main difficulty about going to a college and living at home. There are always plenty of people to talk to and plenty of diversions, besides the time used in traveling. But you have a little time that could be put to good use. If I only had an hour a week to read in I would spend it on the <u>New Republic</u> [*a reform magazine, established in 1914 in New York City; its stated purpose is: "less to inform or entertain its readers than to start little insurrections in the realm of their convictions"*]. **It keeps one in touch with the thinking world, it displays rare judgment and common sense in its editorials, it is a constant stimulant to thought it — I won't go on or you may think I am exaggerating. Besides I am a fanatic on the subject. I get it out here and have just read the issue of April 21 which has some good editorials on "Morale" "The Second Line of Defense" which you should read.**

Well, that lecture is off my chest. . . .

I have been thinking lately and have reached a conclusion as to why I was and am so riled at the numerous Home defense committees and all such nonsense of which I spoke previously. In the first place it is an awful waste of energy that could be put to better use. But more than that it cheapens the countrys position in my eyes. I like to think of the U.S. as stepping in the war without any fear of physical harm nor personal selfish issue at stake but, with a love of right and justice. Or, as Wilson said, as "one of the champions of the rights of mankind." Just as Lafayette helped in the revolution because he believed in the cause and not because he was interested selfishly.

And then, spoiling that ideal and giving it a narrow, selfish color, come a lot of wild-eyed individuals with their leagues for home defence, which are truly ridiculous as the British and French are protecting us far too well for any danger to reach us. They display, arouse

and are a part of hysterical patriotism. Instead of acting on international motives they try to translate our acts to patriotic ones. I do not believe in patriotism at all, as the word is ordinarily used. I think the time has come for internationalism and that patriotism, especially just after the war when a new cycle can begin, will be a hindrance and a drawback to the worlds progress. . . .

May 15.

. . . The best way I have found to describe the modern army is to think of an angle like this with the man in the trenches at the point and behind him nearly all the nation helping directly or indirectly. Right behind to 10 miles back is most of the army who supply him with food, ammunition, relieve him and take care of him when wounded. Most people think of a soldier as fighting most of the time he is taking care of another who is in the front trenches. And even when he does get in the trenches he has nothing to do but stay in his hole in the ground unless there is an attack on. Here a man is four days in front line trenches, 4 in 2nd, 4 in third and then his whole regiment goes a few miles to the rear on repose. Of course when there are any sizable attacks or activity this rule is broken.

Regards to all, Stull. . . .

DIARY: **May 14** [*l917*]

Still no work to do. Lay around all morning and read a little of Carlyle's History of the French Revolution thinking it ought to prove valuable in these days of actual and threatened upheaval. (Here I was interrupted and went out, to where I'll tell later)

Played a 4 inning game of baseball before it rained. I pitched again albeit I was stiff and we were ahead 22-4. . . .

Episode I

To-night I went with Woody, the lieut and Pearl to Reims in the staff car. Reims, the martyred city, used to hold 120,000 people. In it now lives a few thousand too old to leave or who have nowhere else to go. Whole blocks are nothing but heaps of broken stone and many of the walls standing are empty shells, the interior being blown or burnt

Holt took this photograph of a German plane shot down near Muizon. *Holt Collection*

out. The streets are so dead and quiet that one feels awed like at the tomb of a great man.

The Hotel de Ville, which was destroyed by shell and fire while I have been at Muizon, is a disfigured charred heap of walls.

The famous cathedral still stands much to my suprise as the towers are higher than the surrounding buildings but it is utterly ruined. It is covered by a bewildering mass of statuery. You can look at it for hours and see a new detail every minute. It is now all smashed and chipped beyond recognition or repair. The interior is not anymore and nothing but the battered walls remain. Right in front of the cathedral are two big shell holes with the paving blocks that were blown up, piled around them.

We went into the third rear room of a cafe, the front was all boarded up, and there consumed a bottle of champagne apiece and played a phonograph till it was time to go home.

***[On May 15th, Henri Phillipe Pétain replaced Robert Nivelle as Commander-in-Chief of all Allied forces.*[3]]

At School — Wed. May 16, 1917 —

Dear Stull —

I have just finished an exam in Economics, for which I was well prepared by your father, on Monday evening. Any time I want to cover a whole course in a short time I go to him and listen to a two and a half hour lecture and zip! I'm prepared. At least it isn't his fault if I'm not. . . .

Au revoir, Lois —

DIARY: **May 18** [*1917*]

Still nothing to do. Worked on the car this morning taking up the play in the steering wheel. . . .

DIARY: **May 20** [*1917*] **Sunday**

There was a great deal of avion activity to-day. The French are aparently standing and fighting so we saw some good air fights. Little dragon flys manuvering around and going tut-tat-tut with their *metraillueses* [*mitrailleuses — machine guns*]**. Once in a while when in a bad position a plane would dive straight down thousands of feet twisting and turning over as he fell. . . .**

DIARY: **May 21** [*1917*]

The boche came over during our ball game and got two *sauceses*. They went up or rather came down in flames and clouds of black smoke, on the second we made out the observer after he jumped with his parachute but the flaming mass fell on him and must have killed him by suffocation, burning, or by burning his parachute.

May 23, 1917

Dear Lois,

. . . I've been putting a good deal of time on my bus you, as a chauffeur, will understand when I tell you that I cleaned the carbon out of piston and cylinder heads, ground the valves (neither of which had [*ever*] **been done before by the looks of them) took up some play in the steering wheel and did a few other jobs too numerous to mention. . . .**

I read "Kitchener's Mob" by J. N. Hall [*Kitchner's Mob: The Adventures of an American in the British Army*, 1916] **to-day. It is very interesting and gives a good picture of a little of trench life which is awfully hard to comprehend 3000 miles away. I had my hair clipped to-day and I could qualify as a student at Sing Sing easily in that respect. It is the best way to keep out tenants. . . .**

Au revoir

May 25

. . . When I speak of shell fire and shells landing not far away (most of them now are nearly 500 yards to the left of me, I guess) you musn't think it is particularly dangerous. I know I thought and most people home do yet that being that near or nearer to any shell fire however small was terribly dangerous. But it isn't. The soldiers pay no attention at all to it, no one does after learning and becoming used to them. Of course if they hit right they could do damage but the earth is large and one man occupies only a very little portion of it. Shell fire this far away (about 1½ miles) isn't one of the horrors of war.

War is horrible enough. How much so no one person can comprehend fully even tho he had been all thru it and seen a lot. I am just beginning to grasp a little of it. You should read the book I mentioned on page 1. It isn't at all a horror story but is very cheerful. But you learn enough to imagine some more.

When I first went into the outhouse with its roof half blown off and its wine cellar safe far below, a dead man, since buried with a little wooden cross over him was lying in a stretcher outside. He was a typical *poilu*, short, stocky and all the rest of it. A bandage was around most of his head but some parts showed thru. Blood had run down over the stretcher and there was a clot of grey matter which I concluded were a part of his brains. His nose and mouth were covered with blood that had run down and coagulated there. He needed a shave very badly and what made him look worst was the mud, his hands were caked with it and his chin looked as if it had been rubbed in.

. . . Here I quit. Regards to all. I hope you can read this rapidly written scrawl. I have no pen or ink.

As usual, Stull

May 24, 1917.

Dear Stull,

Your first letter from the front came yesterday — creating great excitement in this house. Your people will probably get one soon, but we called your father up this morning in case his didn't arrive to-day. Sometimes they come three or four days apart. He seemed very much pleased and was glad to hear from you even indirectly. . . .

Your chateau must be a wonder. I'd have to see it and explore. Doesn't it make your blood boil when you think of the German's destroying all those old relics of past ages?

. . . I am glad your plans for the future are hazy — You had better keep them so for a while any way and as regards the aviation corps you had better keep them hazy forever. Your Mother would worry herself sick and since there are so many other things to do you had better choose something in which you have a chance to live a little while longer. You are a very inconsistent person, I think. On one page you talk about the joy of living and on the next you talk about joining the aviation corps. If you really feel that you have lived long enough and have done all you could in this old world to make it better [,] why I suppose you might as well die in the air as on land.

. . . *J'ai oublié presque tout que je sachais de francais. Je veux que vous M'aideriez et ecriveriez une lettre francaise.* [*I have forgotten almost all that I know about French. I wish that you would help me and write a letter in French.*]

Bien à vous, Lois.

DIARY: **May 25** [*1917*]

Now at the chateaux at St. Thiery [*St. Thierry*]**. The village, like all French villages, is entirely of stone. The road or street is lined on both sides by a solid stone wall dotted every little space by a side of a house with a few windows. . . . St Thiery has no civilians aparently. Some soldiers are quartered there. . . . The buildings themselves are all smashed up, showing the interior of the solid walls and the arrangement of the houses.**

The chateaux where I am must have been a wonder. On one side you get a beautiful view of Reims and the cathedral, in front across a little valley is Brimont. The house is surrounded by walks, and here

and there a statue or colomn, Now some trenches, evidently reserve, are dug thru them. The grounds everywhere are scarred by shell holes every few feet.

The house itself is badly damaged but not so much but that you can recognize its former beauty, especially of the high vaulted room with a statue of Jean d'Arc in it. You cannot show yourself at any of the front windows or go in front of the chateaux because it is constantly watched by the boche and a few shells follow every appearance. They are going and coming intermittently all around anyway. By going down into a patch of trees on one side and then in front you get a good view of the front lines and Brimont. . . .

The strangest thing is that not a person can be seen. You hear the guns, see the shells burst, see the trenches but never a human being.

I go from here down to the Route National 44 and drive to the left within rifle shot and plain sight of the Germans. I don't go in the daylight unless there is a very urgent case. The four posts are along the road in caves. I will sleep to-night in an old wine cellar under one of the servants houses near the chateaux. It is very deep, dark and damp and long, and full I'm sure of interesting ghosts.

. . . I ate lunch with 5 French doctors by a little light on the little landing going down in the wine cellar. They couldn't speak English so we didn't say much.

. . . Right inside the door is a work bench where a man has the pleasant job of making little wooden crosses. He keeps at it steadily. Not far away is a meadow where his little crosses go. . . .

As soon as it got almost dark I started out with one doctor for the 3rd post for some wounded. We went much nearer the trenches than I thought[,] being within less than 800 yards distant. Lots of shells exploded around us but most of the noise was, I think, from our guns which lined the side of the road and shot over our heads. The star shells which would light and hang over the trench 100 ft. up casting a light somewhat like an arc light. In hasty side glances I could see the trenches plainly but I didn't waste any time. The road was lined by caves and *abri* and after we had gone some distance the doc asked for the post which we found in the side of a little rise. Here all was bustle and excitement, finally I was told to go on to the 4th post and get 1 *couche*. I went on for 1 kilometer of the worst road so far. I would hit

shell holes, you couldn't see them, and "old Henry" would buck like a horse. At the last post there was no *couche* for me, the doctor said, and then said more which I couldn't understand. Finally he asked me if I spoke German and there with real and shell stars, with the noise of guns, with the helmeted me[*n*] rushing around, the French doctor and I spoke German. He said "Es war schrecklich aber man must es tun" [*It was frightful but one must do it*]**. I then went back to the 3rd post. Got 2 *couches*, one of whom moaned every other minute, and a doctor. We started on passing solitary men on foot and hitting shell holes. I was straining to put all my attention on the road and car. The doctor thought I had passed the road to St. Thiery and I had to stop while he ran up the road to find out. I proved to be right and we went on reaching St. Thiery alright. There the *blessés* were looked at and I went on to Chalons. There was more traffic now and I had to take sharp turns in the narrow village roads. I missed the last turn and after passing a regiment going to the front (the searchlights were crossing each other making a spectacular scene) I found myself in Trigny. I went to Chalons found the hospital without much difficulty. It was a long shed with dirty floor and wooden skeleton frame to put the stretchers on. A fine looking priest came up and comforted my *blessés* in a fine way. I crawled out of the hospital grounds on a horrible road and got back to St. Thiery without trouble at passing some more troops and some trench mules. There I slept peacefully in the wine cellar. . . .**

Sunday May 27, 1917

Dear Lois,

You can't complain that I don't write often. But I can complain about you. and hereby do. I am at work again, another 24 hour shift our new work, in a little village. One-half a mile away are two more fellows and we help each if there is need. There has been none so far.

. . . One of the fellows here yesterday had his car hit by *eclat* that killed one of his *blesses*. There are too kinds of *blesses*, *couches* or *assis* (I dont know how to spell it but it means "lyers" and "sitters") We can carry 3 *couches* or 5 *assis* at a trip.

It is very quiet now, hardly a sound. . . .

May 28

This morning I saw two French aviators bring down a boche. It was only about ½ mile away and we all ran to it. The two Germans in it weren't killed. The engine was put out of order by the French fire and the plane fell turning round and round. One of the boche had a leg broken and the other was cut about the face and hands and shaken a little. They were both big, young fine looking men. I'm enclosing a little piece of one of the wings. You'll notice that the outside is painted blue to look like the sky. . . .

Yours as ever, Stull

Ithaca, N.Y., May 27, 1917

My dear Stull,

I learned for first time today your address, hence this note, other letters will follow.

I am deeply depressed by the feeling of being out of things. Two days after the declaration of war I volunteered for the navy, — preferably the torpedo boat destroyer flotilla but was rejected for near-sightedness. Then sought to get into the Yeoman service in the navy, i.e. clerkship, but the recruiting officer HELD that while my eyes were good enough to enable me to be a student in a University and a some-time instructor, yet my eyes were not good enough to enable me to keep accounts on a torpedo boat, i.e. of the number of beans and cans of soup left in the commisary. This finikiness gives me a pain in the royal rectum. . . . Then I went down to a down-town garage which is offering to train ambulance drivers for France, worked at the tricks for two weeks to get at least a beginner's knowledge of the art, passed Dr Munford's physical exam. test, got a Schenectady alumnus to guarantee me funds, — and by the Deity, was rejected because my Mother was born in Germany fifty years ago, and came to the U.S. at the age of six.

I am horribly depressed by the whole affair. How any man of any imagination or gumption can live through the ordeal of staying at home during this conflict is beyond me. My plans are then: I can't get in the military forces proper on account of my eyes I am going down to Washington to see Doc Lunn our congressman, and see if I can get in the clerical service with the army that is going to France if such plans peter out I am going to work on munitions at the General Electric Co. and put aside $150

— which I can do in a couple of months — and come over to the scene of things anyway. Once in France I ought to be able to get into the motor lorie [*lorry*] game or at least on munitions. Enough of this, goddamn the luck.

. . . Now, what is going on in the University? Cornell granted credit for the term to all students who went into agriculture, or the military forces, or industrial work related to the military forces. About 3000 have left, — 500 I should say for the army and navy. 250 Cornell men are at the Officers' Training Camps. Of course, University men being in general the nation's most ignorant, you don't hear the war even discussed here. And if it is mentioned, you never hear a real reason for the war given. Now what is our old Uncle Sam thinking about? Our nation is not taking this war seriously. If they even disapproved of it, such thinking about it would be encouraging, but they neither approve nor disapprove it. There is just oceans and oceans of patriotism — of the "Stand-When-'America'-Is-Sung" kind, of the kind which makes auto-owners put a flag on the radiator, and applauds Gen. Pershing's pictures at the movies, but that's the extent of it. Don't judge the nation's attitude by what goes on in N.Y. City. Being a coast town it is more interested than the rest of the country, but even its interest is mostly newspaper interest. Les Jayne writes me that there is absolutely no interest in the masses of that city, tho from the newspapers you would think N.Y. throbbed with fervor. The whole thing may be summed up by this: I was at a navy recruiting meeting in N.Y. the speaker made an eloquent plea; everybody nodded their heads, say "yup," and went home.

. . . What will be the upshot of it all? I think interest will slowly rise, as in England. When the news papers begin to tell what our troops are doing in France, how our little 25000 are beat[*ing*] the Kaiser, how the subs got a few of our torpedo boats, when the caus[*u*]alty lists begin to coments [*commence*], then interest will rise. If the allies can hold at a year, they will find America a veritable demon out to get the Kaisers scalp. But as yet we're a Prometheous Bound.

. . . Luck and regards from

Bill

DIARY: **June 1** [*1917*]

It is now half past four in the morning. I have just been down to the

post but there were no *blessés*. It is fairly light. Last night we saw a great spectacle, a small *tier* [*tir*] ***de barrage*** [*artillery fire, gunnery barrage*] **about 2 miles to our left. It was so foggy we couldn't see the shells land over the trenches, could only hear a distant rumble. But the French guns were enough. They were far enough away so we didn't get a sharp report but got a muffled exhaust. It looked as if hell were pent up close to the earths surface and at every little distance some one would open a crack and the flames would leap out with a great flash. It awed one and filled him with animal fear the land animals have when they see lightning. Up over the trenches were numerous star shells and joined with them were signals, red rockets, 3 lights on a string etc. Several times we heard the tut-tat-tut of a machine gun showing that somebody saw some men over the top or thought they did. But there was very little of this and after about half an hour it all quieted down.**

After it we sought slumber but it wasnt as easy to find as usual because the rats were very active. One aroused Pat's great indignation by jumping on his bunk and running across his body. Wrote home.

Friday June 1, 1917.

Dear Stull,

. . . The letter you wrote on May 9th got here yesterday. . . . This letter was censored. It is the first that has been. Nothing was blotted out but it had been opened and sealed up again. . . .

You certainly are mad about the fools in the U.S. aren't you? Don't you know that those people exist everywhere. They have to see all sorts of horrors and have terrible things happen to them before they will wake up. Let them drill & charge with fixed bayonetts if they want to. It will keep them out of mischief. The government is not wasting time on them. I don't consider myself one of them even tho I did drill. Our drill consisted of setting up exercises etc. and I dont believe one of us ever expected to shoot a gun. It was good for us and I dont care what you say — it helped to rouse enthusiasm down at school and I'd like to bet that more fellows became interested in the war and were pushed on to take steps toward doing something — enlisting — because the girls were interested and enthusiastic — I can shout and scream and encourage all the boys I know to stand by their country but when it comes to doing the shooting — I resign — I couldn't shoot a cat — even if I were able to hit it I couldn't do it — so how could I shoot a man?

You say they need engineers — well, we have sent some and are preparing to send more. I know a young man who is training right now and expects to go soon. You must not be too impatient with the U.S. Remember that she is all tangled up in politics and she is having a pretty hard fight. If people were only big enough to forget their darned politics at a time like this — but they dont seem to be.

. . . Mother was just talking to your father over the phone. He told her that we have been defeated in a naval battle with the Germans. [*The first American flotilla had arrived in Europe in mid-May.*[4]] The English & American ships sailed into the North Sea to Heligoland [*a small North Sea island*] and were defeated there. The first step toward waking the people up seems to have been taken — He also said that a hospital ship with American wounded has come home. You'll see a change pretty soon in the actions over here. . . . until next week,

Au revoir, Lois — . . . .

DIARY: **June 2** [*1917*]

A boche aviator came very low, so low nobody beli[*e*]**ved him to be boche over us to-day. Two French planes cut off his retreat and we hear he was captured.**

DIARY: **June 3** [*1917*] **Sunday**

. . . In the evening after supper we had a great sight. A boche aviator above us was being chased by a couple of spads [*Spad VII, a French fighter biplane that was the forerunner to the American Spad XIII*[5]]**. These were joined by more until they looked like a swarm of misquitoes around him. Before they had all come up he began leaving a trail of white smoke behind him. He was much larger than any of the French. Suddenly he started to fall with white smoke pouring out of his motor. The spads dived down alongside to be sure it wasn't a ruse to escape. But he was gone and turned upside down as he fell. When a few hundred yds up one of the two men in it fell out and lit about 50 yds from where the plane fell. It was about half a mile from us**

and we ran there. The crowd was awful and uncontrollable by the officers. They rushed on the plane ripping it apart for souvenirs. I could hardly see the plane but got several pictures of the crowd, fighting good naturedly over it. French planes flew down close over the crowd and excitement reigned supreme. I got an aluminum oil tank which I hope to make into several rings. Curtis got the hat of one of the boche (both were smashed all up) from a *poilu* for his Ingersoll watch. . . .

June 3, 1916. [*1917*]

Dear Lois,

. . . I go to Paris on permission in 2 months or so. At least I am supposed to. In the French army you get theoretically, 7 days permission every 3 months. When and if I do I shall certainly look up Dr. Corry, and if I find him the price of champagne will go up 2 fr. [*approximately $0.39*] **a bottle. . . .**

The conductors in Paris are nearly all the wives of men who used to work for the railway company. They earn 3 fr 50 c. [*approximately $0.68*] **a day.**

I am afraid I wont be able to speak French with you. My vocabulary is a jargon of war terms and most of them slang probably, but I can understand a little. It is awfully funny at times. For instance two days ago I was at post with Patterson. We ate with 4 or 5 *sous-officier* [*lower ranked officers*] **in a dug-out and the conversation was marvelous. Pat altho he has been over here a long time has a knack of mispronouncing the 8 words he does know and of being absolutely unable to understand a bit of French. So he speaks English slowly, distinctly and earnestly but of course they dont get a word of it. I had to act as interpreter and it was some job. The things I couldn't understand they would write, as I can read more than I can get by ear. I told them what we ate in Amerique, how many millionaires there are, how many Fords are made a minute. By the time we got to the "*eau de vie*"** [*the "water of life," i.e., wine*] **(it was awfully strong for French stuff it nearly put me out) Pat was passing around the pictures of several American girls and they reciprocated with those of French girls. Everyone understood the other then easily.**

I have to quit now as I have to go to post to-morrow and must fuss

around my car with some grease. In my next letter I'll tell you about the first *tir de barrage* I saw. It was a small one but a most spectacular sight.

Till then
***Au revoir*, Stull**
Regards to <u>all</u>.

June 3

Dear Lois,

This is just a little personal, me-and-you note to go with the other. Your letter came today, Sunday, and — well here I am leaning against [*a*] tree, which is one of the many tall ones that line the little river. Most people would say I was alone but any one with the proper imagination could see that there was someone with me, a medium sized outdoors girl who looks a little thin as if she were trying to do too much and as if she didn't know enough to sit back and look around to see what a nice place this old world is after all. Anyway here we are and here we have been all afternoon. And altho the same thing has been uppermost in our minds all the time we have both carefully avoided it. Just why I don't know but we talked of things generally, or small talk about the trees and flowers nearby or as most of the time were silent. Talk is cheap and words no matter by whom said are inadequate for some things. When you add to that the fact that I am a faltering, ignorant word-fashioner at best, you will understand the silences.

However, I for one was very contented and dreampt a lot about the future and how some day I hope to go on another walk, only then anybody without an imagination could see the person with me, and then I will show that someone all the sights around here and the initials cut in a tree. And then we will call at the chateau and tell the people that I was once quartered there *pendant la guerre* [*during the war*] **and they will take us in and give us some vile tasting light French wine, which we have to take to be polite.**

And then when we drive up the little road leading from the house, it is lined by trees, you will slip your hand in mine and again tell me what means so much to

Stull

DIARY: **June 4** [*1917*]

I am now at post. Took two *malades* [*sick people*] **to Chalons and there talked half an hour with a couple of English speaking French *poilus*. They as usual started off by asking when our troops would be over here. They seemed disappointed at my guess answer and said the war would be over next winter. That France would be bled to death by then and couldn't continue. They alternated between a determined lofty attitude towards the war and a weak we-have-suffered-too-much-let's-stop attitude. The French army is very tired they said over and over again and from what I've seen I couldn't imagine it otherwise.**

They were older than average and working in the hospital is apt to make one war tired. The bodies of the two boche killed when the plane was brought down last night were there. I looked at the one who wasn't all smashed. He was a tall husky young fellow (30) with a hawk like face. . . .

Just about dark I went out to post with a doctor who watched the dust we made apprehensively and asked me to go slower. At the post I got three *blesses*. After delivering them I slept till 3 and then slept on a stretcher in my car. It had some old blood stains but they didn't prevent good sleep. . . .

Friday-June 8, 1917.

Mon Cher Soldat [*My Dear Soldier*],

Before I beat the next mattress [*as a hospital volunteer*] I'm going to give myself a little rest. Do you see how shakey my writing is? Well that's because the pen is rolling around and bumping against blisters, first on one side, then on the other. Yes, I'm a hard working man just now and it's thankful I am at that. . . .

When I read your last letter I couldn't help smiling in spite of the fact that it was a very serious lecture. It seemed so like an old man talking to his — well — grand daughter. What you say is perfectly true and moreover I know it is — I learned it this winter. The "cut" you speak of nearly swallowed up another stagnant brain last winter, but thank goodness that brain found itself locked within the walls of N.Y.U. before it was too late. Then it discovered that it was a well brain but very lazy, and with a little exercise it might be able to stand on its own two feet and show some people what it could do. It has accomplished a little and I guess the rest will have to come thru reading because, owing to some trouble in this household, I'll have to prepare myself to take a position as soon as possible.

. . . American battleships are off the coast of France. Hurrah! *Au revoir*

Lois.

DIARY: **June l0** [*l9l7*]

Everything very quiet except the fleas and they are making things lively for me. Purdy has crabs and Stout some kind of poisoning so we have lively competition. . . .

I have found the reason for the funny color of some of the horses around here. They were formerly white and have been painted to make them less visible. . . .

DIARY: **June 11** [*1917*]

More flea activity resulting in inspection and complete change of clothes.

. . . This afternoon we were entertained by a little bombing party. We have had many lately at night disturbing the peace of mind of many of the fellows. My easy conscience lets me sleep thru them all. But to-days was in broad daylight. The three boche planes were much lower than usual. They were almost overhead when Ned and I ran out to watch the anti air craft guns get into action. We met Purdy and Pat running full speed with arms waving and yelling [“]bombs.[”] De Ville and another Frenchman were lying in the mud next to a house and other Frenchmen were behind trees. The few bombs lit in the open field with one exception which wounded two men slightly. The planes got out of sight safely. I ran to where one of the bombs had fallen and got some of the *eclat* while it was so hot you couldn't hold it.

DIARY: **June 12** [*1917*]

Read “action front” by Boyd Cable, it is pretty good. My bites are worse and are not bites at all I think. I went to the hospital at Chalons for examination and go there to-morrow for treatment. Am starting a letter home. . . .

June 12, 1917.

Dear Folks,

[*Letter continues on June 13*]

. . . For several days past I have been covered with bites (I thought) They itched a lot and spread so I looked for the fleas and then for other bugs. There are several varieties that are very popular with the fellows. But I couldn't find any or any traces so I came over to the hospital for some salve. . . .

I expect to leave here to-night after supper when my salve will have dried up but I wouldn't mind sleeping here all night in sheets. I'll write again in a few days because I know that, altho I have nothing but a French form of prickly heat, you will worry.

Love to all
Stull.

DIARY: **June 13** [*1917*]

Am writing in bed at the hospital. An orderly rubbed me with brown salve that smarts a little. Gamble with a little fever is two beds away. . . .

A priest came in to see us later in the evening and we had a long talk with him.

June 14, 1917

Dear Lois,

Still in the hospital. It seems I have a variety of little bug (too small to be seen) that gets under the skin and there raises — my anger. . . .

My clothes are being disinfected so when I get up to walk around I wear a French uniform. Its owner is now wearing a wooden suit. I know it will sound strange to you for anyone to wear a dead man's clothes but they have been sterilized. Besides it is not unusual. When our fellows wear thru their shoes they usually go to the nearest hospital and got a pair belonging to someone who now walks with wings. . . .

I expect to leave here tomorrow when I will mail this.

— Stull

. . . DIARY: **June 16** [*1917*]

Still treated fine. A colonel dropt in to shake hands.

Yesterday was a bad day for the section. Woody went flying with Chatkoff and both were killed when the machine fell. I don't know any details yet.

. . . They are going to bury Woody from here to-morrow. The saddest aspect of it is that two lives should be wasted at this time when lives can be put to such good use and lost in such a great cause.

Spony and Steve just brought Woody's body here. They must have had a pleasant ride (it was 50 miles) with him. They say he is smashed beyond all recognition. . . .

They have brought the coffin for which they had to go to Epernay. I've been sitting and thinking, I've done a lot of that over here. This is one of the benefits I've gotten. I am beginning to appreciate many things properly, my friends especially, my happy comfortable life, the reality of things, and I also appreciate that I can't go back to them but must "carry on."

This last is an English phrase made since the war. Like many other and great English achievements it earns my respect.

DIARY: **June 17** [*l917*] **Sunday.**

We buried Woody this morning. With quite a number of officers, a platoon of soldiers and all of us drawn up in front of the coffin under the trees, a French parson delivered the sermon and then we followed him to the little cemetery just at the entrance to Chalons. There he lies with Arabs, Russians, Germans, French and others all the same now.

They are treating Gamble and I wonderfully here. The nurses and officers are lavish with us. I got two New Republics. Praise be.

June 18- [*1917*]

Dear Stull,

I received a letter Saturday and another today so I guess I had better get busy. You insinuate in your epistle of May 27 that I have not been doing my duty. Man alive, what do you expect? I have written every week to the best of my knowledge, and have been trying to get Enid to write. . . . On Tues. evening of last week I got Newton to come over to hear "Billy." And — since this was "Billy's" last week in New York I spent most of my time at the tabernacle, the last few days. I took writing paper and intended to write several letters. I didn't write one.

Mr. Sunday has started a wonderful work in New York and I hope to stay a part of that work. He has given me a new ideal toward which I will strive with all my might. I am at last beginning to realize what a useless creature I have been.

It is quite thrilling to have a piece of a German plane in the house. I'll have to frame it and hang it on the wall. Not that I need any reminder of the atrocities those beasts are committing — but it will be a reminder that there is one plane less to do damage.

. . . Saturday I worked in a registration office where Mother is assistant Captain. I wish I had more time to devote to it because it is really quite interesting. Sometimes you have to listen to life histories, family troubles etc. and must sympathize and advise of course. It is surprising, too, how many (women especially) have not even an elementary school education and cannot do even one of the ten or more things asked. Mother is in a pretty good section too. 207th St. and Amsterdam Ave.

Have no more to say just now so

Au revoir, Lois

DIARY: **June 19** [*1917*]

I had a lot of new bites this morning which means I will be here several days more. . . .

DIARY: **June 20** [*1917*]

I finished "Great Expectations" by Dickens to-day. It is very long and took most of the day. I had my usual two applications of sulphur ointment. . . .

DIARY: **June 21** [*1917*]

A big day. First I got news that we were to move immediately to Luvois, on the other side of Reims. Then I got letters from Gertrude, home, Lois and Bill. I answered Bill's which was a peach like he is. Then I got permission to leave which I did after saying good-by all around and went to Muizon where I collected my scattered things as well as I could. It rained quite a bit but stopped by the time we started at about 3, P.M. It was a beautiful drive of 40 km. . . . Here in Luvois

we are very far from the front and absolutely safe, no bombs shells or anything. The civilian population is still here and are interesting. Luvois is in a valley whose walls are high and there is a lot of woods all around. . . .

My letters from home spoke of a naval battle with U.S. ships at Kiel. I have heard nothing at all of it here as yet.

DIARY: **June 22** [*1917*]

It rained most of the day so I have seen little of the very picturesque town. . . .

DIARY: **June 23** [*1917*]

. . . My disease being still with me I entered the hospital in the afternoon. . . .

Sunday-June 24th [*1917*]

Dear Stull —

. . .You sort of suggested that I am "thin" and "tired" etc. If you talk like that any more I'll not write another letter — . . . Maybe I am thin but I'm not tired and . . . I wouldn't stay in hot old New York all summer if I didn't have to. Every nerve in my body shouts & aches for the country.

. . . I expect to trot over to Brooklyn next Saturday. I was to have gone yesterday and Paula was disappointed because I couldn't go — not that she wanted to see me so badly but because I had promised to take your letters over so they could read them. Don't get nervous — I won't forget about the one containing your half-formulated "plans," which you specially requested should be kept a dark and mysterious secret. Paula wanted to take the letters home last time she was here, but I wouldn't let her. I know her too well — Safety first! . . .

adieu. Lois. . . .

June 30, 1917.

Dear Stull,

. . . Paula is telling you fibs about my "promises." I am not in a position to promise any thing. I take life as it comes — making no plans because I can never tell what the morrow will bring forth. I should love to go and will if I can — but — You know I think Paula regards me as she does her little Italian proteges [*Paula taught school on the lower east side of New York, where many Italian immigrants had settled*].

. . . America is waking up! She is yelling with all her might for airoplanes — and airoplanes quick — so it looks like business. Every day there are articles in the paper — "Why we need airoplanes" "The only way to win the war" etc. The writer bids the reader

Adieu, Lois

DIARY: **June 26** [*1917*]

Mailed letter home as well as a lot of postals I wrote. . . . I left the hospital early in the morning.

June 30, 1917

Dear Lois,

I have gotten two letters (June 1 and 8) from you since I last wrote. That is the reverse of the usual state of our correspondence but I'll do better from now on. I was fairly busy because

We have moved about 25 miles south east from where we were. We are now on the other side of R[*eims*]**. . . . The town is so safe that nearly all the civilians are still here, funny little children, funnier old men and women and girls. The entire population is about two hundred I guess. . . .**

My skin disease came back and I went to the hospital here. They cured me absolutely in three days by heroic treatments of long hot sulphur baths till I could hardly stand up; scrubbings with a brush (a foot long with bristles 3 inches long) till blood was drawn; then strong sulphur ointment that would burn like the place Bill Sunday talks about so much. But I got cured.

Our work here is under almost ideal conditions. Six cars are rolling all the time, that isn't altogether true, they are on duty. Four cars are stationed at the village of L. [*Louvois*] **6 miles from here. . . .**

Besides the 4 cars at L. we have two posts up near the trenches. . . . When a car leaves a post it goes to the hospital at L. with the wounded and another car goes out to the post. Each fellow stays three days at a time on duty and then comes back here on reserve for 5 days. . . .

Two days ago all six of us on duty kept going almost the full 24 hours. Mostly with gased men. There was a new man on duty, his first day at post and he got an unpleasant initiation. He had several badly gased men, one of whom couldn't stay on his stretcher but rolled and kicked and vomited all the way to the hospital and there they didn't even take him inside but let him thresh about in the road for the couple of minutes he lived.

I'll try and write a better letter soon when I feel more like it. I've just finished putting in new brake bands and its a nasty job. Regards to all,

Stull.

Schenectady, N.Y., June 20, 17.

My dear Stull,

I appreciate your letters very much, so do others. your last letter has been extensively feted.

. . . I am horridly in the dumps; bluer than hell. I told you about missing out on the French Amb. service because of German parentage. Missed out on Am. Amb. service because underweight. Tried the exams right in the middle of Block Week when I was a physical wreck from my law and English History work. The sergeant told me to report at Allentown in two weeks, saying that I certainly ought to be right for weight by that time. Well, I got into training; lived a la Fairbanks, quit <u>smoking</u>, and drinking, and in <u>five</u> days put on <u>eight</u> pounds, — which was sufficient. Then was I notified that the camp was filled up and no further enlistments could be received. Jesus Christ on a Raft!, — that after I quit tobacco. So here I am, the healthiest damned invalid in America, feeling so damn spry that I am sex conscious (pretty delicate expression, yes?) all day long, and yet inelegible for army, navy, ambulance, and even medical corps all on account of a pair of eyes supposedly bad but which can stand 12 hrs. pull per diem. At last report, tomorrow I am going to try the national guard, — imagine it, such degradation, <u>ME</u> in the National Guard. The U.S. recruiting officer told me that the National Guard is accepting almost everybody that the U.S. rejects, so here goes. I don't know what they'll put me at, anything from the trenches to orderly work at a base hospital, i.e., pushing dung.

. . . Probably the two things you'd like to know about most is what

America thinks about the military situation in Europe, and what America's mood is on the war. Well, of course the common peépul think Germany is already beaten and that it's a mere matter of months now before they throw up the sponge. It is widely believed that the Germans are undernourished to the point of collapse; are making soap and lubricating oil out of human bodies; are wearing paper clothes, and have no more explosives.

But the so-called better opinion has it that the Allies are at present being slowly but surely beaten and they are dubious that American aid can avail much. By conscription we will undoubtedly raise 2,000,000 men but how can we send them to France and keep them in supplies. To do the latter would require tremendous tonnage, — which we have not got. True, we are going to build ships. But Col. Goethals, who is in charge of the ship building program says that the new optimistic forecast is something like 2,400,000 tons in 18 months, and Germany has sunk about that much of English tonnage alone in about six months.[6] Apparently there is nothing that can be done about the submarines except chase them as much as possible, and build as many ships as possible. Germany must be putting out subs at a terrifying rate.

. . . Now what is going on in America? It is the national habit, of course, to be grumpy about our gov't; the inalienable right to slander and be ignorant of our public officials and doings. But the truth seems to be that the Administration is doing remarkably well, in fact surprising itself. Out of that mass of mediocrity at Washington, actually good does come. Of course, the brains of the whole affair is Wilson. Congress obstructs as much as it can, but nobody gives a damn about Congress. The President has surrounded himself by a circle of genius, — Hoover for Food Control, Goethals for Ships, Willard of the B.& M.R.R. [*Daniel Willard was from the Baltimore and Ohio Railroad Company*[7]] for Railroad administration, etc., etc. The Council of National Defense, — Baruch for Purchasing Agent, Edison & Emmet & Hays Hammond on Inventions, Gompers on Labor Conditions, Schwab on Steel, etc., etc., undoubtedly contains the world's greatest personel. It is hampered by want of authority; Congress is jealous of giving it any power but even in its mere advisory capacity it is already doing wonders. Wilson will soon kick Congress in the bottom, and then watch things hum.

As to the mood of our people, Stull, thank God you're in France. To be here and see and hear this stinking thing called the opinion of 100,000,000 freeman, — it makes one ashamed to be an American. Jesus Christ, sometimes I wonder if its worth while to risk one's life to save this mess, our countree.

. . . There is no open opposition, because people are afraid of being jailed. But in conversation, their attitude comes out. They cannot see, in the first place, what business we have to fight over in Europe; they can't see how its our quarrel. "Let the fools go on murderin' each other; taint none of our business, let the damn fools who go on the ocean in these times git drownded" In short they simply can't warm up to it as our battle. In the second place the opinion is very wide-spread that this is a "money-man's war," the argument running something like this: the Am. capitalist class invested a lot of money in Allied war loans, they saw the Allies being beaten, so they dragged America into it so they wouldn't lose their money. The argument never enters these people's head that Wilson is not the agent of the greedy; or that the rich men's and gov't officials sons are going in the infantry, i.e. Marshal Field Jr., young Vanderbilt, Teddy's four sons, Daniel's son, Taft's two sons, etc. and infinitum; or that the Am. capitalists would stand a much better chance of getting their money back now if the Allies accepted the Peace that they may have for the asking, than some years hence where their debt will be tripled. But such argument is water on the ducks back.

75% of the 10 000 000 who registered claimed exemption. The gov't. officially announced that early returns indicated that "at least 60%" had claimed exemption and the "percentage will probably be higher." So I presume 75%.

All this is understandable, Stull. The butcheries of war have been common tea-table talk in America for 3 yrs., i.e. the rats & body lice of the trenches, the stink of the dead, the wounded rotting between the lines, the shell hit men being rent to shreds and their ripped bodies being put into a gunny-sack and burned. America has a mind full of this and is timid.

And all this would be forgiveable, this inability to see across the ocean and the lack of appetite for this hideous business, "war," if only the people would be frank about it. But damn it, they are verbally bellicose. The American flag is cheered in true rah-rah fashion in all the treaties; the same person who has diarhea at thought of the draft, bull-shits the loudest about "wait till WE git at them Germans." I am almost tempted to hiss the American flag when I see the hypocritical demonstrations over it.

. . . Bill

Brooklyn, New York, June 30, 1917.

Dear Stull,

You're a dear boy and I'm a wicked ungrateful sister for not writing more often. . . .

Lois brought all your letters over for mama & papa to read. All yesterday evening they sat and read your letters. Luckly she had abstracted all censorable matter. If you ever try joining any aviation corps or any stunt like that, you will find that you have mistaken the temper of your family. Truly truly it would nearly kill mother.

Lois is having a lot of trouble at home. It's a pretty bad state of affairs. Dr. is suing Mrs. for d - - - on the grounds that Lela is not his. It hasn't gone very far yet, but matters are not so pleasant.

. . . I have finished my motor classes and take my exam for chauffer's license on Tuesday.

. . . Love from all.

Your affectionate sister,
Paula.

DIARY: **July 1** [*1917*]

On post to-day. . . . I made another run to Sillery and after supper to Luvois. One of the men I had was all burnt, whether from liquid fire or the back fire of a gun I know not. His face, then covered with grease was all puckered up and his mustache burnt off. . . .

I finished reading "A Diversity of Creatures" Kiplings latest. In only a few places can be found traces of the real Kipling.

DIARY: **July 3** [*1917*]

Worked all morning on the car washing, oiling, cleaning. . . .

. . . I read some of Seeger's poems and extracts from his letters forming the introduction which were equally good. He was truly a poet, philosopher, a dreamer. He was loyal to his love of Love and a faithful worshiper of Beauty. I find a lot of companionship of thought in him.

DIARY: **July 4** [*1917*]

Read more of Seeger and like him more the better I get to know him. . . .

July 5, 1917

Dear Lois,

We celebrated the 4th yesterday as I suppose everyone did. There were a great deal of fireworks furnished by the French and Germans but too far off for us to witness. We could only hear the rumble. We celebrated in a quiet peaceful way. The big event of the day was the meal. Our chef did himself proud. . . .

Regards to all, Stull

DIARY: **July 6** [*1917*]

. . . I finished Seeger's poems, he is truly a modern Omar Kyaham with the courage of his convictions.

. . . The way the French make a wounded man wait outside the hospital while they go thru red tape always makes me mad and this was especially true about 4 a.m. this morning when I have a grave *blesse* groaning for nearly half an hour while they decided where to send him and wrote *fisches* [*fiches, records; filled out forms*]**.**

DIARY: **July 12** [*1917*]

. . . Last night some boche planes passed en route for Epernay which they bomb on good nights. . . . One of the bombs fell on the shac at Ludes killing Norton. It lit just outside and a piece of *eclat* flew thru the window cutting his throat. The others had narrow escapes. They put him on a stretcher and ran for the hospital but it was too late. . . . Norton was about 40 years old, lives in Goshen and had traveled quite a bit, being with Pearry on one trip and having flown with the Wright brothers. . . .

Thursday — July 12. [*1917*]

Dear Stull,

. . . I have come to the conclusion that your kid sister has a great deal more sense than Miss Paula. When she's Paula's age she'll be great!

. . . From the papers this morning one would gather that Germany is on the verge of a revolution, that Prussia would be done away with in a short time and that Von Bethmann Hollweg [*(1856-1921)German Chancellor from 1909-1917 (he resigned on July 14)*] had seen the zenith of his power.

It sounds very encouraging, but also like a put up job. I suppose there a few little scraps going on in Berlin but I suppose they wont amount to much.

. . . I wish you could come home, just for a few minutes —

Lois

DIARY: **July 13** [*1917*] **Friday.**

I went to Epernay this morning to get flowers for the funeral to-night. Norton was wounded in 6 or 7 places. Gamble was scratched in the shoulder. Aller's coat hanging up is pierced in several places and Elliot was within a foot of being killed. The fellows up there had a bad night what with the shock and the blood and wreckage afterwards. . . .

Esperance is an unhealthy spot. All the fellows have been complaining and yesterday a piece of *eclat* hit Purdy's helmet. They have moved a battery within 150 feet of our *abri* and if the boche locate it we will have to move or some of us will be moved.

We buried Norton after supper when it was so dark there was no danger of being seen by the boche *saucese* [*balloon*]**. First there were services held in the chapel at the chateau here and then we, including some French officers and Andrew, followed the wagon to his grave. It was a pretty sight, the hills just at the end of sunset, and everyone grouped in a semi-circle around the grave. . . .**

DIARY: **July 14** [*1917*]

Bastille Day. I had a little stomache ache which was unfortunate as we had a great spread. . . .

DIARY: **July 15** [*1917*]

At post. . . .

Wrote to Lois. The French made a little *coup de main* [*suprise attack*] **and we rolled from about 11 till after six this morning without stopping. I had one nasty trip out to the second bridge from Esperance. The road, Route 44, is pretty well shot up and I had three grand *couches* who were only half left. One yelled out loud at every jolt but I could do nothing but drive on. . . .**

DIARY: **July 16** [*1917*]

Luckily I had no work all morning and got some sleep which I needed badly. Driving 50 miles or more on dark roads isn't a cinch and when you do it under the conditions we do, it becomes hard work. . . .

Thursday July 19th [*1917*]

Dear Stull,

A few minutes ago I was talking to your mother on the phone. She told me the glad news that they had received a letter. . . . I was sorry to hear you had been in the hospital, but terribly glad it was nothing worse than it was. I hope letters wont be held up again — it's too trying on the nervous system.

. . . Were you very uncomfortable while you were in the hospital? Mother said she thinks it is an itchy rash. If so it must have driven you really crazy. Are you doing something to prevent your getting it again?. . .

Good night, Lois.

19 Juillet 1917

Dear Paula,

Your letter of June 30 (with Lois's) got here on July 15, making the quickest trip yet. . . .

You asked if it was true that there is lice over everything, generals etc. It is and it isn't. All the soldiers in the trenches have them while in the trenches. I've seen them (the soldiers) sitting by side the road, roll up their pants and go hunting. But you must remember they (the lice) are a great deal more prevalent here in peace times than in the American society you know. . . . Of course generals and even lowly lieuts arn't so apt to get bugs and when they do, they quickly remedy the evil. Most of the fellows in the section have had some variety at least once. . . .

Three nights ago at about 2 A.M. the doctor told me to take 2 hours for a run we usually do in 3/4 of an hour. I had three *couché* (Elizabeth will tell you that means "lyers" in French) all terribly wounded. I had gotten one of them, or at least what was left of him, an hour early several miles out nearer the lines. At every jolt and no matter

how slowly or carefully you go there are sure to be plenty of jolts, he shrieked out loud. . . . However, such a one is an exception. Most of the wounded are only slightly wounded and even the bad cases make little noise but go along in a sort of coma.

. . . I'm going to quit now, excuse haste.

Love to all, Stull

DIARY: July 21 [*1917*]

Wrote Enid, got a letter from headquarters saying there was fifty dollars there for me. Got a kodak and 12 rolls of films from home. Jim White, Hanna and Dallin are back from permission with rumours that we are soon to be taken over by the American government and that it is possible to get in the American aviation over here.

The French here are the happiest I've seen yet. They sing and to-night I saw some dancing to an accordion.

Norton has been awarded the Croix de Guerre with a palm.

Wrote home and to Lois.

July 21, 1917

Dear Lois,

Yesterday I got your letter of June 24, five days after I got yours of June 30th. So it goes, you ask in an insinuating tone of voice if I always put stamps on my letters. I never do and don't have to. They go post free because I'm in the French army. That is part of my pay extra to the 5 cents a day. You shouldn't have to pay anything. Tell me if you do. . . .

I get my permission on Aug 2. I don't know yet just what I'll do. I have some business (important and mysterious) to attend to in Paris and it may keep me there all seven days. Or I may go to the seaside for a while. Or I may make a little bicycle tour with another fellow thru the chateau region viz. Orleans, Tours, Poitiers etc. . . .

Regards to all, Stull

DIARY: July 22 [*1917*]

Monkeyed around with three little French boys and taught them to

say "I love the ladies" for "*Comment allez vous*." [*Comment allez-vous? How are you?*]

DIARY: **July 23** [*1917*]

More bustle and more packing till now we are waiting to start. . . .

We went to Epernay and the lieut. got orders to report to Bar-le-duc which means Verdun or possibly Alsace.

From Epernay we went to Chalons-sur-Marne thru Tours-sur-Marne and Conde-s.M. We got to Chalons in time to get lunch at a hotel. Chalons is quite a place.

From Chalons we went to Vitry-le-Francois thru Sogny, Mairy sur Marne etc. We had a supper at a hotel in a banquet room. A fine meal, with table-clothes and songs after it. Weanie sang one to our joy. Vitry is the prettiest, cleanest town of 9000 I've seen. Harold and I slept in a funny little Hotel de Cloche.

The trip over was beautiful but dusty. . . .

We passed wonderful country going thru many little villages where the people would come out and stare at us. Saw some boche prisoners working on the roads. . . .

DIARY: **July 24** [*1917*]

After a good breakfast we pulled out and went thru Perthes, St. Dizier, Chaucenay, to Bar-le-duc. The first half was level beautiful country, the second was very hilly. Bar is walled in by hills. We had lunch and supper at the Cafe de Rochelle. The town is quite dirty and not very interesting. I saw some American soldiers and spoke a minute with them. There were also English, Norton Harjes and other ambulance sections. . . . We slept last night on stretchers alongside of our cars. . . .

[*Norton-Harjes volunteer ambulance sections were organized by U.S. citizens Richard Norton and H. H. Harjes under the auspices of the Red Cross. The ambulance section in which Holt served — the American Ambulance Field Service (AAFS) — was one of many sections organized by A. P. Andrew, another American civilian.*]

Schenectady, N.Y., July 24, '17.

My dear Stull,

. . . The drawings in the draft proceeded calmly. 10,000,000 enrolled men were drafted, to be called in their order, 687,000 as a beginner. I was at the newspaper office when the drawn numbers were flashed in one by one. The whole attitude of the anxious spectators was summed up in the eternal question: "Well, Bill, did they GET you?" I believe the newspapers denominated the first million as "America's Honored Men, etc., etc.," but believe me, Stull, they are a sorry sight. They are scared pea green; they don't know why the country is fighting and regard themselves as mere "French fertilizer" in the cause of American capitalists. Our government is making marvelous strides in the material side of war preparation, but on the spiritual side of telling the mob why we are at war and in creating a morale, we have woefully failed as yet.

Now I anticipate more trouble from the draft than I had previously thought. The Irish are bitterly anti-war, because of their hatred of England, and thousands of Irishmen were drafted. Thousands of Germans, too, were drafted and their loyalty consists in keeping their mouths shut and abstaining from blowing up bridges. The Socialists, also, are anti-war and are sending to the conscripts vivid and lurid pamphlets describing the horrors of war, — "heaps of human bodies, stinking, decaying, etc., etc." It is pitiful to see how the French are banking on us for aid as they have a right to, but I fear the aid will not be forthcoming.

. . . Well, Stull, try to drop me a short line at least once a week so I'll know that you're still whole. For God's sake, be wary of females; the stories we get on this side of veneral disease in the army is horrifying. The losses in the Am. Ambul. Corps seem quite heavy; frequently I notice the death-notices and notices of inquiries of many of the fellows. So drop a line.

Believe me, Bill.

DIARY: **July 25** [*1917*]

Breakfast at half past six and then on thru Rumont and Beauzee to Evres where we are on reserve. It is the Verdun sector and rumor has it that they are preparing a big offensive here. We hope to be out of here and to work soon. The trip to-day was awful[;] the dust from the white chalky roads being so bad that often I couldn't see the car in

After a few weeks of driving at Muizon, Holt's unit was moved to the more active Verdun sector. He took this picture of ambulances near Verdun, 1917. *Holt Collection*

front thru the clouds. We are in a barracks just outside the little village which though now very far back is about half destroyed.

. . . The country all around here is farming country and not vineyards. We hear rumors everywhere of a big French offensive. It is quite something to have been sent to the champagne for the offensive there (which only last a few days) and now to be brought back here for the big doings here.

July 28, 1917

Dear Lois,

Walking stick in one hand, writing tablet and a magazine in the other I sallied forth about an hour ago and here I am in the shade of an old apple tree. That doesn't sound like the horrors of war, does it?

The apple tree is miles and miles from where I was when I last wrote. That last sentence is a delicate way of telling you we have moved. It took us three days to go from where we were to where we are now, in the Verdun sector. . . .

We are living in a barracks (a long wooden shed like the pictures you see in histories of the houses of the Iriquois) and eat in a barn nearby. The quarters are comfortable enough but there is no stream large enough to swim in so we will all be dirty unless we move on soon. We've only been here two days so far.

Paula tells me you are having some unpleasantness at home. I wish I could help but I can think of nothing except to send my best

from, Stull. . . .

DIARY: **July 29** [*1917*] **Sunday.**

. . . My raincoat was stolen in Chalons on the way over here. . . . Saw several very big guns go up towards Verdun, Steve told me that Andrew had asked for the names of two men to lead new sections and Steve gave him Stocky's and mine. If I could be chief I might not join aviation if I could. Aviation school would be long and I might not finish before the war ends.

Monday-July 30 [*1917*]—

Dear Stull —

Such heat. And I just got back from beautiful, cool — wonderful Highland Lake. I went up Friday afternoon with your Father, and came back with him this morning. Just those few days did me a world of good. I sure have a soft spot in my heart for the lake.

. . . Do you remember that I said in one of my letters — some time ago that I felt as tho I must "talk" to someone? Well, that someone proved to be the last person I ever thought it might be — your father. He's splendid, Stull, and he was perfectly dear to me going up on Friday. I feel as tho I could laugh and even shout and dance, again and act foolish. You don't know what it's all about and never mind — you probably have enough to trouble and annoy you now. But your father's a peach — and he talked to me and let me talk to him; so now I feel better. . . .

'Bye — Lois.

DIARY: **July 31** [*1917*]

"Judge" tells me he asked Andrew not to take Stocky and me till

after our work in this attack which we are expecting. More rain and bridge. The lieut and Steve returned from looking over our new work which is in recaptured land in front of Verdun and near Forts Vaux and Douamont. They tell of great guns, traffic, dead mens hands sticking up thru the ground and a smell all-prevading. [*See map, p. 313.*]

DIARY: **August 1** [*1917*]

I left with the six cars that go to work to-day, going along as replacement. We went thru Ippecourt, Vadlincourt, and so to Haudainville, our cantonment. Strater had great trouble because he had almost a gallon too much oil, and I played mechanic. Things certainly look booming, the traffic was dense, I never saw so many *camions* as were on the road and parked along it. Big and little guns were thick as fleas (and that means a lot over here) and all seemed to be in the process of being moved up. Railroads with little two-faced engines cut across in all directions. Our quarters are small and crowded, our auto parc rut[*t*]**ed and mudy but everybody is crowded. Two cars stay at Verdun and go on call from there. Three cars go on call from Caserne Marceau to posts some of which can be only reached at night. One car goes to a little village nearby, Belrupt, and evacuates from there. I rode over there with Strater and back with the relieved French car. I saw two Bulgarians who had deserted and were used by the French for hospital work. They were sturdy little men, much like Italians.**

In the afternoon I walked with Harold up several hills till we looked right down on Verdun. It lies in the bottom of a cup and forms part of a pretty scene. On the high ridge in front we could see the demolished buildings and the few stumps that showed where a wood was once. While we were watching the bustle and activity the boche dropt a few very large shells in the heart of the city.

We had an awful time during the night with rats. Hardly anyone slept. One bit Jim Flyn's toe, Pearl was sitting in bed with a flashlight in one hand and a stick in the other. Purdy and I were lying right at the foot of the stairs and several ran down the stairs and jumped on Purdy's bed. One or two got on my bed. I caught one with the flashlight and he was about 8 inches long not counting his tail. To-night we sleep in our cars. The British and French have started an offensive in Flanders.[8]

DIARY: **August 2** [*1917*]

Rode with the car going to Caserne Marceau. We skirt Verdun and go up the high ridge in front. Everywhere are signs of intense activity, former and present. Munition depots are thick as rats. On the way up we got an awful smell, showing that a shell had dug up some buried bodies.

The army has postponed all permissions.

. . . More and more guns, munitions and all kinds of hate keep going up. We got word we were to be inspected and we all rushed about for awhile. A four striper came and looked the cars over casually. He told Steve he was pleased and that we should learn all roads as well as possible by Aug 10.

. . . I had a wild night. About half past ten they woke me up and by half past eleven Flynn, Strater, Rice and I were leaving Verdun for Haraumont which is out past Bras. It was raining and the road was muddy but we went finely for about one kilometer and then we met a blockade. From then on it seems like a nightmare. We would crawl twenty or thirty feet forward and then wait 5 minutes. Other times we would dodge in and out going thru holes unbelievably small. Then a few shells dropt nearby and it felt lonely sitting up there on the car. We came to a bad spot passing a broken *camion* where Rice got ditched in the mud and I sank in behind him. About 8 Frenchmen helped me out by lifting the front of the Ford up and putting it in the center of the road. Rice stayed in the mud all night. A few yards further on a horse was killed about 30 feet in front of Flynn. But we crawled, skidded and pushed each other along thru Bras, now a heap of stones, and on till we got within less than a kilometer of the post when we were badly blockaded. We stayed there till daylight when the obstructions were removed and most of the traffic which consisted of guns, munitions and food chiefly, went back without unloading. While we were waiting at this place a bunch of shells came in and we all huddled together as close to the bank of mud as we could. The *eclat* of many of the shells fell around us and several times I lay as flat in the mud as I could. When daylight came and the road was cleared we finally reached there after a 7 hours trip (normally less than one) and got back to Verdun without mishap altho the roads were awful and often partially blocked by ditched *camions*. Anyhow I got a wonderful sight, seeing Douamont and Vaux a little to the front and

left. The place had once been a woods but now there were only a few roots showing. It was a mass of shell holes overlapping, nothing growing. I saw old trenches that still retained their outline otherwise it looked like ocean waves of land. On the hill in front there was tons of shells, barb wire and other stuff lying in the open. A little toy engine puffed up several times during our wait. All the way back I saw signs of the coming attack. Gun was next to gun and there were new gun emplacements dug waiting to bring up the canon. It is sure the real thing.

August 2 1917

Dear Lois,

. . . I agree with you Elizabeth is showing signs of real sense. I got her letter written at the beach and it was a peach. I wrote and told her so to-day.

I am having some of the real stuff now. I can't say anything but we have moved up the way I said we would and — I wish I could tell you all about [*it*] but I will some day. This morning I got a whiff from rotting bodies that almost knocked the Ford over. Believe me the "horrors of war" are all present at this little party. So far in writing I have refrained from telling about them and other things and have tried to find other things to say. The letters written home and published are a standing joke with us as they are practically all the semblance and not the substance of truth.

They and the special articles and many books are not to be trusted at all. Just at present the U.S. is full of win-the-war-in-the-air stuff. It sounds fine <u>but</u> the aviation is only one branch of many which are equally essential and which have to include thousands of times more men. In one of the pictorial parts you sent me it shows parts of boche trenches "destroyed by aeroplanes" and then goes on to say the aeroplanes directed the <u>artillery</u> fire. Of course planes are absolutely essential but so are artillery, infantry engineers, chauffeurs, roadmakers, and hundreds of others. I remember in one book, "Italy at War" by Powell he tells how the Allies have the complete mastery of the air and that the boche practically never dare to cross their lines. He probably wrote that in a Paris cafe where most straight-from-the-war news originated. Whenever I used to go to post I could see sever-

Above and below: Scenes at Verdun, 1917, in photographs taken by Stull Holt. *Holt Collection*

al boche planes over the French lines and I remember two times when they flew about 800 meters high in broad daylight about 5 miles in Frenchland and dropt bombs on an anti-air craft battery. Of course by concentrating all machines for an offensive, the Allies do obtain control in that locality like they did in the Somme last year. A lot of other stuff you read by picking up any American newspaper is equally untrue.

. . . If you are real real good and promise faithfully to keep it a secret I'll tell you something. I had expected to be in an aviation school by now and may be soon (providing a slight eye defect doesn't interfere. Eyes and heart must be perfect for aviation, the rest are not so important) but now something else is turning up. I have been recommended for the command of another ambulance section. Our officer here asked that I shouldn't be taken away for a couple of weeks yet because they may have special need. There are only about 30 sections all told and to be the American officer in one means a lot. Although not offically an officer in the French army they wear two strips (the equivalent of a French first-lieutenant) have charge of the entire section, have a staff car (touring) and a chauffeur of their own. If I should ever get appointed I will be the youngest to hold the job. Anyhow its something to be recommended when you consider there are over 2000 men in the service, I have only been over a short time compared to hundreds of fellows who are 10-20 years older than I. Mum's the word. See if you can keep a secret with Stull.

DIARY: **August 4** [*1917*]

More mud, mud, then mud followed by rain. . . . Several cars have broken down and more will if this weather continues. It interferes with the fighting in Flanders but permits them to work during the day getting ready for the attack here. It will come soon and will surely be a big one. We will only work the posts from Caserne Marceau and probably they will be too big.

DIARY: **August 5** [*1917*]

Up at Caserne Marceau to-day. More rain and mud. On the bad night two days ago my new raincoat bought of Jim Flynn was stolen, making the second. Had a quiet day to-day. Finished "Further

Foolishness" by Stephen Leacock. Tonight after supper the sun came out so we could see shadows. There are about 7 155's [*155mm artillery*] **waiting for darkness before they go over the top of the hill. They are still moving guns up so the attack probably wont begin for about a week yet.**

Schenectady, N.Y., August 5, 1917

My dear Stull,

. . . I have not written because I have a job which gob[*b*]les up every second of my time. I am working in the shops of the General Electric Co. at Schenectady. I am working nights from 5:30 P.M. to 6 A.M. plus an hour tacked on each end for getting to and from work. I am working on an insulating machine whereinto enter great rolls of copper wire and wherefrom emerges insulated cables. Much of the work is for the U.S. navy.

You would be amused to see the old scholastic pushing around tremendous drums of copper wire. Physical labor is a welcome change after a Winter of would-be-thought-coddling. The only trouble with the job is that I can't sleep daytimes; I toss about for hours; consequently I get pretty wobbly during the long stretch. I may cave in if I can't learn to sleep days. This war-pay is quite fabulous; I manage to earn about $26 a week.

It is a good bit of human experience to work in these shops I have worked here before, but that was not when my eyes were opened quite as much as now. This is how America's millions subsist and it is good to know of it first hand. I manage to get along with the men; they have not dreamed for a minute that I am going to college, nor would you if you could see me covered with grease and dust, chewing "Mechanic's Delight" tobaccer, and hear my grammar, well besprinkled with "aints" and "gimmies."

. . . If I get any scraps of news of the old crowd, I will certainly send them to you. If misfortune should happen, to you, Stull, I should feel it keener than of any of the men I know.

My very best, Bill.

DIARY: **August 6** [*1917*]

A little sun followed by the usual rain. Steve, Eliott, and Gamble got citations yesterday for work done at Luvois. Got news tonight that we

move tomorrow to Beveaux, the large hospital just this side of Verdun where we take the wounded. It is good news because we can do better work, save essence and leave this mudhole.

Monday-Aug. 6th. [*1917*]

Dear Stull

. . . Father had the bright idea that he would drive down to Red Bank to see Curtis and since I couldn't get out of going & since Paula has a "pull" with father I suggested that we make it a party, so we did — Paula, Newton, a friend of his — Bob, father & I. We left the Battery at 800 A.M.

Continued — Aug-7th.

Took the ferry to Staten Island, Drove thru there to South Amboy — took another ferry to Jersey — First we drove to Red Bank to get Curtis and then went on to Lakewood — stopping at your Aunt's for dinner — It was a great trip — but pretty long — We got home at 1130 P.M. and as father was tired I drove after we hit N.Y. but I could hardly keep my eyes open — I know what it feels like now to drive when you're dead tired — I imagine you must have had to do it many a time — . . .

8th.

. . . I have to walk down past the post office so will drop this on my way — Isn't that an original ending?

Au revoir, Lois —

DIARY: **August 7** [*1917*]

. . . Rumor has it that there is to be a 96 hour artillery preparation for the attack here. I wish it would begin soon as the work is hard and the longer we stay here the less fit we will be for the rush.

This afternoon I made 3 trips to Souilly which is about 30 kilometers away and enjoyed it despite the constant dodging of *camions* and wagons.

DIARY: **August 9** [*1917*]

Had a bad thunderstorm last night which our tent withstood well. Got a letter from papa. Had a run just about dark to Belrupt where I

took three *couche* and an *assis*. They loaded one *couche* on the top stretcher and I suggested to a doctor that as he was badly wounded he would be better down below. The damm doctor said "It is little" but I made them change. Harold was with me and we just started when that *couche* started to groan. He was wounded in the arms and legs and suffered the tortures of the damned. It took almost three hours to get the 30 kilometers to Souilly and several times we had to stop and give him a rest. The night was dark (I used lights for the first time) and it was an awful nervous strain on us to hear his shrieks and to try and do our best for him. It was all unnecessary as the doctors merely were pushing their work on to the next. He should have rested till daylight anyhow. No operation was necessary nor was there any special reason for sending him.

DIARY: **August 10** [*1917*]

Got up nursing an awful grouch, the result of last nights trip. Kept the grouch while we moved all the tents and stuff to the field just outside the hospital yard. . . . Last night there was some very heavy firing the worst I've heard since my first days at Muizon but it didn't continue to-day.

. . . Cleaned the carbon out of my car and am ready and wishing for the attack to begin before we are all tired out and the cars broken.

DIARY: **August 12** [*1917*] **Sunday.**

Tired out but better after sleeping all morning. Luckily my car is A No. 1 so I don't have to work on it. Got a letter from Lois.

It was a wild evening and night. The boche sent a lot of shell into Haudainville Dugny and finally started a fire on top of the hill between here and Haudainville in the old quarry. Pretty soon the munitions stored there started going off and for 4 or 5 hours we got great flames, smoke rings, sky rockets and were kept anxious about flying pieces. Stocky had to run to Belrupt and I went with him right by the explosions. We went as fast as the hill and the Ford could pull us, I walked back to a nervous night. They had been shelling the roads and everything on the way to Haraumont, Oller was a nervous wreck and had to be nursed all evening, Curtis broke an axel, Kreutzberg and Hanna ran into a gas attack and Kreutzberg's mask leaked enough to give him a sick stomache. Purdy brought in a horribly

wounded man, his jaw was shot off[,] **he had a hemorraghe, and his arms and legs were hurt. It was a hard trip and then as they were unloading him here there was an extra large explosion and the** ***bran-cardiers*** [*stretcher bearers*] **dropt him and ran. Purdy caught him and got all bloody before they came back. He was pretty white but after a drink of brandy went on.**

Aug 12. Sunday [*1917*]

Dear Lois,

. . . I haven't written much lately to anyone because I haven't had the opportunity often and the few times I did, I was always very tired. I am in that unfortunate condition now and it's the worst kind of tire, not physical but nervous exhaustion. We have been having a lot of work under the worst conditions almost possible; horrible roads, long trips, lots of them, thick traffic, dark nights, steep hills and a certain amount of danger prooved by the six or seven dead horses you can see after every nights work. These and others make very unsavory odors beside which Barren Island [*at home*] **is a boquet of roses. So altogether we and the cars are getting tired and have been drawing on our reserve strength to keep going. It is a big responsibility to take several horribly wounded men over these roads on a dark night. They get bounced and thrown about even in daylight while you are crawling along on low. And at night the only way to do is to say to yourself; "I didn't wound him, nor build this road" and do your best. You can't imagine what a strain is taken off you when you finally get some bad cases to the hospital. I wish I had time to write more.**

So long, Stull

Sunday Aug. 12 [*1917*] —

Dear Stull,

. . . I am "very excited" about the mysterious business which (takes) — took (a week ago) you to Paris. You are very cruel not to tell what it is. . . . The only thing I beg & pray of you is not to join the aeroplane corps. You threatened to once you know.

. . . Three or four years ago you swore you would be an author; do you remember?

. . . I am getting sleepy so will hie me hence to my little "*lit*" (French for bed — have you heard it used?) *Bon Nuit* —

Lois.

DIARY: **August 13** [*1917*]

I'm first out to Haraumont. A lot of *saucese* up to-day and some big naval guns nearby firing. I am beginning here four days later, the postponement will be explained, and will try my best to report faithfully.

Got some newspapers from Lois, I made during the day 3 trips to Haraumont and one to Verdun. Feeling fine and being first out I asked the lieut if I couldn't start again without a call so as to beat the night. He said yes and a Norton Harjes man (Gordon Bartlett) asked if he could go along. I was willing which was lucky for me later on. We went up to Bras without mishap and there caught up with a line of *camions*. I followed them as far as the road fork and there heard bells ringing and boche shells exploding in front. We all stopt and being suspicious I asked the driver of the *camion* in front of me if the bells meant gas. He said they did so we put on our masks but it was impossible to drive with one on for any length so I kept mine hung around my neck. We only went a very little way when everybody stopt again. The shells were coming in faster so we and a Frenchmen sought shelter in a trench a few feet from the road. The *camions* ahead didn't move so I couldn't. I found out next morning that one had been hit and completely blocked the road. For nearly an hour we sat in that muddy trench listening to the shells that were now coming in very fast and near, but not so fast as the French batteries all round were answering. We crouched into as small a space as possible, hugging first one side and then the other and several times we heard mud, stones and little pieces of *eclat* splash on the ground around us. I was very nervous about gas and soon we noticed a change in the arrives. They whistled more and shrieked less and instead of a loud sharp explosion, went off in a muffled "pfung." I thought I smelt something so we put on our gas masks and started to crawl. I wanted to reach the post, which was only about 600 or 700 yards away where we would be safe and where I could telephone to the others about the gas. We crawled, stumbled and flopped till we reached an *abri*, full of sleeping Frenchman and

one who was watching, where we rested a while and collected our nerve. Then we went on again, the French firing had almost stopt and the whole valley was lit up now and then by a red glare. When the shells got thicker we ducked in another *abri* where the three men were waiting with bags in their hands to fan gas out. We waited there quite some time till there came a lull and we saw some soldiers going by in single file. We joined the line which hug[*g*]ed the side of the hill and dropt every 20 feet or so when a shell came over. Pretty soon the line stopt, everybody put on the gas masks which hung around their necks and then went on. I was holding Bartlett by the hand. A shell shrieked, we all flopped[,] a soldier right on top of me, and mud and stones fell over us. We scrambled up and on but had hardly gone 20 yards when one landed not twenty feet away. I was crouching up next the bank and almost paralized waiting to see what would happen. Several small stones (I think) hit my helmet and then came a big crash that put a big dent in it and raised a bump on my head. If I hadn't had a helmet on it would have knocked me cold if not have cracked my skull. As it was it knocked me flat, my gas mask came off and I got a lungfull. The shell must have been a gas one because the solution was so strong. Water ran out of my eyes and nose, both were smarting, and I had a sharp pain in my lungs. But worst of all I could hardly breath but struggled for air the same way a drowning man clutches at a straw. I was dazed, couldn't see, and would have been a goner only Bartlett grabbed my arm and half dragged me to the post which was only 50 yards away. It was filled with sneezing, choking gasping soldiers. Several times we had to put on our masks and there was a little in the air all the time but I got better. The doctor gave me some dope and I knew I was alright but badly shaken. My sensations came and went so fast and I was so dazed I can't remember my thoughts except that I was scared. Later on the shelling almost stopt, the gas cleared off some and most of the soldiers went on. The doctor asked me to show him where my car was and I went down with him but was intoxicated enough so that he had to hold my arm. Bartlett wanted to drive it back but he didn't know how and the roads were blocked anyhow. I told the doc (it was the lieut) that I would try to make it after daylight. We went back to the post and after a long time someone told me three other cars had reached there. No one came in to see me and I supposed they had gone on when about a half hour later, some big shells

lit right outside. I got scared when Tapley rushed in white, trembling and all mud. He told how they had got loaded and were trying to get past the broken *camions* when the shells came. He wanted to go unload his *blessés* and we got as far as the door when Jim White, Jim Flynn and a Norton Harjes man came up. The sweat was pouring off them and they were shaken and shaking. The first shell should have by all laws killed them all but they like most of us by now, were saved by the daily rains. If the ground were dry and hard the shells would explode towards the sides more and not enter the ground and explode so straightly up in the air. The three cars were pretty badly broken and two of the *couches* in Tapley's car were killed. The doctor who was helping unload got wounded. We sat around and shivered till daylight when we drove home, the cars that could carrying *blesses*. It was quiet then and I had forgotten all my wild thoughts of how to get to Paris.

DIARY: **August 14** [*1917*]

Gamble, who hurt his arm cranking his car so he couldn't drive, left for Paris and the States. . . . I got a few hours sleep in the afternoon and had just said how comfortable the blankets are, at night when Fortan came around and said all cars out for Haraumont. I hated to but we all got dressed (I put on winter flannels) and we started in pitch darkness. Strater in front of me got separated from the rest and soon we found ourselves with Stocky and Rice, working from Caserne Marceau then changing a tire. I stopt and talked a little to collect myself and Rice had a *bidong* [*canteen*] **of rum. Strater couldn't see he said and wanted to wait till the traffic cleared a little but I lead as best I could, although frightened stiff. Pretty soon I heard a welcome voice and the lieut climbed on board. He certainly showed up well in the pinch and surprised me agreeably by his good work. It is nice to have respect for the man you work under. It seems the major had called him up and wanted the whole section. The lieut asked if the three cars on the way had arrived and when he found they hadn't suggested that the roads were blocked and it would be no use to send more cars. The major said you have my orders and the lieut said alright I'll come up myself. So he started but the staff car got ditched near St. Fismes and I picked him up, Purdy, Pat got ditched Strater broke his rear axel, a wagon tipped over on O'Connel**[.] **Curtis**

refused to get up saying he was tired and the lieut told him for all of us that he was a funker. The lieut did wonders, we crawled thru the traffic which of course was blocked everywhere, he would go ahead, clear a passage and call back to me. The French guns were making an awful noise and the sky was flashing but we only heard a very few boche shells. Because of the lieut's efforts we made such good progress that we caught up with the others on the hill opposite Haraumont. (We were using that road because it is safer than the one thru Bras). We finally got there about four o'clock, (I had paper stuffed in my ears) after tiring ourselves out, running danger to ourselves and cars and carrying no *blessés*. We could have started then and done better work. The lieut went in and told the major that he had 7 cars and the *camionette* outside. The major asked for the others and then learnt for the first time that we had six or seven other posts. He said there was a mistake[;] we were doing too much. We worked hard till after eleven next morning using White truck and everything, carrying about 150 *couche* and over 50 *assis*.

DIARY: **August 15** [*1917*]

After lunch I went to Caserne Marceau where I got a few restless hours of sleep before night. I had a couple of runs and (This begins August 15 the third day and night I was working) on the last had to struggle hard to make myself go back. It was pitch black, a thunderstorm came up, and I was worn out. Going on low right in the darkness after a flash of lightning I got off the road and tryed to climb a tree. I was so all in I couldn't work anyhow so I lit my lantern, crawled in my car and shivered. I had gotten wet at least four different times that day. Stout and O'Connel passed me and O'Connell [*sic*] **quit flat so that Steve bawled him out next day. There are about 4 or 5 men who show up a little yellow in this work, admited by even Ned the worst he ever saw, but the rest are fine. It[']s a pleasure to work with them. I got letters from Cornell. . . .**

DIARY: **August 16** [*1917*]

Jim White and Kreutzberg helped me out of my ditch and I went home to a day of rest but could hardly sleep, probably because of all the coffee and stuff I have been going on. I got a letter from mama saying they had just heard of my move to Luvois and she was glad I was

in a safe place. That is what I call the irony of fate. I sent a postal home. An automobile head looked us over and said he was tickled with the work of the men. The lieut showed me the letter he had written at the request of the Norton Harjes lieut telling how Bartlett helped me.

DIARY: **August 17** [*1917*]

We had hardly gotten to bed last night when we heard that Pearl, who had gone up to Haraumont to give Stocky a new spring, was wounded thru the arm. Poor old Pearl got caught after so many of us had such close shaves. It went right thru his arm but isn't dangerous. The major up there cited him right away. Rices car had a lot of blood and holes in it. A Norton Harjes man lost almost all of his left hand last night. Tiring was terrific and I didn't sleep very well.

. . . I know I haven't done justice here to the intense excitement danger and things I've seen. One morning one of the fellows counted 15 dead horses and 8 broken wagons on the road in front of Haraumont. There are patches of blood both human and horse all over. Stouty had to get out and move one dead horse to pass and once he had to run over the neck of one who was not dead yet in order to pass.

Saw a boche get two *saucisse* but it aroused only casual interest. Tried to read a New Republic but couldn't rouse any enthusiasm.

DIARY: **August 18** [*1917*]

Rumors of when the attack is to begin, Monday is the favorite today.

Stouty had a nasty time with a gased men who climbed out of the car and ran around asking to be killed. They got him back in the car again but he was dead when they reached the hospital. Every day some more cars get *eclat* holes in them. The British are doing well in Flanders but it is hard to rejoice. All I do is lie around and rest when it is possible. The weather is good and the boche airmen have been coming over. A big 376 naval gun nearby annoys us by its noise.

Got letters from Elizabeth. . . .

Made a run to-night to Carrier Sud and saw the immense shell hole which had blocked the road. It was fully 30 feet in diameter and had wiped out the road completely.

Pearl is doing better and will probably get the use of his arm again.

DIARY: **August 19** [*1917*]

Another good day and Sunday. The attack is supposed to begin to-morrow morning early. We give up the post at Haraumont to-day to two French sections.

DIARY: **August 20** [*1917*]

The lieut. did fine work again early this morning clearing the road to Carrier Sud which was very badly shot up, parts of mens bodies, horses, and *camions* lying around. He shot horses, drove *camions* to the side and made the genie [*combat engineers*] **fill up the big holes.**

The attack came off as per schedule and this evening the gains are doubtful. Rumor has it that the French have taken the whole of Hill 304 (on the Haraumont side) and have advanced 1½ kilometers in front of Carrier Sud. These facts are certain viz. there has been a steady stream of ambulances coming in here all day; they have made some prisoners, the fellows saw several hundred at least and carried some wounded ones. Purdy after an argument carried off a lieutenants epaulets. Some were very young and all were happy, laughing, shaking hands. They told some of the fellows they didn't want victory but peace.

. . . Saw about 600 boche prisoners go by this evening. Some were very young, some very tired and every little while you would see a real dutch face, broad, glasses etc.

Highland Lake
Monday-Aug. 20 [*1917*] —

Dear Stull,

. . . This A.M. (later) your father, Uncle Jerry, Paula, Eliz & I went to the club and watched your father wipe the court up with all the players over there. I was wishing you were here. The kids think he is a wonder, and were taking notes on service — back hand etc. Their comments were funny.

Tuesday

. . . I hope the mysterious business which took you to Paris was successful — Please tell us about it. . . .

Au revoir, mon cher, Lois.

DIARY: **August 21** [*1917*]

Up and to Carriers Sud by 5 o'clock but there were practically no *blessés*. The attack was a great success (see newspapers) 304, Le Mort Homme, Talon, 344 (all commanding points of great importance) were taken with over 5000 prisoners. It is nice to read about it in the paper and know that you were even a very small part of it. The casualties were unbelievably small (only 500 wounded in our division) and the reason the French stopt was because they feared a trap — several counter attacks were stopt before the men left the trenches. The French are to attack again soon if the boche don't counter-attack heavily.

There was an American officer (a major) being shown around. He was pretty pale which is not so unusual considering the smells, parts of dead horses and men that you have to see on the road, and the shells coming in. He couldn't understand much French and every little while would break out with a "*Ah Oui, oui oui*" just the way we did formerly. Whereat we all smiled.

There were 5 boche prisoners in the *abri*, who had been helping the French *brancardiers*. I talked several hours with them and found that after about a half an hour I got on remarkably well. They said all the boche wanted peace which was no news, as well as many interesting things.

Andrew was out with an American colonel and said we were to be taken over soon by the U.S. army. I don't know the details, money, service etc yet.

Oller is pretty much of a nervous wreck and is going to Paris.

Got a letter from Lois.

DIARY: **August 22** [*1917*]

Lay around on a hot day, rested up with a bad cold and speculated on our date of departure. The roads are still bad in every way and now that the attack is over we all want to get out.

. . . The boche made it damned unpleasant last night. There were a lot of planes right over us that dropt bombs all around the neighborhood. Twice I jumped out of bed and lay on the ground. And when they bombed 5 *camions* loaded with munitions and these started to explode, I left for an *abri* where I stayed for several hours.

Aug 22, 1917

Dear Lois,

I have had almost no chance to write (have only written postals home in the last 2 weeks) and don't feel like writing now but promise a long long letter very soon in which I will tell a lot of news. Of course you know by now that a very successful attack has taken place up here. More of that anon.

Meanwhile — yesterday I got your letter written at Highland Lake for which I thank you. I forsee many a happy talk <u>when</u> I get home.

Will write soon. Till then believe in

Stull

DIARY: **August 23** [*1917*]

The prisoners now counted are over 6000. The paper mentions specifically the good work done in handling the wounded. Everybody is tickled to death with us and we will probably get a good citation (which we deserve) but altho everyone considers the job finished, we don't. The roads are still very bad, and often shelled and we are fagged out. I was tired out and sore all over head and bones. I sent postals home. . . .

DIARY: **August 24** [*1917*] **Friday.**

The number of prisoners mounts[.] [*I*]**t is now about 8000. I lay in bed most of the day but went in the White *camion* with a load of wounded boche to Souilly, where I had a long talk with a pleasant and intelligent young boche. Had a short talk with a boche Oberartz** [*chief physician*] **who had been taken prisoner and was now working hard. He was a fine looking (despite Heidelberg student scars) man and of a type you have to admire and respect even though you fight against them.** [*Dueling with fencing swords was common practice among students at Heidelberg University. Participants proudly wore duel-related facial scars.*]

This morning Pearl left for the hospital at Paris. Dallin left too his time being up 5 days ago. We also lost some of our yellow brethern Curtis, Oller and O'Connell, all theoretically sick actually without character enough to fight their fear. We have gotten 3 new men with more to come. One seems to be the real goods under the label of Mark Brennan, who has just come from 6 months service in Salonika.[9]

We hear rumors of another attack in two days. It doesn't interest me much, as all my interest is confined to getting out of here. There is a French saying that no man leaves Verdun the same as he entered it. That is probably true of all times as the fighting is constantly hard and it is absolutely true of Verdun during an attack. I know.

DIARY: August 25 [*1917*]

On duty the day when the attack is to come off. Got some badly wounded men on one trip from St. Fismes, who hadn't been dressed yet so I waited outside Caserne Marceau over an hour while the doctor fixed them. It was a "hectic" night. Rice wrote a good-by note home in full seriousness. Kreutzberg thru nervous strain and fatigue got sick. Got letter from papa and the Globe which is to come regularly.

DIARY: August 26 (1917)

Lay around and rested up most of the day.

The attack was made and must have been pretty successful as the fellows have seen 4 or 5 hundred prisoners. Rumor has it this afternoon that all this mornings gain was lost in a boche counter-attack. See-sawing is to be expected.

The Italians have been raising hell with the Austrians lately taking over 20000 prisoners and killing many more.[10] Somehow I have a hunch the war wont last another year out.

Got a long letter from E.

The chef of Norton Harjes section had a close call a piece of *eclat* hitting and bending double a watch in his pocket, just the way you read about in books. The boche disturbed us after supper dropping one shell very close, a piece of *eclat* coming in our tent door.

DIARY: August 27 (1917)

Got the very welcome news that Purdy and I go on permission tomorrow. Stocky is going in probably to take out a new section. We had a fine song fest to-night which is Ned's 3rd birthday at the front.

I saw 900 boche prisoners go by this evening. A few weren't over 16 years old if my eyes didn't lie.

Business of packing to-night.

August 27th [*1917*]

Dear Stull —

I received letter of July 28th yesterday and of Aug. 2nd — Saturday — They had to be passed all around the family and then some. The secret still remains between you and me, however, but it was rather an embarrassing proposition. Paula was especially curious as usual — and I had to let her think what she pleased. I am glad I don't receive letters under such scrutiny very often.

Aug 30th —

Dear Stull —

Once again I'm at it. Paula talked me to sleep last night and tried to find out a number of things — She didn't succeed because I am not naturally of a very confiding nature, so she gave up in disgust —

. . . I think it's wonderful that you should have been recommended to command a section — but I knew something wonderful would happen. I hope — Oh! how I hope you'll get it. Haven't told and won't.

Trust Lois —

DIARY: **August 28** [*1917*]

Started early but couldn't take the car to Bar so we went to Revigny but the morning train didn't stop there so Stocky went by and we had to wait till 5:30 in the afternoon. We passed part of the time by speaking to some English ladies running a coffee and tea canteen there and part by getting a haircut and shave the latter being done by a woman and well done. On the train we talked with an American soldier who confirmed the stories we had heard of soldiers shooting themselves in the hand. Arrived at Paris tired and hungry but spent a fine night in fine beds at the Hotel de Calais.

DIARY: **August 29** [*1917*]

Everything is changed. Paris is full of American soldiers and a new kind who I learnt were Portugese. Rue Raynouard is changed, all sorts of offices, bureaus and places with Coulter presiding over one. I had a long chin with him. Everybody had heard of our hard work. The place is full of permissionaires [*pensioners*], **old men, new men**

and odd cases, like Spony whom I met. I spoke to Andrew regarding my chances to get a section and he said he knew nothing now that the government was taking it over but perhaps some men besides the present chiefs would be given commissions.

In the afternoon after getting money I went to the American aviation headquarters and investigated, resulting in my application. I took and passed the medical examination. It was careful and strict as regards my heart lungs and eyes. I did numerous tricks, balancing reading etc.

Went to the Follies in the evening and fell in with several Australian captains about 25 years old, who were as fine men as I ever met. We talked war and they had the English aversion to talk about themselves. They had been thru a few "stunts" at Bullecourt[11] etc.

DIARY: **August 30** [*1917*]

. . . Got letters from Lois, papa. . . . In Lois's she says don't join aviation. It came one day late but wouldn't have made any difference anyway.

DIARY: **August 31** [*1917*]

Bought the "Spoon River Anthology." Went out to Neuilly to see Pearl and am afraid he will lose his arm. While I was there I saw a mother visit her boy for the first time since he had lost his foot.

The aviation people told me to come back in about a week for my mental test but I refused to be put off and am going back Monday. You have to keep right after them.

DIARY: **September 1** [*1917*]

About which I remember little except that I was nearly all afternoon with a decent little French girl I met.

Sept 1, 1917

Dear Lois,

At last the long delayed and promised letter: you mustn't complain tho because I wrote to no one. All I did when I had a chance to rest was to throw myself in bed, dead to the world. I am in Paris now on permission, a month late, and enjoying the luxuries of life including

ice cream, sheets, cafe's and things. What I have done and am doing here I will tell you in a few days, at present I'll only say your last letter (Aug 13) speaking of my trip to Paris, came a day too late.

Now for the Verdun attack. You know of course that the French made (Aug 20) a very successful attack there taking over 10000 [*later estimates state that 4,000 prisoners were captured on August 20*][12] **men, and, what is far more important hills, which cost the boche thousands of lives to take.**

. . . We were in historic ground and it looked it. All the hills (and the country right in front of Verdun is all hills) have been fought over many times and the result is that they are in waves of dirt with one shell hole overlapping the next; no grass or any thing growing; no trees but where there used to be a forest you can see some black spots where the roots remain. . . . Beside the desolation visible to the eye there was the desolation visible to the nose. You could often see old bones, boots clothing and things besides lots of recent ones. Every night before the attack the roads were packed with traffic, guns, munitions and all manner of stuff. These made it bad for us so we preferred and did (counter to orders at first) run in daylight when it was supposed to be more dangerous. The traffic at night would move very slowly, would run into you, would always get blocked either because some one went in the ditch (it was very rainy and muddy at the first) or because as was more often the case some vehicle would get hit by a shell. The roads were being shelled nearly all the time. Every ambulance (all 20) was hit by one or more pieces of *eclat* and three were badly hit killing some of the wounded in them. Just before daylight every morning the traffic would all fade away leaving the roads all day to us alone. Then we could count the nights wreckage. On one curve about 100 yds long we counted 15 horses and 8 wagons one morning all hit during the night. The horses were generally left until after the attack but the pieces of men were usually collected and buried immediately but not always. There was one spot I remember where nothing but a mans leg (naked) lay for over a week. We saw a lot of nasty sights and smelt a lot of nasty smells. I've seen them burying bodies so rotten and full of maggots that the buryers had to wear their gas masks while doing the job, which consists of digging a hole and rolling the body in it. We did excellant work which brought praise to us from everyone. Now that it is over it doesn't seem so bad but during it we

were almost exhausted. . . . It was a routine of work to exhaustion throw yourself into bed, drag yourself out to work again. That was why I didnt write and why it helped so to receive letters. There were 3 of us American wounded, the worst will probably lose his arm. One fellow got hit but was carrying a watch in his pocket. The watch was bent into a v shape and he only got a bruise.

I had a very close call with gas which they used a lot especially in one little valley that formed a pocket for it. There was another American section that came up to take over one of our many posts during the attack and luckily on this night I took one of their men to show him the road. It was just about dusk when we started (my fifth trip that day to the worst post the section has ever had) and we got without much excitement to within about 1000 yds of the post when a big motor truck 100 yds in front of me got hit by a shell (they were comming in pretty fast) and completely blocked the road. I couldn't get by and there were too many shells coming in for anyone to try and clear the truck off the road so I and this other fellow crawled in a trench alongside the road and waited. We huddled there a long time getting splashed several times by mud thrown by shells exploding, when gas shells started to come in great numbers. I decided we had better go onto the post where we would be safer and from where we could warn the others by telephone. We started crawling throwing ourselves flat, crawling again (gas masks on of course). To make a long story short and leaving out several interesting steps we got to within about 100 yds of the post (a great big dug-out almost a tunnel in the hill) when I was about buried by a shell and a few seconds later a big gas shell went off within 20 ft of me. Something hit me on the head, making a big dent in my helmet and raising a bump on my head. If it hadn't been for my helmet my head would have been cracked As it was I was dazed, knocked down and my gas mask knocked off. I got several breathes of the strong solution right from the shell before it got diluted with much air. If it hadn't been for the fellow with me I probably wouldn't be writing this letter because I couldn't see, my eyes were running water and burning, so was my nose and I could hardly breathe. I gasped, choked and felt the extreme terror of the man who goes under in the water and will clutch at a straw. The fellow with me grabbed me and led me the hundred yards or so to the post where the doctor gave me a little stuff and where I became alright again in a few

hours except that I was a little intoxicated from the gas for a while. I had other close calls but that was the closest and shook me up most. I think the hardest thing I did was to go back again alone the next night. I had to call myself names before I got up nerve enough.

. . . I owe about 10 letters and want to get them all off to-day and to-morrow if possible so that I can enjoy myself with an easy conscience. Altho by that time I will have to write again and tell you about how I have — it almost slipped out. Perhaps I'll have two things of importance to tell you one you'll like and the other you ought to.

You know how I want to end.

That way, Stull

DIARY: **September 3** [*1917*]

Went to the infirmary in the Swiss challet at 21 rue R. with a fever of 102.2 and a sore throat.

DIARY: **September 4** [*1917*]

Was sick all day, even too sick to be nursed by Miss Austen who is charming.

DIARY: **September 6** [*1917*]

Better yet, many visitors and much talk. Got letters from mama. . . .

Thursday-Sept-6. [*1917*]

Dear Stull,

. . . I do hope you have had some sort of a vacation by this time. It must be awful to be under such a strain all the time and especially when there is such danger as exists where you are now. I wish I might help you out in some way, but since I'm not near enough to run the machine once in a while to relieve you I don't know just what I can do except knit and that doesn't give you any sleep or rest does it?

I saw the pictures you sent home, for the first time, up at the lake. . . . I like the uniform — it is very becoming.

. . . I have your letter of Aug. 12. that's the last. . . .

Next time you tell me a secret please put it on a page by itself — I have been having an awful time. Have you heard anything more about it?

Bien à vous, Lois

DIARY: **September 8** [*1917*]

Around more. Fussed around the aviation office and successfully passed the mental test which consists of "you want to be a flyer" "I do." Passed.

DIARY: **September 9** [*1917*] **Sunday.**

Got released from my remaining few days in the ambulance service. I had a good time in it, learnt a lot, saw a lot, did some work and am sorry to leave it but such is life — always moving on. . . .

Here ends my first diary, friend to my loneliness, companion to my moments of exhiliration, aid in periods of depression. Always to be trusted, never betraying confidences I found it a habit

DIARY: **September 10** [*1917*]

[*The second of the Holt pocket diaries begins here.*]

Spent most of the day at Versailles. . . .

DIARY: **September 11** [*1917*]

Another one of the lonely restless days that make me dislike Paris. I have to make a decision, am in a city with no real friends consequently lost, am homesick, have nothing to do. The combination is awful leaving me restless, discontented and unhappy. . . .

Sept 11, 1917

Dear Lois,

I've got them bad — all shades from a light violet to a deep purple. And what's more I cant seem to lose them. I'm generally pretty happy and when I do get a blue fit, can kid myself out of it or read out of it. But this one is awful, I've been fighting myself ever since I got in Paris with no result and I've gone down to the new Y.M.C.A. often and gotten real books that ought to coax a smile out of an Egyptian mummy but after a few pages I get up and wander restlessly on. Its just plain

homesickness. What do you advise? Today I got your letter of Aug 6, over a week after I got the one of Aug 12, and instead of making me walk in the clouds as they usually do, I feel worse than ever. It is the first year in (how many?) that I won't be there to guide you safely home when you get back from the country. The other day in the train we went thru a tunnel and I tried awful hard to persuade myself I was on the way uptown and that pretty soon the train would go above the ground at 149 St. But honest it was no use.

Perhaps the cause of all the color is that it is near Sept 17 when I could go home and I know I'm not going. Anyhow when you get this mail please sit down and write me about three letters saying youre glad I'm going to stay and that you['']**r**[e] **glad I've entered the aviation school. It will help a lot because even though I wont need them then I will save them for future use.**

You knew of course I wouldn't come home till after the war and you could probably guess I wouldn't stay in the ambulance service, even though I did have a fine time and was lucky enough to be in one of the sections that got plenty of work. So to make a long story short I applied to the American aviation and go to the school this Friday I expect. The school is near or at Tours in the south of France where I will be comfortable during most of the winter. The course is from 4 to six months. When I know my exact address I'll send it but 21 rue Raynonard [*Raynouard*] **will do till I tell you.**

Incidentally I'll tell you a joke. The physical examination is very stiff as regards the eyes and altho a doctor in Ithaca told me I would have to wear glasses all my life these doctors couldn't find anything wrong with my eyes. Of course I didn't say anything myself.

I consider myself very lucky for many reasons, viz the aviation is the best branch of the service, you live far enough back so that you are safe and can live above ground. How much that means you cant understand. It is the aristocracy of the army the best class of fellows in it, and it affords the most pleasure and exhiliration. And as long as there has to be a war and you are in it you might as well be in a position to get what can be out of it.

(Here I sit back and philosophize sadly for 5 minutes with this result) It is funny. Here I am in France and in love with you very much more than you realize. And I am also in or just entering in aviation. That ought to be a plot for a good letter full of fine inspiring senti-

ments and such stuff. But I fall down horribly and have messed around on 6 pages saying practically nothing but that I hope to be an aviator and that I hope you'll understand. I know you will.

Sept 13,

Dear Lois,

I first decided not to send this but am going to just to show you that we all have our periods of doubt, deppression and dullness. I am all recovered now and in full control of my spirits, the blue fit having run itself out till I was able to drown the remnants in <u>lemonade</u> at the Y.M.C.A.

My papers haven't come back from the adjutant's office yet so I can't "take the Widows shilling" (do you know your Kipling) yet but expect surely to go down to the school in a very few days.

You remember I wrote you that I had been recommended as a leader of am ambulance section. Well the ambulance service is being Fedralized and I would not be certain of getting a section if I stayed in, altho I might. However it isn't sour grapes to say I would rather be in the aviation service anyway. If and when I qualify as a pilot I will get a commission as 1st lieut which carrys a salary above $2200, I think. Thats almost enough to start installment payments on a house at Forest Hills.

To prove to you that I am still as crazy as ever I'll tell you that I have been thinking of and trying to find a way of going to Russia. They sure are having lively times there and I hate to miss them.[13] Don't be worried tho because I found out that to be a Russian aviator I would have to go to the same school I am and then be transferred to the R. army. I may do it but won't have to decide for months yet. What do you think? The prospect is alluring: new places, new people, new customs; plenty of action and best of all unusual experiences that I wont get by staying on this front. Ain't I just as crazy as ever.

After I get down to the school at Tours my mail will be censored by the U.S. so I'll have to be more careful of what I say because they being new to the game will probably be absurdly strict. So when I wrote instead of telling you I took a walk and sat half an hour on top of a hill wondering what you were doing in E 219 St, I'll have to say "what you were doing somewhere in New York"

This letter, you can't complain of its length altho you could and probably will of its coherency, I'm going to send by a fellow who leaves for America the 15th so you will probably get it the 25th. I wonder what you will be doing.

I am now in a little hotel which I have stored in my mind as being on the list for future reference. I don't know that I've told you yet but I intend to spend my honeymoon in France and so whereever I go I naturally lay plans. The ideal way would be to take, buy or rent a Ford and travel leisurely over the places I have and will have been at during the war. It would be cheap as you stay in these little French villages for almost nothing and it would be very interesting. How would you like the trip? (R.S.V.P.)

To get back to hard facts and the little hotel from where I started, I am here and have to write a lot of letters to-night so that they will go on the next boat. I have also to tell the folks that I am going, or going to try, to aviate. I hope they will understand and won't worry but I'm afraid they wont understand and will worry.

So far this letter has been entirely about myself, my doings and little worries. You know thats the secret of all my restlessness and worry. If I could get out of myself and think about someone else for a change it would make all my "blueness" disappear [*like*] **beer at a German picnic. Now for more pleasant things. What whom and how are you doing? What are you thinking of? How do you like school? How is Enid, Lela Curtis and all the rest, not forgetting Aunt (to be) Ethel? What shows have you seen and are they good? What happened at H.L. and who was there. (Mama writes me that Hal was up there, putting on his civils as he didn't wish to pose as a hero. I didn't tell her but when I first got to Paris I got in a room all by myself and had a dance of joy in mine) For goodness and my sake send me some news. Whats the matter with you anyhow!!!**

Now for the real dope on the war. Here is my guess. The war may end this winter the right way i.e. Germany absolutely beaten. There is a chance of this but it is not very probable now after the turn of affairs in Russia has bolstered up the very low German morale so it may stand the winters strain.

The war may end this winter a wrong way i.e. a draw or its equivalent, not an overthrow of Billy the Kaiser[.] **I trust the English but am afraid of the French. They are awfully low in morale because of**

Russia [*Russian Bolsheviks were organizing and receiving support from within the French government*] **and even to-day formed a new cabinet with no socialists in it. That is good news because the socialists or part of them were getting stronger and were pacific. France was awfully near a revolution (or at least a flat refusal to fight on the part of the men) last April. Only the fact that the U.S. really came in saved the day in my humble opinion. More than one regiment shot its officers and refused to leave the trenches when they ought to**[,] **thus contributing largely to this springs failure.**

But I'm an optimist and honestly believe the war will survive the winters cold and last another year. What will happen then even my great brain can't predict but every day longer that it lasts means that Germany is so much nearer and surer of defeat. . . .

Here I am (in a little hotel) writing page after page to you when I have at least 15 other letters to write. There is a lot I could tell you about and wish I could but it is hard to write. All the things you see, the people you meet and the conversations with the different soldiers. I have a great and healthy respect for the English, both private and officer, English includes Australians, and have little respect for our "heroes" over here. Our officers are worse junkers [*militant aristocrats*] **than the Prussians and our privates have already, long before they've been in danger, begun to shoot themselves in the hand. I know for a fact there has been a good deal of that. But of course the next bunch of new men will be of a different class and real men.**

Enough of the worlds troubles now for yours and mine. My worst one is that you are so far away. Whats troubling you? But the war will be over some day and then —

Look out for Stull. . . .

Tuesday Sept. 11. [*1917*]

Dear Stull,

. . . .No letter came last week but one did this A.M. so I guess that was delayed from last week. You must be terribly busy if you haven't even time to write. Why do they work you so hard? Can't they get fellows enough to shift once in a while? . . . I'm terribly afraid you will break down badly if you aren't relieved soon. I don't see how you have stood the strain so long, as it is. . . . If you don't write and say you have had a vacation soon I'll have my head worried off.

We have been to the movies this afternoon — Everything is soldiers, marching, fighting, in camp. German aeroplane brought down — etc. It makes you thrill — then feel like killing every boche in sight — then like just crying good and hard. . . .

. . . I was talking to your father on the phone the other day about this good news you may have for him soon. He asked me if I knew what it was. Were you coming home, etc, etc. . . . Eliz. says you told them you had "good news" and the only good news is that you are coming home — , you are coming home. Q.E.D.

Au revoir, Lois.

DIARY: **September 12** [*1917*]

Read some more and tried to get better control of my spirits. Had a long talk in the afternoon with some fellows who are anxious to go to Russia where Kerensky and Gen. Kornilof are having a little argument and Russia another revolution [*the attempted Kornilof coup opened the door for a Bolshevik takeover, which was successful in mid-November*]. **It seems almost impossible to get there and what I would do I don't know. But the prospect is alluring, new places, scenes and people. The drawback to the aviation here is that it is too crowded and regular with none of the advantages accruing to the pioneer. . . .**

DIARY: **September 13** [*1917*] **Thursday.**

My papers haven't gotten back from the adjutants office yet so I can't be sworn in and needs must hang around longer. . . .

Sept 13, 1917.

Dear Folks,

. . . I have severed my connection with the ambulance service and did so with real regrets. There were some fine fellows in our section and we accomplished something. Incidentally I was recommended as a good leader for another section which is quite a compliment because it is a fairly responsible job and because there are so many older men in the service. But the government is taking over the entire service and

I don't know whether I would be given command of a section or not. . . . As for me I've done or am doing what I have wanted to for a long time viz. getting into aviation. . . . The course is from 4 to six months so I will be there (in southern France) most of the winter and when I pass it successfully (as I have no reason not to) I will get a commission as 1st lieut, which carries a good salary. While in the school I will get a private's pay.

I hope you will understand, approve and not worry. I've had to decide alone without consulting your wishes at all and have done what I thought right and best. It isn't so dangerous as most people think. In fact the whole war isn't as you will see if you consult statistics[14] (see Literary Digest for Aug 18 (?)) And the air service is even less dangerous than the others, contrary to popular opinion. It also has other numerous and great advantages viz. you are stationed back far enough so that you are safe and can live above ground. You can't understand how much it means to not have to live underground. Both sides are turning and concentrating their efforts more and more on aeroplanes because if either could overwhelm the other absolutely in the air it could end the war quickly. The air service includes the best type of man as a class. You don't have to fight hand to hand which while necessary is messy. You do get some joy and sport in flying and if there has to be a war and you are in it you might as well get what you can out of it. Altogether it is the best, cleanest, healthiest, least dangerous and most effective (?) branch of service in the war.

. . . I hope again that you will be pleased with what I have done. Write frankly about everything. I do.

Love to all, Stull

DIARY: **September 14** [*1917*]

My papers haven't come back yet worse luck. Rice is in and says the section goes on repos to-day. He has heart trouble and a nervous breakdown. Heywood reached here to-day and hopes to go to the aviation school too. . . .

POST CARD

Sept 14. [*1917*]

Dear Stull,

I don't suppose you'll have a very happy birthday, but I hope it will be as happy as it can. Our cards ought to reach you in time to let you know we wont forget Oct. 2nd

Lois

DIARY: **September 16** [*1917*] **Sunday.**

Went right after lunch with Heywood to Versailles where they were having some kind of a big fete for the blind. We sat in the woods and listened to good music, we wandered about seeing races, a baseball game, fencing, duels with wax bullets and best of all the polygot [*mixed*] **crowd. Such a crowd all nations, ranks and ages. In the evening we dissipated further by going to the Follies Bergére and witnessing that crowd. It is a great sight.**

DIARY: **September 17** [*1917*]

Six months ago to-day I sailed from New York. I can remember the day well; how it rained, how we all met at the pier; waited there and how with a sinking heart I set sail for new experiences, which I have enjoyed and benefited from. And to-day appropriately I may have paved the way for another set of still more interesting times.

No my papers haven't come back yet but I refer to Russia. All my inclinations point to Russia now as the place for most excitement, new experiences and different ones. Even fate seems to help in luring me on. This noon while sitting in a little cafe eating lunch with Heywood and Long a little civilian came in and asked me to order lunch for him. He spoke English with a very funny accent and said he was Russian, that he had deserted from the Russian navy 4 years ago, had been in Italy and wanted now to return to Russia but couldn't get papers to go on past Paris. His story didn't sound right to me in several places and I wonder what he really is. Of course as Brace, of the Herald who is trying to get to Russia, says we are all suspicious now but there is a chance he might be anything from a Russian spy to a German prince. He heightened my natural curiousity by asking if it were possible to buy a gun here. I left him waiting for the naval attaché to return from lunch.

That is only an incident that adds to my desire to get to Russia, where a new field, new honors, new things to be done, awaits the one who dares to do them. I went from Russian consul to Russian military

mission and from there to 59 rue Pierre Charron where resides Colonel Bobrikoff and General Fankevitch, who have charge of Russian aviation. After walking in as if I owned the place I secured a fine interview with the Colonel and he said the best thing to do was what I wanted viz go thru the American Aviation school, get a commission, then go to him and he would ask the U.S. army to attach me to the Russian army. He said it can surely be done. I hope so. . . .

DIARY: **September 18** [*1917*]

. . . My papers have at last arrived and I was told to return tomorrow to be sworn in.

In the evening after a good talk with Charlie Muller we went to the Olympia and again I enjoyed the sight of the soldiers from so many nations with the French girls. We got talking with a couple of American privates, then an English officer and an American aviator in the *Lafayette Esquadrille* was added. Both were slightly drunk but that loosened them up. Soon another American aviator drifted into the conversation. He proved to be Lufberry the best American and one of the best aviators in the world. He gave me the impression of being very level headed but ordinary, like many others who like him were mechanics or chauffeurs before the war.[15] Home and to-bed where I finished "The Valley of Fear" by Doyle. Altogether an interesting night.

Tuesday-Sept. 18th [*1917*]

Dear Stull,

The last letter I received from you was written on Aug 22. and in it you didn't mention anything about being gased. I don't understand why if it happened on the 15th as your father says it did. The fellow who went thru it with you wrote to his father who told your father — Why didn't you tell us about it?. . .

Won't you please come home now? Even if you go back later, I think you ought to get away and rest up for a while —

Can't write any more — Lois.

DIARY: **September 19** [*1917*]

A momentous day as I took the Federal oath this morning after

much finger-printing and such like. It was an opportune time as I was told I might go to the school at Tours tomorrow and was sent to the quartermasters where I got my uniform which I can see becomes me. Such is the vanity of man. But I am real proud to wear it and I liked the business like way it was given out. When the Americans really get in the war it is time for Germany to look out. . . .

DIARY: **September 20** [*1917*]

Around to the aviation headquarters. . . In the afternoon I was told I was to go to Tours tomorrow early so I left to get ready. . . .

Home quickly, packed and had my baggage checked at the station because I leave early tomorrow morning at 7:something. My last for a while night in Paris I'm spending alone and broke in my hotel. Now for some letters. Wrote to home, Bill Smith and Lois. . . .

Sept 20, 1917

Dear Lois,

This is my first letter to you since I became a member of the U.S. army and I'm sorry it wont be a better one. Somehow I never seem to have time to write a long, thought-out letter to you. But I ought to have soon, because tomorrow morning I needs must leave my soft bed, which I will do cheerfully, and go to Tours where an aviation camp is. After this I wont be able to tell you where I am but I will be at Tours. . . . my new address sounds like a recruiting poster it is: American Expeditionary Forces, Air Service, France, via New York.

Yesterday was the momentous day; my papers had been properly red-taped so I took my oath and gave it to them and then they took my fingerprints. In exchange they gave me a new uniform and outfit. It just becomes my style of beauty and I had to call a gendarme to protect me from the girls (are you jealous).

. . . However I will say this, namely; in all my vast army experience both in the French army (where I earned 5 centimes [*1 cent*] a day) and in the American (I haven't even bothered to inquire about salary) I have never worn any uniform as comfortable as "civils." Even tho my one suit was all crushed and wrinkled and it is wartime, I have been wearing them here in Paris. And in the pockets I found some money, real U.S.A. money. It looked as welcome as a man does at a

summer resort. Besides that I found some theatre ticket stubs for Mar 14. Remember it — the "Kiss for Cinderella."

. . . I've been having a great time and great experiences lately in Paris, having recovered my health nerve and spirits. I think I forgot in my previous letters to mention that when I first reached Paris after Verdun I went to bed for 6 days with a fever of 102½ that lasted three days. No wonder I felt homesick and blue. . . .

Will write you soon and often from Tours.

While I think of it, you mentioned several times about the "mysterious business" that was to take me to Paris. There was nothing mysterious about it only I didn't want to write home that I was going into aviation and then find I couldn't pass the physical test. They might worry for nothing. If I couldn't get in nobody would ever know or worry[.] **If I could get in, I would then tell them. That's all, no mystery.**

. . . I had intended to write a lot to-night (it is my last night in Paris for some time and I'm spending it alone at home. Sherlock Holmes would deduce from that and correctly that my financial status is not the kind that Bradstreet would rate A no 1) but this is my third and last letter, if you can call this a letter.

I'm in the American army now so it[']**s your patriotic duty to keep me cheered up with many and long letters.**

Now to bed, so as to be up bright and early tomorrow. For tomorrow I go to new faces, new fields to conquer, new problems to meet new things to see and the same girl to think of. *Alors je suis content* [*Therefore I am satisfied*]**.**

Stull

Part Two

Learning to Fly in France

September 21, 1917-August 27, 1918

HOLT EXPRESSED PLEASURE with his initial experience in aviation school at Tours, but his early exuberance began to fade as he moved through flight training. The joy of flight for W. Stull Holt may have lessened when he had to cope with the French Nieuport airplanes and their rotary engines, which he encountered in the later stages of instruction.

The training aircraft employed in the winter of 1917-18 were quite similar, no matter what national insignia they wore. They were of wooden construction, braced internally with wire, and covered with a light fabric that was then painted with a compound that drew the fabric taut. This compound, called "dope," made the fabric inflammable. The training machines were two-seaters, with the instructor and pupil seated in two open cockpits, usually with the instructor occupying the rear seat. Both men were exposed to the elements. These aircraft had no heaters, brakes, or parachutes.

The biplanes had wings externally braced by a forest of wooden struts and wires. Inevitably, all this wood and wire dragged at the air as the aircraft passed through it, especially since the two non-retractable landing wheels were also supported by similar struts and wires. This drag drew heavily upon the engine's available, and sometimes meager, power.

But it also must be said that instructors and students often saved themselves considerable harm by side-slipping into the ground when a crash seemed inevitable. It took some time for all the wire, woodwork, and fabric to crumple up as the wingtips met the ground, and this could sometimes soften the impact of the aircraft's arrival.

Stull Holt trained upon Caudron machines, among others, at Tours. These awkward, two-seaters were powered by stationary, air-cooled, Anzani radial engines, with cylinders set in a star pattern around the propeller shaft. The available power and speed of a radial engine depended upon the number of cylinders it contained, and this could vary from three to nine. The instructor — the "*moniteur*" — and his pupil sat in tandem in a "*nacelle*," a bathtub-shaped fuselage, with the motor sitting out in front.

This aircraft was certainly unsophisticated, even by the standards of 1918. Holt successfully managed the slow, steady Caudron machines and after approximately a month of dual instruction, he soloed — the first to do so in his group he proudly recalls. He had some misadventures and forced landings, which often could be ascribed to the chancy performance of the aviation engines of the period, particularly those which were being overworked by amateurs in training. Generally, however, Holt got along alright, and the Caudron seems to have been a relatively safe and forgiving machine to fly, unlike the aircraft he encountered later.

As 1918 arrived, Holt and his friends saw day after day of foul weather and little flying. For example, he did not get back into the air for four weeks after his solo flight. But Holt finally completed his basic flight training in late January and received his French pilot's badge — a wing in a wreath — and his American Air Service wings. Eventually, his Federation Aeronautique Internationale certificate, dated 30 July, 1918, caught up with him.

Holt's papers make it clear that some of his post-solo flying at Tours — including some long distance flying and altitude tests — was done on what he called "Rhone" Nieuports, by which he meant, "LeRhone," a French rotary engine. To understand some of Holt's decisions during his advanced training at Issoudun, a general knowledge of rotary engines — a type of internal combustion motor long forgotten by the public until it reappeared in the modern Mazda automobile — is warranted.

The rotary engine of the 1917-18 period was the result of attempts to design an air-cooled aviation motor with power-to-weight ratio more favorable than the heavy, water-cooled, in-line powerplants of the period. The latter were burdened with the weight of radiator, water, hose and pump of their cooling systems. It was thought that a radial engine, which looked like a rotary but was fixed in place, did not receive sufficient cooling air flow past its cylinders. By contrast, a rotary engine's crankshaft was fixed to the motor mount in the nose of the airframe, and as its separate cylinders fired, the entire motor rotated around the fixed crankshaft, turning at the propeller's speed. Thus, as the air passed by the cylinder, the heads were being spun through the enveloping air. Gasoline was fed into the hollow crank shaft, as was the lubricant, and the whole engine became an air-cooled, whirling dervish!

Imagine some 200 pounds of engine metal, with a heavy wooden propeller, set spinning at 1,300-1,400 revolutions per minute. A rotary tended to spew unburnt fuel and lubricant — castor oil — from its exhaust valves. This ejected mist of fuel collected inside the metal cowling around the engine, where it mixed with air and constituted an explosive fire hazard. The castor oil spray was also inhaled in some quantity as it blew back into the pilot's face.

The fuel and air mixture levers that governed the operation of most rotary engines required sensitive adjustment. They had to be set with extreme care for takeoff and climb, and the relationship of one lever with the other had to be carefully altered for level flight or landings. Engine vibration alone could move them out of adjustment, starving the motor of the fuel and air mixture it required and stopping it in mid-flight. If it could not be restarted, an immediate emergency landing was inevitable. And of course when a rotary engine was attached to a light wood-and-fabric frame, this weight of swiftly turning metal created gyroscopic forces that had to be experienced to be believed. Controlling such an engine, especially when it was mounted in a nimble, light aircraft, took a delicate touch.

On February 1, 1918, Holt, having completed all the requirements at Tours, was enrolled at the pilot's "finishing school" at Issoudun. There at Issoudun he ultimately came to the conclusion that he did not possess the piloting skills required of a fighter pilot. In his diary entry for the period

February 5-18, 1918, Holt wrote, "The course is divided into roulers, 23 meter Nieuports double control, 23 meter single control, 18 meter single, 15 meter single acrobatics, and then 15 meter with 120 hp motors. A great many fellows only go thru 18 meter work and then go to observation or bombing schools." In the French system, aircraft were sometimes designated not by a model number, but by the area in square meters of its wings, so a "23 meter" Nieuport had a wing surface area of 23 square meters. The 15 meter Nieuport of 120 hp was the smallest and fastest of the aircraft Holt mentioned. All had rotary engines

The "roulers" were Morane-Saulnier monoplanes with their wings clipped short so they could not fly. Almost all aircraft of the World War I period were "tail-draggers," — they rested on two main wheels forward, were non-steerable and without brakes, and on a "tailskid" at the back. Steering the aircraft on the ground, using only the propeller airblast over the rudder surfaces, was a difficult process. The clipped-wing rouler, Morane, was used for teaching ground control. It also introduced the student to the sensitive control adjustments required to operate a rotary engine.

At Issoudun, the trained pilot was led through a succession of numbered fields where he learned maneuvers of increasing complexity on machines that were ever-faster and more sensitive to fly. Only in the initial stages at Issoudun did one receive much dual instruction, and this might have sufficed provided that the weather permitted daily flying. But in February 1918, the weather at Issoudun was not conducive to flying. Moreover, the French instruction system was based on the belief that personal gallantry and a sincere desire to fly were all an aspiring pilot needed to successfully complete training. It was reminiscent of the methods sometimes employed in teaching novices to swim: hurl them into deep water to give them the incentive to learn quickly.

As the weeks passed and the American officers at Issoudun struggled to organize and operate their newly acquired instructional facilities, Holt became fretful. He was increasingly annoyed by the teaching methodologies, the inferior state of aircraft maintenance, the poor food, low morale, sickness, and especially the winter weather that eventually prohibited all flying. Although he frequently denied it, Holt's confidence was being eroded away. The diary will show Holt's growing uneasiness about his lack of "touch" in the air. Ultimately Holt was convinced that he was too ham-fisted to fly the very maneuverable but demanding rotary-powered

French Nieuports. But, of course, one had to master these aircraft if he hoped to fly in an American frontline fighter squadron.

On February 22, 1918, he crashed and recorded the incident in his diary. Many pilots far more experienced than Holt made the mistake of turning back under similar circumstances, trying to regain the field from which they took off. Most of those who made this decision died for it. Landing at a high rate of speed across the furrows of a plowed field, Holt's Nieuport sank its wheels into the mud, instantly somersaulting to an upside down stop. Perhaps because he had cut the ignition, or perhaps because his fuel tank remained intact, the aircraft did not burn. Holt was hanging head down, suspended from his safety belt.

Holt was cleared of all blame in this crash because he had done everything possible under the circumstances to prevent it. He had crashed and walked away from it, which was all that counted for a pilot in that era. But his nerve appears to have left him, despite his protests to the contrary.

He had reassured himself, and his family and fiancée, that the sights he'd seen as an ambulance driver on the western front had not shaken him. An exploding gas shell had torn off his steel helmet and left him choking to death, but he had overcome that too, and had won the *Croix de Guerre* for his bravery and determination. Yet this brave youngster, a fine, natural tennis player, did not seem to possess the eye and hand coordination needed to control an agile combat aircraft. He decided to transfer to bombardment, ending any possibility that he might join one of the new American fighter squadrons.

There is irony in his decision, because had Holt continued his training, remaining with the slower machines until he felt more comfortable in the air — a choice offered to him by his *moniteur* — he might have gained that touch for which he sought. He might have passed out of Issoudun as a competent, if not brilliant, *chasse* pilot and gone first to gunnery school at Cazaux and then to one of the newly formed, American fighter squadrons. Moreover, he decided to go to bombardment, not as a pilot, but as an observer-gunner, bombardier, photographer, jack-of-all-trades.

The first American squadrons to go into action flew the most up-to-date of the Nieuport machines, the rotary-powered 28's, but in July, 1918, these machines were replaced by the newest French fighter aircraft, the Spad XIII. This chunky, sturdy, and very fast biplane was powered by a 220 hp, eight-cylinder, in-line (and non-rotary) Hispano-Suiza engine. It could achieve speeds of up to 138 miles per hour. Moreover, the Spad was strongly built and its pilots came to believe it could dive forever without losing its wings. As a consequence, they put their trust in it, despite initial problems with its "Hisso" engine. Not everyone liked the Spad, especially those who preferred the maneuverability of a Nieuport, but in spite of this, Americans began to run up big scores on the machine.

Stull Holt might have found the Spad to be an ideal mount for aerial combat. With its straightforward throttle, the Spad was relatively simple to operate. The Hisso engine, when functioning well, gave the Spad a higher top speed than almost any other frontline fighter, which allowed its pilot to accept combat or eschew it. It also was a very steady platform for the two synchronized Vickers machine guns mounted on the cowling in front of the pilot. This heavy, squared-off, tough little fighter proved to be an ideal weapon for Eddie Rickenbacker, Frank Luke, Charles Biddle and other high-scoring American fighter pilots.[16]

Note that the number of letters written by Holt was very much reduced during this mid-winter period of turmoil. He wrote to Lois Crump on December 1, 1917, but the next letter she received was written on February 3, 1918. Other than Christmas letters, his parents fared no better than she did. He speaks of a post office fire at Tours which may have destroyed some of his letters. In mid-January Holt sent a very brief cable to his parents that read, "LETTERS DELAYED EVERYTHING ALRIGHT."

Was this dearth of letters simply because — as he said — he could not find sufficient privacy in the training barracks to allow him to write? His diary writing also became quite sparse at the beginning of 1918, and he eventually stopped keeping a daily diary in April of that year. He later reconstructed the events from April through July from a perspective in September 1918. Then he quit writing a diary entirely once his squadron entered combat. [See map, p. 314.]

DIARY: **September 21** [*1917*]

Up early so as to write short notes to Steve, Miss Mingame and Heyward. To the train and off. The trip was uneventful save for the little French girl I talked with all the way out. The country was not very picturesque being very flat all the way. Arrived at Tours and went out in a motor truck to the field which is 4 or 5 miles out of Tours. Tours is a city of 80,000, a cathedral and other sights yet to be

seen by me. All I saw was the ordinary quaint squat French city altho with fewer soldiers than most I have seen and less warlike, naturally as the war itself never reached here.

At the aviation field everything seems to[o] **good to be true. There are about 200 students here including about 50 in the French army. It only takes from 6 to ten weeks to get a *brevet*** [*certificate*] **and commission. In that time, depending on yourself and weather conditions, the course here is finished and afterwards it is necessary to go to another school for acrobatics and fancy work. . . . I recognize several men here I knew either at Cornell or in the ambulance** [*service*]**, notably Wilmington and Brewer. Everyone is enthusiastic and looks in fine health.**

The country is naturally adapted for aviation schools (I hear there are more nearby) being flat and not wooded. We are in a great big enclosure, with lots of good barracks and more being built by boche prisoners, Algerians, Adamites [*Annanites? i.e., Vietnamese*] **and women dressed in overalls. Above the field are a lot of planes going up and coming down all the time. . . .**

DIARY: **September 22** [*1917*]

. . . Saturday. . . . Had some coffee, bread and confiture [*jam*]**, and did practically nothing most of the morning except a little red tape.**

They talk a strange language here, all about "wing slips," "taking their first hop" "solos" etc but I suppose I'll be a veteran soon. And after reading the U.S. army rules about mail I don't think I can write anything at all. That too I guess will be learnt in time.

Had a real meal at about 11 and as we had nothing to do I went along with the auto truck which visits Tours after lunch. Tours is a very old city, with narrow streets even for France. I did nothing but look around and buy a paper which told of a new and seemingly successful British [***Second Army on 20 September***] **attack at Yhers** [*Ypres*]**.**

Got back from Tours just in time for a little lunch at 3 and then spent the rest of the afternoon watching the flying and learnt something by so doing. It looks easy and I think it must be. It was a fine day and they must have been able to put in a good deal of time. Which redounds to our benefit as the men ahead will not clog our way so much.

Another meal at 8, the fourth, but none too many. The air is wonderful and I can feel myself getting healthier.

DIARY: **September 23** [*1917*] **Sunday.**

Hung around and watched others fly nearly all morning, learning a lot of more or less obvious things.

We had a lot of equipment issued to us including flying-helmet, goggles, woolen cap, sweater, leather coat, gloves for flying and underwear, shirts and any other things of the regular uniform we wanted. In the afternoon some of us in [*the*] **charge of a *moniteur*** [*a prefect in charge of the students*] **went off to another field nearby and some of the fellows flew a little. The only thing noticeable was that once in landing it** [*the training aircraft*] **tipped up on end.**

DIARY: **September 24** [*1917*]

Up before six again and saw the sun rise for the fourth day in succession. I was the first to go up this morning, riding over to the other field from here in the plane. It is an Anzani with double controls altho I played a very little part that way. The wind from the propellor was awfully strong at first but I seemed to get used to the pressure. We started off, rose slowly and rode very steadily all 25 minutes, making a few turns which I endeavored to assist in under directions from the *moniteur* who would tap me on the back. The steering, right and left is done with your feet on an ordinary rudder arrangement, a plain board. The balancing up and down either lengthwise or laterally is done with a perpendicular stick, which you push in the direction you wish to go down. I wasn't so greatly thrilled because I knew I would get a lot of flying from now on but it was certainly a great and new sensation. The whole country looks different, naturally, and very small and neat especially the little groups of houses that rushed by way underneath. The landing didn't seem to be so difficult. The motor was stopt and immediately we started downward sharply which we continued till it looked like we were going thru but before we hit, he pulled back the stick and we skimmed along bumping a very little at first. So it was, my first flight of many thousand I hope, nothing so very wonderful when you do it but strange when you think about it.

Thirty six new men blew in last night after a week in France and

as long in England. They are mechanics, engineers, aviators or something no one seems to know exactly. They are a fine . . . bunch. . . .

Drilled a few minutes in between a couple of meals and after went out to the field to fly but didn't because they didn't get around to me. I have a new instructor, M. Baret(?), who speaks good English and is one of the best instructors according to common report. He looks efficient and I am glad of the change.

DIARY: **September 25** [*1917*]

Very foggy and rainy all morning so there was no flying. We all lay around. I read "The Mutiny of the Elsinore" by J. London, again and lots of periodicals. In the afternoon there was flying but not for me. Our man had hard luck breaking wires and tires which took some time to fix. But I am not in the least impatient everything is far better than I expected, but some of the fellows grouse a bit.

I met Kurtz an old section one man here yesterday. It is a lazy and healthy life we lead, open air[,] **plenty of meals, no dissipations (as yet). I can notice myself getting fatter.**

Tuesday Sept, 25th [*1917*]

Dear Stull,

No letter yet — and everyone is worried now. I don't know whether or not to send your sweater. It is finished and ready to send but I think I had better wait until I hear from you before I send it.

. . . The Tribune this morning quoted part of a speech made by Major General Woods and the words are exactly what you wrote me quite a while ago — "America cannot win the war in the air as so many people seem to think — It will take men and sacrifice." I have noticed similar statements made by others — We seem to be waking up. Socialists, anti-war people and I.W.W.'s [*Industrial Workers of the World or "Wobblies"*][17] should be behind prison bars now, after the revelation of all the German plots and intrigues, of the past week. According to records made during or just after the Spanish American war, Germany was planning then to crush England and France and then to come to the United States and help herself to our gold. It seems odd to me that those things have not been revealed sooner. . . .

Your father says in his Market Letter that war will be over before January 1st — I am optimistic too — It must end by that time —

Here's hoping that it will —

Au revoir, Lois

P.S. Have you learned any French?

DIARY: **September 26** [*1917*] **Wednesday.**

Another foggy morning but it looks as if it would clear up in time. The weather assumes a position of utmost importance in my new profession. No flying in the morning but some, not including me, flew this afternoon. I did nothing but lie around on the grass and watch and read. Its a great life, the war seems a million miles away. . . .

DIARY: **September 27** [*1917*]

Foggy and misty again so that no one could fly this morning but this afternoon we got in some good licks. I had 2 trips running part of the time in the air alone and most of the time I ran it and the *moniteur* followed along. It seemed very easy altho I realize I have a lot to learn but it seems easy to do so. . . .

DIARY: **September 28** [*1917*]

. . . The morning was again so misty that we couldn't fly but I made a couple of trips in the afternoon. My instructor was very pleased with me and I was too. Of course I don't know anything about flying yet but I can see I can learn. . . .

Friday-Sept. 28 [*1917*] —

Dear Stull,

I am so happy and proud that I am using my bran[*d*] new writing paper on you. There was no one home yesterday when I received that long looked for letter so I had to make a perfect fool of myself and dance around all by my lonesome —

. . . The United States is becoming aroused to the fact that there is as much danger lurking within its territory as without. Just at present every patriotic man and woman too, who is capable of talking before an audience is demanding that all suspicious characters be put out of the way, especially those who hold high positions and by their speeches influence the ignorant — who cannot or do not think for themselves and believe all they are told. Several senators will have to explain their actions before long, and methinks it will go hard with them. Detectives and police in New York are doing great work in rounding up — I.W.Ws. "pacifists" etc. In one night there were several hundred locked up. Things are humming over here now.

One indication that we mean business now is — that all boys over sixteen must train three times a week. Curtis went last night, for the first time. It is no longer empty talk. . . .

Au revoir, Lois.

DIARY: **September 29** [*1917*]

No fog so I got up feeling fine like I do all day. I find myself singing every little while and capering for joy and animal spirits. It was so windy in the morning we had to quit but I got in a ride, being especially picked out. At noon we had general inspecting, which included some marching, . . . and other stuff.

The afternoon was windy at first but I got in another circle and seemed to do pretty well altho I was kept jumping by the wind. My arm is pretty tired tonight this flying ought to develop it.

A new bunch of 20 arrived here to-day including Heyward.

We hear 50 more are to come in about a week. I'm lucky to be ahead of them. Everything here seems too good to be true. Even the moon is wonderful now, big, full and romantic. I'm reminded of one of the Bairnsfather's cartoons.[18]

DIARY: **September 30** [*1917*]

. . . This morning was very windy and foggy that we couldn't fly but stood around and waited for several hours. In a long talk I found that Barett my *moniteur* lived in Brooklyn seven years and is a member and all round sportsman of the Crescent Club. He knew well a lot of people I know by name or a little by person. He is going back after the war so I may see him there.

For a couple of hours at mid-day I spread my bed clothes out in the sun and soaked in it myself. Believe me this life is great, good food, sleep, no dissapations, plenty of fresh air, wonderful country. Even

when flying the air is pumped thru your skin at a great rate. I am feeling pepier and pepier every minute. I sing and dance around all the time.

There was some flying this afternoon but I didn't get up. After supper Heyward and I took a long walk cross country under a wonderful moon, picked a few apples and talked a lot.

DIARY: **October 1** [*1917*]

A beautiful day; a beautiful night but nothing of great moment transpiring. I've discovered two drawbacks to this place viz. no tennis court and lack of privacy. This latter is a bad feature of every army at all times but after I get a commission it will be better.

DIARY: **October 2** [*1917*]

My 21st birthday. Was up and out on the field earily enough to see the sun come up. Flew a little and did poorly because my arm and shoulder was so stiff, sore and weak I could hardly manage the stick.

The day took the usual course of meals, drill etc. Heyward bought me some lunch to celebrate. Incidentally I have only a few francs (3) to start my 21st year and those few are borrowed.

. . . So ended my 21st birthday, miles from home, in a great war, without a cent or a sou [*French "penny" equal to five centimes*] **but perfectly happy.**

AMERICAN EXPEDITIONARY FORCE
Oct 2 1917

Dear Lois

This is quite a unique letter, my first since I came to the aviation school and the only one I will ever be able to write you on my 21st birthday. To-day, as you probably know, is the great day. Way off in the future the school children will probably have to memorize it and maybe they will get a holiday. But though it will be important then to me it seems like all the rest except for one or two things. As usual I got up in time to see the early morning stars and to watch the sun get up. And after breakfast and a wait but long before you would ever think of getting up, I tried to navigate an aeroplane with only indifferent success. Of course I dont fly alone yet but go up in a machine

that has double controls, one of which is held by a *moniteur* and the other by me. But I have progressed far enough so that almost all the time in the air the *moniteur* doesn't touch anything; which pleases me muchly. . . .

I cant begin to tell you what it is like up in the air because I can hardly realize yet that I am not dreaming it all. Of course you know it must be great sport and it is. I feel just like the illustrations you can see in almost any current magazine in a story entitled "The Conquest of America" "Wars of the future" etc. and not like a plain ordinary citizen who used to ride in the subway. There is little sensation of tremendous speed because (I think) there are no stationary objects whizzing past to judge your speed by like there is on the ground. The most obvious things are the noise of the motor (not so great as I had heard people, who had never flown, tell of) and the great rush of air from the propeller. The ground looks awfully funny which is probably because I've never seen it from an aeroplane before. Altogether it's great sport (as you will learn some day) and I can hardly wait till I get a machine all to myself and can get way up and off by myself.

That time will come soon too, much sooner than I had dared to hope before I came here. Everything here is beyond my fondest hopes; the country is fine, the course is much shorter than I expected, we get 4 meals a day. For the last week there has been a most wonderful moon and another fellow and I take a walk every night borrowing a few apples or grapes here and there in the surrounding country.

However this letter is not to tell about the school, I'll do that in future attempts. . . .

Yours, Stull.

Tuesday-Oct 2.nd [*1917*]

Dear Stull,

. . . If the weather is as beautiful over in France as it is here you have had a beautiful birthday. It is just cold and snappy enough to be glorious here — . . . .

I would fight for . . . [*Mayor Mitchell of New York*] with my dying breath and one of the biggest reasons is because of his loyal and splendid support to the country, President Wilson and our boys at the front. He is working for all besides the fine things he has done for the city. He represents the anti-German & anti pacifist socialist and anarchist. . . . Your father doesn't approve of him, I don't know why not — but he's going to vote for him I guess. He said he thought he would have to.

You ought to hear me electioneering — What you really ought to hear, tho, is how many seemingly intelligent men know practically nothing about their city or its administration. There is going to be a hard fight this election and the eyes of the whole country, perhaps the world will be on New York. . . .

Au revoir,
Lois.

DIARY: **October 3** [*1917*]

Was the last one to fly and it was the most enjoyable trip yet. No wind and the machine was as easy to handle as a tennis racquet. Nothing else out of the ordinary.

DIARY: **October 4** [*1917*]

Wind all morning and a little rain added in the afternoon to prevent all flying for the day. The seargant read us all the Articles of War. One of the fellows, Beaumont, got a letter from his father which could pretty nearly fit me. He mentioned that B. was not yet of age, an only son and after much worry and thought his father thought he oughtn't to enlist. It is only by these occasional times that we realize at all that a great many people at home consider us more-or-less heroes. Luckily we are all unconscious of the fact. Personally it doesn't seem strange or heroic at all and I can say truthfully I haven't felt a bit of fear as yet or any doubt of outliving the war. . . .

Thursday-Oct. 4th [*1917*]

Dear Stull,

Well, you have gone and done it! And now all the papers are spreading abroad the fame of this Brooklyn youth — I spent more money on newspapers today than I ever did before — but I would have spent my last penny — It's wonderful for you to have won the Croix de Guerre — but then we all knew you would as your mother says. I think you created more excitement in this house than you did in your own. Anyway I congratulate you with all my heart — so does the rest of the family.

. . . The enclosed account is from the Herald. It is the best I have seen. Isn't it nice to think it happened on your birthday? But how did the news get over here so soon? . . . My cousin just called up and asked if I had seen the Herald this morning. She is excited too —

. . . Time to say — Good night,

Lois.

Ithaca, N.Y.,
Oct. 4th., 1917

Mr. Byron Holt,
New York City.

Dear Mr. Holt,

Perhaps you will remember me as a friend of Stull's. Enclosed you will find a clipping from the Ithaca Dailey News of his latest escapade. I am sending him a copy to France which ought to cause him a bit of amusement.

The "Era," a University publication, would like to get a picture of him in Uniform. If you have such photograph will you please to send it to me? I will see that it is returned to you. If it is to be published it must be in by next Tuesday. Will you therefore send it to me by special delivery postage, which is enclosed?

Very truly yours,
Wm.D. Smith.

DIARY: **October 5** [*1917*]

Again no flying all day. We got rifles issued and drilled a little altho what aviators need rifles for I don't know. I got 2 letters from Lois, one from mama and one from Purdy. Tonight after the nightly walk with Heyward, on which we got some apples, I passed Bridgeman and he mentioned casually that he saw by the paper that I had gotten the Croix de Guerre. It took a little time for me to confirm it by the paper. Dallin, Farnham, Purdy (good news), Kreutzberg, Stout and I were the lucky ones. I'm intoxicated with joy, it means and will mean so much, especially to the folks at home. Whoopie —

Brooklyn, N.Y.
Oct 5, 1917

Dear Stull: —

. . . I want to write tho to tell you of the happenings this week in connection with your war cross.

. . . I got home at 7 and found a young fellow, Mr. McCabe, from the N.Y. Herald. We gave him your photo, copy of your letter of Sept. 1, . . . and other data about you. As you will see from the enclosed clipping from the Herald of the next morning, he gave you a good sensibly written article — by far the best in any paper. I got 50 copies of this Herald and will send them to those who will call most for them. I also got 50 copies (by mistake) of a later edition with the abbreviated story of you.

. . . when I got to the office on Thurs. A.M. your Herald photo and article were up on the bulletin board. Many there congratulated me on my hero son. I told them that I was proud of you but that I feared that you would again go into extremely dangerous places, minus the happy accident that saved you on Aug. 15.

You may think me cold and ungenerous, or even cowardly, perhaps, but I put little value on the opinions of the world at large and great value on one[']s own opinion of himself. I don't doubt but that you deserved the cross for doing your duty at such awful risk, but as I see it, crosses will make little or no difference to you 100 years hence or, perhaps, even 10 years hence. Your highest duty is to yourself — to live to develope into the greatest and noblest of which you are capable. When you are doing that you must approve of yourself and it matters but little what others think of you.

Personally, I doubt if your duty to yourself, family, country and world, should cause you to return to death's valley. Besides, you should be entitled to promotion that might diminish your risk. I hope you will get it. Whatever happens take no unnecessary risk and take care of your health in every way possible.

. . . The weather is getting cold. Be careful about sleeping or staying in smoky rooms more than is necessary. Your lungs are not strong.

Your proud and loving father

Byron M. Holt

DIARY: **October 6** [*1917*]

Past a restless night with pictures of rows of medals and decora-

tions. Flew a short time in the morning but did nothing else all day to earn my pay which is about due now. I wrote to Lois and home breaking the news to them gently.

Fifty new men, ground school men from America, got here from Issydown [*Issoudun*] which is still in the process of being built. I dont think they will fly here for awhile as the school is pretty full.

AMERICAN EXPEDITIONARY FORCE
Oct 6 1917

Dear Lois,

Yesterday two letters came from you, written on Aug 27-29-30 and on Sept 11. I hate to think of all the good times I missed this summer up at the lake but am glad all the rest of you had them. My turn will come again. You mustn't understand that to mean that I am not having a good time here because I am. In fact since about 4 months ago I have become the greatest-enjoyer-of-life since Pollyana finished her run at the theatre. I smile a very superior smile when you express concern about working too hard. We did that alright, so much that we all lost weight, got nervous (two of the fellows are in the hospital yet from shell shock) but we managed to get a lot of fun out of it by making everything a joke. There was one dead horse, at least it was the hind legs and part of the body of a horse, at a place where we had to turn, with the legs striking up in a funny angle. We called him affectionately "Old Wrinkle-Belly" and bets were laid as to how long he would last before he got hit again by a shell. Everybody swore faithfully that on dark nights they steered by smell. When it got beyond the enduring point we knew we had to turn on the road to the right. And then the fellows were always making agreements and conditional trades i.e. if one got killed the other was to get his kodak and pictures, some body else his shoes and so on. These are only typical of the way everybody took everything as a joke.

. . . At present I have only 2 sweaters, one my big white one you may remember, and the other, just given to me. That may sound as if I were oversupplied but not so. In my present profession sweaters are as necessary as music to the movies. This morning before the sun had been up half an hour, I was up flying. And altho I had both sweaters and a leather coat on I don't remember that I was bothered

by sweat running down into my goggles. And winter is yet to come. . . .

Now for my news . . . you may remember I hinted a month and a half ago at good news. (If I had known it would have been so long delayed or that it would have raised suspicions that I might return I wouldn't have written) Then I knew that I had not only been recommended for the command of a section, but I also knew that I had been recommended for the Croix de Guerre. It was so long delayed that I thought it hadn't gone through and I gave up all hope and regarded the incident as closed. But last night one of the fellows told me to look in the paper and there I saw a little news item saying that I had been cited and given the croix de guerre. The paper said something about working "under heavy bombardment and through clouds of gas" and the joke is that that is almost true. As yet I haven't gotten official notice and the citation, they were probably sent to my old address and will reach me in a day or two. When they do I will send you a copy of the citation.

Of course it has tickeled my vanity so I could hardly put my helmet on for flying this morning. It is quite an honor to be decorated and the medal will make a nice momento of the time I was in the French army. But you mustn't get the idea that it is anything great or extraordinary. It seems so more in America where as yet practically no one has gotten a chance to get medals or get killed.

I'll tell you more about it in my next letter which will be soon. Regards to all, and more to you

from Stull.

P.S. I can't resist from an addition. I notice you said you saw in the movies a German aeroplane brought down. Dont believe it. It isn't done in the best of families. Take it from me as an old veteran, who has seen several brought down in his day, that in this war they don't stage little acts for the movies the way they did in Mexico. Every air fight I've ever seen (and they are actually in the hundreds) was so far up no camera could possibly take it. They might take a picture of the wreck after the fall. I have several of that kind myself.

DIARY: **October 7** [*1917*]

Couldn't fly all day and had a hard time passing the time away. No

privacy so it is hard to write or read good stuff. It is only a taste of what we will get in large doses if we stay here. There are constant and well-talked-over rumors that we may be sent to Egypt to a school there. Of course I am wishing that this rumor will turn out to be fact. New experiences, new places and we would probably learn to fly as quickly as here. . . .

DIARY: **October 8** [*1917*] **Monday.**

I saw in yesterday's paper that Ned, Red Day and Plow all got Croixs. Section 1 certainly showed up well. Fifteen citations from 43 days work at Verdun.

It was windy and rainy again preventing all flying. Heyward and I went to Tours but didn't pretend to see the sights only doing a little shopping.

I forgot to say that yesterday the clocks were all put back an hour to the winter time. There is now only 5 hours difference between N.Y. and here. Took a long walk with H. on a dark and windy night. We at least are making some little efforts to keep in condition. Unless they begin setting-up exercises or something most of the fellows will have colds and worse this winter. Some are beginning now.

DIARY: **October 9** [*1917*]

More wind and rain and no flying. I woke up with some bad bites which after investigation and consultation I concluded are bed bugs. Now for the war with them and no quarter given.

. . . Also in the mail I got a letter from Steve with my citation in it. The citation is *Service de Sante 32 Corps d'Armee, II Armee, Ordre no 131. It reads "le conducteur Holt, William Stull de la S.S.U. 1 volontaire americain: "conducteur de grand sang froid et tres grande bravaure. S'est particulierement distingue la nuit du 17 Aout 1917 où apres avoir été intoxiqué par les gaz et rendu presque inconseient, il a repris la volant de sa voiture 3 heures apres et a continué à transporter les blessés pendant 36 heures sur une route lourdement bombardeé."* [*The ambulance driver Holt, William Stull, of the American Volunteer Medical Service Section 1: a driver of great self-control and very great bravery. His bravery was particularly notable on the night of August 17, 1917, when, after having been exposed to poison gas and made almost unconscious, he after three hours, regained control of his ambulance and continued to* *transport wounded soldiers for 36 hours on a road which was under severe bombardment*]. . . .

I went downtown with Heyward who as always was ultragenerous and bought me the medal and the ribbon which I now have on my uniform and right proud am I. . . .

Tuesday, October 9, 1917

Dear Stull,

I found out Sunday night why my "letter of Aug 5th came too late." It must have been the one in which I asked you please not to join the aviation corps. You say "too late" just as if it would have had some effect if it hadn't been too late. These contrary people who always do what you ask them not to do —

We didn't get any letter at all last week but we know all about you just the same. See what comes of being so notoriously famous. "Young Brooklynite who won war cross joins Aviation Corps." A long account of "Our Hero" was printed in the Ithaca paper.

. . . I suppose it is all right and you ought to know what you are doing, but don't try to get any more crosses — one's enough — You will have to study (on the ground) for two months or so before you fly, *n'est pas*? . . . Please be careful, don't take unnecessary risks and be a good boy —

Lois.

P.S. Does the gov't censor mail from the U.S. to France.

Your last letter was not censored. . . .

DIARY: **October 10** [*1917*]

A little flying in the morning before it got too bumpy or too something else. I didn't participate. I have a new *moniteur*, M. Barret having left much to my regret, about who I know nothing as yet.

Had a lecture on motors after lunch at which I learnt little knowing already the fundamentals. It seemed funny to be sitting at desks again. Real country-school desks too.

Two more Globes arrived Sept 12 and 13. I wrote to Lois.

I flew twice in the afternoon but the first trip he wouldn't let me take control because it was so rough and the second time I misunderstood and didn't take control when I should have. It was a beautiful

day with a fitting sunset. After supper H. and I rode to town in the truck, walked around a very little and then walked home.

AMERICAN EXPEDITIONARY FORCE
Oct 10 1917

Dear Lois,

Not much news in the aviating line, wind and rain have prevented all flying for several days so I am probably not as good an aviator as when I last wrote. Since then I have gotten my citation, however, and will now copy it as I said I would in my last letter. (That is put in in case you shouldn't get my previous letter. I wonder how many if any of my efforts are lost) . . . [*citation follows*]**. . .**

You can translate it better than I could. There are a couple of mistakes in it viz, the date I got too closely acquainted with gas was the 13 and not the 17 and 3 *heures* after I reached safety (40 ft underground) I was lying on my back coughing, sneezing and it wasn't till at least 6 hours afterwards that I or anyone else could go on because the road was impassible. Another error, that I can afford to admit to only a few intimate friends, is that instead of being "*tres grande bravoure*" I was scared worse than I ever had been before or since.

Nevertheless it is a nice citation as is the medal too. . . . Of course I never wear it but I do wear on my uniform a little ribbon, made of the same material as the ribbon in the medal, to show I have received it.

(Here occurred an intermission of all afternoon during which I flew or tried to and nearly extinguished myself.) Even though I didn't shine particularly I enjoyed it and the perfect day to-day was. Imagine a flat, most picturesque country, a wonderful sunset, and best of all cool, fresh air that would make a man with no legs get up and dance.

. . . Believe me, we aviators led a hard life. I'll blush with a guilty conscience when I get paid.

I suppose by now you must surely have gotten my letter telling you I am in aviation. I'm anxious to hear what you have to say about it. Also what your family and mine have to say. Give my regards to all and tell Lela I will write the letter I owe here, soon.

***Au revoir*, Stull.**

DIARY: **October 11** [*1917*]

No bedbugs last night, glory be. It is very cold, I have on my heavy underwear, regular clothes, two sweaters and a leather suit over that. What it will be like when real winter comes I hate to imagine.

One rumor has become fact as a notice was posted that we receive $100 a month.

Flew this afternoon and did much better. I may learn yet. That sounds as if I have had doubts, which I have never had yet. H. and I had a long talk to-night in which we decided to try and fly across the Atlantic after the war. The talk naturally was mostly "in the air" but stranger things have happened. The big things of life belong to those who dare to take them.

DIARY: **October 12** [*1917*]

Columbus Day which was celebrated by a hard rain all day. We had two lectures on carburetors and things, which were the full days work.

The "Herald" printed more good news of section 1. We got a section army citation, our fourth citation the record so far. The paper printed a picture of the section, the one taken at Evers, and said it was the hardest work ever done by an ambulance section in France. Again I appreciate my great luck in being in Section 1. . . .

Friday-Oct. 12. [*1917*]

Dear Stull,

For the first time in ever so long I have had time to read — and read I did without ceasing. The book "Over the Top" is the most exciting and in some places the most horrible thing I have ever read. It is said to be a true story of the war and I guess it really is — most of it anyway. . . .

Oct. 13th.

You ask what I think of going to Russia. I don't think you ought to. They do such crazy things and kill each other just for the fun of it. You might not come home at all if you went there — No — please stick to France —

Don't worry for fear your folks will worry about you. They think aviation much safer than Ambulance driving and your father is quite pleased to think you are practically out of danger for a few months anyway. He cheered me up quite a bit the last time I was over there —

. . . My pen is running out — to bed. *Bon nuit.*

Sunday-14th.

Dear Stull,

Today I learned how downhearted a soldier can really get. You have doubtless heard of the Columbia War Hospital which has been built over here at the Columbia Oval. There are about forty men there now and after today there will be two hundred who are now on their way from France. The young people of our Church — (and some of the old) go over every Sunday afternoon, sing, hold a very short service and then go around the wards. I, being the President of the League, naturally have a lot of talking etc. to do. Today I met a fellow who goes to France tomorrow. He was as cheerful and full of fun as anyone could be, but the fellow with him was as blue as you must have been — He had received a letter from his sweetheart and very likely it was the wrong kind.

. . . There were several fellows at the Hospital with legs or arms shot off, also about a half a dozen who had lost their minds. It makes me feel horribly weepy — But I won't weep. What good are wailing females? I'll just do all I possibly can to help — in every way I can. . . .

Bon nuit, Lois

DIARY: **October 13** [*1917*] **Saturday.**

No flying. Heyward took me downtown and bought me a supper. We enjoyed the people who were even more than usually interesting [—]more than the meal. Later on we got called down by an American officer for not having our overcoats buttoned up, much to our disgust and mental annoyance.

Saturday-[*October 13, 1917?*]

Dear Stull,

While I wait for further orders I'll scribble something to you to cheer up your poor dear heart and change your color. Perhaps just at the time you needed cheering most I wrote a horrid letter. Tis the nature of the beast.

Many and Many a time tho I thought of nice things to say but I didn't say them because I didn't want anyone else to read them. But just this once I'll take a chance and tell you that I surrendered long ago and I love you. Or if you like it better in French — *Je vous aime de tout mon coeur* [*I love you with all my heart*]. I am awfully glad you are in aviation and I know you will do wonders <u>without</u> taking risks. I am awfully sorry I let you get the "colors" but I tried hard not to. You are absolutely <u>always</u> with me wherever I go and I never put on a dress or hat or plan to do anything without your approval. (You're right on the bureau) . . .

Yesterday I volunteered to act as chauffeur for members of the Mayor's Committee — Navy League or something like that. Well, as a result, here I am on 45th St. & Vanderbilt Ave — waiting for orders to take someone somewhere. I have been on one such errand this A.M. but expect that won't be the last. It is great to serve the city & country but like lots of other people I'd like more action. Waiting is not my strong point. . . .

I was, of course, terribly disappointed because you didn't come home — but I <u>knew</u> you wouldn't and while disappointed I am glad. It gives me a chance to sacrifice a little for "Democracy."

France and Switzerland are my pet countries and <u>I</u> should certainly love to take that trip thru France on <u>your</u> honeymoon. . . .

. . . It is now 3<u>00</u> P.M. and after three trips I am having a solitary lunch in Schraft's. It is great tho. I like it. Very exciting (<u>driving</u> in New York — not the waiting part) and as you see I am having lunch with you — I said solitary but I meant that to the rest of the people here I look solitary. This is between courses when we have a chance to talk. . . .

This is a very delapidated looking letter but I guess I'll send it. . . .

Lois

DIARY: **October 14** [*1917*]

A fine flying day but I didn't get up. In the afternoon Heywood, I and two others were to our great astonishment sent to landing school. With only four of us and a fine *moniteur* we will get in a lot of flying and will progress quickly. We are thrown off our mental balance by the promotion.

. . . Lois mentions in her last letter that papa found out from Bartlett's father about our little party when I got "gased." Its great how they find everything out. They must have worried a lot.

DIARY: **October 15** [*1917*]

Didn't fly in the morning because of a thick fog but in the afternoon got my first ride with the new *moniteur*, Coldefy. He speaks almost no English, was a prize fighter before the war, has lots of guts, and is a gentleman. Consequently I had a most wonderful ride, staying up steadily for a half an hour. Most of the time we were up about 600 meters and the sensation up there is too great to seem real. Tours looked like a little village and villages looked like pebbles. While way up Coldefy started to look for a landmark, turned off the gas and we started on a long coast down. I gave him control of course and tried to find what he was looking for. He told me that a comrade *moniteur*, who got killed a little while ago, was buried there. And when we got within 50 meters of the ground I saw the white cross in the middle of a field. Coldefy shot on the gas, I took control and then he, in the superb way only a Frenchman can do, saluted the grave.

Ithaca, N.Y., Oct. 15, 1917.
Godam the Germans if
they sink this one.

My dear Stull,

. . . Now as for the University in war-time. The fact is, Stull, that the heading of this paragraph is a misnomer, for it isn't war time; the all-pervading rigor of war, reaching every woman and child, hasn't struck our country yet; the realest that the war hits us is to see a uniformed man on the streets occasionally.

About 3000 are back, — about 1500 of them Freshmen; very few upperclassmen are back. Many of them are back because they feel (1) they weren't drafted, (2) they have only one more year in college, which they had best finish, (3) the war will last long enough for them to get killed anyway, so stay for one year of [*illegible*]. Very very many are back because physically deficient. You would be surprised to see how noticeable is the number of men this year who are crippled, hunch-backed, short-legged, etc. of course, they were here before, but now they stand out like eloquent monuments.

The classes are conducted the same as usual, the dull drone of the lecture is the same as ever, — the war is never mentioned in the class-room; Chaucer and Spencer are. But their standard of scholarship has gone up tremendously; there is none of the rah-rah; the men are here for business, and they're plugging hard; it's really amazing how the students are working.

In trying to describe to you the campus atmosphere, I am confronted with two contra thoughts which are both true observations and both conflicting: (1) The students don't talk, read, or even silently <u>think</u> war; it is not table talk; it is not read; yet (2) A very serious air pervades the whole University; there is practically no drinking; foot-ball is not discussed on the front page of the <u>Sun</u>; we lost to Williams last week, and nobody turned a finger; there is absolutely no horse-play down town; no cheap wit in the theatres, i.e. no bursting of pop-corn bags when the hero & heroine kiss, no groaning when the dolly gets down to her corset cover, no jamming and cave-man stuff at the theatre entrances; very little rushing of co-eds; no dances — there hasn't been a fraternity or downtown dance for studes this year. I can reconcile the two only this way: the average student[,] as we have discussed him together oft times, hasn't enough brains to realize the tremendous and awful and truly terrible thing that has happened to our country; he can't reason on it; but subconsciously he knows that the old ways would be hideously uncalled for these times; so he is calmed down and serious, really not knowing why.

I suppose, Stull, old fellow, you have to chuckle and pinch yourself when I tell you they're still playing foot-ball at Schoelpopf field. But it's sane. There is no training table; no organized cheering; no practice before Sep. 29th, the day of registration; the boys are not blue when their team loses; everybody confidently expects to lose every game, i.e. Colgate who buys her teams and Penn. who has 9 veterans back — but nobody gives a rip. Truly, very truly, Stull, Cornell has this year put her athletics on such an amateur & sportsmanlike basis that you'd think we were English.

The fraternities are limping along as best they can; in fact they are doing what the Allies are doing, i.e. democratising themselves & howling democracy out of necessity and policy; they're taking in many men who would have been "barbarians" in peace times. Alpha Delta Phi has 5 men back; Beta Samach has the largest percentage back; Gamma Eta Gamma is threatened with a sale of their house for inability to pay taxs, etc., etc.

My Senior Law Class is typical: 15 persons back out of 50, — two women, two cripples on crutches, one released from Training Camp without commission ("mental ineptitude"), one on furlough, and five that I personally know have been rejected by the army surgeons, — which accounts for 11 of the 15. A noticeable thing about the men back is their extreme youth; its the boys that are back; kids 17, 18, & 19; I know only a few companionable men in the U.; I feel like a Professor Emeritus.

The faculty has done well; several full professors are in it; practically all the Instructors have gone so that the U. is really hard up for its teaching staff. Six instructors went from the English Dep't; five from Chemistry 1, and four of the five in History Dep't — MacKenzie, Mcguire, Jack Schurnan, and Townsend, — leaveing ME.

. . . In my earlier letters I told you the people of our country did not yet even know we are at war. This is changed now — the sight of 670,000 drafted men already in the camps, and Pershing's men in France, has informed them. The startling exposés of German diplomatic treachery involving O'Leary, Judge Cohalan of Sup's Ct. of N.Y., the Argentine & Sweedish affairs, etc., etc. which I presume you know about, are known by the people. But while the people now know we are in war, and while the exposés are gradually showing them why, it is still true that America is not converted to the cause. Your narration of Pershing's men shows this. This mobilized militia — 400,000 strong — are savagely sore at going to Europe. The Liberty Loan campaign is ½ over and only ⅛ the sum has as yet been subscribed. The nation is not behind the war.

. . . My next letter will be entitled: "Experiences as Clerk to an Exemption Board." This is news to you, isn't it? I worked for two months this summer for a Draft Board in Schenectady, my official title being "Chief Clerk." This may seem bragging, but let our intimacy pardon it, — what "Chief Clerk" amounts to is this: You run the office, and the whole affair, and let the members of the Board, most mediocre men, take the credit; can you excuse me for that self-praise remark. My God, Stull, if you have seen battles, I have seen the very souls of men when I cross-examined them on their claims; I have seen men as noble and courageous as Horatius of the Romans; I have seen men as cowardly as a nigger raper; I have had men confess to me that they were not married tho the public thought they were; one X needs must explain to me why his affadavits states (1) he has been married 2 months, (2) and his wife is 4 months pregnant; I have seen a man who delivered the Fourth of July oration in Schenectady on "Our Duty toward the Flag" claim exemption as a County Supervisor (claim denied), and I have seen humble men simply say: "I don't like to go, I don't like to think of my wife having to put up at a rooming house, but it's my duty; no, I guess I won't claim exemption."

The draft army is going to be a marvel, Stull, of morale & efficiency, contrary to my former predictions. Dont believe the gossippy stories otherwise; they are going to be the world's greatest troops. It's hard to reconcile the fact that the nation isn't truly back of the war and the fact that the draft army is going to be a marvel, — but its true. More in my next letter.

Yours till Sunday,
Bill.

Did you get my long clipping from the Ithaca Dailey News concerning your decoration? I am as proud of you, Stull, as any man dare be who is himself not at the front; or, in otherwords, tremendously proud, but quiet about it. Always tell me the date of the last letter received from me so I can tell if you are receiving them all.

DIARY: **October 16** [*1917*]

Notable only for the long 50 minute flight I had. We spiraled over a nearby town to the admiration of the populace whom I could see with upturned faces in the street, we landed but didn't stop in several fields, and best of all we passed a machine going in the same direction; it seemed as if suspended motionless in the air, the ground below looked like scenery in a theatre. Altogether it was a great sight and a great flight. Coldefy said I did very well and that he would take me over the river tomorrow to see if I could land well enough for solo work. Height record so far 800 me.

AMERICAN EXPEDITIONARY FORCE
Oct 16 1917

Dear Lois,

Two days ago I got two letters from you (Sept 6 and 18) and like a dutiful boy answered them that night and then, like I often do, let the letter lie around till it is so creased and old I have to write another. . . . The paper is inaccurate in its list of gased and wounded, only one of the fellows named got hurt, and he lost an arm.

That's probably the last time I'll have that kind of news for you for some time because there are no honors where there is no danger. I played the coward and left the ambulance where there was sometimes real danger and am now enjoying some real sensations but no danger

in learning to fly. I seem to be really learning for I have been promoted out of the kindergarten to the next grade. I still have a *moniteur* in the machine with me but he very seldom touches the controls. I had a beautiful ride yesterday afternoon, flying for half an hour around 200 feet. . . .

Both in your letters and in those of the others, you talk as if I should have gone home (when I could have after my ambulance time was up) and rested up. I wish you could see me, I'm getting fat by inches and never looked or felt better in my life. By the way I don't think I told you, so I had better now because you would find out somehow anyway, that when I got back to Paris I was sick in the infirmary six days with a fever and sore throat. It was the result of overwork and getting wet too often. . . .

If you think aqua-planing is some sport just wait till you try aero-planing. Way up so far that a city looks like a village, and a village looks like a few pebbles, with air rushing by so fast it blows right thru you and makes you feel like jumping out and try flying by yourself. Thats where I'm going now.

Stull

DIARY: **October 17** [*1917*]

Flew half an hour and did well in the morning but a light rain stopt all proceedings in the afternoon. Rumors of pay day still continue active despite many false predictions; hope springs eternal.

Wrote to Lois and home.

DIARY: **October 18** [*1917*]

Couldn't fly all morning so I finished "The People of the Abyss." It was somewhat of a disappointment probably because from the nature of the book it doesnt permit Jack London to use his best powers.

Flew a little in the afternoon and again earned commendation.

DIARY: **October 19** [*1917*]

Payday rumors still flourish. A thick fog came up in the morning just as we went out to fly and it delayed proceedings. But altogether the day was my biggest so far as I totaled 80 minutes and 26 landings. Coldefy complimented me and promoted me so tomorrow I fly alone.

Heyward is also to make his first hop tomorrow so we are still together and incidentally the first in our platoon to get that far. I learned a lot while with Coldefy, he has lots of nerve. Sometimes he'd smoke, more often read and always turn around and grin. . . .

DIARY: **October 20** [*1917*]

Up early and out on the field to make my first "hop." We had to wait quite a while for a fog to lift, which it finally did and off we went. I didn't get very far, primed by inside dope, I pushed too much on my right foot, corrected too much and made a *cheval de bois* [*spun the plane around*]**. I kept my presence of mind enough to stop the machine, so trouble was averted and I went back and flew the length of the field alright, altho I was probably in a daze. Heywood went off like a nigger chaser firecracker which was just the way I felt. Later in the evening we made our first tour de piece** [*tour de piste: take off in the plane, circle the field, and land*]**, which I did very well, landing exceedingly well for a beginner — Heywood was not so lucky and fulfilled his many prophicies by breaking his machine in landing. It is a new and great sensation to fly alone and I enjoy it to the limit. I feel tickled with myself and satisfied the way I used to in times gone by when I had played good tennis and won. I was the first of the bunch that came here with me to fly alone. . . .**

To bed tired but very happy and proud. So far I haven't felt any fear in flying nor lost my absolute confidence for a minute.

DIARY: **October 21** [*1917*] **Sunday.**

A fog prevented all active war operations in the morning but after waiting all afternoon I made one *tour de piste* and did well, I think. I was more nervous about it than anything yet but not very much and what there was came from waiting too long.

. . . To-day's papers tell of the defeat of a zeppelin raid in which at least 4 were brought down. A real defeat for Germany costing trained men, much material, money and morale.

DIARY: **October 22 (1917)**

No flying in the morning but in the afternoon I made 3 *tour de pistes* and landed finely everytime. My confidence amazes me all the time, it is so different from the before-the-war-Stull.

Monday-Oct. 22, [*1917*]

Dear Stull,

I got up before breakfast this morning so I can talk to you for a little while — First I want to ask you why you haven't said anything in your letters about getting the Croix de Guerre — I expected a detailed description of the whole thing and you haven't said a word.

Next I have some good news — that is, good for me — After Nov-1st letters can be sent to soldiers in France for 2¢ — Won't I save money tho? All mail in the U.S., however, will cost 3¢ instead of 2¢. Isn't it good you're in France? . . .

Just at present I am head over heels in "things" which I am doing or attempting to do. I'll tell you a few of them — Party for the Infant & Intermediate Classes in church — Halloween — Thurs. afternoon of this week have to play the piano for a rehearsal of the Country School we are giving — Tonight cut corn stalks etc. to decorate Y.M.C.A. for a big community Social a week from tomorrow night. Am Chairman of Publicity & Refreshment Committees for that. Besides all this I am <u>working</u> (real work) in school — I passed my first test and hope to pass the second this Friday — I am awfully glad that I have so much to do tho — I'd die if I had much time to sit around and think. . . .

No letter and my spirits fell 40 degrees — but one will come tomorrow surely — You usually say practically the same thing in my letter as you do in your letter home so I'm going to get ahead of the mail man this time, call Paula up and get all the news before I get my letter — Now! You will be good —

You said in one letter that I never tell you any news, or what I do or think etc. You're a fibber, but anyway I'm now going to tell you what I think at this very moment. By tonight I wont think it so listen now while I tell you. I am thinking with all my mind of a place far away from here out in the woods — no people near, just a small tent and trees, and trees & trees — beautiful ones — leaves of all colors — I am wishing with all my heart that I could be there away from everybody & everything just for a little while. Some day I'm going to do it, just as sure as you live —

. . . You are coming home as soon as the war is over aren't you?

Love, Lois.

DIARY: **October 23** [*1917*]

No flying all day, the first break after 8 consecutive flying days. The

good weather has bolstered up everyone's hope so that now we can see ourselves finished and commissioned by Christmas.

To-day I finished a delightful experience I haven't had in a long time viz. being drunk with a book. This particular drink was "Desmond's Daughter" by Maud Diver. Especially inspiring and intoxicating was Thea. She was a peach.

I had two of my letters returned by the censor. All letters going to the base censor should be put unsealed in a blue envelope. There were none here so we were told to use any envelope and to mark it blue envelope. But the straight-laced censor couldn't stand for such actions and back came my two letters dated Oct 6. I expected some dam foolishness with our censor but none as bad as this. More of my letters will come back probably so the folks home wont hear from me for over a month unless I cable which I am thinking of.

DIARY: **October 24** [*1917*]

Another windy and troubled day but I got up once. We were entertained on the field by several smash ups but as usual no one got hurt. They say we will get paid to-morrow. . . .

DIARY: **October 25** [*1917*]

No flying all day but there were other big events. All doubts were put to rest by the coming of the paymaster, for who we all lined up and before whom we singled, receiving our pay. My share was 75 francs [*approximately $14.48*]**.**

Most everybody piled downtown after supper and I went along too. Did a few errands. . . .

I had to wait a long time for the truck back to camp and I spent it in walking around. I went to the cathedral which was beautiful in the moonlight. Some parts dark in the shadow, some white from the moon and in between every grade of gray. The whole effect was subdueing and added to the medeval and past-world impressions that the cathedral gives one even in bright sunlight. . . .

. . . Thursday-Oct. 25-[*1917*]

Dear Stull,

What have I done that I should be punished like this? Not a sign of a letter in two whole weeks — I suppose you have been working terribly hard tho, and haven't had time for such things as letters. I must keep right on writing tho, because the government says so. As I was reminded — it is my patriotic duty —

Yesterday morning I got one of the biggest scares I have had in a long while — I was reading the Tribune (as usual) and in spite of the difficulty of turning pages in a subway train I got over to the third page where I saw an article entitled "Brooklyn Boy killed in French Aviation School" or something very similar — I held my breath and I never read anything so fast as I did that article — to find the name — Since you have never been in such a position you can't imagine the sensation — I'm not anxious to experience it again —

. . . I am now going to practice taking dictation at 90 words per-min. I take the 90 test tomorrow — Please hope that I get through even if it is three weeks late —

Tout à vous [*all the best to you*], Lois —

DIARY: **October 26** [*1917*]

Another overcast day, pretty windy but we managed to fly a little. I got one turn and was just going to have another when the last available machine was broken, not badly as so many have been but only enough to put it in the repair shop an hour or so.

Went down to Tour[*s*] **after supper with Vinx and walked a lot, most of the time thru the old part of the city. That is really jumping back into the past. We were both characters in one of Dumas novels. We could be nothing else in those narrow dark streets, overhung by houses hundreds of years old, dimly lit by lights extending a little from the house walls. The houses individually are if anything even more interesting.**

Friday-Oct-26th [*1917*]

Dear Stull,

I have a supply of 5¢ stamps which I must get rid of before Nov. 2nd therefore this extravagance —

Your letter of Oct 10th just arrived and from a remark in it I infer that one letter has found a watery grave — That is the first and I hope the last

— It must have been on one of the two French ships which were sunk (last) two weeks ago —

Just this minute I received a call to drive the auto again tomorrow for the National Food Com. That's only one more thing added to the list — It's a great life if you don't weaken —

Maitenant [*Maintenant*] je *veux faire mon compliment à M.W. Stull Holt parce qu ´il a recur le croix de guerre pour l´exposition de grande* <u>*bravoure*</u> *dans l´ attaque de Verdun — Il a dit qu´il n´a rien de courage mais ce n´est pas vrai. de est un jeune homme brave, malgré cela qu´il a dit* [*Now I want to pay a compliment to Mr. W. Stull Holt because he has received the croix de guerre for demonstrating great bravery during the attack on Verdun. He has said that he displayed no courage, but that is not true. He is a brave young man, despite what he has said.*]. . . .

Au revoir, Lois

DIARY: **October 27** [*1917*]

A wonderful flying day, so good that most of it was devoted to the newcomers in the class and I got only one trip. The sunset was wonderful, a profusion of color such as I have hardly ever seen before.

DIARY: **October 28** [*1917*] **Sunday.**

Another wonderful day for this or any other time of year. I got three trips and was with Vinx and several others promoted to the next class, which does practically the same work only with Anzani motors. With good weather we can finish in three weeks, a subject which is discussed from every angle.

The days and especially the nights are getting very cold but during the sunlight I feel full of pep and energy. This doesn't take the form of letter writing, I can't seem to settle down in the confusion of the barracks.

. . . Had a long walk in the great moonlight with Dudley. This same moon means lot of bombs and bad sleep just behind the lines.

DIARY: **October 29** [*1917*]

The new class doesn't seem to be very active, the instructor being poor and there is a shortage of machines. So I didn't fly although it was a beautiful day. All men possible were being rushed thru to

show on the month's record, so we ought to have plenty of machines soon. . . .

DIARY: **October 30** [*1917*]

A windy and unsettled day of no flying but with several more very interesting and instructive lectures by Hamilton.

The Italians seem to be still getting it in the neck [*at Caporetto*] **which means more work and sacrifice for America especially. It is pathetic to see France, after bearing the brunt of the war, after being honeycombed by countless intrigues, plots and German traitors, so dangerous that a breakdown was imminent several times. And yet with all her rotten politics, intrigues and losses, she not only continues to fight well, witness Verdun this summer and now the Aisne, but is talking of going to the aid of Italy. My admiration and genuine respect for France grows daily. . . .**

DIARY: **October 31** [*1917*]

A new *moniteur* to-day who seems to have lots of pep, thereby restoring all our hopes. I didn't get up but know everything is O.K.

. . . it seems the papers published news of my Croix, some with a picture, Bill had my letter to him put in an Ithaca paper and everyone knows me for a blooming hero. Consequently I feel like a hypocrite, even tho I had no hand in spreading the news. Also what is better, everyone approves of my transfer to aviation — I think they expect a peace thru Germany's collapse before they think I will be ready. The present Italian picnic may enlighten them.

Wednesday-Oct. 31st, 17

Dear Stull,

Last night our famous Social came off — They tell me it was one big success — . . . .

Saturday —

. . .Yesterday, during the lunch hour I had a very interesting talk with a young man in the class — who is not a Socialist but so near it that he might easily be — It reminded me of a lesson in Economics — I hope to continue the conversation next week because it makes me reason and think —

a thing I haven't done any too much of lately — His arguments are very hard to answer as is always the case with that kind of a person. It is impossible to pin him down to anything and every word he utters means something — He takes every thing that is said literally and if you don't know what you mean it's good bye — He told one girl she better not talk if she didn't know what she wanted to say — . . . .

Do you still want to go to Russia? I wish you wouldn't. Something seems to tell me you ought not — Please tell me what you are planning to do won't you?

Mother[,] Enid & Lela send their love — also —

Lois.

Oct. 31, 1917.

My dear Mr. Aviationer Stull,

. . . I always feel abit stiff about writing you; the thought of one young man in France and another safely cuddled in America is not itself inspiring; then, too, I always am a bit ashamed for not having written oftener. But anyway —

. . . Now let me tell you about my work this summer on the Draft Board. Five weeks did I labor and toil on cables at the General Electric Co. Then was I offered a job as Chief Clerk to the Local Draft Board in Schenectady. There did I work two months.

The draft was a marvel of administrative efficiency; I remember of once arguing at the Telluride House against Universal Service on the ground that we did not have sufficient administrative ability in our politics to run it. I take it back. The War Dept. was called upon to select 675,000 men; clothe, house, arm, and equip them; do so without injuring our industries; do so without causing hardship from dependents left behind, — all in three months. The War Dep't had to start with a blank page; there were no local boards that could be utilized for the purpose.

First came the appointment of the civilian Local Boards, — a total of about 10,000 members. The governors were called on to nominate them. The governors called on the political parties; i.e. in Republican localities the Board was to be of two Republicans and one Democrat; in Democratic localities vice versa. The political war-horses, the pigmy local chairmen actually responded well; they appointed men of ability regardless of whether those men were wont to cut their ballots on Election day. The

Chairman of my Board was the President of the Non-Partisan League, hated by both parties.

And the men appointed were free from all political bias: witness, (1) our board denied the claim of a Republican supervisor who, as Chairman of the Bldg's Committee, had granted the Board the use of the County Bldg. for offices. (2) The Medical member of our board was a veteran of the Civil War, an old time James G. Blaine Republican who liked Democrats like St. Patrick took to snakes; a man 85 yrs. old and spry as 40. Well, in a certain fishy case that was pending, the Republican District Attorney writes the Doc: "Do what you can for Mr. X." Whereupon the Doc's perfectly enormous stomach contracted, his face flushed, and he exploded: "What the hell does he think this is, a Republican caucus?" The Doc was a man of finess so he apologized to our stenographers, who, by the way, had not been offended.

Who were the men of these boards which were to decide the fate of the nation, to send one man to his doom and save another by exempting him; what was their calibre? They were honest men of sound sense, — retired grocers, active real-estate men, lawyers, doctors, insurance agents, clothing store proprietors. They had not read Mill on "Liberty" or Aristotle on "Justice," but they could tell a fake a block away. This was the average man of the 10,000.

Of course in some of the districts, like the East Side of New York and Hinkey Dink's ward in Chicago, the Boards were not models, — chiefly because old Diogenes himself couldn't find three honest men therein resident. Right off the bat, the gov't sent four of them to Atlanta prison for two years, which had a good effect on such like boards of, well, say the Barbary Coast in 'Frisco. This gave the Boards a black eye with nonthinking people, but believe me, Stull, the Boards were save in those instances above reproach.

Well, the Boards being chosen, the rules of the Draft had to be laid down, and the Members instructed. . . .

The General [*Provost Marshall Crowder*] first got out a little pamplet called the "Rules and Regulations," which is plain language and without technicality, arranged every detail and answered almost all conceivable questions. (New York Court of Appeals please notice.) Everything was done automatically. The gov't printed millions of forms, 176 varieties. Did a man want to claim exemption as a regularly ordained minister? "Boy, get me form 113." Did he want to claim as a married man with Dependents?

"Boy, get me form 130, a." Had he registered in Chicago, and was he now in Schenectady? "Boy, get me forms 176 and 176, a." Did he claim exemption as the sole support of an aged parent? "Boy, form 109, please." These forms asked all questions calculated to elicit the required information. The claimant simply filled in the blanks and swore to them before a notary.

Well, the boards being appointed, the rules laid down, and the forms provided, push the button. All registrants were numerically listed according, to the order in which they had been drawn in the great gamble at Washington. The Board simply took the first 100 men on the list, sent them form 107 which called them for examination, and the fun began.

Each board examined approximately 100 men a day. A staff of around six doctors went over and through them like lightening.

At first the old regular army standards were maintained. Of course, ridiculous results followed: great tennis players were deemed to have flat feet; champion wrestlers were too short in proportion to weight; cross-country-runners too light in proportion to height. During the first few days, only about one in four was accepted. It seemed that the Gov't wanted Paul Swann's rather than soldiers. Later, of necessity, the unimaginative military changed these hockus pockus rules, — changed them; not lowered them, and things went better.

The men were examined at the rate of about one every three minutes. From this one would think that only superficiality could be attained; but the doctors got so they could tell a soldier by looking at him. Very few men were later thrown out by the army surgeons at the Camps, where the men were examined every day for thirty days.

Gossippy human nature had to have it that many men had faked the doctors and were exempted as "physically deficient." Don't believe it. Faking was practically a psychological impossibility for two reasons: first, just before the examinations were about to begin, the newspapers were full of stories by eminent physicians on the easy detection of faking. Second, the details of the examinations were so arranged as to terrorize a faker. Suppose X had planned to pretend near-sightedness. He sits in the waiting-room sweating rivulets for fear he will be found out. Suddenly the door is thrown open, his name is barked out, the doctor takes him by the arm, rushes him across the room, fairly pushes him into a chair; a Boy Scout is already pointing out letters on the eye-chart, the doctor snaps his questions, and almost before X knows it, his eyes have been examined. For the ordinary man the experience is so unusual, the excitement so great, the fear of detection so great that his well-laid plans vanish into vapor. There was no faking. Some loud-mouths bragged of how they faked the doctors. One . . . in our district said he had faked his hearing; whereon the Board made public that [*he*] had been rejected for syphlis.

The causes of physical disability varied with different districts, of course, e.g. hook-worm in the South, tuberculosis in the mine regions of Pennsylvania, etc. On our district they were, in order of importance: rupture and condition favorable to rupture, heart-murmer, flat-feet, defective vision, tuberculosis, and venereal disease. As a comment on the last mentioned, it might be stated that the "one in every three" "statistics" of the alarmists are rot; not one in twenty-five men examined were afflicted; but what was noticable was this: — that of the veneral disease that was found, gonnerea & syphlis ran neck and neck for numerical supremecy, — contrary to the usual notion that syphlis is rare.

As for the grounds of exemption, the most used was (1) aliens [*4 million aliens were living in the United States*[19]] and (2) dependents. There were a multitude of other provisions for exemption but they were seldom used, — i.e. ordained ministers, licensed sea pilots, employers [*employees*] of state arsenels, state officials, etc., etc. Nil for conscientious objectors. One was exempted who had "dependent on his labor for support" (1) wife, or wife & child, (ii) aged and infirm parent, (iii) widowed mother, (iv) motherless child or orphan brother or sister under sixteen — The classification was rigidly held to: you might have a dependent mistress and three children, or four dependent grandparents, but as the law made no provision for such, — no exemption.

As for the exemption of aliens, it seems hideous to penalize men who have taken out first papers, and exempt the useless dogs who don't become Americanized. But much is to be said for the esprit of our aliens. 46 out of 130 in our district waived their claims. The district, I have read, with a low record of exemption claims was a German-American locality in Brooklyn.

As to what constitutes a "dependent wife," when there are no children, there was terrific confusion. Some boards treated any wife — so long as the right to her had been acquired prior to the war — as an exemption ticket. Other boards, like the one home in Schenectady, held that if a woman was healthy, she was not dependent; and if she whined: "I'll starve," they offered to get her a job in the General Electric Co. at $3.00 per diem.

Under the new regulations just passed, all men owning wives are to be put in Class Z and are not to be called till Class I (single men) is exhausted, — which will never be. Stull, if marriage were what we like to think it is, if all marriages were like the few we know, I should believe in the exemption of all married men, even tho they have no children. But so many of the marriages that I saw in my experiences with the board were mere meal-tickets, mere bed-partnerships, that I dissent. Imagine the ordinary hoodlum coming in with his boistrous wife, and saying: "Here is my little exemption ticket." It is not that an injustice would be done the single men, for it is no injustice to any man that he be ordered to take his part in this war; it is simply that a rediculous and vapid privilege of being a piker is extended the married man.

My board was strict. Five of the first seven picked were married. Only eighty married men were exempted from the total of 600 names drawn. Of these eighty, all but fourteen had from one to five kids; and of the fourteen, twelve were pregnant and two were cripples.

Some of the boards were NOT strict, getting only one out of every ten or twelve called; my board got better than one out of three.

One glorious thing about the draft was its total disregard of technicality and its aim at substantial justice. My God, it was a relief, after my year in the Law School. The motto seems to have been "Justice; and to hell with the law." Lawyers were not permitted to plead the cases of any draftees before the boards. My chairman put one lawyer out bodily.

Now after the above dry analysis that you will probably boredly skim over, meanwhile playing with the propeller of a French biplane, allow me to narrate a few cases I thought amusing. One . . . claimed exemption, not as a conscientious objector but as a "loyal Irishman." One . . . , a Cornell Ag. student, claimed exemption on two grounds: (I) piles, (ii) industrially indispensable, — an ag. student. The mother of one . . . claimed exemption for him, tho he had claimed none and wanted to go; she alleged the boy was crazy and the fact that he was anxious to go proved his insanity. The wife of one . . . , a colored gem'men, implored the board to send him. One . . . took an appeal for exemption to President Wilson, alleging that he [*the draftee*] had syphlis. One . . . , of wealthy and prominent family, who had been married forty days, claimed his wife was pregnant. The Chairman dropped that old-timer about "I'm from Missouree" [*the "Show Me" state*]. The most conspicuous case of a piker was . . . the chairman in Schenectady County of the N.Y. State Military Census. On 4th of July he delivered the city's patriotic speech. He was a County Supervisor. When drafted he claimed exemption as a state officer. Claim denied. In the primaries he received 22 votes, — of which one was his own and one his fathers. He is now in Camp Devens. He even carried his case to the U.S. Federal Court but was calmly told to go home.

The above instances may make you think that the draft took the men unwillingly. So far as I could judge this is absolutely untrue. What this country is suffering from right now is no considerable opposition to the war, but rather a most oppressive and wide-spread apathy toward it. The drafted men were not opposed to going; they were simply somewhat surprised to find that the war had come home so quickly to them. As one of the draftees said to me: "The draft is like an alarm clock; when you hear it go off in the morning you don't want to get up to stop it, but once you're up you're glad you're up." The course of least resistance for the average man was to stay home; all the other average men were doing it. It was not opposition; it was inertia; it was the same thing you say you had to fight in making up your mind to go to France. Now that they're drafted, they're glad they're in it. You may feel that the draft has a black eye shade to it; it was certainly not so looked on by our country; in not one part of the country (save some Indians in Oklahoma) was there any ostensible opposition; the draftees were somewhat dazed, but they went with good heart & will make a wonderful army.[20]

# # # #

Here ends the draft bull.

The University had a little spy hunt lately. Tuttle discovered that Prof. Faust (of the German Dep't) allowed his name to be used as a Vice President of some God-damned German League. Whereon a wild stink arose in the U. Tuttle wrote some really able editorials. It was all cleared up by the revelation that Fausts activities were of the year 1915, and by a profession of loyalty by Faust, who is of American birth.

A group of us studes, 70 in number, sold \$100,000 worth of Liberty bonds in a house-to-house canvas down-town. It was chiefly among the poor people who would not otherwise have bought. They bought the \$50$^{\underline{00}}$ bond, payable \$1$^{\underline{00}}$ a week, most of them. I must have interviewed at least thirty-five families. I raised about \$2400$^{\underline{00}}$. Practically every householder in the U.S. now has one or more bonds. The students themselves failed lamentably. Unwilling to deny themselves a movey show a week, [*they*] slunk into a piggy ease & refused to buy.

Previously you have known me as a man of the proletariat, a scourger of corporashuns. But look at me now, a BONDHOLDER in the U.S. Gov't, a bloated bond-holder. Now I'm a man of the interests. . . .

. . . Jesus Christ, what a lengthy letter! Notice, I started it Oct. 31 and I end it Nov. 7. . . . Sunday I will write you of the Elections [*for mayor*] in N.Y. The approximate outcome is Hylan [*John F., Democrat*] 280,000; Michel [*John P., Fusion-Independent*]149,000; Hillquit [*Morris, Socialist*] 142,000; and Bennett [*William, Republican*] 56,000.

My very, very best, and be as careful as you can about that aviation business.

Bill.

N.Y. State went for suffrage by about 150,000.

DIARY: **November 1** [*1917*]

Rain in small quantities all day precluding everything but lectures and shop work, the latter being merely an inspection of the repair shops here. Even they show clearly that our Liberty Motors and 100000 aeroplanes are things of the future.

The camp is I think officially American to-day. As a result we have stricter and unreasonable rules, such as no more trucks to town, but no improvement nor break in the monotony of boiled meat and potatoes.

DIARY: **November 2** [*1917*]

Again no flying for me. I finished The Forty Five by Dumas, which, as always with Dumas, was good but not too good.

We drew up a lot of rules, satirizing the damn foolish ones posted to-day.

DIARY: **November 3** [*1917*]

No flying in the morning, everyone sat around and crabbed. In the afternoon I broke a long idle period by making 3 *tour de pistes* in an Anzani. More grousing at night. In the morning I went to Lieut Knight and complained about the food and conditions but got little satisfaction.

DIARY: **November 4 [*1917*] Sunday.**

Another misty, damp day with nothing to do but talk about our troubles, which everyone did with a vim. More fellows have gone to complain to the lieut. and mutinous talk is rife. Goodness knows we have enough grounds. In the evening the lieut. came up, was raked over the coals and promised improvement and all sorts of things.

I flew some more in the afternoon and got promoted. On the next flying day I go on a voyage which means that in two weeks at the most I ought to be through.

DIARY: **November 5 [*1917*]**

Nothing notable except it was very cloudy so I flew only with the Anzani class.

DIARY: **November 6 [*1917*]**

The results of our crabbing are showing themselves, we got a fine meal and a speech with reassuring promises by Knight.

It was a banner day for me, one of the few when I was full of confidence and could dare and do anything. They have made new rules requiring a certain amount of time before going on voyages, so I am and will still be in the Anzani class for a time. It was very windy in the morning and 3 of our 5 machines got broken on the first *tour de piste*. We waited a while and then the *moniteur* asked who wanted to go up. I volunteered, and make progress in a "rough sea" getting between 50 and 100 meters up when suddenly my motor stopt completely. I was so low, and the air so bumpy I couldn't waste time to look for the cause but had to pay full attention to my landing. I managed to veer off from a tree and with the devils own luck hit a good little spot and instinctively made a fine landing. After making sure nothing was broken, I looked for the cause of the trouble and found the contact was cut. In moving my left arm my sleeve must have caught the button and broken the contact. I got out, cranked my own machine (a risky business), taxied around in the muddy and rough field and then decided there wasn't room to leave. Later when the *moniteur* came with mechanics (he located me by flying overhead and waving) he agreed with me and we had to taxi and roll the machine over ditches and stone piles before he found a field large enough to go off in. It was a good experience to have gone through safely.

. . . I got a big mail . . . Nearly everyone enclosed clippings and made a great fuss about my croix de guerre. I am afraid to deprecate the incident as I truly want to because they will think I am trying to play false modesty. I also got a package from Lois, with a wonderfully knitted sweater, soap, toothpaste, cards etc. I ended a perfect day by a little walk alone at night.

DIARY: **November 7** [*1917*]

The good food continues, white bread for breakfast. The wind continued its pro-German efforts. We tried to fly a little, had several smash ups and then quit. I made one tour with a frightful machine literally full of frights, but finally landed O.K. keeping my record still clean of even a broken wire. . . .

Nov 7 1917

Dear Lois,

I am enclosing with this one, a letter written and sent on Oct 6. It was returned a little while ago by the censors, not because of anything in it, but because of a red-tape regulation violated in the envelope I used. It wasn't my fault either. I am afraid that more of my letters have been, are, and will be delayed or lost. So if you don't hear from me for a long time dont worry or scold. You needn't worry because nobody with my luck could get hurt; and don't scold because I write letters even if you dont receive them.

My luck was working overtime yesterday, beginning early in the morning in flying . . . up I went. But not very far. I only got about half a mile away and between 50 and 100 meters up, when suddenly my motor stopt completely. I was too low and the weather too rough to try and find the trouble, I had to use all my efforts in getting down alright. With my usual luck I just cleared a tree and landed perfectly in a cleared spot next to a house. . . .

It is little incidents like that, which keep the thrills in flying, because in calm weather straight flying is so easy, I am afraid that some day in the distant future it may lose its thrill for me. . . . I am progressing steadily, in less than a week I ought to start making voyages to parts of the country within a radius of 60 miles or so. . . .

. . . Despite your electioneering I didn't vote for Mitchell. Neither

did I cast my vote for woman suffrage. Whereby I probably lost all pull with your mother. But the truth of the matter was that for some reason unknown to me we didn't vote at this camp (it was probably too small and out of the way to bother) so I have never voted yet and Mitchel didn't get one vote he would have. . . .

To get back to and finish the history of yesterday as a perfect day, a package also came with sweater, soap (was that a hint because of marks on the paper) et al O.K. I had to take a walk at night and test the sweater. It passed with a mark of 121½%. Thanks for all. Regards to all.

From Stull. . . .

Holt took these photos of wrecked airplanes at his flying school. *Holt Collection*

At bombing school, Clermont-Ferrand. Holt is second from right, front row. *Holt Collection*

Wednesday-Nov. 7th [*1917*]

Dear Stull,

Well, New York has again made a fool of itself — Hylan elected — Nuf Ced — I am sick and disgusted — I am going to move out of the city of which I am ashamed — Woman Suffrage also won by a 70,000 majority or something like that — Will you be home to escort me to the polls next November?

. . . Remember Aunt Ethel — to whom you referred in a letter no long ago? Well, she bet her young daughter that I am engaged — and am not saying anything about it. . . .

Au revoir, Lois.

DIARY: **November 8** [*1917*]

A long busy day despite a high and puffy wind. Made 3 tours in Anzanis, 2 of them with motors that coughed and spit, little diversions that made me sit up and take notice. Forced landings are no joke even with my luck. Vinx brought down his third French plane so far.

After flying was over, it was lunch time and after lunch, there was just time to get to a lecture in time and after the lecture I had to run

to catch the truck going to the spiral field, where I have been promoted to. There I had my only rest of the day while waiting for the machines to be repaired. They are [*le*] Rhone [*rotary*] Motors. Finally I was sent up with directions to do a hairpin but just when I was reaching my altitude my motor went bad in loud explosions and I started losing altitude. I looked around for a good landing field but hesitated too long over possible ones, and then tried to limp back to the regular field. I couldn't quite make it, so landed with the wind in a good patch and rolled into a cabbage patch. I expected to turn over and "hang like a ripe apple" but with my usual luck stayed right with nothing broken.

DIARY: **November 11** [*1917*] **Sunday.**

Very windy but a little flying. I brought a machine home from the spiral field and had a lively time. No flying after lunch, so I finished "The Green Mantle" by John Buchan, a very good but wildly improbable war story altho I don't doubt there have been many episodes already more improbable. He probably wrote it in odd moments to kill trench ennui. . . .

DIARY: **November 12** [*1917*]

Made my hairpin in the morning which consisted of nothing but turning around and coasting down 200 meters. In the afternoon I passed my spiral successfully, coming down from 600 meters and landing within 50 yards or less of the T. I was told to go on voyage tomorrow.

Monday-Nov 12-[*1917*]

Dear Stull —

Received yours of Oct-16th today. . . . The letter was late as is all mail nowadays — . . . .

One of your packages has been sent off — and the other will follow in a few days — I am dividing things up in the hope that if one pack doesn't get there the other will. . . .

I am glad you are feeling well and getting fat but that isn't the reason we all wanted you to come home —

. . . What do you think about Russia? . . . Because the capital is in the hands of Russia doesn't mean that the country will make separate peace with Germany but it certainly was disheartening news which was printed in our papers last Thursday — Once again I beg you not to go to that crazy place. . . .

Lois.

DIARY: **November 13** [*1917*]

Cant go on a voyage till 14 hours of flying. But I flew 1 3/4 hours in the morning and can now start voyaging on the first good day. I was supposed to go up to 1000 meters this morning but my altimeter wasn't working and altho I went quite high, I dont know how far. A bunch of new men arrived, ground school men from the states lately building barracks at Issudon [*Issoudun*], **and a fine looking bunch. From their tales Issudon must be a hell hole. While the army itself learnt lesson I think from the horrible mess of the Spanish American war, the aviation branch which is all new has a lot to learn. There will be a good many young aviators, "America's Best," killed by poor mechanics, faulty machines, mistakes of leadership and similar details.**

DIARY: **November 16** [*1917*]

Again the fog but it cleared off around noon. I went up to pass off my altitude test but when I got 900 meters up I ran into big clouds and the day was generally hazy so I came down. I changed to an Anzani and made a petite voyage to Pontlevoy and return. It was a wonderful trip, except that the clouds and haze prevented clear visibility. My motor was perfect, so perfect I could take my hands off the stick, the day was calm and I knew from the map exactly where I was all the time. On my return trip I cut across a big forest, over cities and down the river, a foolish proceeding because I was under 300 meters high and so would have no opportunity to pick a field if I had motor trouble. But the motor ran perfectly.

I got home to find my pay envelope waiting for me, 513 francs being $100 a month minus the installments for 2 Liberty bonds. Also a letter from papa dated Oct 27 and enclosing a draft.

DIARY: **November 17** [*1917*] **Saturday.**

Fog worse than ever. As Vinx says we will probably do our flying in the afternoons from now on. . . .

DIARY: **November 18** [*1917*]

Being written up on Dec 9 the delay being partly due to absence and partly to lazyness. So a very interesting period will be noted down in topic sentences. A bad motor prevented a voyage and I enjoyed a beautiful day by reading "The Definite Object" by Jeffrey Farnol about which nothing need be said except that it is Jeffrey Farnol.

Sunday Evening, Nov. 18, 1917
Ithaca, N.Y.

My dear Stull,

. . . The U. has taken a turn for the worse. I wrote you that the men had some sense of self-respect, or rather, sense of humor, and had cut the rah, rah!! stuff. It has worn off. Fretting over foot-ball is in style again. Groans at the movies are come back. Even a Frosh-soph rush on the Dutch. But, cheer up, the second draft [*for men as young as 18 and old as 45, an additional 13 million men*[21]] will be pulled some time this spring and the colleges will be finely combed. The new draft system is to put all men in five classes and draw the whole of one class before touching the second, etc. Class one consists of unmarried men with no indespensible or valuable industrial pursuit, i.e. college students and other parasites generally.

. . . Well, Stull, they say the Lord takes only those He loves best, so I guess you'll pull through. But in Christ's name, don't be fool-hardy, especially in training.

My very, very best,
Bill.

DIARY: **November 19** [*1917*]

An overcast day but I made my first triangle flying to Chateaudun and Pontleroy at low altitudes. I had lunch at Pontleroy with a French family. The trip is about 125 miles so I was pretty tired.

Monday- noon. Nov. 19th [*1917*]

Dear Stull,

. . . As you probably know — the Y.M.C.A. is also trying to raise money to send men, equipment — etc. to France. . . . I should like very much to have some first hand information on the subject of what the Y.M. is doing in France — Won't you give it to me? Everything you can think of — Since you use Y.M. note paper you must have some connection with it in some way & know something about it.

Enid paid your honorable household a visit this past week end — She said there certainly was a houseful all the time — Mr. Pope dropped from somewhere in Montana. . . . She was very much amused at your father and Mr. Pope — The latter would discourse for ten minutes or so on some subject or another — Russia for example — then end by saying "What do you think, Holt" — Short but expressive reply being, "I think you're crazy." The performance must be repeated at every meeting between those two because the very same thing happened when I was over. . . .

. . . Do you still think the war will last three years?. . . Paula has something up her sleeve which interests me greatly — Teaching the blind — . . . .

[*Lois*]

Nov 21, 1917

Dear Lois,

Since my last letter I have received two from you (Oct 22 and 25). In both you add to the conscience troubles I have by complaining about receiving no letters. Because of the justness of your complaint, because I know my own unworthiness and because there are lots and lots of interesting things I want to tell you, I have registered a vow to write a letter a day for 7 days. Now will you be good.

. . . Things over on this side of the big drink are still going flyingly. In about 3 more flying days I will probably be finished at this school and am then supposed to be a sure enough aviator. In reality I am no more an aviator than a girl coming out of a stenography school is a stenographer. She may manage to make funny marks in a book and to make a noise with a typewriter. In the same way I somehow let an aeroplane carry me about from one place to another. I have been carried a good deal lately. Several days ago I made a trip of about 50 miles and had a good time. The day was very foggy and hazy so I couldn't go above 1000 feet. Below 2000 ft isn't nearly as safe as above but I had a fine motor and machine, so good that I could take my

hands and one foot off the controls and lean over the side and wave to the people in villages I passed.

The next day I made a trip of over 125 miles. They give you a machine with a map in it and tell you to fly to such-and-such-a-place, land, have a paper stamped; then go to another s, a s, a p. get your papers stamped and then fly home. It[']s great sport, only then it was a pretty rough and bumpy day so I was pretty tired when I got home.

Yesterday I started out again on a 100 and some mile trip. It was very hazy so I had to stay low and even then I couldn't see far. According to the map I had to go along one side of a forest. When I reached the forest I thought I didn't have to pay any more attention to my course, so I sat back, enjoyed the scenery, waved to people and only looked now and then to be sure the forest was still on my right. It was, and continued to be, even after I had flown near it for an hour, when according to its size on the map, it should have been far behind me. Then I started to look for other landmarks but couldn't find myself on the map. Generally if you know your general locality you can fly around a village, count the roads going to and from it and then find the village on your map. But that didn't work because I didn't even know my general locality. Of course I could have gone on round and round that forest until I found myself but I was tired and hungry so I picked out a field to land in and landed. Then the fun began. The first one to reach, was an old cluck who had been working in a nearby field. He seemed to regard me as his special prey as tho he had first claim to me and explained how I landed and all about me to the rest. "The rest" included everyone within sight. There was a little village about a mile away and it turned out *en masse*. Old women, bent double and shriveled up toddled out to see their first aeroplane. The young ones were there, too, in big wooden shoes, dressed just like the girl in the picture "The Angelus." In fact the French peasants are all members of past history. They look, act and live just the way they did in Dicken's time. Remember we saw the "Tale of Two Cities" in the movies just before I left. Well everyone over here looks like the characters in that. I don't know which caused most staring, the machine or I, but I was at least a close second. I must have looked like a strange animal to them, dressed up in a big fur-lined suit, helmet and goggles on. The children would look at me in awe and wonder, and seek safety in their mothers skirts when ever I moved, and the mothers would tell them to look at me for I was an American. I picked out one little fellow and made him proud and happy by placing him on guard with order to let no one touch anything — Then I went over to the village, talked a while to the pretty girl in the post office (she told me I was the first American ever in the village) then went to a funny, quaint, ancient-history hotel (such a one as you wouldn't believe possible but so common that I am sorry to say I am getting *blasé* to them and no longer thrilled the way they deserve). Here the host made me drink some wine with him and I had to lie and say it was "*trés bien*" even though it tasted like strong vinegar, because he told me it was made there in town. After lunch I sat around the big open fire and swapped wisdom with him but often had to concurr when I didn't know what he was talking about. He was so fat it interfered with his talking and I could only understand a little here and there. About 3 hours after I landed I went back to the machine and found that everyone including children and dogs were still waiting — I had to warn them to keep way back when I started because there have been cases when they didn't know any better and got in front of a machine, which is apt to break the propellor. Then I gave the boy who had guarded it ten francs, whereat he almost fainted. The girl from the post office gave me a couple of roses; I cranked my motor, got in and away I went. They had told me the direction of a certain city nearby, I found it easily, examined its cathedral as seen from the air and then went on and reached my first destination where I landed and put up for the night. This is a fairly large town and altho the people and it are ancient history, they are used to aeroplanes and aviators because lots of both come here when "making voyages." When forced to stay here over night we always stay with a certain French family. The father used to be chef in a London hotel and the daughter is very pretty so we feast with both our eyes and stomache.

This morning I was supposed to go on to a place about 60 miles away, land and report; and then go back to the school which is 60 miles away from there. But it is raining and blowing a gale so I have to stay and use some of my writing paper which I brought along for just such a contingency.

The biggest reason, I think, why I haven't been writing many or good letters is because I am living in barracks. There is always talk,

confusion and something going on so I cant sneak off by myself and write decently. I think up fine, long letters of all the interesting things I see or hear but never seem able to get them down on paper. However I am beginning now to reform and will do better in the future, especially as I expect to leave these barracks within a week or thereabouts.

I must go and feast (my stomach as its time and besides I saw the ex-chef skinning a rabbit this morning).

My best to all, Stull.

Nov 22, 1917

Dear Lois,

Here I am again after an interesting day, It was drizzly, and rainy all day so there could be no flying. Such being the case, the two fellows, who are marooned with me here in this little village till better weather, and I took a sight-seeing trip. We got on the funniest little jerk train that ever puffed along and after an hour and a half reached a city about 15 miles away. I had seen it several times before from the air but never before from a man's eye view. The city itself is small and old and like all such is full of winding narrow alleys with overhanging houses. But the chief point of interest and where we spent most of the day, was in the chateau, which is as full of history as the ocean is of water. Less than a month ago I read "The Forty Five" by Dumas and that includes this particular chateau and many of the people who lived there. As well as I can remember Francois I, Louis III, Henry III, Duc de Blois, and a few others hung their hats there at one time or another. Personally I would prefer to hang mine "somewhere in the Bronx" because my ideas of comfort dont coincide with the old style. The rooms are dark and tremendously large so that it takes a long time to walk from one low, narrow door to another. And then the tapestry, panels, wall paper and ceilings show a funny taste. Catherine de Medicis bedroom looked like a cubist nightmare out on a drunk. However if it pleased them, it interested me, as did the prison cells underneath and the secret hiding places and all the rest of the paraphanalia that belongs in a perfectly proper middle-age chateau.

We inspected the cathedral (every city of any size has one), sno[o]ped around the old streets causing much staring by the inhabitants; tested the "*petite gateaux*" in several "*patisseries*" [*tested the* *cookies in several bakeries*] **and then bumped around for an hour and a half to cover distance that I have done in 10 minutes in an aeroplane.**

Back at the village, had a fine supper (we have a good pull and strengthened it today by buying a box of candy for the proper party) and then sat around telling the ex chef and his family; how many Fords are made in America a minute; how tall the buildings are; how much pay a chef gets; how all Americans arn't millionaires; and goodness knows what else,

It[']s a great business, this aviating,

Believe me, Stull

DIARY: **November 23** [*1917*]

Still too bad for flying. We hired bicycles and rode to Chaumont on the Loire about 12 km from here and there went thru a wonderful chateau. A prince is living in it now but part is reserved as a museum. The furniture of Catherine de Medici, Henry III and other former inhabitants is kept intact and of course is very interesting. . . .

Nov 24, 1917

Dear Lois,

We didn't take the trip I told you we had planned, neither did we fly. In the morning it rained and in the afternoon it blew a gale so all we did was to take a long walk in a nearby woods. The two fellows who are marooned here with me are both California boys and like all Californians talk about nothing but the good points of California and how rotten the rest of the world is in comparison. Some day I'm going west to find out why all Californians are afflicted that way. I myself think that the W.K. [*well-known*] **town of New York is quite some place but I dont go around like a living real estate advertisement. And I can recognize that even such an outlandish place as the Bronx may have its advantages. However East is East and West is West, and its not up to me to mix the two or to write a brief on their respective merits.**

Speaking of fellows perhaps you'd like to meet the two I am with most when I am at the aviation school and not touring France. Let me introduce Mr. V.E. Heywood of Worcester Mass., commonly known as

Vinx. You may have heard of him before as he was one of the seven fellows who came over with me on the boat. He and I were in the same stateroom but hardly knew each other till we got on land because he was sick all the way over. He is 28 years old, and was an expert machinist and machine designer for the U.S. Envelope Co. He is very quiet and backward and before he came over here never had lived because he was always working hard or because he was afraid he would make a break and attract attention. He has been cured of that and can now be as human as anyone else. We got to be pretty good friends before we got sent out to different ambulance sections. When I got back to Paris I saw him again and we both signed up only I beat him by a few days. Since then we have had some very enjoyable times together and will probably continue to do so in the future, only I am afraid we may get separated as I am about 2 weeks ahead of him in flying. He is going to make a very good aviator despite the fact that so far he has "brought down" three machines. None of the smash ups were bad ones however.

Now for the other. Meet Mr. Lew W. Springer, home somewhere in New Mexico but living the past few years at Washington D.C. He is 27, holds several different kinds of degrees, is a member of the bar; knows more about mechanics than any of us, must be rich as he has a Pierce Arrow to play with; moves in the best society; is a real student; very quiet and reserved; will make a wonderful aviator of the careful, exact, dependable type. Not the type that does crazy, brillant stunts and gets away with them. . . .

Stull

DIARY: **November 26** [*1917*]

Flying but very windy, so that when over half way to Chateaudun I was so tired, cold and bumped about that I landed in a field and rested for some time. Reached Chateaudun in time for dinner at the Hotel St. Louis (Chateaudun being large enough to have several hotels) with some other voyagers. I was too tired and the weather too windy to go on in the afternoon. Instead I visited the very interesting old chateau. . . .

DIARY: **November 27** [*1917*]

No flying bad weather. Mac Kinney, Davidson and I hired an old

two lung auto in which we made the 50 km ride to the city of Charters [*Chartres*], which we "did." The cathedral there is wonderful especially the stained glass windows and the carvings.

DIARY: **November 28** [*1917*]

More unflyable weather . . . joined a party (McKinney, Davy, Estey and Hamilton) going to Sens where there are some American nurses who had invited Estey and friends for Thanksgiving. We took a chance that the weather would continue to be bad to-morrow. . . .

DIARY: **On Nov 29** [*1917*]

Thanksgiving Day reached Sens. . . .

DIARY: **November 30** [*1917*]

Overcast but maybe flying . . . took the 5 am. back to Chateaudun.

DIARY: **December 1** [*1917*]

Where we found out everything was as bad as could be. There had been flying both days, fellows were up there to fly our machines back and we were to go back by train which we did but not till night which was the first train. Found the camp all changed, by guards, new rules, majors and things. Woke Vinx up and had a talk.

Dec 1, 1917.

Dear Lois,

You didn't get the rest of the promised letters but you will and they ought to be interesting ones. I have been to several more cities, visited several more chateaus, cathedrals etc; widely scattered, and haven't been back to camp yet but am going to-night under arrest. I want to mail this now because you may not hear from me for a little while as I may be in the cooler. You see it was this way. Several of us had been kept here (at a town to which we flew from the other place where my former letters were written) for several days by bad weather and the night before Thanksgiving suddenly decided to go to a hospital far away where there were some American nurses who had invited one of

the fellows to bring some of his friends to Thanksgiving dinner. We took a chance that the bad weather would continue and prevent flying for one day more. Well, we went, had a fine time (including turkey et al about which I will tell you later) but the weather was good enough for flying and we couldn't make train connections so we missed another day and didn't get back here till early this morning. Here we found that they had been telephoning and trying to locate us, and there were orders to report to camp at once by the first train. It doesn't leave till to-night so nobody knows yet what is in store for us. But we will probably get a few weeks at some work around camp or maybe the guardhouse. So maybe I wont have an opportunity to write but when I do I will tell you all about everything.

If it had rained, been very foggy or done anything else to prevent flying, everything would have been alright. As it is we had a good time and now that the dance is over we have to pay the musicians. We took a chance on the weather and lost. But aviators are supposed to take chances.

Excuse the haste, brevity, bad writing and other little errors in this note

From Stull.

P.S. I would rather you didn't say anything to anybody in Flatbush about this. When the episode is finished I will tell them myself.

Saturday-Dec. 1st. [*1917*]

Dear Stull,

The first day of the last month — how startling! One month left in which to win the war — this year.

We had a very interesting time on Thanksgiving Day. I told you we were to have two soldiers to dinner, well, the people over here are so anxious to do something for the soldiers that we had 115 more people willing to entertain than there were soldiers to be entertained. Consequently we only had one left for ourselves. He was very interesting indeed and talked a blue streak all the time. We had plenty to talk about too after the experiences he has been thru. He was born in Oklahoma, has lived in practically every state west of that, had been to the Border under Funston, calls General Pershing, "Black Jack" which he says was his nickname among the western troops before he got to the top of the ladder — Our soldier had been to Camp Mills where his leg was broken and he was then sent down here to the Hospital. His home before he went to Camp Mills was in Seattle, Wash. He said he hadn't had many home dinners in years. Once, three years ago, he remembered one but that was about all. He was so grateful he couldn't thank us enough. I am very glad we got him. . . .

I finished another helmet the other day . . . you must have a heavy sweater. . . . It will take me quite a while to make a heavy one with sleeves but you don't mind waiting (in the cold) for a while do you?

. . . *Bièn à vous*, Lois.

P.S. I guess you must be Lieutenant Holt by this time but I don't dare address you thus until I hear for sure — . . .

DIARY: **December 3** [*1917*]

Many and continued rumors as to our punishment dismissal etc but nothing official. Read "Salute to Adventures" by John Buchan. Very good. Vinx, an aviator left for Paris.

DIARY: **December 6** [*1917*]

Were told our punishment which is two weeks on the ground doing fatigues. Altogether it is lighter than I had expected. I was afraid we would be an example.

The morale here is awful and Issoudon [*Issoudun*] **seems to be worse.**

Friday-Dec. 7, 1917.

Dear Stull,

I worked so hard today that I am really tired.

. . . This letter ought to reach you about Christmas — It will be a rather lonesome one for you won't it? If thoughts could only carry people across the sea what a difference it would make — You would have a crowd of friends for Christmas dinner. But Christmas will be strange to everyone this year. In this house there will be no presents — Everything will go to some kind of Relief or other or Red Cross etc.)

Do you remember last Christmas Eve? . . . Don't forget you are going to spend part of Christmas day with me — Now don't let's talk about it any more — it makes me feel — "all in."

. . . You said you were well & happy so without being ironical I can wish you a Merry Christmas & a Happy New Year — Everybody wish me to send their love to you —

Lois

DIARY: **December 11** [*1917*]

A very ordinary day which means much crabbing, more wasted time and nothing accomplished. . . .

DIARY: **December 12** [*1917*]

Papa's birthday. He is 60 to-day, which is pretty old. Nothing else transpired except that time passed. What a cow-like life. . . .

DIARY: **December 13** [*1917*]

On guard in the afternoon and night and altho the night was fair it passed slowly. I have a cough like everyone else, and as I haven't been able to get any outside food for some time am actually under nourished.

DIARY: **December 14** [*1917*]

Passed without anything worthy of note. There was a very fine YMCA meeting at night at which a fellow named Barker sang. The best was a war talk by Mrs. August Belmont (Elenor Robson). They ought to give us more and more of that kind, except for those minutes when I get off alone and think, I forget the war and what it is all about. It was a good war talk.

December 14, 1917.

Dear Stull,

. . . I have a feeling inside me that worries me. It is that these two weeks before Christmas are going to be full of action on the part of the Germans. It seems as tho it must be "now or never" for them and I am terribly afraid it will be "now." That is until the Americans get over there. Of course, we hear many wild reports but I don't think they are the cause of that little worry inside of me. . . .

Later —

The skating pond which I mentioned . . . is ruined — Covered by about 2½ feet of snow. You have probably read that the city is tied up — The cars are not running up here at all.

. . . Your heavy sweater is more than half done and if people will let me alone this week end I'll finish it. Surely this one ought to keep you warm when worn over the other —

. . . You have been gone nine months Mr. Holt, do you know it? Some times it seems years and years and others it doesn't seem long at all — Most of the time it's years —

Tout à vous — Lois.

P.S. Are you considering going to Russia now? . . .

DIARY: **December 15** [*1917*]

Slipped by without much trouble except that caused by moving into another barracks. Ours was needed for incoming American mechanics. They have fine and plenty of food while ours is absolutely bad. So all our crabbing has foundation. Even so I get awfully ashamed of it at times. At night I got 12 letters, all fine. They are beginning to realize the war in America, I can tell from the general tone of all the letters. Incidentally everyone is sending me numerous Xmas packages. I hope they all come. . . .

Sunday Eve — Dec. 16th [*1917*]

Dear Stull,

. . . Last Sat. (yesterday) I received no less than four letters and two post cards — You certainly did punish yourself to my great joy — Those letters are the most interesting you have written because they were about an interesting topic and written in a place where you could hear yourself think. . . .

I [*k*]new you would come home just as soon as the war ends but I wanted to hear you say so yourself — You have done so for which I am very happy — and I know you will come home as good and as true as you went away —

Lois —

DIARY: **December 17** [*1917*]

Just blew away between coughs and sleep and eating bad food. Springer is quite sick.

DIARY: **December 20** [*1917*]

First day of freedom my two weeks on the ground being completed but to-day was the same as every other one being cold, snowy, windy and no flying possible.

Thursday — Dec. 20th. [*1917*]

Dear Stull,

. . . Saturday I had the great privilege of using a friend's ticket for the concert at Carnegie Hall. It was wonderful. I haven't been going at all this winter (one year I had a season ticket) and it was a real treat — . . . I was an hour late for that concert because I went to see your Dad before it — At 2:30 P.M. he started to wash his hands (he was going up-town too) and at 3:15 he didn't have them washed — Such a life in Wall Street —

. . . Your sweater is ready to send but I think it would be better to hold it for a while because it might get mixed up with the other thousand things in the mail and never see France —

Au revoir — Lois.

DIARY: **December 21** [*1917*]

Another move to another barracks where there is no water anywhere near to wash in, no lights, no latrines but much wind coming thru the sides. We are getting used to it.

DIARY: **December 22** [*1917*]

The shortest day of the year. How I hate winter. My soul shrivels up and I can only live for spring. No flying much wind but glory be letters from . . . Harry Kaplan, papa, Lois-Enid and Lois.

DIARY: **December 23** [*1917*]

The afternoon was officially a holiday but just the same as the morning there being no flying and much cold and no pay yet despite many rumors. The war still goes on more actively than usual in winter. . . .

DIARY: **December 24** [*1917*]

After many rumors and delays we finally got paid, my share being 640 francs [*approximately $123.55*]. **I immediately walked downtown with Simpson, had a bath, haircut, got a room at the Hotel Universe with Cadbury. At night the four of us, Cadbury, Springer, Simpson and I went to a horrible vaudeville screeching and then enjoyed a night of civilization; fine beds, water, a fireplace and such things. . . .**

I read <u>The Light that Lies</u> by McCutcheon in bed at night.

DIARY: **Xmas day** [*1917*]

Nothing much accomplished except that I bought a fountain pen. In the afternoon, after a dinner really French with "*Alouettes*" [*skylarks*] **for fowl, we four sat in our room around the open fire, wrote some letters and soaked in civilization generally. I rode out to camp to find a letter from Bill and a package from Lois containing sugar, prunes, and a finely knitted helmet and wristlets. In the evening we went to the Municipal Theatre, a fine place, and enjoyed hugely an operaetta. So passed by first Xmas away from home, my first in the war. I took a long walk after the theatre.**

DIARY: **December 26** [*1917*]

Went back to the cold, barracks but might just as well have stayed in town as the cold northeast wind still prevented all thoughts of flying. . . . We talk and argue a lot about the war and are all, especially myself in fine spirits.

DIARY: **December 27** [*1917*]

Damn the cold. Sherman must have made his famous speech [*War is Hell!*] **in winter. No flying possible, much arguing. Took a long walk with Davidson and Simpson in the afternoon. Got a letter from Vinx, also put in an application for assignment to the school at Clermont figuring that the work would be more interesting, more apt to give promotion and safer than trying *chasse* acrobatics with my inexperience. . . .**

Thursday-Dec. 27th 1917 —

Dear Stull,

. . . .Your letter of Dec. 1st stating that you were about to be given a "ball

& chain" came on Christmas Eve — what a Christmas present! But I am very glad you let me know that I might not hear from you in a year or so because we might worry over here — I am waiting anxiously for the next letter to see what they really did to you — I hope nothing very bad because it really was an awful temptation.

In spite of the fact that we weren't to have much Christmas this year we received some very nice presents — Father gave each of us a $10 check and mother gave Lela a muff and Enid & me each a set of furs. . . . Think of those poor tots in France & Belgium going around without half enough to eat let alone wear while I get a new set of furs — it makes me cry — Well, I'll be working soon — and won't I work! Then I'll have money of my very own and can give every cent if I choose — (except what it takes to live on).

. . . Your father must be a very busy man today — yesterday also — The government has taken control of the r.r.s[22] you know and Wall St. has been lively in consequence —

. . . *L'espere que vous né soit pas dans le* "guard-house" [*I hope you are not in the guardhouse*]

Bién à vous, Lois.

DIARY: **December 28** [*1917*]

Colder and windier than ever. One of the fellows has gotten spinal meningitis and the whole camp is under a strict quarantine. . . .

DIARY: **December 29** [*1917*]

I hope that nobody in the future tries to tell me that France doesn't get cold in winter. However it was dry today and we all felt good after drilling in the light snow. There was some flying by a few "voyage" men only in the afternoon but it was very windy and cold and I didnt get in on it.

DIARY: **December 31** [*1917*]

Again no flying for the same old reasons. . . . So ended the year and a momentous one for me as well as for the world. Just think of all the undreamt of things that I have done and had done to me. The end of it finds me supremely happy having found myself and a cause. To be able to do ones part in such a crisis as the present one and to realize

that fact makes one serenely happy. I wish I could get privacy so as to explain that more in this choppy, incomplete collection of odd moments.

DIARY: **January 1** [*1918*]

How different it entered from other years! I wonder what it holds in store for me. Of one thing I'm pretty certain and that is of much action, many sensations, joy and progress condensed in a short time. Had the usual and interesting debates with Springer and Simpson, in which I learn a lot and find inspiration adding to my growing interest especially in aviation. The weather prevented actual practice again. . . .

DIARY: **January 2** [*1918*]

No flying nor will there be any voyages made till the quarantine is lifted. Several more fellows are taken sick and are suspected of having spinal meningitis. An epidemic would make this camp a hell hole of horrors. No water, even to wash in except a quarter of a mile away and not always there, no light, few and bad latrines, bad food. What a field for an epidemic. . . .

More reading and debates on aviation. The romance of the idea is getting me more and more every day and as my knowledge, small and meagre increases. . . .

DIARY: **January 3** [*1918*]

Sterritt one of the last foreign legion men here got killed to-day falling near Pontleroy. He is the first death since I have been here altho several have been slightly cut or bruised. Sterritt was a quiet gentlemany fellow, there are many here who could be better spared.

DIARY: **January 4** [*1918*]

Quarantine still in force, a mechanic got hurt cranking a motor. They let us make altitude tests and I tried to make mine, flying for the first time since Nov 28. It was windy down low but steady cold and clear up high. My barograph dropt off and didnt work properly so I didnt go above 1000 meters but came right back to the field. I wasnt too anxious to go higher as I hadnt flown for so long and the machines are in such poor shape everyone's nerve and confidence is gone. I

woke up in the night and passed a bad time with the horrors. It was good to fly again. Flying is truly a great game but confidence is necessary and good machines and food are essential for confidence.

DIARY: **January 5** [*1918*]

Bumpy down low but fine up high. I started on my altitude with a [*le*] **Rhone motor and climbed quickly to 2400 meters (7500 feet). I only stayed above 2000 m. 15 minutes as I wanted to take no chance on getting cold or fainting. And my goggles leaked air which made my eyes water so I was afraid I might not be able to see clearly. From way up high the view is more wonderful than I dare to attempt to describe now. I seemed to hang suspended because of the great view the ground under me moved very slowly. . . .**

Saturday, Jan. 5, 1918.

Dear Stull,

. . . We have all been skating all afternoon on the great and mighty Bronx River. It was very rough in places but we managed to have a ripping good time — First we skated hard up and down the river to get warmed up, then we did stunts, snapped the whip, etc —

. . . I have finished school and now await a position. Before Christmas I took the Civil Service Exams, for service in Washington, D.C. but have heard nothing from it. Different girls have told me that it takes six weeks and more so I still have hopes. The test was a cinch and I am sure I passed it.

. . . Another box is on it's way — containing a sweater and a few bars of chocolate which I lied about — I told the post office clerk there was nothing but a sweater because I wanted to stick those in and couldn't take the trouble to buy a tin box [*and*] pack them in it which is the only way they allow you to send candy. . . .

For two weeks I have been wondering what happened [*to*] you when you reached camp under arrest. All I know is that they didn't supply writing paper and ink or pencil. I have been watching the newspapers, but I guess it couldn't have been an event of international importance because there has been no account.

Today we were asked if we could spare a little coal for the poor and they came for it this afternoon. We have been doing without a kitchen fire and so can give them that coal. New York is being supplied now tho so I guess the trouble will soon be over. Think of being without heat, having water pipes freeze & burst — gas freeze etc. That's what some people have gone thru this past week. Something for us to be thankful for — comfort. . . .

It won't be many months now till you have been gone a whole year — It seems years longer and oh how I wish you were coming home — . . . .

Love — Lois . . .

DIARY: **January 6** [*1918*] **Sunday.**

There were some American aviators, Seth Low, Cord (?) Meyer Rickenbacker and several others in Nieuports played around doing such crazy and daredevil *vrilles* [*tail spins*], ***turneaus*** [*tourneaus — turn-arounds*], **climbing spirals and other stunts that everyone had to swear in admiration. It made me feel glad they were American and filled me with envy and ambition.**

I did no flying mainly because the school stopted all afternoon to bury Sterrit. Springer and I acted as pallbearers (my first experience). A bishop held a very unsatisfactory service at the school, and then we all followed the hearse on a long walk to the cemetary where after a few more sterotyped words and a volley of shots, we lowered him, his hopes and dreams into the clay. The two nice features about the funeral were the aeroplanes circling overhead during the funeral and the way in which all the French people we met on the road either crossed themselves, saluted or removed their hats.

Rumor has it (1) that there was a new case of spinal menigitis yesterday and that he and another died to-day (2) that there is mumps in camp (3) that the mechanic hurt cranking a machine died (4) that Wilson who got hurt in a forced landing yesterday is hurt badly but no one can get any news.

The fact is that the wind has changed now coming from the south and the air is almost springy. Would that were true. . . .

I read "Damaged Goods" by Brieux with an introduction by Bernhard [*Bernard*] **Shaw, both of which were very good and likely to make anyone sit up and think.**

DIARY: **January 7** [*1918*]

No flying, much discontent. I stayed in bed all day, reading

"Fannies First Play" by Bernhard Shaw; and talked much to little purpose. . . .

DIARY: **January 8 — February 1** [*1918*]

This is a poor excuse for a diary; but as I remember the big features; the quarantine, bad food, no flying and discontent continued till about Jan 18 or thereabouts, when we got paid. From then on I didn't eat another meal in that old swill-hall. Cad, Springer, Simpson and I walked down the road to the Petite Arch and there ate as finely as I ever did anywhere, consequently I could feel health and good spirits come back. We went to the Municipal Theatre, a beautiful building, and heard Mignon and Carmen, both very fine production. About Jan 22 I tried to make a second altitude hop but after trying to pull up an Anzani for half an hour above 1700 meters I gave up and came down. And made my altitude a couple of days later easily in a Rhone. And Finally on Jan 28 I made my last triangle with an uneventful trip. . . . On Feb 1 I left Tour[*s*] **for Issoudun with a three days stop over at Paris.**

I had a good time at Tours and had a lot of new experiences, learnt a lot and changed my whole life in a few months. I saw a good school more or less ruined by the Americans, altho they may make, and probably will, a good school finally after months and months of horrible bungling.

. . . There has been little activity in the actual fighting but there are persistant rumors of a coming German offensive. Aparently all the guns and men from the eastern front are being concentrated on this front. Is Germany to make a great and final effort before the U.S. can get many men over here, or is it only a bluff as people say the reported strikes in Germany lately are. . . .

Wed. P.M. Jan. 16, 1918.

Dear Stull,

I don't know whether I'm "me" or whether I am somebody else just at present because there seems to have been a complete revolution in my life. I have become a part of the machinery of a business office and yet I feel like the "Spectator." It is a very odd sensation. I watch the suffering Jews in the Subway at night and altho I am jamned in between them so that I can't even get my arm out to scratch my nose — I do not seem to share their suffering — just watch it. Tonight I really had a very enjoyable time — My itching nose, being scratched by the paper on a bunch of flowers that my neighbor had the courage to bear into that cattle car, gave me no trouble — At 42nd St. — Guards yelling at the top of their lungs "Let 'em off" held back the surging mass behind them while those inside the car expanded into the space that those alighting had left — until the mob made their usual stampeed. One Jew sighed & remarked, "Ah! Dat's better ven dey get off" — But another soon destroyed his dream of comfort by saying, "All the more ven dey get out de oders comes in" — How glad I am that I don't take up much room —

I told you in my last letter that I had a position in Rev. of Reviews Magazine — Well, I haven't. I am in the Home Pattern Co. 114 Fifth Ave — Hours 8:30-to 5:30 I leave at 7^{00} A.M. and get home at 7^{00} P.M. Your father could have gotten me a good position but I didn't say any thing to him about it. I wanted to get one all by myself and get some real experience before inflicting myself on any one your father knew —

. . . There hasn't been a letter from you since the one written on Dec. 1st. I have heard that mail has been held up again so probably there is a nice long letter — oh — two or three telling what happened in the guard house — etc — etc. If they only knew how badly I wanted it they would send it up immediately I am sure. . . .

Love from us all, Lois.

COMPAGNIE FRANCAISE DES CABLES TÉLÉGRAPHIQES
[*January 18, 1918*]
BYRON W ITOLT [*sic*] ROBERT
GOODBODY ET CO 42 BWAY NY
AMERICA
LETTERS DELAYED EVERYTHING ALRIGHT
STALL [*sic*]

Monday Jan. 21$^{st.}$ [*1918*]

Dear Stull,

This has been a day without precedent in the history of the city of New York. I, being less fortunate than some of the poor unfortunates, had to go to work. The subway was comfortable, plenty of room to turn a page of the newspaper. Nobody stepped on me or pushed me out of the way. The train was not stalled & I took my time from 14th Station to the office. There everyone was muffled up in coats, sweaters etc & all complaining about the cold. We had no heat of course, it being against gov't orders. I shivered all morning, but went back after lunch expecting (as every one did) to be sent home. We were kept till $4^{\underline{00}}$ P.M. By that time I was really warm — having worked all afternoon. My hot dinner helped some too. At $4^{\underline{00}}$ we were informed that every Saturday we were to work all day & until $1^{\underline{00}}$ P.M. Mondays. That's the way they are evading the "Order" Heat left over from Sat — used Mond. morning —

I have never seen New York as it looked at noon today. Not a store open except Deng. & Resturants — I went into Riker's to get some cough drops & was informed that they were candy and they couldn't sell them.

The war has come to us at last and it's a good thing. I am glad of it, because some people will have to wake up. I am willing to go without cough drops — (how self-sacrificing *n'est pas*?) shiver all morning & even get a worse cold in order that that awakening may be quick. Some people are really suffering tho & I wish I had a "million" — . . . .

Today I received word that I passed the Civil Service, but have to wait to be appointed — Such red tape — They yell for Stenogs. Then take months to hire them when they are to be had for the asking. . . .

Love, Lois.

Saturday Jan. 26, 1918.

Dear Stull,

. . . Tuesday I rec'd a telegram from Washington asking me if I would accept appointment — I wired back that I would and now await further orders. In the mean time Hal is looking up a boarding house for me. He will have to be my guide, councillor & friend when I get down there — he & Darwin, because I don't know the first thing about Wash. and even tho I'm not going on a visit I expect to explore —

. . . I am going to cry some more too if I don't get a letter pretty soon — The last was written on Dec. 1st — which makes it nearly two months since we have heard from you — Letters are coming from France because I know several people who have received them — Therefore I can't console myself with the thought that the mails are being held up. Also your last letter was not especially reassuring if you remember, you left yourself about to take a train for camp under arrest, where practically anything might happen. . . .

Bon soir, Mon cherie

Wed-Jan. 30th [*1918*]

Dear Stull,

Tomorrow has turned out to be a couple of days hence — but never mind because I had in my own hands a very important Cable gram which lifted such a weight off my mind that I almost floated away — I don't know what kept me on earth unless it was my feet —

It was a relief to hear from you tho even if it did cost about $\$2^{00}$ too much. Your father said you used too many words. Isn't he the ungrateful person? I think it was perfect even tho Holt was spelled Itolt.

I am breathlessly waiting to hear from Washington again. Hall. looked up my telegram and it arrived safely so I expect I'll hear from them soon — Then it will be Washington for mine — and when the war is over (?) you will have to come way down there — to see the Popes — Then I'll take a weeks vacation and come home with you. . . .

Bon soir — Lois.

DIARY: **February 1 — February 5** [*1918*]

In Paris stopping at the Calais Hotel in a very little room from which I would sally forth going mostly to the YMCA and the Soldiers and Sailors Club libraries where I read a lot. At the Y.M. where I ate several times I fell in with a Canadian captain, a doctor, and we held long and interesting conversations. I learning a lot.

I saw only one place where damage had been done by the last aeroplane raid of a few days ago (the biggest Paris has had yet) but rumor has it that much damage was done in the suburbs.

I bought, or think I did, a French bond with the half hundred franc [*approximately $9.65*] **note I have had so long.**

The first day I went to Henry's and tried to get my long lost baggage but didn't. I looked thru all that we had stored and saw lots belonging to Ned, Judge and Red Day but not mine. I wrote to Steve about it and congratulated him on his book "At the Front in a

Flivver" which is a continuation of "Ambulance No 10" and the History of Section 1. The book stops before I joined the section.

So after storing a trunk at the American Express Co, my Paris trip ended without the recovery of my baggage, without the purchase of much equipment but with much reading especially in Nelsons History of the War by John Buchan.

Feb 3, 1918

Dear Lois,

Here I am again in Paris, this time on a three days leave. Paris is just the same as it always is so I am not experiencing many new sights. In fact I would have gone somewhere else on my holiday only I had some business to do here, viz. trip to find some baggage I have lost. So far I haven't succeeded and as it has been lost for over four months I have almost given up hope. There wasn't very much of it but I hate to lose what there was. However it is wartime and war always means losses of one kind of another. Witness last night when I sat up in bed till — (I am ashamed to tell) reading.

I am now a real aviator and wear two wings thusly [*drawing*] **on my uniform to prove it. The wings are made of some kind of silvery thread and are on a blue-black background so they show off for nearly a mile. Consequently I enjoy myself immensely by strutting down the main streets with my chest thrown out so far I couldn't get anything out of my pocket. Despite the wings I have still a few things to learn and next Tuesday I go to Issoudun (a little town some 50 miles southwest of Tours) to a perfectioning or finishing school. "Finishing" is a badly chosen word. It will probably be about two months before I leave there, depending on luck and the weather. I sure did have bad luck and weather at Tours. I should have finished by all indications around the 1st of Dec but as you know, only just finished near the end of Jan. It was just one thing after another 1. I was put on the ground for a week for taking French leave on Thanksgiving 2. the awful spell of winter in December 3. the quarantine, which you know nothing of so far. In Jan. when the weather reversed itself and became springlike, we were all quarantined for spinal meningitis. Of course I couldn't tell anyone about it on account of the censor, but that was why I was delayed so long. As soon as the quarantine lifted, I did too. It takes**

real philosophy to have to sit more or less idly for almost two months and not get ill-tempered.

I have one more thing to grouse about and that is the mail or rather the lack of it. You write I know and so do others but I dont receive. The last I have received from anyone is yours of Dec 17. That isnt true either because one came at the same time from Enid dated the 19th. I am afraid you haven't been doing much receiving either. There was a little fire in the postoffice just after Xmas and some at least of the Xmas letters I wrote probably never arrived. I hope yours wasnt among them.

Having relieved my mind of all worries, lost baggage, delays and mail, I feel better which means a lot as I feel pretty good all the time.

There isnt much to tell that is real exciting or interesting like there was and what there is, is uncensorable. Probably there is a whole lot of things that would be very interesting but I don't realize they would be so. We all become so *blasé* about flying and flyer's that it is hard to remember the curiosity and awe of those poor unfortunates who never get any higher than they can walk. I myself was just such a one and had just such awe of flying not six months ago. Every once in a while the non-flying point of view is brought to our minds and it always startles. For instance the other day I fell in with a captain (infantry) and as he was going out to the aviation school we went together. He was going to see a friend and I suggested that he take a ride with his friend. He didn't seem at all enthusiastic saying that altho he had driven in automobile races he didn't like the idea of trusting himself in the air. But I talked him in to it or had done so when we nearly reached the school, and right across the road was what had formerly been an aeroplane. Some fellow had tried to cut a tree down using the machine as an ax. I looked at the wreck with professional interest and laughed, just the way you would at an auto that had hit a lamp post or something. But the captain was very interested and when we got inside the school and saw right in the middle of the field another machine piled up like kindling wood, he decided then and there that the afternoon was too late to think of making a flight. Some of the smash ups do look awfully bad and you wonder how the fellows get out of them safely as they always do. Most of them occur when a fellow first begins to fly alone, because then he is mentally paralized in the air. That is the only reason (except when the machine or engine

goes bad) there are ever any smash ups. All one needs is a level head and a lot of conceit and he will not even break a wire, witness me. I talk big on the ground but don't always feel quite so center-of-the-universe when in the air. Especially at high altitudes. The other day I was up pretty high and I felt so small I would have had to stand on my toes to look a snake in the eyes. It is a funny feeling, you feel as if you were up there all alone and the funny part of it is that you are all alone.

Incidentally I had a new sight that day flying for the first time above real clouds in any large quantities. Flying in or above clouds is dangerous because when you lose sight of the earth you lose your sense of equilibrium and without knowing it you might go into a wing slip (fall this way [*drawing*]**) or go straight down and think all the time that you were flying level. Then if the clouds were very low you might not see the ground in time. Therefore it is dangerous to play around with real clouds and consequently I didn't. What I did do was to fly up to the edge of them and a little over but always keeping sight of the ground behind. I was about 5000 feet above them and altho they were fairly high above the ground it looked as if they were lying on it. They looked for all the world like raw cotton rolled between your hands into long strips and layed side by side. There wasnt a bit of ground to be seen through or beyond them.**

To-day is Sunday and the hour being meal time I have to stop, eat and then take my weekly promenade. Only this time I will flash a pair of wings upon the eyes of the admiring multitudes. O! Vanitas vanitatum!

I have been intending a long time to write to you about the Y.M.C.A. as you asked and will do so before the week is gone. In that as in other things

Believe me
Yr. most obed.t serv. t
Stull

P.S. Some ending a la Geo Washington

DIARY: **February 5-February 18** [*1918*]

Reached Issoudun, saw a little of the little dirty town before a long truck ride and beautiful night to camp about 8 miles away from everywhere. Here I met Vinx and from him I got all the "dope." There are

between 4 and 5000 men here (the place is enormous) but only about 260 fliers (and these are scattered in several fields nearby). I was the 439th aviator to enter the school and as all aviators in France go thru here that shows that the American army wont have so many ready this year. The course is divided into roulers, 23 meter Nieuports double control, 23 meter single control, 18 meter single, 15 meter single acrobatics, and then 15 meter with 120 hp motors. A great many fellows only go thru 18 meter work and then go to observation or bombing schools.

Besides the actual flying of which there appears to be plenty in good machines with good mechanics, there is a lot of ground work including trap shooting, pistol practice, machine gun theory and stripping etc. We are divided into sections of about 10 with a section leader (ours is Captain Parks) and the section flies half a day and goes to classes the other half. The officers (there is a distinction here between officers and flying lieutenants) are treated the same as we are except that they have a separate mess and it is nice to see Lieuts. Meredith, Davis, Capt Parks etc. out doing Kalisthenics and marching with us. They have all showed up well under the severe test viz. lording it at Tours in command and now treated very disrespectfully by other officers and as equals to us.

The food (we eat with mess kits, a very extravagent, dirty and wasteful way) is not good. It is all very heavy, meat, potatoes, rice and heavily cooked. Canned vegetables which could be more easily cook[*ed*] [*and*] **transported arn't here at all. And there is no way of buying any outside.**

There are no flying clothes here at all. They have a demerit system, a lot of funny rules such as blanket folding, no suitcases in sight. We sleep in those accursed double bunks but luckily the barracks are pretty empty so we manage very well. The weather has turned cold after a spell of real Spring and we all have a hard time keeping warm at night.

There are several hundred cadets here who haven't begun flying yet and among them I found Al Fuller. He has been doing guard duty and k.p. for 3 months, coming here in October after graduating from ground school. We went for 2 months here without taking a bath. The Red Cross has now donated showers in a tent, where a bath may be had once a week. The Red Cross and the Y.M. which has a large build-

ing are the only monotony relievers. The Y.M. stages fights, wrestling, concerts, music, speakers, and runs a little store, and best of all gives real movie shows. They are good.

We started work almost immediately and in about two days I finished with the roulers, which are Moran[*e*] parisols with clipt wings. Then waited a few days for room, and good weather and flew my first trip in a Nieuport on Feb 15. Of course the 23 meter is large and unwieldy compared to the 15 but even it seemed very fine to me. They seem easy to run, requiring almost no lateral correction the way the Caudron does. I got 3 more trips on the 18th and enjoyed them despite the cold.

Springer came along a few days after I did and is in the section behind me, with Ted Meredith etc. He bunks right opposite me, and Sayre on the other side, so we have great debates now and then. Cadbury showed up a couple of days ago and we expect Simpson soon.

I have been reading a lot of magazine articles on the war, The Last Days of Ft. Vaux etc so am full of war interest again. If I can get out of this hole soon and either at the front or at some place where conditions to think, write and do are only fair I will be very happy.

I have just begun to receive mail, getting several letters from Charlie Muller, Lois and home. Also some very fine chocolate from Mr. Barker.

The nervousness along the entire front is reaching the breaking point. Every day there are bigger and bigger raids in all the sectors and a big attack is due any time. The Germans have made peace with the Ukrains, a part of Russia, and for a time a unique condition existed. Russia refused to sign a peace treaty and denounced German rulers but declared the war was over.[23] Germany only yesterday said that meant war, which I hope is true, because it would hurt German morale and military strength too even a little.

Every little helps because the U.S. is aparently unable to accomplish much for a long time yet. I have seen the horrible mess made of the air service and I think it is almost as bad elsewhere. Investigations in the States are revealing bad conditions and over here they are worse. Springer's brother-in-law, a medical major is wild over army methods and Capt Parks told me that the artillery has no guns but is wigwagging all day long. Meanwhile there is a threatened German drive and the tension increases. Naturally the activity in the air is very great and

likewise the number of R.F.C. [*Royal Flying Corp*] **men in the Roll of Honor.**

Washington, D.C., Feb. 6, 1918.

Dear Stull,

. . . Here I really and truly am — in Wash. with a really, truly government position. I am in the Bureau of Standards, but don't know what sort of work I will have to do, having gone today for the first time, and not in the place which I will fill permanently.

The B. of S. is out of Wash. very near where Popes live and since Mrs. Pope has been good enough to allow me to board here with the family it is going to be very handy. I can walk back and forth — and in that way get the exercise I need to keep me thin —

. . . This is a great old town. I haven't seen it all but what I have seen I like — Popes live way out of the city in a beautiful section — at least it will be beautiful when Spring comes — There are some of the dearest houses on this very block — I know you would love them — one in particular which has a great big porch — is big and square with fine bay windows — Looks as tho there were plenty of room inside — I'll bet my life there are fire places in it — big ones — oh — how many and sweet are the memories those words bring back — Popes have them too, but there is always some one in the room to talk to me and — well, we will have our own some day — *n'est pas? . . .*

Mr. Pope firmly believes that the war is no where near its close and he also believes some other very painful things. I don't agree with him on a good many subjects — I couldn't and exist.

. . . I wonder what you are doing now. Sleeping I guess — because it's about 3:00 A.M. in France — I hope your dreams are pleasant — wonder what they are — You are nearer than when I started this anyway — You're the dearest boy that ever lived or fought for a good cause and I love you.

Lois.

Sunday Feb 10, 1918

Dear Lois,

Last night, after nearly a month of no mail, I again had that schoolboy at-three-o'clock feeling which comes with mail over here. As

usual you didn't fail me (it was dated Dec 20) and I was also lucky enough to get one from Lela (Jan 4). While speaking of mail it would probably do no harm to repeat: Package no. 1 with helmet wristlets, prunes etc. came O.K. and are doing excellant service but package no 2 has failed to appear as yet. When it does get here I bet I find "Don't open till Xmas" written on it. . . .

As for that Y.M. and the Red Cross, they both do fine work. At the other school I used the Y. a lot even tho there was a large city only a couple of miles away, But here where the nearest town is about 8 or 9 miles away it is the only form of dissipation we have. There is a Red Cross branch here too which does similar work and just as well. You can buy candy, crackers, sandwiches, and other eatables; towels, soap and all such essentials; and can get magazines etc to read. Besides they provide lots of entertainment such as movies (real honest to goodness just like New York movies) several times a week; lectures, music, basketball and a few other things. This is quite a sizeable camp so they have quite a large building. At the other school there were two females, one fairly young and fair and the other fairly old. Here there must be 8 or 9, I havent been here long enough to know how many yet. . . .

I am enclosing a couple of pictures which may or may not be of interest. That funny looking wreath with one wing in it is the French student aviator's insignia.

My best to everyone, Stull

Wash., D.C., Fri-Feb. 15th [*1918*]

Dear Stull,

. . . This week has been very quiet. I have been in every night but one — that being Tuesday — when I went with Rob to hear Billy Sunday. Poor Billy — Washington doesn't seem to love him as much as it might. . . .

It sure will feel good to get hold of another "letter from France." Think of it! — not a word (except cable) since Dec. 1st — en route to — the guard house — I suppose your Dad knows about that wild escapade by this time — Wonder what he thinks?

. . . Mr. Pope has, thru careful study and calculation, found the solution to the wheat problem. He is "going" to put it before Mr. Hoover. I'm sure you will be interested. This is it in a sentence — Pass a law forbidding the use of talc — & rice powder — and thus save 400 barrels of substitute for wheat a month — . . . .

He often remarks — "I wish I had Holt here" (something he & your Dad disagree on) and I think to myself "Gee, I wish you did too."

I hear less about the war down here than I did in New York. It is odd — Read a good article in the Sat. Eve. Post. on the German Peace Offers — but am not up on current events like I was at home. Think I'll have the Tribune sent down here — . . .

With best love — Lois.

DIARY: **February 19** [*1918*]

I flew 4 trips to-day, 3 with my own monitor and 4 with Springer's friend Harding. The whole class was passed and tomorrow we will make our first trip alone. I also, for the first time was able to hit a few birds at traps and enjoyed it. Then came more mail than I have received in a dogs age viz. . . . mama and Lois.

DIARY: **February 20** [*1918*]

Flew alone making three trips with pretty good success, finding little tendency to *cheval de bois* [*spin the plane*], **and the landings easy.**

Simy arrove today full of the latest Tours gossip which is of no great moment.

. . . There are a lot of interesting sights here and some fine machines. All kinds of Nieuports, a couple of Spads, an occassional Caudron, a Sopwith, and a Morane parisol which can almost *vrille* upwards. It goes thru some great stunts, making a terrific noise with a 160 hp Gnome monosoupape [*single valve rotary*] **motor.**

Read some horrible stuff about the American Army and what it is going to do and one little article that was fine in Colliers of Jan 12 on the Sins of the Censor. What we need is a Lord Northcliffe and an entirely new set of officers. [*Lord Alfred Northcliffe (1865-1922) was a prominent journalist who organized a propanda campaign within Britain throughout the war and in 1918 against a dispirited Germany.*]

DIARY: **February 21** [*1918*]

Rain and no flying. Wasted afternoon on ridiculous lectures. Got a

letter from papa and Elizabeth dated Jan 28th. Went to the movies after a compulsory bath but they weren't up to the usual. Fine article by H.G. Wells in the mail on the League of Nations.

DIARY: **February 22** [*1918*]

Washington's birthday and a noteworthy one for me. Flew one trip in the morning alright and on my second the motor stopt while I was turning, I almost went into a wing slip, righted, glided, motor caught then stopt and I landed with the wind (vineyards prevented any attempt to turn in the wind) going over 90 miles an hour on a plowed field. I made a fair landing but should have pancaked very high and dropt. As it was my wheels sank in the mud and because of the great speed, the landing gear broke and over I went. I got no sensation and felt no fear. The belt held and I hung upside down until I undid it and crawled out. The landing gear, wing and rudder were well broken but nothing else. The officers in charge who witnessed the whole performance said I was not to blame and said I wouldn't have it charged against me on my record. So ended my first smash of anything large or small. So far I haven't felt any nerves about it.

Heyward was around tonight. He had a smash up to-day too. He left the hospital (?) last night and warns us not to go there no matter how sick we get. They had no medical attention altho the swelling went down with him, no fires nor blankets so they almost froze, very little food (old Vinx would divide up the bully beef on the six plates resting on the floor.) . . .

DIARY: **February 23** [*1918*]

The usual uninteresting ground classes given by inexperienced youngsters in the morning. Flying in the afternoon, I went to the 23 meter field to get in a few more rides while the rest of my section went to the 18 meters. I made 2 landings, neither of them very good and the *moniteur* told me I had better stay with the 23s a while. I used too much rudder in the air and flew nervously. The rest of the section flew 18s and A.H. Wilson, the musician and gentleman, had an accident and got killed. He got into a very steep spiral and then went into a nose dive straight to the ground. He was killed instantly.

Such an accident always brings thoughts but we will probably become more accustomed to them later on. They have little visible

Flying training at Tours and Issoudun, 1917-1918. Above: Stull Holt in front of a Caudron airplane, and below, beside a Nieuport (with propeller missing). *Holt Collection*

effect now, the fellows laughing and joking as usual, but I can tell they think.

Davy, the old bag of grit and guts, had another little smash and is back on the roulers with a new bunch of men from Tours.

Went to the movies at night but they weren't very good.

DIARY: **February 24** [*1918*]

Sunday and work, the latter being contrary to custom on Sunday. I am in another section with McKinney etc. and we put in a very uninteresting morning while some infant tryed to explain and did in a way, deflection in aerial shooting.

. . . Read an awful bunch of newspapers Springer has received and noticed particularly the great howl that went up when the coal saving 5 day shut down went into effect.[24] Compare that to what all businesses have suffered for years over here and it makes an American feel cheap.

Wrote to home and Lois.

Wash., D.C., Sunday-Feb. 24th. [*1918*]

Dear Stull,

. . . There are a great many soldiers in Washington and I really ought to be used to them by this time, but somehow I always feel a queer little stir inside me when I see one and feel like shouting. Do you know what a wonderful feeling it is to have a soldier in France? No — you don't — But it is wonderful — Next to being there yourself —

Paula & Enid, like two angels, copied & sent me your two letters written on Christmas Day — one to your dad & one to your mother. I think mine must have found a watery grave. Paula also sent me a photo which I could look at and return immediately — I looked — and looked, and looked before I realized what the matter was. O: Stull, where did you get that mustache? I'm so upset I can't even spell it. Of course, it may be very becoming, but if so, it will be the first I have ever seen that was — I am assuming that you are going to let us see it.

Mr. Pope is the most pessimistic man I have ever seen. He has nothing but criticism for the administration, sees only the weak spots and nearly drives me wild with his conceit. I once applied that word to you I believe — I humbly entreat you to forgive me — You don't even know what it means. And the worst of it is Mr. Pope really has nothing to be conceited about — He thinks he knows more than anyone else because he predicted a wheat shortage — Well, who didn't? He keeps harping "I told them so," but never divulges what remedies he suggested. He is really such a boy that I suppose it's only talk, but O! I wish he wouldn't criticize.

Washington is a dear old place, Stull — I like it more and more — It is dreadfully crowded now, of course, but it must be just wonderful in normal times. . . .

Give Fritz one for me — Lois.

Feb 24, 1918

Dear Lois,

I will now complete a very interesting Sunday afternoon and evening in the proper way i.e. writing to you. I lay on my back all that time and read news papers which kind and thoughtful friends (that is not a hint as I get all the papers I can possibly read) sent to my bunkie, Springer. Reading about the war, and especially about aviation, in the Sunday supplements of American papers is one of the best forms of amusments we have. After this I will never believe anything I read in any newspaper, I wouldn't even believe my own death notice if I read it.

The aviation business still goes along airily, I might almost say breezily. I had a new experience last week that was amusing, viz I had a smash up, my first one but very thoroughly done. I had a "forced landing" which means my motor went bad and naturally I was forced to come down. Which I did very gracefully but I had to land with the wind (I couldn't turn into the wind because I was too low and because of a vineyard under me). I lit in a ploughed and muddy field, going over 90 miles an hour. My wheels sank in the mud and because of my great speed, the landing gear broke and over I went *comme sa* [*like this*]

[*Stull's Sketch*]

Of course I wasn't hurt a bit, such things just aren't done by the best people this year. I wasn't even jarred because the belt kept me from falling out when the machine went over. I hung there a minute till I undid my belt and scrambled out, laughing because I felt so foolish

while I was hanging upside down. The damage done was to the machine which suffered external and internal injuries. I was not blamed at all because it was, as they told me, just one of those unavoidable accidents that happen once in a while.

That is all the interesting news about me except that I try every day with only indifferent success to hit bull eyes, clay pigeons, targets and things with shot guns, machine guns and pistols. When I get home if I am good for nothing else I can get a job as a first class gunman. I might even introduce a new idea and instead of making a "getaway" in a taxi I could use an aeroplane.

The news of your "job" came as a big surprise. It doesn't seem quite right and yet I am glad in some ways. The only things I ask of you are 1. Don't be foolish and hurt your health by trying to overwork 2. Be polite but dont get too well acquainted with any embryo editors or literary stars (I am too far away to withstand any competition) 3. Dont change too much, or even as much as I have changed from the fellow you used to know — . . . .

Yours, Stull.

DIARY: **February 25** [*1918*]

More ground work including an interesting lecture on bombing, I want to get on one of those Breguets [*French bomber plane*] **more and more every day.**

Philipoteaux got killed today landing in a *vrille*. Altho he knew practically nothing of the mechanics of flying he was a good flier and they used him as a tester. They say that because the Nieuports are not being used at the front any more they are not so carefully made but are thrown together compared to the hand work they used to receive.

We buried A.H. to-day on the hill up the road. There was the band, the pall bearers and one squad as a guard. Davy, Tom Reed, McKinney and I were part of the guard. I wonder how many more of us will stay over here. A.H. had a bad day to end his stay on earth as it rained during all the funeral. I can remember the time he and I had lunch with a young Englishman at Chateau[*dun*]**.**

I got a box of crackers from home. It was pretty well banged up and the crackers stale but they tasted good.

DIARY: **March 1** [*1918*]

Much wind and no flying but the usual poor ground work. Read some, more men arrive, forming now section 48, (I'm in 36) but they will go slowly because we and every one is held up by 23 singles. With them once past we should go very fast because the rest of the school is pretty empty.

Vinx was over. He has quit flying here, the rotary motor, his poor physical condition, and bad treatment when sick have gotten his goat. He has asked to be sent to another school at any other work. He confirms our decision about bombing especially in Breguets at Clermont. I wish we could all go there together. . . .

DIARY: **March 3** [*1918*] **Sunday.**

Nothing much doing except a run after reveile in the morning a new feature. It leaves us from 6 to 625 to eat breakfast, fix bunks and go to flying which means eating too near exercise. It is another example of annoyance. No discipline, endless petty annoyances.

DIARY: **March 5** [*1918*]

Ground classes, too muddy for flying (the result of picking these bare fields for a school) much talk, little accomplished, much thinking, a Charlie Chaplin movie at the Red Cross at night. . . .

DIARY: **March 6** [*1918*]

I didn't fly altho there was some flying done. Lt. Perrault got killed in an 18 meter. I have been thinking a lot of transfering and becoming a bomber. More of that anon. . . .

3214 Newark St., Wash., D.C.
Wednesday-Mar. 6th [*1918*]

Dear Stull,

Mail is beginning to travel again thank goodness. I have rec'd a letter and a postal in two weeks. I hope you are getting some too because you need it more than I do — . . . .

Later —

When I got home from the Bureau this afternoon I found another letter waiting for me — written Feb. 10th. I am very glad to hear that you have at last received your mail, but very much disappointed about the sweater. It was a very heavy one — much warmer than the first one I sent.

The war situation looks gloomy indeed —

. . . Now for the pictures — if I were not naturally a truthful person I would say they are both adorable — but, being as I am, I must say that I would never recognize you in the one where you are wearing your hat. That hat does not suit your style of beauty nearly so well as a peaked hat would. Can't you buy or steal one somewhere?

. . . I was terribly disappointed last week when I learned that we are to have no vacation at Easter time. . . . It means that I won't get home until May 30th — I am not homesick or anything like that, but I hate to have my plans all spoiled. . . .

Bon soir, Lois.

DIARY: **March 7** [*1918*]

The usual very heavy ground fog but it cleared off in time to give me three trips in the morning. I landed and took off alright but don't know how to fly these machines in the air. In the afternoon I had three more rides (two in a lumbering double control machine) and could have been laschayed [*an Americanized use of French, i.e., to be released, to be let go*] **with the rest of the class if I made a couple of more turns. But I told him I would prefer not to fly as I didn't feel well. There is absolutely no sense in going on when I don't know how to fly these yet. These machines are super sensitive and I dont know their flying position nor how to turn or manuvere them properly. All of which added to a poor condition (headache, cough and general lassitude) makes me have a slight case of nerves. I would put in a request for a transfer as a bomber only I am afraid that I am afraid of Nieuports. A bad quandary causing much thought. I think I would prefer the bombing but am afraid that the nervousness enters into the argument.**

Got letters from Lois and papa.

DIARY: **March 8** [*1918*]

Didn't feel well so made no attempt to try to fly. Others are in a somewhat similar position as I. The weather is becoming more and

more beautiful. I have about made up my mind to get the bombing job[.] Harry Agerter is going to and McKinney may. It is a coming service, offers more chance of promotion, is more interesting I think but I want to know how to fly (the machines are double control) and I dont want to quit. I know I can fly these and only need more time and a little more instruction.

We had some excitement at night. About 9 all lights were put out and we turned out to witness an air raid. They got news that an attempt was made on Paris and failing it started south. There was a lot of scurrying all around, in motorcycles and autos, two shots were fired either thru nervousness or at a fancied plane but no boche appeared.

DIARY: **March 9** [*1918*]

A beautiful day, warm and Springlike. Rumor has it that Tours was raided last night; which I doubt.

As was to be expected the paper proved rumor was wrong, there was a raid on Paris but Tours wasn't even thought of by the boche.

I put in my application today to be transferred to Clermont as a bomber.

Ithaca, N.Y., March 9, 1918.

My Dear Stull,

Are you dead, or dying, or on a Secret Service Mission to Kahrlsrue, — or why in hell have you not written. Neither Dan, nor Harry, nor Jack, nor any of us have heard from you, and all say they have written. . . . I am still a chair-warmer at Cornell College. Thank God! I get thru as a full-fledged candidate for the Bar this May. The Draft Board saw fit to reject me altogether on account of my eyes. But I expect & hope that such rigid regulations will be revoked in time and I will be made an army pen-pusher, or interpreter, or something or other. I plan to brush up on my French & German this Summer. I used to be able to speak German like a native.

. . . Well, more later. For God's sake, drop a card. I am hoping for your safety, Stull.

Bill.

3214 Newark St., Wash., D.C.
Sunday-Mar. 10th [*1918*]

Dear Stull,

I had a big surprise today in the form of a fair maid and a sailor boy. Yes sir, Paula & Newt. "dropped in" to dinner. Newt. is stationed at Annapolis. . . . we had a hard time to crowd all we had to say into one small afternoon.

. . . Tuesday-A.M.

. . . Last night I made a remark which brought forth a lecture from Mrs. Pope, . . . I said "If I should inherit enough money to keep me for the rest of my life I would remain an old maid & travel all over the world." She gave me a most est scornful look and said, "Do you think you'd be happy? No sir, you would be miserable. It's a home with "Daddy" coming home & kissing you each night, and children always clamoring for attention — and the thousand & one little cares that make one happy, etc — " I said not a word. How could I when I knew she was speaking my own thoughts and dreams? . . . .

With love, Lois.

DIARY: **March 12** [*1918*]

Told by Major I would be sent as observer and bomber. Pleased Springer gets active orders and is now camouflaged as a lieut. Paris is raided again. Great aerial activity all along the front, also many raids.

DIARY: **March 14** [*1918*] **Thursday.**

Still waiting more or less impatiently. I sneaked off this afternoon and took a walk alone over to a pine woods near the 18 meter field. It is delightful to get all alone once in a while and I lay down in the sun and soaked up lonliness. I hate this school, feeling like a prisoner in it.

They are rushing everyone thru as fast as they can, once past the 23's which block results because of their scarcity. The result is I dont think the fellows get decent training and they will lose good potential pilots. For instance, Pike broke a tail skid (a little thing possible to anyone) coming down from an altitude in 15 meter and was almost

sent as an observer for that. The fellows are all hounded and the atmosphere is all wrong psychologically.

Got a letter from Margi Fawcett. Went to a lecture in the Y.M. and had an entirely new sensation[:] **I almost fainted. That shows I am in not very good condition.**

DIARY: **March 15** [*1918*]

Passed without incident. Major Spatz [*Carl "Tooey" Spaatz, later to become famous as a World War II general and chief of staff for the U.S. Air Force*] **gave a talk in the evening and it was pretty good. According to him the English sure have got the boche buffaloed in the air.**

DIARY: **March 16** [*1918*]

A big day. Newton D. Baker [*Secretary of War*], **Pershing and a flock of lesser lights arrived in camp. There was some fine flying shown for their benefit, formations galore, sham battles, acrobatics and other side shows. I got only a fleeting glimpse of the notables but it was enough for me.**

In the afternoon Ed Butler met his [*death*] **flying in an 18 meter. He skidded around a turn and *vrilled* to the ground. I will always remember him in connection with the New Years party in the barracks at Tours. I was one of the guard at the morgue, my watch being between two and three. I sat up till 12 talking with old Sayre and then read and finished "Married" by Strindberg until I had to go on guard. It is nice to show respect for a friend and I really enjoyed the solitude and reflection.**

"Married" is a collection of very short stories by Strindberg. There are very fine, all dealing with the marriage problem. How Bill Smith and I would enjoy talking and reading them over together.

DIARY: **March 17** [*1918*]

Sunday and a beautiful day. It was just a year ago today I left New York. How little I knew what was in store for me and how little I know of the next years prospects. It was a year I enjoyed immensely and did I think a world of good for me. It ends with me very very glad I came and yet pretty homesick.

We buried Butler this afternoon on the top of the hill. It is not nice to think of leaving just when life promises so much.

Vinx (he and I have been thrown together a lot) [*and*] **Cadbury are leaving tomorrow for the front by a roundabout way to fly artillery observers. It seems to be a law of war (life too for that matter) that you meet, become good friends and are immediately separated. . . .**

Mar *[17?]* **1918**

Dear Lois,

Probably by the time you get this letter you will have changed your occupation and place of residence several times. However I am keeping up with you the best I can. The latest reports say that you are in Washington helping to run the government. A big bunch of mail came all at once, letters from you dated Jan 5, 17, 22, 31 and Feb 9. And, believe me, they made me sit up and take notice. Among the things particularly noticed were those little pictures and the sweater which came O.K. with the chocolate. It sure is a peach. I didn't know they could be that good.

I cant get accustomed to the idea of your being all alone down in Washington and at work. Going to work was bad enough (it was really good I mean the suddenness of it gave me a jolt) but migrating off to another city and living alone exceeds the limit. It must have been awfully lonely at first and hard for you to get adjusted. Ill bet you had a lot of funny experiences, too.

The war business has been going pretty slowly by me. There isn't much to say about my activities lately because I havent been very active. And what there is to say the censor wont let me say it so I wont say much. You can tell Woody [*President Woodrow Wilson*] **the next time you see him that his friend Newton** [*Secretary of War Newton Baker*] **stopt in to see me the other day. At least he was here in camp and if he didn't see me he needs a new pair of glasses. Also we showed him some real flying such as they wouldn't believe possible in the states. But I had no hand in that.**

. . . A couple of my best friends are leaving here tomorrow and I expect to go in a couple of days. (Where and why I will tell you later.) Thats the way it is in an army, people are like combs and brushes, i.e. they meet but to part. . . .

Gute nacht, meine liebe [*Good night, my love*], **Stull.**

March 17, 1918.

Dear, dear Lois,

It was just a year ago to day that I kissed you good-by and you cant guess how much I want to repeat the performance only it must be hello next time. It has been a long year but one that I will never regret, am about steen times more fit to love you and make you happy. All I ask now is the chance. But the war prevents that and will for some time. Even after the war, altho I want to marry you as soon as I can get to Washington, that wont be possible because I dont think you could support me in the style to which I am accustomed and I know I wont be able to earn enough to keep you supplied with knitting needles not to mention open-fire-place-wood. I have always wondered how I would be able to separate the public from enough of their money to keep that fireplace going and when I get back it will be worse than ever. The only thing I will know anything about will be war and we are fighting to make future, wars impossible so I am fighting myself out of all chance of a job. It's a sad world. I sometimes think they only started this war to keep us separated. Why couldnt they have waited another ten years.

Joking aside, dear, I want to thank you for all your letters. They mean everything to me. You are more wonderful than I dreamt any girl could be, And I love you. That is an old old song but a sweet one and one that should be punctuated with kisses. If my punctuation is bad blame the 3000 miles and not me.

You are with me all the time, we take walks together, fly together and are happy together. I try to think of what you are doing in Washington and to be with you and also plan all sorts of trips there together. Also trips in the future to all sorts of places (we arent going to be like most married couples) and always there is a home to go back to. You are all the world to me and I love you.

Do you remember last year to-night you were home alone and cried. Well I felt pretty bad that night too (it wasn't seasickness) and for quite a time afterwards, but for a long long time now have been very happy knowing that you love me. That would make me happy under any conditions. Whenever you get lonely or tired and things are all going wrong just remember that I am waiting and long for the

time when I can take you in my arms and keep away all unpleasant things.

Good night, my love,

P.S. If this isnt a good love letter it is because I have had no practice. I can't write thru a censor. . . .

DIARY: **March 18** [*1918*]

A very uneventful day till evening and then I was called up and sworn in as a first lieutenant. I swore to defend the constitution and all sorts of things and am now an officer in reserve waiting for orders to go on active service.

DIARY: **March 20** [*1918*]

Took walks with Si Kloski who, we are all glad, has stopt flying. He would have killed himself surely. . . .

DIARY: **March 21** [*1918*]

More walks, hear we will go to Clermont about the 28th, Springer like the wise man he is may go there as bomber. If he doesn't he will waste special genius. Got a . . . letter from Lois. She is a peach, wait till I get back. Spring is here actually and calandarically.

Washington, D.C., March 21, 1918.

Dear Stull,

. . . Washington is a lovely place in Spring, e.g. just at present the frogs are letting forth their outlandish croaks and nearly setting me loony. That's because it is a rainy night. Really tho, I do enjoy my walk to and from the Bureau and I guess it agrees with me, because tonight at the dinner table Mr. Pope was talking most earnestly about something or other — 8 hour law, I guess — when he looked at me & all of a sudden — came out with "Lois, you're getting fat." I suppose I'll get still fatter if they pass that law. It will compel all clerks to work 8 hours. As I understand it the extra hour will be added in the morning, so that with that & the daylight saving law I will really be going to work at 7-A.M. It will be 8 by the clock, howsoever. It will be nice to work early in the A.M. and have an extra hour of light in the evening.

Paula and I will follow your advice and stay here where we belong. We all get foolish ideas once in a while you know so you must make allowances. If anyone should ask me if I would go to France & really offer me the opportunity, I would accept like a flash — Don't worry tho I don't think it will be offered. . . .

With love, Lois

DIARY: **March 22** [*1918*]

The fireworks have begun. The Germans attacked the English on a 50 mile front south of Cambrai with about 40 divisions. I'm betting on the English to hold well and expect the real crisis and, attack on the French. The fighting is very severe, but that is all we know yet. It is the biggest attack on the English yet.[25] These are interesting times.

DIARY: **March 23 (1918)**

Heavy fighting continues with no reports except that all goes well. Let us hope so. Rumors of daylight air raids on Paris.

DIARY: **March 24** [*1918*] **Sunday.**

A lot more men arrive. The Plane News gets out an extra saying the boche are shelling Paris 70 miles away with propellor driven shells, causing panic and damage. What next?

DIARY: **March 25-March 29** [*1918*]

The big battle is on and is more awful than anticipated. History will give a better account of it than I can, but things are at boiling point and anything might happen. Oh for a chance to get in it.

DIARY: **March 28** [*1918*]

My active orders came, making me a full fledged lieutenant on active service, and also an order to report to the chief of Air Service at Tours. This is a mystery and threw great consternation into camp. What does it mean!!

DIARY: **March 30** [*1918*]

The battles goes on to a degree beyond comprehension, the big guns

still shell Paris while I get up at 4 in the morning (having said goodby last night to some real men and friends) with my detachment of 3 cadets and go to Tours via Vierzone passing many and large American camps on the way.

Reporting to hdq. I find out that I can go to Clermont — eventually. It is full now and I have to wait till Apr 15 at St. Maxient [*St. Maixent*] **then go to an intensive machine gun school at Gondrecourt and then to Clermont. I shrug my shoulders. It['\]s the army.**

DIARY: **April 1-3** [*1918*]

Waiting in Tours for orders to move on, stopping at officers hotel, meeting some fine men and some who often make me ashamed of being an American. The smug complacent, we-are a-higher-civilization kind and the look-at-the-little-engines-no-wonder we-had-to-come-over-and-win-the-war-for-them kind. . . .

The battle is quieting a little, aparently the boche is held but it looked bad for a time and he has gained lots of ground.

DIARY: **April 3-5** [*1918*]

Up at 4 AM and to St. Maixent, a town west by south about an hours ride from Poitiers. The barracks are right in the town, mine in the back of an old old church. A lot of cadets have been here 5 months waiting for training. They have had and still have a pretty hard time. But I as an officer am pretty well off, having the run of the town, which is very nice. . . .

How I hate the army. When peace comes and I get out I will have a load lifted off me. Altho when I finally get to the front I will be very very happy.

DIARY: **April 6** [*1918*]

I am officer of the day but it means little work except to hang around in barracks. Wrote to home, Lois, Bill Smith. . . .

Apr 6, 1918

Dear Lois,

. . . you can tell Mr Pope what I told you almost a year ago viz. that I wont be home till the war is over. There is too much danger from

submarines to think of ocean travel during the war. Besides we only get 7 days leave every 4 months so that there would be hardly time for an extended visit.

All of which discussion shows that more mail has arrived including three from you (Feb 16, 25 and Mar 7) which I am immediately answering. I would like to send you whole boat-loads of the kind of news you requested so as to confront, confuse and confound Mr Pope but I couldn't do it for two reasons, the censor and the truth. . . . However there is no need to become pessimistic. Sometimes I get mad, sometimes ashamed but never pessimistic. In fact I incline to be what my old friend Bill Smith would call a sentimental optimist. Just why, I dont know, probably because I am putting my faith in human nature and banking on the hope that some fellows I've met are not exceptions but are representatives of a large class. I have met some wonderful fellows, real men and I have noticed that most of them come from the West. It may be a coincidence but I will have to investigate when I get back. Besides they play tennis all year round in California.

I don't wonder that you didn't recognize those pictures and it isn't the fault of the hat (now relegated to the scrap heap never to be worn again) but don't worry, that mustache is only on for duration (a war attrocity) and goes when war does. The year has made other changes in my external appearence, for instance I am "strutting" in a Sam Brown belt [*officer over-the-shoulder belt*] **and wearing silver bars on my shoulder (meaning, as you undoubtedly know, that I am a 1st Lt) I think I neglected to mention that change in my previous letters, but it has existed for some little time now.**

As for the internal changes they are many and large but come too slowly for me to recognize them. I know that when I came in from the front last September I was very tired and nervous from too much work but I felt better than ever before in my life. I was full of the right kind of spirit and felt almost exalted as everyone must who can share even a little in the joy of accomplishing a great and big work. But now I have to get alone and remind myself of what it is all about before I even approximate what I consider the proper attitude. . . .

This is a proper letter according to censorship rules but I am ashamed of it as a civilian. With the greatest war of all going on, during the greatest battle of all, I am not supposed to write about or dis-

cuss any of it or of even the small part I am doing or trying to do. Can you imagine anything worse.

Regards, Stull

P.S. I thought it would do no harm to thank you again for the sweater as my previous letter in which I did, may get lost. You now have 2 sweaters, helmet, wristlets and me doing service in France. I hope I can do mine as well as they are doing theirs.

P.S.2. (Later after Sunday) Heard some records on this phonograph at the local Y.M. and finally (I think the last thing I heard was "Selections from The Mikado") got so homesick I grabbed my hat and walked miles and miles thru a beautiful country till I found the proper place, which happened to be a stone wall with a tree to lean against, and there I sat contemplating things till I regained poise. It is no wonder that so many of our great men started in as farmers' boys. They have a chance to acquire a depth of thought and character that we poor city bred mortals haven't time for.

Anyway such a treatment is the proper one for me. The only human beings who bothered me were a few old women who walked by and only attracted my attention long enough to say good day. They were worthy of more attention however because such women couldn't be seen in America. Nor could their black shiny wooden shoes nor their funny bonnets. Today being Sunday their faces which are weather-beaten like a sailors, are all clean and shiny. Women of their age in America would consider that they had an inalienable right to be cranky and at least a semi-invalid. But here they are aparently always happy and contented and I know they do an unbelievable amount of work. They not only have to keep the farms going alone (in a great many cases there are no old men or young boys to help) but they send money to the soldiers at the front. You know the French soldiers only get 5 cents a day and altho they complain about it and want more they are secretly proud of the fact because it shows that they are fighting for their country, the glory of it. At any rate they can't be accused of being professional soldiers.

I have just finished reading Wilson's anniversary speech. You ought to be able to use it as ammunition on Mr. Pope, because Wilson certainly can handle ideas and ideals. Whether he can equally well get and handle the men to execute them I dont know yet altho I have

my suspicions. However I'd rather have it this way. Imagine how much lower our moral position would be and how much worse international relations would be 25 years from now if some hasty, ill-balanced man like Roosevelt had negotiated our entry into the war. . . .

DIARY: April 7 [*1918*] Sunday.

The battle goes on apace with renewed vigor. Carry on you English and hold you sons of Napoleon. . . .

DIARY: April 8 [*1918*]

I like the town pretty well, there is a fine place to eat in a erstwhile *patisserie* run by several women, altho expensive; lots of well stocked little stores.

Last night 800 Chinese arrived, fresh from China where they had been recruited by a French officer and about 6 men to work for the U.S. The whole town was at the station and laughed at the funny sight they made as they piled out of the smelly freight cars. They were dressed in all manner of ways, straw hats, slippers of all descriptions. I helped to herd them into the barracks where they are quartered thicker than a swarm of bees. They are mostly big fat jolly birds huskier than any others I have seen in France. I imagine they will fare pretty badly at least till they move on from here as the captain in charge is a little fussy New York office man and he only has 2 interpreters to help him.

DIARY: April 9 [*1918*]

Orders come that a bunch is going to Gondrecourt, 45 cadets and 5 officers. At first my name isn't on the list whereat I am scared so I see the adjutant and find it is a clerical error and I am going.

DIARY: April 10 [*1918*]

Leave St Maixent this evening after a very pleasant stay. We go in two coaches and a baggage car and the journey will take several days. We arrive at Poitiers at 10 — and try to sleep in the cars till 4 — when we are attached to the back of a freight and reach St Pierre (Tours) a little after seven. Here after a wash I feel almost human despite many

bites (flea?) caught possibly from the evil smelling Chinese. There are several other similar cars here filled with men who had just landed at Bordeaux.

DIARY: **September** [*?*] [*1918*]

This is now written in the middle of Sept, after a lapse of five months crammed with many experiences, new sensations, beautiful sights that I cant pretend to even mention here but I remember all the places I was at, the dates, and the headlines of the big events. I was sorry to discontinue this diary and often meant to start again but that is an old story.

DIARY: [*April 11, 1918 - May 28, 1918*]

My trip to Gondrecourt took two more long days going thru Dijon, Is-sur-Tille, Neufchateau. At Gondrecourt we went to the First Corps Infantry school where we spent two weeks, one on the Lewis and one on the Vickers. I learnt a good deal not only about the guns but more about infantry work. I lived in a barrack with a lot of old captains marine, U.S. and national guard. They were a happy lot despite the fact that they like everyone had to do close order drill every day, play funny English games in lieu of calisthenics, and work hard on their field problems, my respect and hopes for our army increased manifold from my trip to the school.

I walked one day to Amanty, nearby where there was an aviation camp and some fellows I knew. They weren't working over the front but practised on old A.R.s [*aerial reconnissance aircraft*]**.**

There was a good Y.M. [*YMCA*] **where they had some fine shows; one, scenes from Shakespeare by a Mr Craig whose boy got killed in the Ambulance. Here also I read a good deal — to wit Stevenson's wonderful essays "Virginibus Puerisgue" and some of Nelsons Short History of the War by John Buchan.**

The last night Springer came up with another bunch and we had a grand pow wow.

The trip back to St Maixent was much better than coming, we went first to Chaumont where we spent 5 or 6 hours in which I did the town, interesting now because American Headquarters is there. At the station I saw 2nd Lt R. Norris Williams all dolled up, meet a General. I stood at a distance and worshipped. From Chaumont we

rode all night on the American "special" which runs to Tours. It was very comfortable and had real nigger porters who got blankets for us.

Thence back to St. Maixent where I was again assigned to the barracks in the old cathedral-monastery. But I had lost my blankets traveling so went to a hotel.

* * * * * *

It was now May 1 and I stayed almost all month at St. Maixent, expecting all the time to be ordered out but having a delightful time. I did little work — had charge several times of about 400 of the Chinese who had been quarantined for mumps and had to be exercized. They are a funny, happy, child like lot. I was also assigned for a while to a company of "casual" men who are waiting here and incidentally quarantined. I drilled them some, made them play those English games I learnt at Goudrecourt [*Gondrecourt*], **hiked them and censored their mail, and gave them talks; learning a great deal more about handling men than they did of anything. Censoring their mail was a revelation to me, showing me as it did their secrets and home life. The most startling feature to me was the general ignorance. I gave the general public more credit than they deserved.**

Here I learnt from Major Peyton about the charges he brought against Capt Tiddle because of conditions at Issoudun. Later I learnt Tiddle was sent home in the hold of a boat. Peyton used strong terms about Issoudun and gave me the inside dope.

John S Pfaffman of Harvard was at St Maix. and with him Oh joy of joys I played some tennis. They had built a court which was fair up at Coiffe (the main barracks) and he and I played quite often. Of course I was wild and stiff and generally awkward but I did better than I expected. Pfaffman was a real man, full of the right spirit and a fellow after my own heart. He and I talked tennis (also the war and other things) and he told me lots of interesting stories we were good friends. I was sorry to hear several months later that he had been killed training on a Farman [*one of several designs of Henri and Maurice Farman*] **near Chartres.**

In the middle of May Springer came back and we had a fine time together arguing long and deeply about the war and the good that will result. Every night he and I would repair to my hotel The "Ecu de France" which is very quaint and more of an inn or a hostelry than a

hotel, and play chess. Joffre [*French commander before Nivelle*] **had once stopt at the hotel and had kissed Mlle André. She was a very nice girl of about 19. I bought her some quartermaster candy and brought her bouquets of roses from the courtyard of the monastary whereupon she would thank me nicely and Springer would ask me about my girl in America and suggest, that probably somebody was giving her candy. André was a nice girl and could play the piano well.**

There is a French officers school at St. Maixent and also they were training a lot of Czecho-Slavs. These were an interesting lot, I talked pigeon French German with some and heard their tale — how they were in the Austrian Army, gave themselves up to the Russians and were now going to fight for their land which the "Deutchschwein" had taken from them. I realized how in the midst of the world war they were fighting to throw off a yoke of oppression as heroically as any of the precedents in history and I was thrilled. Lucky are the few who are big enough to appreciate all that is going on in the world upheaval to-day.

The weather was beautiful, Springer and I found some fine food; so I had some regrets when I finally got orders to go to Clermont-Ferrand on May 27 or 8 and said good-by to André and St. Maixent.

I stopt in at Tours en route saw Jim White and tried in vain to fix it so Springer would go to Clermont with me.

April 24, 1918.

Dear Stull,

At last you have told me in so many words that you are a really truly officer. I could only guess before. I am just as proud of you as I can be — in fact so proud that when Mr. Anderson congratulated me on my "engagement" and wished you and me joy, I simply asked him how he knew so much about it. Guess I was a little fussed as well as proud —

. . . After dinner.

. . . We are having a Liberty Bond parade this Friday. I have been trying to enthuse the female personnel of the B. of S. and get them to turn out 100% — I have the distinction of being Capt. Crump. for this one occasion. We have been having lots of fun about it & I hope it will be successful — . . . .

With love — Lois. . . .

Schnectady, NY
AM. [*April*] 28, 1918.

Stull:

The enclosed is one part of a whole letter, in which I gave you the general gossip of what goes on in Ithaky, and then proceeded to dilate on our old discussion of the war aims. I have separated it into two letters in the hope that you will at least get one part. This part contains said dilations.

Bill.

. . . The fruit-fulness of Wilson's war-aim discussion in this country is beyond question. The Radicals are now swinging in line. "The Masses" has become "The Liberator" and is supporting the Wilson War, tho none other. Max Eastman, Morris Hillquit, the Socialist party generally, & Bill Bryan have seen the moral grandeur that he has brought into this dirty business. If we are not deceived by self-adulation, it is fruitful in Europe as well. The war-weary masses of Europe find consolation in this new leader, if Van Loon tells me aright.

. . . Witness, most tragic of all, the pooh-hooing of the Le[*a*]gue of Nations. Not only Clemencea[*u*] & Sir Edw. Carson and the diplomatic "geniuses" of Europe (whose only claim to that distinction is a waxed mustache, a well-fed look, and a sneer at the rights of humble men), not only these men but all the audible opinion of America sneers. Senators rise in the Senate Chamber and laugh at it when some men are dying for it. The agitation is keen in this country for universal military service after the war, — and few see the joke of it.

. . .Yet, withal, the war is holy. I believe that Wilson, Henderson, Thomas, etc., are still in the minority, but they will triumph. Wilson and the British Labour Party are converting England. Wilson will win in America. The soldiers, after the war, will be with Wilson & the Liberals, — from what I can gauge from Van Loon & from a Canadian aviator on sick leave (in one of my quiz-sections.).

. . . The draft is going like clock-work now. Baker, now elevated in public esteem, says we will have 3,000,000 in it by next year <u>if we can get the ships</u>. Anything you read in the papers to the contrary notwithstanding, the shipping program is proceeding wonderfully in America. We've made a miserable fluke of air-planes,[26] but the ships are dropping into the water in good fashion. I've seen Hog Island [*shipyard*][27], so I know a bit about it. The concrete ship plan, also, looks good, and concrete ships multiply like guinea-pigs, you know. The spirit in the Draft Camps is astounding,

Remmie Ostrander & Harington tell me. The men are just nuts to get across and "at the Kaiser."

. . . Good luck to you; by God, I hope you pull thru. If any of my German 2nd, cousins are aviators, give them an extra one for me. Here's hoping for you,

Bill.

May 8th 1918.

Dear Boy,

I received your letter written on March 17th after that written on April 6th. Thank heaven I did receive it, because it was what I have been waiting for, for one whole year — I know it is abominable to have to write thru a censor but you won't have to again if you don't want to — I can read this one over and over till I know it by heart — I wish I could tell you how much good that letter did me — . . . .

Last week we were working on a "War Work Report" for the Sec. of Commerce — It was very interesting, even tho it took a pile of time. Friday and Saturday nights we stayed until 10^{00} P.M. to finish it.

. . . Stull, I think Paula is really married. I have heard so from several reliable sources tho she has not deigned to inform me herself — I think no one is supposed to know it, but everyone seems to. Don't say anything about it when you write home, please, will you? I'll tell you for certain — later. . . .

May 9.

. . . Very soon I will have to add another year to those piled up behind me — It does not seem possible that I can be twenty-two, but that is what I'll have to admit after next week — . . . .

Au revoir, *Mon cher ami*, L.

May 11, 1918

Dear Lois,

You have probably imagined me as being at the front for some time now but unfortunately I havent been and probably wont be for some time yet. The delay has been due to a multitude of causes over which I have had no control so all I can do is grin and carry-on but it is hard

at times. I want to get to work as much as I ever wanted to get anywhere.

. . . Below me in the street I can see a very warlike scene. And when I say warlike I mean it because the scene is typical of many armies in many countries. My first sergeant and two other Americans are fraternizing with a French family. Its a low, stone red[-]roofed house; madam is sitting on a chair in the doorstep which is level with the street, around her are seve[*r*]al daughters (buxom Tennyson would call them, husky and rosy cheecked I say) and a group of indiscriminate small children from the neighborhood. One of the Americans is doing a jig, my sergeant is whistling and clapping his hands, the kids shrieking with joy.

Such is war, or at least a part of it. Men are sometimes made brutes, in some directions; sometimes made more sympathetic and considerate in others.

I read a story the other day which is wonderful in that it is so true and universal. Some one was talking to a wounded French soldier "Oh! so you were one of those heroes who held Verdun" "Heroes!" said the *poilu* "always I hear talk of those heroes. There were none of those people there, we Frenchmen held Verdun"

Everyday, as my knowledge increases, I respect and admire the French more. They have a simplicity and nobility, as a racial characteristic, which is hard to beat. I wish you could meet and get acquainted with the French. I consider that one of the greatest opportunities of my life.

I have to finish up now. It is beginning to get dark and I am Officer of the Day. I have to inspect my guard, make sure they know their orders, and look very severe so that they will be afraid all night that I am watching to catch them if they stop "walk(ing) my post in a military manner keeping always on the alert etc —"

I have one little shaver (19 yrs old) in my company about as tall as Curtis, freckled faced and awful young. When we are out hiking and pass a French girl of six or seven all the fellows yell "Shorty look the other way" etc. whereupon he blushes if I am around or tries to answer back if I'm not.

Please, please keep on writing often as you have been doing to

Your Stull

May 14-1918 —

Dearest Boy,

I swore to go to bed early tonight, but I cannot seem to find a minute to write to you so I must lose my beauty sleep once more.

Your cablegram came Sunday — at least it was phoned to me on Sunday. I received a copy of it yesterday — Wasn't that very quick work? It was dated "France May 12th — & I received it same day. It was sweet of you to do that — I know I have never had and never expect to have a birthday that will make me happier — You seem so near when it takes only a short time for a message from you to reach me — Thank you for that message. . . .

Love, Lois.

May 15, 1918

Dear Lois,

Some day I hope to be with you on your birthday so as to celebrate it properly. I never have as yet altho this is the fourth you've had since I've known you and goodness knows how many you had before then. Last year if I remember correctly I sent you a long letter full of most excellent advice. It was written out under a big tree on the Champagne front where big things were being done, where the guns rumbled all the day and the drone of the planes over head never ceased; so of course the advice, whatever it was, must have been good.

This year, when you, as today, pass another milestone and balancing the debits and credits of last year make good resolves for the next one; I'll let you off easy and wont pull any of that advice stuff except this which is: —

Now that you are of necessity more or less alone stretch out your good right hand and grasp the opportunity to read: not stuff like the Saturday Evening Post or McClures but the real cream of literature, to wit; — Lately I have read, (and while doing so often sat back in my chair slapped my knee and chortled in my joy because some idea of my own was expressed so perfectly and clearly) that collection of Stevenson's short essays that goes under the title of "Virginibus Puerisque." You couldn't help but enjoy them both because of the ideas expressed and the methods of expression. The ones entitled "An

Apology for Idlers," and "Crabbed Age and Youth" and "Aes Triplex" are especially good.

I am not going to write a book review but I want to mention one more, The Diary and Letters of Alan Seeger. His poems too are fine. You ought to get acquainted with him for he was not only a real man, but was also one who was fortunate enough to have the genius of expressing his thoughts. Some of these are the same as I have on those occassions (far too seldom unfortunately) when I can detach myself from the narrowing influence of everyday circumstances, and getting a better perspective realize again all the war means and the opportunities offered to everyone to live so intensely. Incidentally, too, I have been thru most of the country Seeger was in (I wrote letters sitting in the same doorstep that he mentioned in one of his letters) and I worked at the place he got killed.

Here ends the lecture and the advice which you couldn't escape but dont have to follow.

I hope your day today has been as happy as mine was (it is now after 11 at night). Listen to this schedule: Got up in time to hold reveille at 6; Gave the men calesthenics; latter in the morning drilled them a while; then delivered a very fine lecture (it must have been fine because they paid the closest attention and laughed hard at the right places) whose central theme was (they were a squadron of aero mechanics). To remember the war; they were apt to be way behind the scene of all fighting and work hard all day the way they would home in a machine shop. : they were apt to forget what the war was about, that they were soldiers and that they were playing a man's part in winning it. I elaborated this till I included the whole war; a description of every kind of fighting, and several jokes I had ready beforehand. Then I marched them all to the bath house and made them indulge. The afternoon too was passed profitably and then O joy of joys from 6 till dark, I played tennis, real, smashing tennis. I am getting so I sometimes hit the ball back twice in succession, a real thrilling sensation. After tennis a shower, then supper and here I am writing to you. If I had been playing tennis right along over here I think I would have won the war by now. Because after I have sweated all the laziness and mediocrity out of me by several sets of fast tennis followed by a shower I am so full of pep and enthusiasm (especially for the war) that there is nothing I believe I couldnt do.

Incidentally I have to philosophize here to the effect that: — Enthusiasm is the path to success, the Bluebird of Happiness, the key to accomplishment, the secret of love.

I find that in my resume of the days doings I left out one thing to wit: — I bought a can of Lowney's chocolates and bonbons from the quartermaster and did present them to Madamoiselle André, the daughter of the family who own the hotel where I am stopping (I lost some baggage again including blankets and bedding roll so I am staying at a hotel being lucky enough to be near one). They don't make candy or confectionery any more in France and Madamoiselle André is a charming young lady, albeit perhaps a little spoilt. I thought perhaps you wouldn't mind, it being your birthday. Besides I wouldn't sit up till midnight (it's now 12:20) ever to write to Mlle, André.

I have thought out a fine scheme. Usually I remember a lot of clever and interesting things about half-an-hour after I have sent a letter to you. This time I will be foxy and leave some room so that to-morrow morning I can add all such brilliant after thoughts.

Till then, Lois-one-year-older-than-yesterday, Good night.

Good morning. My scheme didnt work. So far I havent remembered a thing I had forgotten

. . . in a recent letter my father [*said*] **that your folks, mine and Browns are probably going to the lake this summer. I dont think I will go this year. When I get my vacation I will run down to Washington to see the sights and how they are running the government. — especially the bureau of standards. Some people might not think so but to me the b. of. s. is about the most important department.**

Au revoir, ma cherie. Je t'aime comme toutjour [*Good-bye, my love. I will always love you*]

Stull

P.S. How do you like my French?

Schenectady, N.Y.,
May 26, 1918.

My dear Stull,

Your last letter received was of the date, April 6.

First, as to the reason for this letter at the present time, when I ought to be studying for Bar examinations: I connected with a dose of poison ivy, the genuine virgin-foliage variety and not the fig-leaf kind. My arms are bandaged up with sugar of lead. A bit of the poison has got on my procreative organ, which keeps it constantly stimulated and lo! incapacitated, — Dante's 13th hell. I'm getting a lot of "scratching," but not the famed sort.

Well, I'm all gradiated. I'm a virtual attorney and counsellor at law, — with the exception that I must pass the Bar Exams, a mere wave of the hand, for one who went to Albany Law or N.Y.U. Law, or other tutoring school. Have a good opening in local district attorney's office; also in Wait's office in N.Y. But I feel as much like practicing the more useful profession of public scavenger.

Life in this country for a young buck now is like a tomb. All my old cronies are in and over . . . I can't find a soul in the famed "Louis's" to sip a glass of beer with, — Dante's 14th. hell. All of Class I in this town — about 3000 in all — are drafted and in camp; the last 368 went last Saturday. June fifth, those just coming of age register and are all expected to be in camp by the end of July. We are fast becoming Canadianized; you can't find a young fellow on the streets any more.

If I can slide into the service now, besides feeling more decent, I will automatically pass my bar. Ergo, I am reconoitering with the Adjutant at Camp Devens to find out what use he has for a whirl-wind, eats-'em-alive administrator with 4/200 vision. If you could see the letter of recommendation written by the chairman of my exemption board, you would think I was the nations savior at the 11 3/4 hour. Am awaiting developments and studying listlessly.

The military preparations are beyond all imagination. The following facts have been officially announced within the last couple of weeks: (1) over 500,000 in France; (2) over 300,000 in the navy; (3) 2,038,000 grand total under arms in the Army; (4) proposed maximum of 5,000,000 for the army[28] removed and no limit yet, Wilson saying: "Why fix <u>any</u> limit?"; (5) 90,000 men shipt to France in the first <u>ten</u> days of May, (6) ships launched exceeded in tonnage ships sunk for the first time since 1915; (7) over one steel ship a day is being launched; 60 are promised in July; (8) the concrete-ship "Faith" is apparently a success, especially as a tanker; (9) the Browning machine gun is a world's wonder and, if I remember rightly, being put out at about 200 a day.

The only flea in the ointment, the aviation scandal, which Wilson diplomatically appointed Hughes to investigate.[29]

The nation's morale, which I was so dubious about last summer is coming around. The third Liberty Loan was over subscribed without any campaigning; the 2nd Red Cross fund of $100,000,000 was way over-subscribed, 300% in Schenectady. This improvement of the morale is not due to any sudden enlightenment of the mob but to a feeling that something is loose in the world that must be put down (with no realization that it's loose all over the world, but in a most aggrevated form in Germany); due to the constant repetitions of the newspapers; due to the fact that now most families have a son in it; and due mostly to a religious faith in Wilson.

Teddy is barking and farting around as usual; he aims to be the "Win the War" candidate in 1920; if the war progress is at all fair by that time, Wilson will walk all over Roosevelt. So far as I can see, Teddy is America's chief Prussian (next to Lodge and Du Pont) with his "big stick," "armed fist" diplomacy, viz, Panama; with his jibes at Wilson's idealism viz, League of Nation's including Germany; with his cry for perpetual military service; and his lack of sympathy with the Bolsheviki. If Wilson does not stay in control, I dare say this country will emerge the most reactionary of them all. Prof. Bretz, a good pro-ally-ist is with me on this.

The Republican party, whose platform I enclose, is running true to form. It opposes the gov't building of dwellings for the ship-builders; is keen for limiting the duration of gov't control of railroads, and is wildly in arms against Macadoo's [*Secretary of Treasury*] proposed tax bill to raise $8,000,000,000 a year by 80% tax on incomes, inheritences, and war profits. But so long as Wilson is in the ring the Republican party isn't a fart in a gale of wind anyway.

. . . Well, *au revoir*, Stull. My very best to you. My God, I hope you pick through, Stull, old fellow.

Bill. . .

DIARY: **At Clermont May 29- July 31** [*1918*]

Clermont had some new sights for me. It is a large city about 150,000 and right at the foot of the nearest to mountains I had ever seen. The highest peak (Puy-du-Dome) is 1,400 meters high. Clermont is a historic spot, the fine main square is where Lafayette first spoke in favor of America, there are several Roman churches, fortifications,

roads; the field we fly from is the one on which Caesar licked the Gauls of the neighborhood.

Clermont has large and well supplied stores, relatively few Americans, good cafés and so was a nice place.

The camp is about four miles out of town, past several large factories, of which there are a lot around Clermont, including the second largest munitions factory in France. The workers include besides many women from the neighborhood, old and decrepit Frenchmen in equally old faded blue uniforms; a lot of evil looking and smelling Morrocans and Turcoc, and a raft of Italians reputed to be from the infamous Second Army who laid down their arms last fall. All the workers are stained a funny yellow color from the explosives or chemicals.

At school we didn't begin work for a couple of days as we waited for the class ahead to finish up. In it were many friends Tom Reed, Harry Strauch, Cap Parks, Gatton etc.

. . . Work began and proved pretty interesting. First there were numerous lectures and ground work on divers subjects such as bombs, machine guns, the methods of bombing and how to do it, also practice on a rolling carpet, on which scenery was painted, using the bomb sights and dropping little bombs with pins in their end which would stick on the target showing results.

Before I forget, I met Baret, my Tours instructor here for a few brief moments. He was killed shortly afterwards in a flying accident, which thus ended a good man's career. I remember his fiancé[*e'*]s chateau near Tour[*s*] and how he would often fly with me over it waving to her below.

Then the pilots and observers teamed together, flying first over a camera obscura which would record their flight. Then we would shoot Very pistols [*flare guns*] instead of dropping bombs and the camera obscura would show our results. After some practice at that we next dropped smoke bombs on a field nearby. This was followed by much formation flying with Very pistols and smoke bombs and lastly by cross country work. This is, of course, only a list of the headlines and there was a lot of detailed work. On the whole the school was the best I had been in. While I was still there some of the best men, Ellis Inglis etc left so the school may fall down. . . .

There were about six observers with no pilots, among them me, and

we stayed after the regular class finished and with six pilots rushed there we finished in about three weeks while the new large class was getting under way. These were all good men and we did good work. I teamed up with MacWhirter (Donald) who is as Brooke says "a simple egg" but a very good pilot and a decent fellow. What he lacks in brains and ideas and ability to keep still he more than makes up for by fine flying and good nature. I would (not?) try at all to tell of how we bombed and rode the awful bumps around the hills and mountains. Suffice to say that when we left we were both marked excellent, a not very common mark, and there was talk of sending us to a new school as instructors after we had been at the front a few months.

Brooke Edwards, another part of the six teams, is a S.S.U.1 man having spent most of 1916 in it. Consequently we have many mutual friends and hold frequent reminisence-swaping contests. Besides he is quite a tennis player from Philadelphia and we gossip a lot about that. He is a jolly individual, inclined to be corpulent, with a great leaning towards *pinard* [*wine*] **but with a very good head on his shoulders.**

Sunday-June 9th [*1918*]

Dear Stull,

This has been a wild week for me — that's the reason you have been neglected. I have hardly had time to write home and let the folks know I arrived safely.

Of course we were on the "go" every minute while I was home — which I rather regretted as I needed the rest and knew I couldn't get one after I got back here. Miss Bailey, the other stenog. in our office is on a short vacation. She told me she was going to take a week as soon as I returned, so I was prepared for the worst. I learned yesterday that she isn't well and won't be back till the end of next week. The work piles up and worries us all. Mr. Hubbard & I have been working from 8:30 A.M. to 6 P.M. every day but one when we stayed till 7[00]. He looks as tho he'd give out any minute, and I admit I get kind of tired. . . .

Tuesday — 6/12/18

. . . I have been able to muster up a little more pep than I had on Sunday so expect I can finish this epistle if not disturbed by yon howling mob. . . .

Do you know I would give anything to see Lt. W.S. Holt commanding a bunch of chinks? You must have had a wild time. . . . Why are perfectly good aviators, who are ready to do real work wasted thusly? I am forced to conclude that we haven't the planes — . . . .

Good-night dearest boy — Be careful & dont take chances — I know you wont.

Love — Lois.

. . . Yours of the 11th & 15th received. I don't mind advice — It doesn't worry me at all — However, when Popes have gone to Montana (more on that subject anon) and Frances gets a job and poor little me is left all alone I shall haul out yours of the 15th & act on said advice — I blush to admit I have read nor prose nor poetry in months. . . .

Tuesday June 10, 1918

Dear Lois,

It is over two weeks since I last wrote you which is very bad especially as I had many great and glowing thoughts to set down and opportunities enough to do so. Please don't fail on your end as aften as I do on mine. You haven't so far, to wit: Since I last wrote I have received 5 (five) letters from you in this order Apr 5 and 25; March 13, May 15 and 16. Each has already been read innumerable times and the four pictures of "We Four" looked at as often. You see, I want to keep well enough acquainted so that an introduction wont be necessary when I get back.

In the latest letter (May 16) you say you have gotten reports that I sounded home sick. Dont believe it. Once in a while I feel as if I would like [*to*] feel the sting of a Flatbush misquito or spend a week end on the subway — Mt Vernon car lines. But those times are few and far between. I realize that the opportunity of all time is offered to me (and others) to do and see things, to live life to its fullest intensity, to crowd more sights, impressions and emotions into a week than most people have a chance to do in their lifetime.

. . . I have already plugged in the social swim and am going strong. My entreé was made thru my special friends who happen to be the family of a professor in the University here. They all speak English so I dont have to exhibit my *poilus* French (with which I make many *faux*

pass [*sic*] **using probably the worst slang in France) and are very charming, especially the beautiful young daughter. Yes, of course, there is a beautiful young daughter, there always is.**

On Decoration Day we had a little social whirl of our own at camp. . . . Another fellow and I picked out a group of nurses who looked old, fat and safe so that they wouldn't expect us to propose before the day was over, and showed them around camp exhibiting the machines and enjoying their funny questions. As usual we had to explain the biscuit gun [*the large bore of the Very pistol*] **to them and how we shot biscuits up to the poor fellows whose motors stopt thus preventing them from coming down.**

. . . About the war there is little I can tell you. But because I dont talk about it dont think I am indifferent. I spend a lot of my time going around with a large map of the front under my arm and on it I make new marks after every new communique. I'd give anything to be up there now (patience is one of the very first essentials for a good soldier) altho there will probably be plenty left to do when I do finally get to the front again which I hope will be in about a month. . . . take for yourself all of my very best love that I can cram in a letter.

Stull

Washington, D.C., June 13, 1918

Dear Stull,

. . . Well, by God, if it isn't one thing it's another. I'm in Washington now with the Food Administration. I was just beginning my cram for the Bar two weeks ago when I got an offer to come down here so I scooted. Now I am glad to be doing anything but law and yet are rottenly disappointed. And for reasons below.

There are thousands and thousands of men and women here civilians, working in the various gov't departments, — 2000 in the Food Administration alone, then the Fuel Administration, the Foreign Trades Board, the War Industries Board, the Council of National Defence, etc. etc. Practically none of these gain exemption from draft; most are "cripples." One would at first say, and I at first thought, "Here's big stuff; if the draft don't want you, go down and use your brains; help feed the Allied world; help blockade Germany; swing the American propaganda in America; you've got brains; raise intellectual hell and you'll be worth a hundred bayonets."

Shit, shit, shit; vain delusion. Of several thousand people in the Food

Administration; which is typical, not more than ten use the beans or have opportunity to. They are Hoover, and then the so called "commodity men," viz, the Sugar man, the meats man, the wheat man, etc. All the rest, regardless of their high sounding titles, are only higher or lower degrees of "clerks," with all that that drab term signifies. Government work is so confoundedly systematised that there is no room for versatility; you just sit on your bottom and watch the machinery work. The food reports come in from the dealers, are sorted more or less automatically at the Mail Division, slide on to the Enforcement Division, where credit is given for the report; appended letters are slid to the Communications Division to be answered (that's the shell-strewn danger zone in which I work; the communications division); then to the Editing division for inspection; then to the Statistical Division for tabulation; then (here begins the brains) to the commodity man in pill form, and then to Hoover. The above is not submitted for your memorization but just to show the dreary mechanical work that the thousands do. Everything is so labelled, tagged, blue & red penciled, checked, and coded as to make it fool-proof, even against the bulls of the many ex-school teachers here.

Now, I'm in the Communications Division; we answer all the mail; there are only six of us and we needs answer about eight hundred letters a day. To do this we are surrounded by dictagraphs and have over some hundred stenographers and lesser clerks down to the bell boys. This sounds unmechanical, but wait. The dealers' problems are so similar and their inquiries therefore so similar that we have form letters, ligniotyped, to answer at least three-quarters of them. When I shoot into the dictagraph "Jones, 0428, I-1," that means — a letter to Jones whose fuller name and address is to be found in file 0428, has gone out of business and should cancel his license, Jones get busy. "Jones, 0428, Enforcement A"; if old Jonsie doesnt get in that back January report we'll close his business. Poop, poop, poop. So it goes, the machinery works without you, it slides before you like a panorama; I become an intellectual adding machine. And if anybody in the crowd takes himself too seriously I say: "Whoops, boys, we just held Ludendorf back an eighth of an inch."

And I am told all the other departments are the same way. But why not become one of the upper ten who <u>do</u> use their brains. Impossible. The upper ten don't know you're alive. The uppers are chosen on what they were before the war and not what they became during it.

I am going to get out of this mechanical stuff. I am going to try to get into the Dep't of Justice, think of the secret service!, or the Enemy Property custodian, or Committee on Public Information. I hear they need some lawyers over in the War Insurance Board, running down fraudulent insurance claims by fake wives and the like. If I can't get into something where I can use brains, I quit. Am told I can get a 1st. Lieutenancy with the General Staff, the two essentials now being (1) brains, (2) inability to pass the army physical examinations, — the latter resulting from the Congressional stink over holders of "bomb proof jobs." My present feeling, however, is that it[']s bad enough to be a clerk in civilian clothes without the stigma of clerical puttees more of this anon; I enjoy the uncertainty of what will I be doing next.

Give the "slackers" [*draft dodgers*] in Washington credit. They are working like hell, the pace here is feverish at a necessary job no matter how drab. They are not exempt. They are working in the hottest god-damn climate you ever saw. A new press in a suit survives the sweat only one day here. We work under fans to live. The man whose desk is beside mine used to be a consul to many tropical S. American countries and says the heat here is new to him. They are earning very little, and are putting the surplus that the profiteers don't get (viz, I'm paying $25[00] a month for a bedroom 3 miles from heart of the city) into gov't bonds, etc., which we now call "investments["] but which I believe will be gifts. The New Republic says of these bomb-proofers that they're not heroes but they certainly are martyrs. Ha, ha, the above is known as the psychology of self-defense.

. . . The submarines have been with us the past two weeks and are still here; apparently working in relays; have sunk some twenty coastal ships. The Germans are now doing for us what the Zeppelins did for England. The results of the sub. war over here are (1) no stoppage of troop — shipments; (2) no withdrawal of destroyers from the channel; (3) increased enlistments; (4) added war-savings stamp sales; (5) more vim in the ship yards.

Well, Stull old fellow, I hope you get a bit of pleasure out of this letter. Rip off a line to me if you can, so far as a fighting mood inclines to letter writing to healthy bucks on this side who are waxing fat.

My very best wishes to you, — and hopes.

Bill.

For God's sake, Stull, old fellow, be careful with the women. Don't be tragically forgetful, which advice is untasteful but well-meant.

Tuesday-June 18th [*1918*]

Dear Stull,

Latest news from the front — Popes go to Montana June 30th — whole — family. I begin tomorrow to find me a new home. Truly, it is a funny world. . . .

June 19th —

Aprés le travail [*after work*] —

. . . Stull, doesn't anything ever go wrong in France? You're such a dear about overlooking unpleasant things and writing cheerful letters you make me ashamed of myself — There must be some things it would do you good to tell someone. I always keep one ear turned your way & if it will relieve you to confide your troubles once in a while, please use it. But love to the dearest boy who ever fought for Uncle Sam.

Lois

June 24, 1918

Dear Lois,

Still hard at work, doing nothing for the last two weeks on account of bad weather, but not as happy as when I last wrote because there has been no American mail since then. The last I have from you is that of May 15th.

There has been a little flying in between the rain and what there is I enjoy a lot. This is the most mountainous country I have ever been in yet and viewed from the air it looks pretty good. Early the other morning there was a whole range of mountain tops covered with snow, the first I have seen so far.

I am enclosing a letter which is self explanatory. I thought, perhaps, as you are on the spot you might call and get my commission for me. If you do I dedicate it to your care, if you don't please save the letter. In case they should ask what relation you are of mine, tell them — anything you want to. . . .

As a matter of fact, all is off. To-day shedding many a bitter and salty tear I had my first crop shaved off. My heart gives a wrench when I think of the loss now and rub my finger over the smooth space which feels and looks to me to be about a yard wide. . . .

your lover, Stull. . . .

Washington, D.C.
June 28, 1918.

Dear Stull,

First of all please note the radical change in address — I start to move next door so soon when I finish this letter. . . .

Your letter of June 10 arrived today. From May 15th to June 10th is a long two weeks but I'll take your word for it that a letter or two may be down near Coney Island — washed up on the shore.

. . . Stull, (this is a serious question) do you suppose the boys who have been fighting, both in the air and on *terra firma*, will be able to calm down and reconcile themselves to doing the ordinary things of life? I cannot imagine, for example, a boy who has been driving an airplane — say a bombing plane at the front — for even a few months — ever sitting quietly at a desk in an office at Lower New York — That's a problem which must be solved — . . . .

By the way — if you see a small pamphlet (size of a 20 fr. note) floating around in France, entitled ["]How the French Measure" or "How they Measure in France" (something like that) edited for the American soldier etc — etc. get it & read it. Mr. Hubbard dictated most of it to me & I have worked many an hour overtime on that thing —

. . . Best lover, Lois

Sunday June 30, 1918

Dear Folks,

. . . I thought I told you of the time I smashed up a plane. There is no reason why I shouldn't have as there was little danger in it. We had a funny accident here last week, one of those freaks of fate that you occasionly read or hear about but never believe. Two planes were up practising combat work and during the manuvering the observer in one was thrown out of his plane. That wasn't so freakish or unusual but just then up jumped Fate and the observer instead of falling to the ground fell on the tail of his plane, with such force that his knee broke thru giving him a firm grip and he lay across the body of the plane like a drowning man across a barrel. Realizing he couldn't stay on where he was he collected himself and crawled along the top of the body of the plane back to his seat, all the time thousands of feet up in the air and going over 100 miles per hour. Can you beat that?

Stull,

July 4, 1918

Dear Lois,

I like to please you but sometimes you ask too much, to wit, in your last letter received (June 12) you ask me to scold you for not writing often and yet since last Sunday[,] a week when I wrote to you[,] I have received three letters May 10, 24 and June 12. While I get three for one I can't scold, you can't make me mad no matter how <u>many</u> you write.

To-day (see above) is a great day and this letter is part of my celebration. All France is doing herself proud in honoring us to-day. Here, in Clermont, there was a big parade this morning of American soldiers, with bands, flags on every house, much ullulation and cries of "*Vive l'Amerique*," crowds and confusion. . . .

I had intended to sneak off alone and climb the highest mountain nearby (Puy-du-Dome, 4500 feet) but it looks too much like rain. So instead of writing on top of a mountain I am using the writing room of the best hotel. . . .

I can and often do imagine you and I happily married but my imagination isn't good enough to see the children. I can't imagine myself as a father but I know I will be some day if the war doesn't get me and you are willing. I wish I could sit down with my arm around you and have a real heart-to-heart talk. Letters are poor mediums for heart to heart talks but they are the best we have now. Wont we make up for lost time when I get [*home*]! Meanwhile I am proud to sacrifice the happiness I would have had with you, if I can help win the war by being here. I know you feel the same way.

I send all my love, Stull

P.S. Here are two kisses, XX.

Washington, D.C., July 14th — [*1918*]

Dear Stull,

All hail Bastille Day! We are celebrating over here in various ways.

. . . I received your letter of June 24th, also the story [*on wartime marriages*]. You ask what I think about it and that is the hardest question you could possibly ask. The Girl's arguments have been mine in several cases which have been discussed either at Pope's or at home, but whether I should have acted as she did is more than I can say. . . . As a child I was easily influenced by what other people said, but I have over come that to a great extent and feel that I can depend upon my own judgment more than I used to — in fact — entirely. But I am sure that I could not have done so a year ago. You know that I hurt you terribly as it was because I didn't realize what your going meant, but I woke up and when a girl wakes up she is no longer a girl. I cannot tell you what I think, because I try not to think. If you were holding my hand I could tell you, but pen & ink are unsympathetic instruments. . . .

My best love & all of it, Lois.

3212 Newark, July 24th [*1918*]

Dear Stull,

Even tho I'm too tired to say much, I can't neglect you any longer — so here goes.

I received the picture & letter of commission — The less said about the former the better — I can only hope and pray that it lies. As for the comm, I have called several branches of Sig. Corps and finally located the place where it is, probably. Expected to go yesterday to get it but was too busy — . . . .

Do you remember I told you some time ago that Paula & Newt were married? You never commented on the news at all. It is true all right so please tell me what you think. It's a dead secret at least so Paula thinks. I am the only one she told and that was necessary since I am going to visit her in Annapolis week after next.

. . . I have been so excited watching the progress of the Allies this & last week that people thought I was crazy.[30] Mr. Hubbard swears the war will end this fall and tho I cannot believe it, it is a great comfort to hear him say it. Stull, if you come back this year I'll never let you go again.

Goodnight dearest boy, Lois.

N.Y. City, July 30, 1918.

My dear Stull,

Your long letter of June 11th was a bear. I hope you got two from me written while in Washington. In your letter you compliment my talk on the war philosophy, et al. That is the hell of it; I <u>talk</u> well, while the

Cohen's, and O'Brien's, and Luigi's are dying for Anglo-Saxon rights. I hardly have the gaul to write you any more, — you on the other side. I am in N.Y. now — Woolworth Bldg. — big law stuff — million dollar cases. But you cannot imagine the hell of being out of the army now. A young man of military age is no longer to be seen anywhere in civilian clothes. All who are out are constantly on the defensive. Imagine my impressions as I look out from the 17th story of the Woolworth building, out over the docks, and see the strangely camouflaged ships, pointing down the river, their decks crowded with men taking their last look; or when I see, daily, the drafted men going down Broadway for the L.I.R.R. [*Long Island Railroad*] station, the bands playing. One thing seems certain: I can't get into the American army. I have written my draft Board, the members of which I know intimately, and have asked them to kick through and draft me if they possibly can. My self-respect demands that as soon as I pass my Bar in October, I join the British; they take anything that walks. . . .

# # #

What the country is doing on the war really dumbfounds me, you cannot pick up a paper, & read the accomplishments without pinching yourself to see if you're awake. 2,500,000 in arms; 1,200,000 [*July 15*] in France; more than two ships a day being launched, — the record 6000 ton ship being launched 14 days after her keel was laid; Schwab says 10,000,000 tons in the next 365 days; draft age to be altered from 21-31 to 18-45; Crowder to call 300,000 in August. Ships are dropping off the ways like guinea-pig pups. Airplanes seem our only failing. My God, think back one year ago, when no one dreamed of anything save merely supplying the Allies with money & munition and a handful of men and flags for moral support! Appropriations for first year, — 30 billion, about 6 billion to the Allies.

How good the morale is, I don't know; I don't know how it will stand losses, but of one thing, I am certain, — it is uniform. There is no opposition to the war. It is no "Hurrah-Boy ain't it great to have a war just like the others" moral; it is a unified, cold and unimpassioned conviction that the Kaiser and his crowd must beat it before a man can ever again say his soul's his own. Doc Lunn, our Congressman told me that one year ago he would have been defeated because he backed the war in the early days; in fact the man he supported for Mayor of Schenectady was beaten because of his support, but that now his Lunn's re-election was a mere formality.

Dropt in to see your father last Sunday. He was leading the batchelor life; your folks were in the country. Because I knew you, your father treated me like the President of the Western Hemisphere. We rustled a lunch together, viz, I poured the tea and your pater did the rest. God, Stull, when I thought on what a intellectual-dialectic basis your Dad thinks our relationship in school was, I have to laugh on the fire-place stories and that venerable suit case of Schlitz. What a story I could write on the Tale of a Suit Case, or, Fire-side Tales of Tail, or, Omar with Local Color.

Quite a mustache you have.

More later, Bill.

Sunday P.M., August 11th [*1918*]

Dear Stull,

I received your letter of July 4th & also the newspaper — It was very interesting indeed — a number of people have found it so. . . .

The War Dept. had quite a little fun with me the day I went for your commission. You are a dummy! Don't you know better than to write such a thing as "If they ask what relation — — etc where they couldn't help but read it? I had to show the letter to prove I was authorized to get the comm. One man read it & when he passed it to the Officer who had charge of Commission Div. he said, "Don't read too much." Then grinned diabolically at me. He asked — after he had written my name "Lois Crump" on a pass, if I was Mrs. Holt — I said "No" — "Not yet,??" says he — Frances nearly killed herself with enjoyment — and I guess everyone had a good time so I should worry — But I hope you appreciate what I have endured for your sake!!!

. . . I am wondering if you are now at the front. Things are very lively there now. Wherever you are I am always sending you love & good luck —

Lois

Friday, Aug. 15, [*1918*]

Dear Stull,

. . . I wish you were here, Stull, or rather I wish it were possible for you to be here. And if that wasn't possible I wish I could go over to see you.

. . . If the war isn't over by next year I think I'll enlist in the aviation. I don't see why they don't have girl aviators. Girls, nowadays, this is some of 'em, can keep their heads as well as the majority of men and I'm sure they're just as capable of killing the Germans as the men are. I know I am. I'd take great delight in it.

. . . Lots of love, Elizabeth —

Aug 27, 1918

Dear Folks,

I told you in my last letter that we were to start for the front on the next day but it was all called off. However we leave early tomorrow morning. This makes it quite a coincidence for me because it was on Aug 28 last year that I came in from the front and left the ambulance service. To increase the coincidence I am staying to-night in the same hotel and in the very room that I went to a year ago tomorrow night.

It has been a long year for me, crowded with many and varied experiences, but a happy one. I have made a great many friends and a few very intimate ones. One of my best, Simy (short for Leslie B. Simpson of Los Angeles) was in Paris a couple of days last week and we had a fine time together, the high spots being a trip to a French *esquadrille* at the front and "The Tales of Hoffman" at the *Opera-Comique*.

I wish I had time now to tell about both and many other episodes but it is going on to ten and I have to get up early tomorrow. After I get out to the front I will write oftener and in greater detail. I am delighted at the prospect of getting back. . . .

My mail hasn't caught up yet and probably wont now for weeks. . . . As soon as I learn my squadron number I will send it to you which should expedite matters.

Don't worry about me because there is little cause and also because it does no good.

Love to all, Stull.

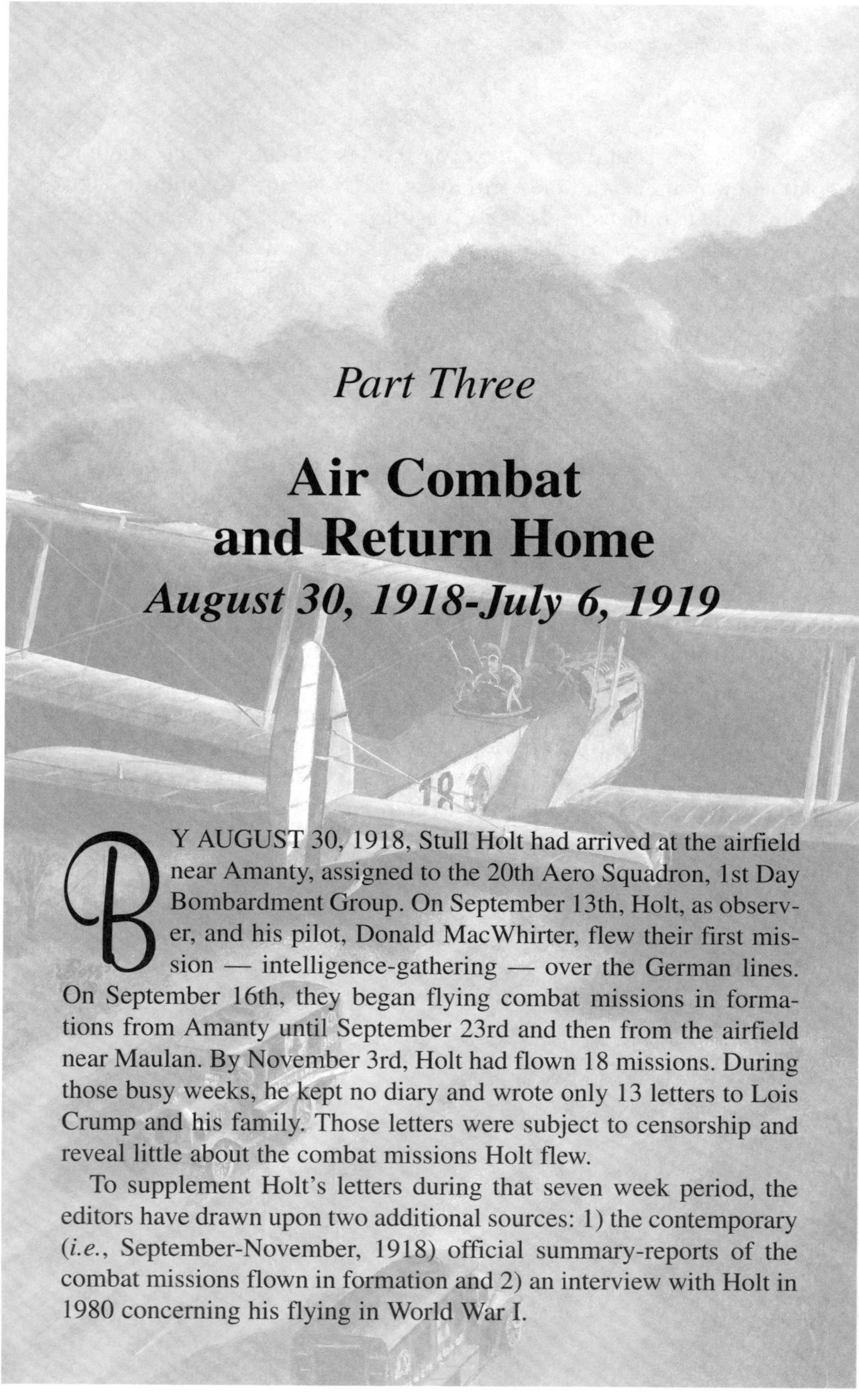

Part Three

Air Combat and Return Home

August 30, 1918-July 6, 1919

BY AUGUST 30, 1918, Stull Holt had arrived at the airfield near Amanty, assigned to the 20th Aero Squadron, 1st Day Bombardment Group. On September 13th, Holt, as observer, and his pilot, Donald MacWhirter, flew their first mission — intelligence-gathering — over the German lines. On September 16th, they began flying combat missions in formations from Amanty until September 23rd and then from the airfield near Maulan. By November 3rd, Holt had flown 18 missions. During those busy weeks, he kept no diary and wrote only 13 letters to Lois Crump and his family. Those letters were subject to censorship and reveal little about the combat missions Holt flew.

To supplement Holt's letters during that seven week period, the editors have drawn upon two additional sources: 1) the contemporary (*i.e.*, September-November, 1918) official summary-reports of the combat missions flown in formation and 2) an interview with Holt in 1980 concerning his flying in World War I.

TheTwentieth Aero Squadron crews flew their combat missions in the de Havilland DH-4. The DH-4 was designed by the well-known British de Havilland firm, but the planes flown by the crews of the Twentieth Aero Squadron were manufactured in the United States — the only American-built plane to reach France in time to fight on the western front. It was a two-seat, dual control biplane — which meant that it could be flown from either seat — designed for bombing or observation work. It was of conventional wood, wire, and fabric construction, which meant that it was inflammable. The DH-4 was heavily armed for the time, carrying one or two forward-firing Marlin guns — later, Browning machine guns — for the pilot's use, and twin Lewis machine guns on a Scarff mount for the observer. The Scarff mount could be rotated through 360 degrees, allowing the observer-gunner to cover those portions of the sky not masked by the wings, fuselage, or tail of his own aircraft. But it was necessary for the observer to restrain his enthusiasm since his guns could, and on occasion did, shoot off vital parts of the aircraft's structure, including control wires.

The DH-4 was not an outstanding aircraft and many American pilots and observers much preferred the French Breguet. Still, the DH-4 was a good, serviceable plane, although it did need design changes, many of which ultimately were accomplished to the considerable improvement of the machine. The marriage with the Liberty V-12 engine — the British DH-4s used a Rolls Royce "Eagle" V-12 engine — was astonishingly effective, albeit marred at first by motor and fuel system problems.

One major design flaw of the aircraft was the fuselage location of the main fuel tank. It was positioned between the pilot and the observer, separating the two men by more than six feet. Communication between them, even with speaking tubes, was almost impossible over the roar of the 12-cylinder Liberty engine. Denied verbal communication, and unable to reach a pilot by hitting him on the shoulder, some observers maneuvered their pilots to the bomb-release point by tying reins to the pilot's arms.

Moreover, the metal fuel tank, which was not self-sealing, could be struck in combat and set alight by tracer bullets that contained burning phosphorus. There were complaints, too, that the tank was so poorly secured in the fuselage that it immediately left its supports in a crash, crushing the pilot against the engine. The motor was also believed to be inadequately secured to its bed. The crews suspected that the rubber connection to the metal fuel line, which ran parallel to the engine, could heat up and part company with the line, showering gasoline under pressure all over the red-hot exhaust stacks. The fact that the DH-4's fuel tank and fuel system was pressurized virtually guaranteed that the aircraft would explosively burn if punctured.

The big Liberty engines required American spark plugs, and these were not always available, which meant that French plugs had to be substituted at times. These latter were not designed to handle the compression loads, particularly on a Liberty-powered de Havilland trying to hoist itself into the air from a muddy field with a full warload of bombs, guns, ammunition, fuel, and crew aboard. The French plugs blew out of the cylinders and the DH-4 came down at once. Such an accident brought Holt and his pilot down prematurely, as we shall see, on the worst day the 20th Aero saw in France.

The German fighter pilots soon knew all about the strengths and weaknesses of the DH-4s, including the placement of its fuel tank between pilot and observer. It made sense for a fighter pilot to fire at the juncture of fuselage and wings of an enemy aircraft, for this was where the crew was seated. Some German pilots came in from below and astern, attempting to kill or disable the gunner, which would leave a two-seat bomber undefended from the rear. In its original configuration, the DH-4 was a fighter pilot's dream target. If he strove to kill the observer and missed, he was likely to hit his opponent's pilot or the fuel tank; and if the German pilot was content only to spray his machine gun fire in the general direction of his opponent's wings and fuselage, the results were likely to be spectacular. The crew called their de Havilland DH-4s "Flaming Coffins."

Their German opponents in the air basically were the four *jagdstaffels*, or "*Jastas*" — "hunting squadrons," Numbers 12, 13, 15, and 19, which made up *Jagdgeschwader II* (JG II), a "hunting group." If the JG II *jastas* did not have the reputations of the German Air Service's premier fighter group, *Jagdgeschwader I* (JG I) — which Manfred von Richtofen commanded until he was killed on April 21, 1918 — they were still a crack outfit, and Holt commented on their aggressive bravery. As was common among Allied airmen, some pilots and gunners in the 20th Aero mistakenly believed they were facing von Richtofen's "circus" because two of JG II's squadrons painted the noses of their aircraft red, a color associated with von Richtofen's JG I.

JG II was equipped with the latest German fighters, Fokker D-VIIs, using Mercedes or B.M.W. in-line engines of up to 185 hp and capable of efficiently fighting at the altitudes where the American de Havillands flew.

The Mercedes-powered D-VII could reach the 20th Aero Squadron's bombing altitude — approximately 12,000 feet — in just over twenty minutes, and the B.M.W. D-VII could reach those heights in ten or twelve minutes!

Late in their frontline service, the men of the 20th Aero encountered a new German fighter, the Siemens Schuckert D-IV, powered with a Siemens Halske Sh IIIa of 200 hp. A rotary engine which employed eleven cylinders, the Siemens Halske Sh IIIa was technologically advanced but delicate, suffering from some of the problems often encountered in engines hastily brought from the drawing boards to service. But by late October, 1918, some of these barrel-shaped, stubby, fast-climbing D-IVs — they could reach 12,000 feet in less than nine minutes — had found their way into Jastas 15 and 19, where they made their presence known to the men of the 20th Aero on at least two occasions late in the war.

The four *jastas* hurled themselves at the DH-4 squadrons wherever they could find them. Despite the massed firepower brought to bear on them by a flight of ten or twelve de Havillands, the German pilots often drove into and through the American formations, their guns firing, much as their Luftwaffe successors were to do in the next war. The Germans continued to harry the bombers to the bitter end of the war.

Nearing the lines, Holt would have stood upright on thin wooden floorboards, facing the tail, with nearly half of his body exposed in his wood-and-fabric open cockpit. The aircraft usually would be at 12,000-13,000 feet on a bombing mission. Though it was autumn, his cockpit was not heated, nor was his flying suit. We must imagine Holt, clad in layers of clothing for warmth, with a 115 mile-an-hour gale droning through the wires and struts between the wings and beating against his body. At his back was a 66 gallon tank filled with gasoline, waiting for the passing tracer bullet which would bring it to incandescent life. No oxygen equipment was carried on bombers to save on weight — with crew and a full war load, the DH-4s could carry only about 300 pounds of bombs aloft. The plane had no armor plate and the pilots no parachutes. Add to this the ear-splitting roar and vibration of a huge Liberty engine slamming against his ears through a thin leather helmet, coupled with the lurch and sway, the bounding motion of a flight of de Havilland DH-4's pounding through an ocean of turbulent air, and the reader can get some idea of what Holt and his colleagues experienced mission after mission.

Holt wrote on the back of this photograph: "We went through Clermont-Paris-and to the front together. Standing (left to right) — Joe Endler, Everette A. Taylor, myself, John Y. Stokes, McRae Stevenson. Sitting — Brooke Edwards, Dick Mathews, Donald MacWhirter, Arthur E. Seaver, Les Harter." *Holt Collection*

The gaily colored fighters of *Jagdgeschwader II* succeeded all too often in reaching the heights where Holt and the others sought to make their way; or they were already there, waiting, and they shot the young Americans out of the sky. Twenty-seven aircraft from Holt's 1st Day Bombardment Group fell to German guns. Forty pilots and observers from the Group's four squadrons were killed. Some of these men burned to death in the air. Others jumped to their deaths to avoid the fire. Seventeen men crashed with their machines behind the German lines to become prisoners. Five more men died in crashes that were not combat related. We get some clue to Holt's reactions to these aerial losses when he wrote his family on October 15th that "a 50% casualty list in 7 successive days is apt to cause a little thinking."

As these sobering statistics were accumulating in France, Holt continued to receive a variety of messages from friends and family in the United States. Bill Smith, with his usual vividness, describes a Bolshevik meeting, blind patriotism, and what he considered America's ill-conceived bent to avenge herself on Germany. He also alludes to Holt's love life and expresses his own love interests. Both Smith and Holt thought that Holt's father shared the view that Germany must be invaded and punished, and both Smith and Holt championed instead the peace-making effort of President Woodrow Wilson.

Letters from Holt's parents point to an incident that pits them against Lois's mother. However, Lois mentions only the need to discuss the conflict upon Holt's return.

Aug 30, 1918

Dear Lois,

Out at last and in just the sort of place I have always wished for. We are on the top of the biggest hill in the neighborhood and consequently from the flying field which is, of course, open and very large, there is a wonderful view. But the best part is that most of the hill is covered with very thick woods so thick that you can't see any of our barracks either from the ground or the air. When I look out the open door I can see nothing but very thick underbrush that makes me feel just as if we were out on a camping trip — which is the exact truth. The air, too, is very cool and invigorating the way it is up at the lake in the fall. We

Holt flew combat missions from the region of Bar-le-Duc to Toul, September-November, 1918.

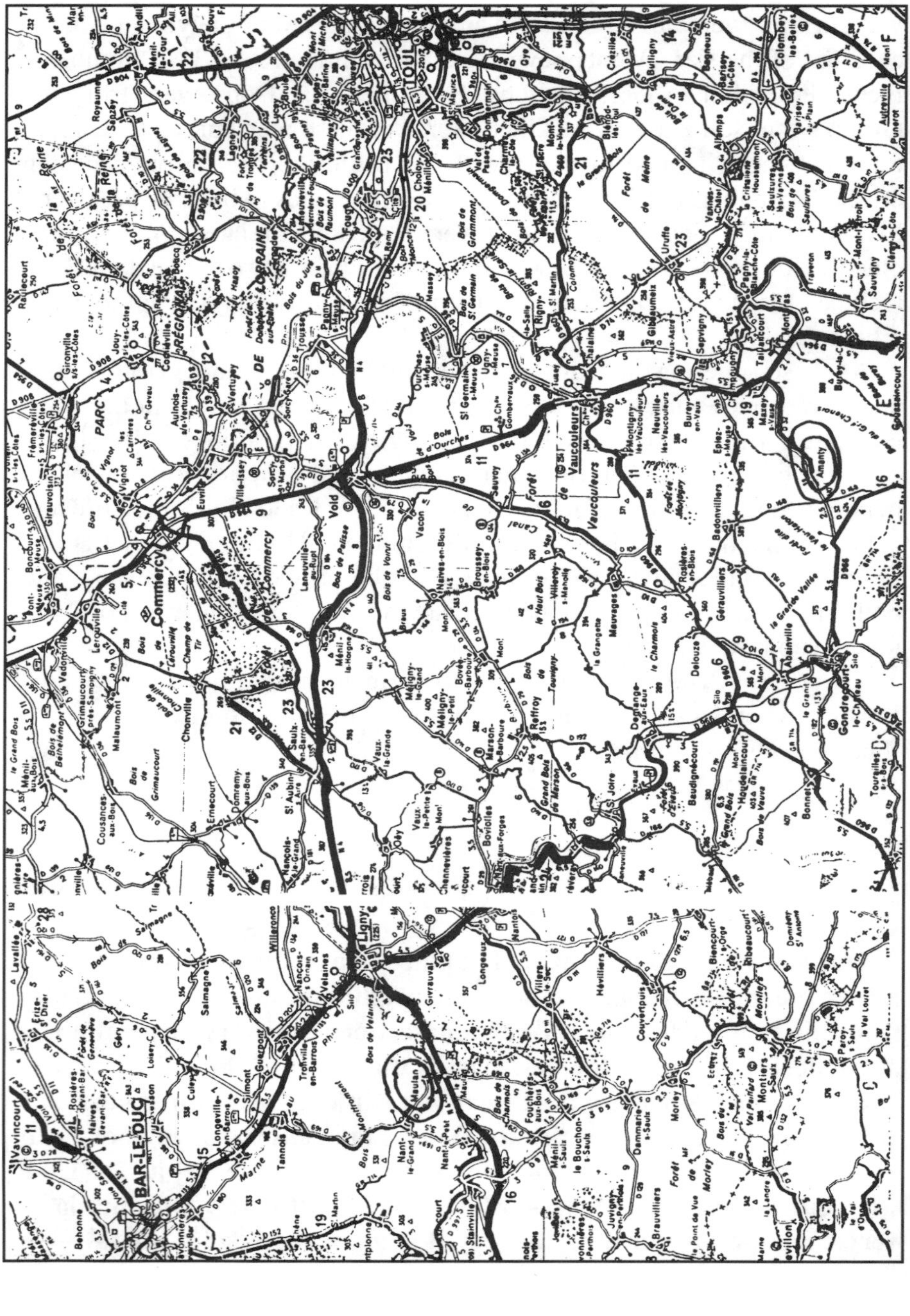

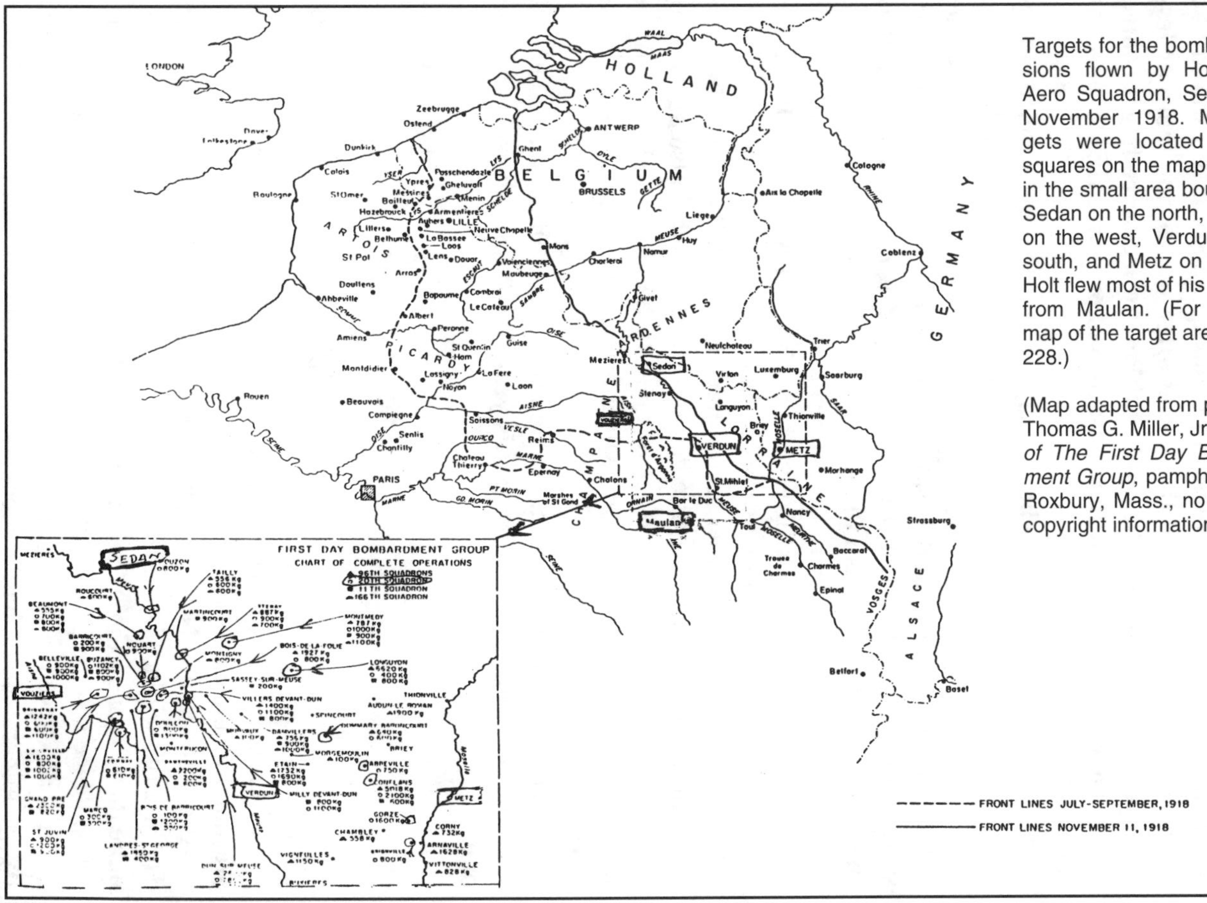

Targets for the bombing missions flown by Holt's 20th Aero Squadron, September-November 1918. Most targets were located (as the squares on the map indicate) in the small area bounded by Sedan on the north, Vouziers on the west, Verdun on the south, and Metz on the east. Holt flew most of his missions from Maulan. (For a larger map of the target area, see p. 228.)

(Map adapted from page 3 of Thomas G. Miller, Jr., *History of The First Day Bombardment Group*, pamphlet, West Roxbury, Mass., no date, no copyright information)

have only just gotten here and so aren't settled at all . . . it will be about a month, I think, before we begin to make life unpleasant for the huns. . . . Sometimes I think I wouldn't be able to settle down and live in a city, not even New York. If I could speak Spanish I would like to try South America, you'd think that after wandering more or less for a year and a half I would want nothing but a chance to get rooted in one spot but I have the wanderlust as bad or worse than ever — at times.

All my mail for some time back is chasing me around France but by some very lucky freak of the postal service your letter of July 24 (the only one I've gotten here) came here in only two moves. You ask me what I think of Paula and Newton but I noticed you didn't express your opinion. The fact that they got married is no great shock, it[']s their own affair and I wish them luck and happiness. But I don't like at all the secretness. Why in the name of goodness they did that I cant imagine, nor easily sympathize with. I wish you would ask Paula for permission to tell me so I could write her.

I agree with you — it does seem queer for you to be in Washington alone and working. I cant quite get used to the idea. I also agree that it does everyone, even you, a lot of good to be alone and away from home. That's one of the reasons why a fellow and a girl too should go to college away from home.

I[']ll bet you werent half as excited about the allied successes as I was and am. But it won't finish this year. We'll have to wait another one.

Love, Stull. . . .

New York City, Sep. 2nd., 1918

Dear Stull,

. . . Probably I have written you I quit the feminine pen juggling at Washington and came to N.Y. City. . . .

As a greenhorn in N.Y., I am the victim of ten thousand varying moods. The size of the place bewilders me. From the Bowery to Fifth Ave. is a bit more than a stone's throw; yet in that short distance is illustrated the greatest opulence and the greatest misery in the world. When I walk down Elizabeth & Roosevelt and Mulberry Streets, and see the shabby hulks drifting, shambling along, hardly recognizable as humans, I am a Socialist, or any other -ist that attacks all that is. I think the thing which strikes me most in this city is not the deep misery of the Bowery district or the puffy, gaudy display of Riverside Drive, but rather the general run of down-right crassness and stupidity of the city's millions. . . .

Was over to a Bolshevik meeting on the East side the other night. One John Reed, who found himself in Russia when the Revolution broke out, and who became famous because he happened to be under indictment for something or other here in the U.S. at the time, I.W.W. stuff, I guess, a brilliant young writer, I judge from his articles in the new Radical paper, the "Liberator," was to speak on "The Truth about Russia." The police prevented the meeting. It is very embittering to think that in our own U.S. ideas, right or wrong are stifled; but I am convinced it is necessary if we are to win the war. The suppression of free speech has been complete here; there have been only a few prosecutions, but the 20 year sentences in these have cowed all others. The result is an amazing one-mindedness of the people, and its results only that will beat Germany. Things that are said as a matter of course in England and Germany would throw a man in Leavenworth prison in 5 minutes; Maximilian Harden & the Daily Mail wouldnt last long here.

. . . From what I have seen of the East side here, we will have a Socialist Mayor of New York in ten years, unless the Socialists queer themselves too much in this war. I am studying up on Socialism now; if I can believe in it, I am going to try to ride the whirlwind; but I don't think I can believe in it. The people can't successfully rule themselves now; God help them if they try to rule industry.

The country is behind the war fanatically now. I see a Berlin paper states: "Every inclination on the part of the Allies to peace talk is met by the war craze of America." Good God, Stull, assure any doubtful friends that the war is all over so far as the final outcome is concerned. America is in to the hilt. The ships are dropping like guinea-pig pups; new draft 18-45; 4,000,000 in Europe by July 1918. The war is won. America is 100,000,000 howling dervishes after the Kaiser's fore-skin. The only danger is that we shall come out of the war the most re-actionary of the Allies. Sam Gompers [*English born founder of American Federation of Labor. Gompers was an ardent supporter of the war and a vigorous opponent of socialism and pacifism*] is now in England trying to show the British Labor party how ridiculous its Program is. For once the N.Y. Times is backing Gompers. Roosevelt in a speech the other day said that all who favored the League to enforce Peace were either "fools" or "pro-Germans." Here our hope is in Wilson.

. . . Your folks must be back from the country by now. Guess I'll drop over and tell them about their son next Sunday. I'll be discrete.

Blame on the beer the rambling nature of this letter.

As ever, Bill.

Sept 6, 1918

Dear Folks,

. . . The biggest and best piece of news I got was that Bill Smith has moved to New York. I hope he stays there and also that you get well acquainted because he's a great friend of mine. I notice that papa says (loosely I think) that he, Bill, "still has pacifist ideas and would [*not*] **smash Germany if she quit." I don't think he has retained any pacific ideas but what I consider mental poise. I am another who doesn't want to "smash" Germany no matter whether she quits now or it lasts ten years more. "Smash" might be applied to Germany's military power and organization but not to Germany. To smash her would be in accordance with her own philosophy, not ours (at least not with what I hope is ours). It is the same idea that the old prison systems and wardens acted on — and not Osborne's or Rusby's** [*Thomas Osbourne was on the New York State Commission on Prison Reform (1913) and introduced self-help programs while warden at Sing-Sing*]. **I don't blame Germany either individually or collectively any more than I do a criminal but that doesn't make me any less anxious to fight Germany or arrest the criminal. Would you "smash" Roosevelt or Henry Cabot Lodge for being protectionists, advocating what tends to create in a small degree such a system as caused the war, and what runs counter to evolution and progress? I am afraid that our victory may be abused and that too many will want to "smash Germany" Thank goodness for our Bill Smiths and W. Wilsons. The nearer and more certain our ultimate victory appears the more anxious I am that the opportunity it gives won't be wasted even in part. . . .**

Love to all, Stull

P.S. I notice in papa's market letter that he expects great trouble in the demobilization. The readjustment will be a critical period, fraught

with dangers, of course, but I think he overestimates one danger viz. the reluctance of the soldiers to return to employment and civilian pursuits. Remember this war is like none of history. Wars used to consist of long periods of idleness, wild jamborees, much looting and occassional big battles with periods of camp life in between. Nowadays it is 9/10s work and one tenth fighting, no looting, very little jamboreeing. A great majority of the men are working as hard or harder than they did in civilian life and never fight or see any fighting at all. And the work isn't so different, many are baking, chauffering, building roads, chopping trees etc like they did in civilian life only they haven't as much liberty to quit their job or get drunk on Saturday night.

Did you notice on the envelope that my initials are changed again. I am now A.S. U.S.A. meaning Air Service, United States Army. It is a speedy man that can keep up with his latest title.

Highland Lake, Conn
Sept. 8, 1918

My dear Lt. Boy:

. . . I wrote you 10 days ago about Mrs. Crump. [*This letter has not been found.*] Developments have come fast since then. She told Mrs. Brown that Ken and Elizabeth were in bed together in the Lookout — Pope's study house. The facts were briefly, that Elma, who did not feel well, had gone to bed early and had asked Eliz. not to leave her. Ken, who had a headache from being hit with a chair when he was refereeing our tennis match was lying on the kot and E. was rubbing his head when Enid and Waldo Brown burst in on them. Mrs. C. admitted that she had not told Mrs. B. correcly, at the conference when Mrs. B., Mama, I, E, Enid and Ken, were present.

We also find that Mrs. C. has been systematically speaking evil of Paula and E. (lately of Elma also) as well as of others — Hal Bannon etc. It seems to be a disease with her. Last winter she told Mrs. Brown that our home was not a fit place for her boys to go. Also that because the Holts were not Christians it would be wrong for the two families to intermarry etc. [*Mrs. Holt was interested in Theosophy — a form of religion in which one believes in God through mysticism and the occult.*]

We had a lively seance and the end is not yet. I had a talk with Lois — interrupted. She has not declared herself but does not seem at all shocked or even much displeased at her mother's conduct. I will talk with her again soon. If she still thinks that your sisters are unfit to associate with, I think you should weight matters carefully, before proceeding further.

I asked Lois why, if her mother wanted to reform the morals of our daughters, she did not come directly to Mama. Lois said she supposed it was because the same thing had been going on all summer without Mrs. Holt making objection. This is, of course, untrue. It indicates that Mrs. C. stops at nothing to defame and malign.

All of this time, the Crumps have been friendly and (unasked) have visited us frequently.

Apparently, Mrs. C. — as I told Lois — is schooling Enid and Lelia to spy for her and to propagate her vile slanders. I can't take time to go further into details. Mama is furious and has kept me awake several nights planning what to do. We think that the Popes have been warned against letting Darwin visit us. He has not come lately.

We think well of Dr. Crump now and wonder at his patience. He is the worst hen-pecked husband I ever saw. He should paddle Enid's and Lelia's backsides until they are black and blue. Their treatment of him is scandalous.

Plainly, we think that Mrs. C. is insane on some things and that if you should hook up with Lois and she should not cut entirely loose from the family, you would find a "hell on earth" — mama's words. . . .

Be careful of yourself! Your loving father

Byron W. Holt

Sept. 8th [*1918*]

Dear Stull,

. . . You said you would probably leave for the front the day after your last letter was written. That means you are there now. Please, please dont take needless chances, Stull. That may sound foolish as you read it, but it isn't. If you should be sent back as an instructor, it would mean in France behind the lines I suppose — Why couldn't it be over here?. . .

It made me mad when I saw that "oniony" picture of you stuck up in the Club House up here. I don't know how it got there, but never mind — if people will do such things as win crosses — etc. they must suffer the consequences. . . .

Lois.

From the 1980 Holt interview:

> **On 12 September 1918, four or five of we pilots from the 20th Aero were sent to a fighter field 40 or 50 miles away. We were to protect the fighters! We were supposed to fly behind the Spad fighters and to protect their rear. We did not even know the pilots from this unit, much less what they did. We [*Holt and MacWhirter*] couldn't fly the protection mission because that field was wet and we picked up a stone which broke our propellor. We telephoned our unit and they sent over a truck which carried a new propellor, but it did not arrive until late in the afternoon. . . .**
>
> **That evening I received orders to fly over to another empty field near Headquarters from where I was to fly on the next day. We flew over to the field and the squadron truck followed with gasoline and mechanics. . . . Early the next morning I received orders to fly over the St. Mihiel salient. The commanding colonel said that the Americans were supposed to meet at the town of Vignevills. This was right in the middle of the salient and he wanted us to observe and to find out if the Americans were there. . . and to fly low enough to see the uniforms on the soldiers and to see if the roads were in good condition to carry guns and trucks. I don't remember the name of this colonel but his telephone number was "Running Water 33." It was raining lightly and low clouds were blowing by. From my days in the Ambulance Service I knew all of the territory on the French side of the lines and down through the salient. I knew it quite well.**
>
> **We crossed the lines at a very low altitude. We could see enemy tracer bullets as they passsed above our plane. Then we got lost. We wandered about for about an hour on the German side of the lines — looking for our troops. Of course, MacWhirter would steer our D.H.4 anywhere I told him to go. We must have gone quite deep into Germany because we flew over a German train. I was so green and overwhelmed with the importance of my mission that I did**

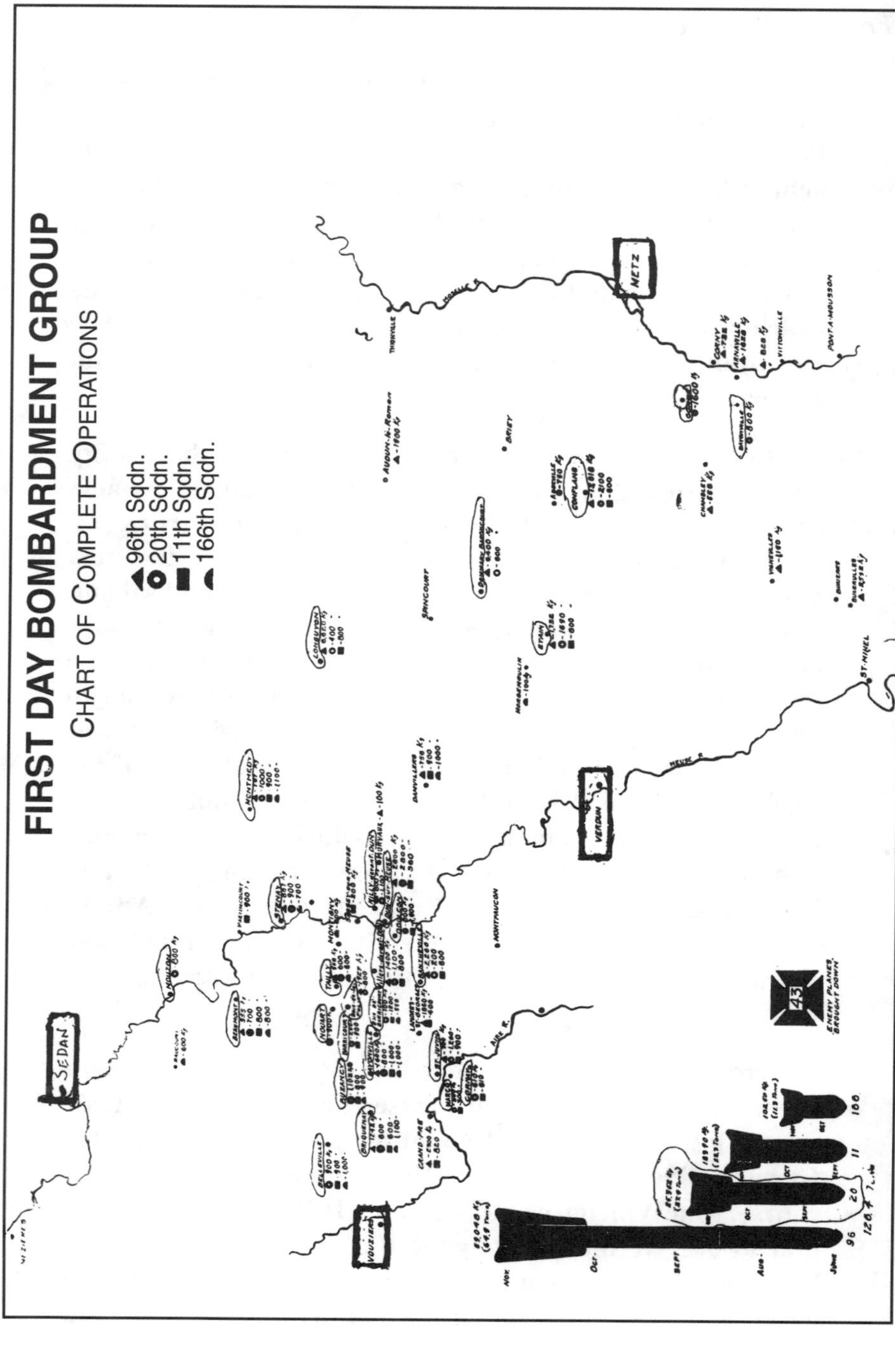
FIRST DAY BOMBARDMENT GROUP
CHART OF COMPLETE OPERATIONS
96th Sqdn.
20th Sqdn.
11th Sqdn.
166th Sqdn.
SEDAN
METZ
VERDUN
VOUZIERS
THIONVILLE
MONTFAUCON
SPINCOURT
BRIEY
ST. MIHIEL
PONT-A-MOUSSON
ENEMY PLANES BROUGHT DOWN
43

not do what I would have done three weeks later when I was a veteran. I would have shot up and strafed the German train . . . but this time I did not do that. The aircraft's compass was spinning around and I finally knew enough to fly west where we landed at a French airfield. I called the phone number "Running Water 33" but by this time the colonel had plenty of information from other sources that he did not give a damn about what I had to report.[31]

Monday Sept 16, 1918

Dear Folks,

. . . While I think of it, I have bought on the installment plan 2-$50 Liberty bonds. They are all paid for but I have no receipt or anything to show for them. I couldn't get any information over here as to how to get the bonds but was told to write to the Depot Quartermaster at Washington. I did so and told him I would like to have the bonds delivered to you in N.Y. (I think they were bought thru the Federal Reserve bank in N.Y.) As yet I haven't heard from him but if by any chance you should get a notice about them don't be surprised.

* * * * *

You will know long before you get this of the American attack in the St Mihiel salient and because of it we naturally have been working hard.[32]

. . . There are several other squadrons at this same place and Springer is in one and Simpson, another of my best friends, is in another, so we see a lot of each other.

. . . I told you before I think that I will probably be called back as an instructor after a few months up here. I am working as an observer and not as pilot. I thought the work would be more interesting and a bigger job — more chance for headwork. The machines are all double control so I get all the chance to fly I want to but over the lines I'm working as an observer.

Opposite: The First Day Bombardment Group, chart of complete operations. Targets bombed by Holt's 20th Aero Squadron are circled. (Map adapted from a copy in the Holt papers, no source cited.)

There is lots to tell that is interesting but I can't seem to do it as some of it is censorable and there is a buzz of conversation all around which prevents good letters.

Love from, Stull.

The combat mission reports which follow, each chronologically placed in the text, are composite documents assembled from selected 20th Aero Squadron operation orders and from the squadron's post-operation reports for each bombing mission. The source for these documents is the Gorrell Histories.

At the close of the war, Colonel Gorrell was assigned the task of assembling the American Air Service documents from which a history of its wartime experiences could be compiled. This mass of paper, some of it consisting of faded carbon-copy typescripts or the blurred, purple results of 1918 multiple-copy systems, eventually was microfilmed by the National Archives. It was later published by the Office of Air Force History in four volumes. Maclyn Burg, the initial compiler of Stull's diaries, consulted the appropriate microfilm rolls, but found that Barth's History of the 20th Aero Squadron, *was a more legible source. Originally published in 1919, it was written by Lieutenant Clarence G. Barth, the officer who had compiled the 20th Aero's contribution to the Gorrell Histories.*

The reports selected are primarily those for missions in which Holt took part. On the operation orders, the pilot was listed first, followed by a slash, and then the name of the observer, (e.g., MacWhirter/Holt). The operation orders included each aircraft's position within the formation. To promote greater bombing accuracy and to provide better machine gun coverage from the formation's rear-seat observer/gunners, the 20th Aero usually put its de Havilland DH-4s into a "vee," with the aircraft echeloned — stair-stepped — up and back on each side of the lead. Frequently, a DH-4 was placed so as to close the open end of the "vee."

Readers will find that many of the post-mission reports describe the types of German fighters which intercepted the bombers, and in the post-mission debriefing sessions, the American pilots and observers often cited specific colors or markings painted on their opponent's machines. This information helps to confirm the fact that the four jadgstaffels *of JG II, Numbers 12, 13, 15, and 19, were their usual opponents in the air. In some cases the reported colors help to identify which* jadgstaffel(s) *attacked the 20th on a particular mission.*

The 1st Daylight Bombardment Group statistics show that the Group's squadrons, including the 20th, made numerous trips without loss, and then suffered their heaviest losses on only two or three bad days during their two months of front-line service.

Finally, it should be kept in mind that Holt's correspondents at home never saw these documents during the war. It is not clear that Holt himself ever saw them during the war, either, although he and his flying companions doubtless were questioned after flying a mission.

Tuesday Sept 17, 1918

Dear Lois,

. . . We have been very busy (you probably guessed as much when you read of the St. Mihiel salient attack) and I have had a lot of new and strange experiences. They are so many that I am swamped when I try to put them down. One of the queerest was on Friday the 13th. I

TRIP NUMBER: 6TH Date: September 16, 1918
Objective: Conflans Railroad Yards
Leaders: Lieut. Howard and Lieut. Parrott
Teams Leaving the field: 8 Teams reaching objective: 5
Formation:

(1) Howard/Parrott
(3) Wiser/Christian (2) Edwards/Endler
(5) Koepfgen/Hicks (4) Harris/Ramsey
(7) MacWhirter/Holt (6) Tucker/Faulk
(8) Sellers/Payne

Departure Time: 12:45 Return Time: 14:30
Altitude: 12,000 Bombs Dropped: 16
Enemy Aircraft Seen: 7 Enemy Aircraft Encountered:
Type: [*Unspecified in report*] Markings: Red nose with white wings and fuselages
Region: Rounds Fired:
Remarks: [*None*]

was doing special work, about which I cant tell you now but was very interesting and responsible. I crossed the lines only about 5 or 600 feet high (so low I could see the men in the trenches) in the rain which poured at intervals and thru the clouds which ranged between 700 and 1000 feet. Because of these we (there were two of us in the plane) couldn't see much and promptly got lost. For over an hour we sailed around Germany trying to find ourselves and accomplish our mission, we went over boche trains, airdromes, towns et-al., probably causing them a lot of surprise to see an Allied plane come charging thru the rain and clouds so low. They shot a little at us both cannon and machine gun (I could see the tracer bullets from the machine guns coming up at us) but neither came anywhere near. We couldn't find ourselves so finally headed southwest till we crossed the line and then landed at a French airdrome and found where we were. The most interesting moment was when our motor started to miss and we were 20 or more miles on the German side.

Yesterday I went over in one of 5 planes and bombed an important railroad junction and yard with fair results. The anti aircraft fire was pretty heavy, I counted over 100 bursts in the air at once and they kept coming up. A lot of them came close enough so that I could hear the loud crrrr-ump of the explosion above the roar of our motor and the plane would rock with the force of the explosion. But none of our planes were touched at all. In fact nobody pays much attention to the anti aircraft fire except to figure out how much it costs Germany. About 8 boche planes came up after us, they had bright red wings and white bodies, ran right into their own anti aircraft fire which tickled us, chased us a while but didn't get near enough to fight and then withdrew.

That is a very brief and bald account of a couple of incidents. I wish I could collect myself and write full accounts the way they deserve. But the censor would very rightly interfere.

I noticed in your letter you wondered if I could ever settle down "at a desk in an office in Lower New York." I have often wondered too. Of course I could if I wanted to and probably will just thru force of circumstance and inertia. But I feel at times as tho what I want to do and what would be better, is after a few months home to grab you and start out for some new country the newer the better — South America, Alaska or South Africa. What would you think of that? To do that

would mean breaking home ties and what is harder overcoming inertia, which after all plays the largest part in most peoples lives, holding them here or there or in this or that business. It is only those who have the courage and will to shake off inertia and live their own lives, that really know life.

However I am getting philosophical which means it is time to stop.

. . . I wish I weren't away and then your arm . . . would be squeezed in one of the biggest hugs you ever heard of. I am starving for a chance to make love to you.

Love, Stull.

Washington, D.C., September 19, 1918

Dear Stull:

Here I am back in Washington, and the most disappointed mortal you ever saw. I fully expected to be greeted by two or three letters from the other side of the world and there isn't a sign of one yet. . . .

My vacation was all too short.

TRIP NUMBER: 8th Date: September 18, 1918
Objective: Mars-la-Tour
Leaders: Lieut. Howard and Lieut. Parrott
Teams Leaving the field: 7 Teams reaching objective: 5
Formation:

(1) Howard/Parrott
(3) Townes/Bunkley (2) Wiser/Christian
(5) Edwards/Endler (4) Leach/Wilmer
(7) Harris/Forbes (6) Koepfgen/Hicks
(8) MacWhirter/Holt

Departure Time: 16:10 Return Time: 18:20
Altitude: 12,000 Bombs Dropped: 16
Enemy Aircraft Seen: 9 Enemy Aircraft Encountered:
Type: Fokker Markings: White stripe near tail and black fuselage

Region:Rounds Fired:
Remarks: Bombed Abberville instead of objective

. . . Glad, Fran Young, and I are now keeping house by our lonesomes at Popes'. Some fun. Me for the batchelor life — it's great.

. . . Mr. Hubbard has been acting loony lately. I simply cannot get any dictation out of him during hours. I have stayed three days in succession to take the next day's work and last night I just went home.

. . . Enid is finishing her first year at Hunter. Thank goodness she will get a college education.

. . . Best love, Lois.

115 B'way, N.Y. City
Sept. 20, 1918.

My dear boy: —

. . . We assume that you are in the thick of the fight not far from Metz. We notice that there are several bombing planes "missed" each day. Please keep out of this variety of plane.

I do not think that Mama has written to you after having had a long talk with Lois about affairs. I also had another talk with [*Lois*] which was more satisfactory, altho she was still inclined to think that her mother was not as bad as we thot. I have always liked Lois — and still do. I would not, however, want to mix up with the rest of the family. I told her that my greatest objection to her was that she had too much ambition and would wear out too soon. In presenting these facts I simply want you to have them. I am not trying to prejudice or influence you.

. . . Your loving father
Byron W. Holt. . . .

Friday, Sept. 20, 1918.

Dear Stull,

. . . By this time you've probably heard all about the "Crump affair" but I thought I'd add my two cents and explain matters more fully.

. . . Mrs. C. stopped Mrs. B & said that Ken & I had been in bed under the covers etc. Mrs. B. got the two boys & told 'em what Mrs. C. had said & of course both boys denied emphatically any such occurrence. Well! I told papa & mama what had happened and they got Mrs. B. & all of us together (Mrs. C. included) & Mrs. C. had to take back what she said & apologise. . . .

Well! Lois didn't know very much of what had happened & when papa told her she felt dreadful. You see it[']s realy harder on her than it is on anyone. Lois said she couldn't believe that her mother said all those things. . . . She also told papa that this year away from home made her look on things differently & she justified her father in the things he did. . . . Poor Lois, she feels awfully badly over all this & she isn't to blame at all. . . . I can't begin to tell you of the unhappiness Mrs. C. has caused me but I wouldn't hurt Lois for worlds.

. . . Mrs. C. has done her best to spoil Lois' life. You know she always blamed Lois for any unpleasantness that occurred in their house.

. . . I hope, Stull, that you won't feel too badly over everything that's happened & I'll wrote a longer letter real soon.

Lots of love, Elizabeth

N.Y. City., Sunday, Sep. 22 '18.

Gents:

This is a letter to my friends Holt & MacTaggart, written via carbon paper copy. The reason for this time saver is that I have gone into virtual confinement in an effort to fool the N.Y. State Bar Examiners on Oct. 15th, 16th. Having taken the enemy's first line, viz a college degree, we now proceed to the mopping up party. I have a whole trunk full of notes thru which I must wade. . . .

. . . You may think there are horrors of war, but there are horrors of peace, too. All the clerks in the drug stores nowadays are women. You go into buy a "for medical purposes only"; a woman clerk asks you sweetly what will you have. My God, what can you say? I say "Beacham's Pills." One afternoon, I trotted from drug store to drug store that way and bought enough physic to floor an army. . . .

\#　　　　#

Really, fellows, I don't believe you would know the U.S.A. if you came back. Talk about back of the war and going strong! Good God, we're at present the most warlike of the lot and the least willing to make peace. It has got into the marrow of the people that the Kaiser must go and they'll never stop till he goes if it takes ten years. And . . . the whole damn country is slowly moving to France. Gen. Mach announced yesterday that

1,250,000 were over. On the first eight months of this year, 482 ships were launched, tonnage 2,800,000. Everywhere you go its war — "Men 18-45 inclusive register there"; "Classes 19-22 and 31-37 to have 2,000,000 men over by next June." "Send milk to the French babies," "Join the ranks, treat 'em rough"; "The Ship-yards want you"; "Drop your last nickle here for the Y.M.C.A."; "Chocolate bars for the soldiers, give till it hurts"; "If you can't go across, come across."

The soldiers are treated like lords. When Pershing sent some veterans back to help the Liberty Loan, civilians saluted the privates. N.Y. City is, of course, the great embarkation point; here comes the men from Texas, Minnesota, Porto Rico, Alaska who never saw a town of over 2000 people and they land in N.Y. They are met by the Community war service committee which feeds them up free; then they are tooted around free in private limousines and Fifth Ave busses; up the Woolworth Tower for nothing (it costs us 55¢); sleeping quarters for 20¢; free theatre tickets; dances put on all over town for them. All this makes these boys, raw simple fellows wish they had the Kaiser by the foreskin, if he has one. "Smilage Tickets" is quite an institution; the civilians chip in a pot at the street corners and buy best seats at the best Broadway attractions and give them to soldiers. Whoops, boys, it's war everywhere.

. . . Every paper in the U.S. favored rejection of the peace offer but one. That one you would expect to be some Socialist paper. But it was none other than the howling-dervish, pro-war-till-1918 New York Times. Why the Times backslid is the question of the hour. The popular gossip is; and I have it confirmed from a fellow in the legal dep't of the Tribune, that the men of wealth in the country and the world over are getting afraid of the war, because it is spreading radicalism. And the Times is, of course, the leading spokesman in this country, of the men of wealth. Here is the government taking over R.R.'s, Telephone & Telegraph lines, some coal-mines, the Smith-Wesson munition factory for refusing to let its employees form labor unions, fixing prices of coal, oil, platinum, steel, and God knows what, taking incomes as high as 80%, taxing the sacred profits of all firms engaged in war work, building homes for war workers. In short, pseudo-Socialism, and total disregard of the "rights" of wealth. Also trade has gone to hell; they say what you can export, and import and how much and when. Europe is so eating itself up that it will be a poor market for American trade. Senator Sherman openly denounces Wilson as a Socialist; Ford is opposed in Michigan as a labor radical too dangerous for the Reconstruction period. In other words, is the supposed idea of the Times, let's end this God-damn thing before the people get too radical and before the world becomes too impoverished for trade. This fear of the Times is undoubtedly justified; if I had oodles of money I would think the same. But they haven't the chance of a snow-ball. The country, and Wilson in particular, is on the way to semi-Socialism. Curious, — wars in the past have often begun to stop radicalism. It was a favorite trick of Lord Palmerston [*1784-1865*] in the last century, where grumbling got too hot in England, to start a blustering foreign policy to take the peoples minds off their complaints. And here is a war, which people of his type are trying to stop to prevent radicalism. The conflict between labor & capital in this country after the war is going to be an awful fight.

. . . Here ends the profound political observations of Blackstone Jr. . . .

My best in a hurry, Bill . . .

Monday Sept 23, 1918

Dear Lois,

Only a short note because we are moving again this time to a place about 30 miles north of here. It has been a rainy and windy week, so much of both that we had little excitement in the flying line altho the week before we had enough to last all winter and longer. . . .

A couple of days ago I got two letters from you (dates Aug 1 and 12), and before I forget it will answer about the stamps. I have never had to pay any postage on any of your letters since the first couple I got in Paris and the winter before last.

. . . Hours later — we have a hurry call to move. Excuse brevity — lots of love

Stull.

Monday Sept 23, 1918

Dear Folks,

This last has been a very quiet week, rain or high winds preventing flying almost entirely. I know you will have noticed in the papers that five bombing planes were lost in a raid and will be worrying about me so I think I will cable in a few days. I knew some of the men who were lost but they werent from our squadron.

. . . Despite several very unpropitious factors I have been very happy here and am feeling fine. We all get up in the morning singing and fooling which is proof of good condition. But I am afraid we are all inclined to eat too much and exercize too little. I haven't had an opportunity to do any hiking lately but intend to take all the chance I get. We have been living in a little barracks [*drawing*] about 60 feet long and 15 feet wide at the bottom. It is divided into 3 partitions; four men in the front room, six in the middle and four of us in the back. Here Brooke Edwards, MacWhirter, Joe Endler and I have our kingdom, which consists of our cots with our bedding rolls thereon, our trunks and other baggage; many home made shelves, tables, stands and other appurtences. The biggest drawback is, as has always been true in the army, the lack of privacy but it isn't as bad here as most places I have been. Still I don't get the solitude to do the reading and writing I want to do. I have done some lately and expect to begin sending some books home which you are to keep for me.

We have very good food . . . and good equipment issued to us. My particular pride and joy is a three quarters length fur-lined coat with a broad fur collar. . . .

I am getting flying pay now, 25% extra for participation in regular and frequent aerial flights, which brings my salary to about $222 a month minus insurance. That is quite a hefty sum so I expect to be ahead of the game soon. So far I've done little better than keep even. There is practically no chance to spend money out here so we have to save but intend to make up for missed opportunities whenever we get a chance at Paris or any city again. . . .

Love to all, Stull. . . .

Friday Sept 27, 1918

Dear Lois,

You said in one of your letters that if I had any troubles I should share them with you. I wish I could because I sure am low to-day. My spirit is so low that it would have to take an aeroplane to get to hell. It shouldn't be because the Germans were never in as bad a position on every front as to-day — but we all have our high and low days and today I'm in my cellar one.

It has been raining all day so far and I have been doing a little

TRIP NUMBER: 9th: 1st Formation Date: September 26, 1918
Objective: Dun-sur Meuse
Leaders: Lieut. Koepfgen and Lieut. Payne
Teams Leaving the field: 16 Teams reaching objective: 14
Formation:

(1) Koepfgen/Payne
(3) MacWhirter/Holt (2) Edwards/Hicks
(5) Townes/Bunkley (4) Mandell/Frank
(7) Tucker/Faulk (6) Baker/Ramsey
(8) Seaver/Stokes

Departure Time: 8:50 Return Time: 11:10
Altitude: 14,000 Bombs Dropped: 56
Enemy Aircraft Seen: 6 Enemy Aircraft Encountered: 6
Type: Fokker Markings: White band on fuselage, black body.
Region: Clery-la-Grand Rounds Fired: 550
Remarks: All bombs dropped on Dun-sur-Meuse. One fire started. The enemy aircraft attacked our second formation from side and rear. Five of our planes are missing and one enemy aircraft went down in flames.

TRIP NUMBER: 9th (2nd Formation) Date: September 26, 1918
Objective: Dun-sur-Meuse
Leaders: Lieut. Howard and Lieut. Parrott
Teams Leaving the field: 16 Teams reaching objective: 14
Formation:
[*K=Killed; P= Taken Prisoner*]

(1) Howard/Parrott [K]
(3) Wiser [P]/Richardson [K] (2) Rhinelander [K]/Preston [K]
(5) Matthews [K]/Taylor [K] (4) Cooper [P]/Leonard [P]
(7) Harris [K]/Forbes [K] (6) Potter/Schultz
(8) Leach/Wilmer

Departure Time: Return Time:
Altitude: Bombs Dropped:
Enemy Aircraft Seen: 6 Enemy Aircraft Encountered: 6
Type: Fokker Markings: White band on fuselage, black body.
Region: Clery-la-Grand Rounds Fired: 550
Remarks:

house-cleaning, overhauling all my stuff and repacking my trunk. I had a tremendous collection of letters which I ran thru and then burnt them all except yours and a few others. I have all of yours that I have gotten since I have been over here. . . .

I have heard and believe, but can not be sure, that after a year and a half's service in the army in France one can get a leave home if he has had no leave over here. I have had no leave yet and have been in the army one year and eight days so if I can last out the other 176 days I hope to get a trip home which means you, of course. If I do I will bring a diamond ring with me. You have three guesses who it will be for. And when I get back may buy another ring — that depends on you.

I am feeling some better already since I started this letter because I got a train of thought that is my best hope and dreams.

Don't worry about me because of this letter. I am in fine health only a little weary and nervous and needing a little cheering up. How I wish you were here to do it! Only then I probably wouldn't need it.

Love from, Stull.

P.S. Please send some more pictures; I like to keep up to date so I will recognize you quickly when I get back.

P.S.2. Excuse this horrible excuse for a letter.

Sunday Night, Sept 29, 1918

Dear Lois,

Am feeling much better than when I wrote you the day before yesterday but am still below normal. Since then I have made three trips into Germany all with a reasonable amount of success. To-days trip was the best yet; we started very late about a quarter to five and got back at almost seven. It has been very cloudy all the time lately and to-day was no exception. We were about 14,000 feet high while the clouds were only about 10,000. They look for all the world like a snow field and when the sun was setting the red light on them was beautiful. Our raid was pretty successful, we smeared the town we aimed at. It was the first time I have ever been over without seeing any boche planes and we were flying over territory where Richthofen's circus

Holt and his pilot, Donald MacWhirter, in front of their DH-4 after a mission. *Holt Collection*

TRIP NUMBER: 11 Date: September 27, 1918
Objective: Mouzay
Leaders: Lieut. Koepfgen and Lieut. Payne
Teams Leaving the field: 6 Teams reaching objective: 6
Formation:

(1) Koepfgen/Payne
(3) Mandell/Frank (2) Edwards/Hicks
(5) Townes/Christian (4) Baker/Goodell
(7) Seaver/Stokes (6) Tucker/Faulk
(8) MacWhirter/Holt

Departure Time: 17:05 Return Time: 18:45
Altitude: 3,200 Bombs Dropped: 15
Enemy Aircraft Seen: 6 Enemy Aircraft Encountered: 6
Type: Fokkers Markings: [None specified]
Region: Etain Rounds Fired: 200

Remarks: 20th, 11th, 96th Squadron went in one formation.

Holt in the observer's cockpit of his DH-4. This photo was taken by his pilot, Donald MacWhirter, from the pilot's cockpit. *Holt Collection*

has been operating. Altogether we had a great and glorious time, even Archie (anti-aircraft guns) didn't bother us as much as usual all the bursts being more inaccurate than ever, with one exception that burst nearby and put a little hole in our plane. . . .

The war news continues to exceed anything I could have dared to hope for, even the little Belgians have slipped their few words into the argument. Perhaps the war wont last more than 3 or 4 years longer. And when it's over you'd better look out because I'm going home with many plans in my head.

(I am going to stop for to-night but will finish tomorrow morning. Good-night my love. I hope I dream of you)

Next afternoon at 3 o'clock.

It has been a fine day for aviators so far, a high wind and low rainy clouds. If the bad weather keeps up an hour and a half longer I am going to walk for exercize to the nearest town which is quite sizeable and only three miles away. I have several things I want to do, among them buy some writing paper this being absolutely the last sheet.

I know a fellow over here who told me he shot down a boche plane

Above and below: DH-4s from Holt's 20th Aero Squadron on the flightline at Maulan.
Holt Collection

in our lines and that when they went to bury the boche they found he was a she. I wouldn't swear it was true but have no reason to disbelieve it. Rumors have been constant that they are using women soldiers in all branches. I rather approve of the idea, just think of the fine times you could have with a bunch of girls in the squadron. Those Germans sure have the right idea. . . .

Love, Stull.

Sept. 30th 1918.

Dear Stull,

I am simply starved and in a bad humor. . . .

I rec'd yours of Aug. 30th which is the first letter since July 4 — I have had. However, I knew your folks had received several so didn't feel so bad.

. . . Stull, I wish you would sit down and tell me just exactly what you are doing at the front. What sort of aviating are you doing? Bombing, scouting or something else — Do you (or will you when you get started) attack in formation or fight in single combat? I havent the slightest Idea which kind of work you are doing and I want to know.

. . . We are very busy at the Bureau as usual — rather more so — I should say — No matter how hard or how long I work I cannot get caught up — . . . . And what is it all for? To get men to test and improve the instruments you use on your airplane — Or if we have the men, to keep them from being drafted — etc.

. . . I hope the handkerchief I sent from H.L. doesn't find a salty grave, but reaches you in safety. It was about all I could think of that would go in an envelope.

Best love, Lois,

On my 22nd birthday MacWhirter and I went over the lines alone and dropped some bombs to celebrate my birthday. So you can see that our morale was not completely bad. But in the day bombing missions it sank lower and lower as time went on because of the heavy casualties.[33]

Thursday Oct 3, 1918

Dear Lois,

Yesterday was the big day and I had intended to celebrate it by writing you but went on a raid in the morning and stood around watching the sky waiting to start on another in the afternoon. The hanging around is so tiring that by evening I just was able to crawl to bed. But if I didn't write I thought a lot.

To-day we are given the afternoon off, for which let us make a joyful noise, and I am going to start *toute de suite* [*immediately*] for town. It is only an excuse for a town to disport in (I hope to show it to you

sometime on a trip thru France) but any change from camp and the sight of aeroplanes is desirable.

To quote your letter of May 15 — I am sending my best birthday love

Stull.

Thursday, Oct 3, 1918

Dear Folks,

I had intended to write you yesterday (to send congratulations) but didn't get around to it. In the morning I went on a raid and was to start on another right after lunch but the weather was not good enough so we hung around and waited for it to clear off which it didn't. The hanging around and watching the sky is so tiring that I didn't feel able to write last night but went right to bed where I spent a good twelve hours. Yesterday I sent a cablegram by one of the fellows who says he has sent it. I hope you get it alright.

The raid yesterday morning wasn't very satisfactory in one sense and was in another. The clouds were so thick and the visibility so poor that we don't know whether we hit our target or not. However, here's the good part, we saw no boche. The anti aircraft around the places we have been going lately is very inactive and inaccurate but where we were going a couple of weeks ago it was very heavy and apparently accurate altho it did no damage other than a few holes in several planes.

In our job the idea is to have as little to do with the boche planes as possible and when we do meet them we never attack but get home as fast as possible, if we have dropped our bombs. They never attack us unless they outnumber us (a sound policy) altho frequently smaller numbers of their faster scout planes will hang around the end of our formation looking for stragglers and exchanging a few long distance shots. Five hundred yards is a long distance for shooting in the air. . . .

Love to all, Stull.

October 6th 1918.

Dear Stull,

. . . I had an argument with Grandma Pope today about Wilson, the war and the German inhabitants of Fontennel — her home town. She says the

TRIP NUMBER: 17th Date: October 5, 1918
Objective: Ancreville
Leaders: Lieut. Koepfgen and Lieut. Payne
Teams Leaving the field: 10 Teams reaching objective: 9
Formation:

(1) Howard/Hicks
(3) Edwards/Bunkley (2) MacWhirter/Holt
(5) Derge/Willis (4) Potter/Wilmer
(7) Woolfolk/Graveline (6) Mandell/Ramsey
(9) Weimer/Brodeur (8) Townes/Johnson
(11) Murphy/Fulton (10) Tucker/Faulk

Departure Time: 16:05 Return Time: 17:50
Altitude: 13,000 Bombs Dropped: 18
Enemy Aircraft Seen: 3 Enemy Aircraft Encountered:
Type: Biplanes Markings: [Not specified]
Region: Cunnel Rounds Fired:

Remarks Burst on road in southwest corner of Ancreville and southwestern part of town. One fire started. One machine dropped two bombs on Doulleon making a direct hit. Two bursts of illuminus balls similar to tracer bullets and much larger were fired from the ground near Romagne. The balls of fire died out at about 8000 ft.

town is forcing the Germans to buy bonds if they own property — Good! said I. But the crops failed this year. . . . I hate the Germans, even those who are seemingly American (with just a few exceptions) because they have always proven trecherous when tried out. — It lasted quite a while — neither one of us won. She hates war, hates to see our boys go and of course you can't blame her much because she lived thru the Civil War and knows the horror of it. The younger generation thinks of the war as beating the Germans — down with tyrany — victory for the Americans — She knows and consequently thinks of the result — in the future, after the fighting is over.

* * * * *

Stull, I wish you could see Washington now. Rock Creek Park rivals the mountains in beauty. . . . The are no more rooms in Washington evidently.

I am short three clerks & lost another Saturday because he couldn't get a room — after hunting two days. Conditions are really pretty bad and if we don't get our Housing facilities to a point where they can be utilized soon, the people on the job now will be working night and day.

. . . Stull, I hope you don't get the wanderlust so bad that you never get over it. That would be pretty hard — and I'm afraid I wouldn't keep so cheerful as I have been — not lately — most of the time — If you keep talking about that wanderlust — I'll — get it myself I guess — . . . .

Bestest love — Lois.

Tuesday - Oct 8th. [*1918*]

Dear Stull,

. . . I suppose you read about the explosions at South Amboy. I never was so disgusted at the people in N.Y. as I was last Saturday. To begin with our whole family were up all night with the explosions. When the TNT went off our house rocked from side to side and glass smashed all around but not in our house. Well! Stull, after spending a sleepless night — Paula and I had to go to N.Y. We were going to meet Hall there and have supper. The subways had stopped running 'cuz they expected a great big explosion in the afternoon and no one was alowd on the bridge. Paula and I were taken to Fulton Ferry and jammed on a boat. It was terrible! The [*people (?); this corner of the letter has been torn off*] acted insane — They broke windows and climbed up poles jumping down on top of the ferry boat and the crowds just chimed in. You'd think they thought the world was coming to an end. When we got to the other side I was afraid that someone would be shoved into the water between the boat and dock, however ten lovely southern soldiers and a big man who said he had to go to Jersy City still — formed a circle around Paula and I and laid on the people so that they couldn't push forward so much. They were about the only sane people on board.

. . . Lots & lots of love — Elizabeth

Wednesday Oct 9, 1918

Dear Lois,

No mail yet and these last four have been long, rainy days. My last letter from you was dated Aug 12 and that seems a long time ago.

We have been sitting around and arguing about the peace movement but can reach no conclusion. Sometimes we would walk up and down in the [*mud*] and argue but with the same result. This afternoon it cleared off and we quit talking and participated more actively in the war. It was a pretty good raid considering everything. We didn't see any boche planes and archy was very inaccurate and inactive. What more could an aviator want?

Yesterday evening Springer, Don Malcolm and I walked to the little village nearby and passed a pleasant evening such as many I have had. We had ordered a dinner in advance — roast chicken, French fried potatoes, peas, string beans, bread & butter, wine and (the crowning feature) a chocolate layer cake. We supplied the sugar for this last and a pretty young girl made it. It was very good but not as good as a certain blackberry pie I can remember. . . .

Over the enormous and wonderfully cooked meal we sat and

TRIP NUMBER: 18th Date: October 9, 1918
Objective: Bantheville
Leaders: Lieut. Howard and Lieut. Hicks
Teams Leaving the field: 13 Teams reaching objective: 13
Formation:

(1) Howard/Hicks
(3) Edwards/Bunkley (2) MacWhirter/Holt
(5) Derge/Willis (4) Potter/Wilmer
(7) Woolfolk/Graveline (6) Mandell/Fiske
(9) Weimer/Brodeur (8) Townes/Johnson
(11) Murphy/Fulton (10) Tucker/Faulk
(11) Seaver/Turner (10) Koepfgen/Payne

Departure Time: 14:20 Return Time: 16:15
Altitude: 13,000 Bombs Dropped: 26
Enemy Aircraft Seen: Enemy Aircraft Encountered:
Type: Markings:
Region: Rounds Fired:

Remarks: Fires were observed in town of Mareq and Fleville. Formation was well protected by Allied Chasse.

chinned as only people can who have a well-filled comfortable feeling. Springer told us about his New Mexico, the life there, the wild scenery, the cattle et al. His folks own thousands of acres there, also the coal mines, a few railroads, lakes and a collection of odds and ends. I've told him he must get up a house party and invite us (you and me). We certainly must go out West and at least look around if we don't settle.

Speaking of settling the war news has certainly been startling during the last few days.[34] The prospect of peace is intoxicating and alluring (just think what it would mean to be sure of going back) but personally I don't expect it now. Nor do I think we are ready for it yet, altho we may be. I don't know enough of the real facts to form an opinion. But Wilson probably does and I trust him to the limit.

I am enclosing a picture which you may recognize. . . . The doctor

TRIP NUMBER: 19th Date: October 10, 1918
Objective: Devant Dun
Leaders: Lieut. MacWhirter and Lieut. Holt
Teams Leaving the field: 14 Teams reaching objective: 11
Formation:

(1) MacWhirter/Holt
(3) Townes/Johnson (2) Koepfgen/Willis
(5) Seaver/Stokes (4) Mandell/Fiske
(7) Potter/Wilmer (6) Baker/Goodell
(9) Murphy/Fulton (8) Tucker/Faulk
(11) Woolfolk/Graveline (10) Derge/Brodeur
(13) Weimer/Turner (14) Sellers/Payne (12) Howard/Hicks

Departure Time: 7:00	Return Time: 9:05
Altitude: 12,000	Bombs Dropped: 22
Enemy Aircraft Seen: 2	Enemy Aircraft Encountered: 2
Type: Fokker	Markings: [Not specified]
Region: Region of Nilly Dun	Rounds Fired: 820

Remarks: No burst observed on account of heavy fog. Enemy Aircraft did not come close. A fight between Enemy and Allied Chasses was observed in region of Denvillers. One plane was seen to go down out of control.

examined me the other day and reported my blood pressure, heart and lungs as being in perfect condition. . . .

Lots of love and a couple of kisses from Stull.

Oct. 11, 1918.

Dear Stull,

I wish I knew what you think of the war news now. To me it seems mighty like the Germans were a "little" weak in the knees. I hate to get unduly excited but I sure did dance a really truly jig after reading last night's news. Tonight's was practically the same — The Germans seem to be on their way home.

You have read, I suppose, of the dreadful time we are having with the influenza epidemic — It is really serious because of the shortage of doctors, nurses and proper hospital facilities. We had one case here of five girls who were rooming together all being sick at the same time with no one to take care of them. A Red Cross worker finally found them, half starved and very ill. I am going to offer my services tomorrow at one of the hospitals where they are terribly rushed and very short of help. I am willing to do anything from answering the phone to actual nursing — that is, nursing I could do. If I find I can help more there than at the Bureau I shall take some leave and go on helping in the hospital. We are dreadfully short of help at BS but no one would die if they shut the whole place up for a few days. . . .

Your letters came at intervals of from three weeks to a month now. One reason just now may be that the P.O. is short of help. . . .

Best love, Lois.

<u>October 12, 1918</u>. *Holt describes the mission on this date, "Trip Number: 20th," in the 1980 interview, although he places it incorrectly on October 10th:*

> **Potter and Wilmer were lost on 10** [*12*] **October. Little Willie Potter. . . . he was very nervous, always chewing on his handkerchief. His father was president of one of the big banks in New York. He was from Harvard. I remember so clearly seeing him go down. Potter was over right on my**

TRIP NUMBER: 20th Date: October 12, 1918
Objective: Villers
Leaders: Lieut. Koepfgen and Lieut. Fiske
Teams Leaving the field: 13 Teams reaching objective: 11
Formation:

(1) Koepfgen/Fiske
(3) Seaver/Stokes (2) MacWhirter/Holt
(5) Baker/Goodell (4) Townes/Johnson
(7) Tucker/Faulk (6) Potter/Wilmer
(9) Murphy/Fulton (8) Derge/Brodeur
(11) Weimer/Turner (10) Woolfolk/Graveline
(13) Sellers/Payne (12) Edwards/Christian [W]
(14) Howard/Hicks [W]

Departure Time: [11:00?] Return Time: [Not specified]
Altitude: 13,000 Bombs Dropped: 22
Enemy Aircraft Seen: 9 Enemy Aircraft Encountered: 7
Type: Fokkers Markings: Black fuselages, red noses and light bodies.
Region: Region of Ancreville Rounds Fired: 1500
Confirmations Requested: Two
Credit for Planes: Lieut. Howard and Lieut. Hicks, 1 plane. Lieut. Edwards, Lieut. Weimer, Lieut. Woolfolk, Lieut. Murphy, Lieut. Christian, Lieut. Turner, Lieut. Fulton, and Sgt. Graveline, 1 plane.

Remarks: Two combats. Burst observed in center of Village, direct hits. As formation approached Ancreville going to Villers at 12:20 seven enemy planes...attacked aggressively from the rear. The fight lasted about fifteen minutes during which time the formation bombed Villers and made a left turn for our lines. One enemy plane was seen to fall in flames and another out of control in the region of Villers. Lieut. Hicks received two wounds in the leg. Lieut. Christian received a tracer bullet in the leg. Both [*men*] were observers. Lieut. Potter and Lieut. Wilmer were forced to land with steam coming from radiator headed into Germany in region of Villers. Two enemy aircrafts [*sic*] followed this plane to the ground. Another formation of twelve chasse was seen south of Ancreville, followed our formation to the lines but did not attack. One Enemy Aircraft is believed to have been brot down in flames by Allied Chasse south of Clery-le-Petit.

> right wing and I was looking over there and the Germans were coming in. I saw this one particular German plane come in and turn — and Potters gas tank burst into flames. The plane turned over and it went down. I did not see him fall out but I knew that he was dead. Poor little fellow! It is traumatic. I had seen others go down before, but this was the most vivid. Harry Wilmer was a Canadian. Why he was in the American Army, I do not know. He had been on the ground with the British Army and had won a Military Medal.[35]

Tuesday Oct 15, 1918

Dear Folks,

. . . I have so many ideas about the peace notes, and the notes are following one another so rapidly that I won't talk about them at all. Last night we got by wire the text of Wilson's answer to Germany's second note.

To get back — in the midst of such a crisis I dont seem to be properly worked up as the situation deserves but go on serenely except when I worry about the mail. It is the same way with the flying, I am not *blasé* about it, I appreciate what is going on and what it means but I don't go wild about like some of the fellows who write long books about everything and who fail I think to get the proper perspective. There can be no doubt however that an air fight is an ultra-thrilling and wonderful sight. On the last raid (Oct 10. I made two before one o'lock. Since then it has rained, the beginning of the rainy season which is long and solid in this part of the country) we had the hardest fight I have been in yet and one of the best yet. I wasn't in the thick of it (being in the front of our formation and it is the rear planes that generally bear the brunt) and there wasn't even a bullet hole anywhere in the plane as there has been on other occassions. The most salient feature of air fighting is the rapidity with which things happen. Before you realize what is going on it is all over. After a little experience you get used to the speed of events and then you are more able to take care of yourself. Of course the whole idea of fighting way up above beautiful cloud banks, at unthought of speed, where most mortals have never and never will be, has a romantic lure that stirs any

adventuring spirit. The way the planes maneuver, diving, spinning, twisting and climbing straight up, adds to the effect. But thru it all I have astonished myself by my matter-of-factness, I really think my pulse doesn't jump 2 beats even when I see a German coming straight at me and the smoke coming from his four machine guns.

. . . Some more mail got here yesterday including letters from Elizabeth and Papa (Sept 20). Papa speaks about reading a certain thing almost daily about bombing planes. It was all about the outfit I am with, bad management which fortunately has since been reformed was responsible. The experience was a great test, in fact any experience in the war acts as a crucible and frequently jolts the men tested out of a lot of their previous ideas. When, as we were before, men are faced not by the possibility of death but the almost certainty of it, they are stripped of all sham and are apt to get down to fundamentals. I have seen a good many quail and under the circumstances don't censure them at all but I am glad I found that I didn't. Consequently I have a confidence in myself I never had before and a feeling of satisfaction and pride to know that I am a member of that great fraterni-

TRIP NUMBER: 21st Date: October 18, 1918
Objective: Bayonville
Leaders: Lieut. Koepfgen and Lieut. Fiske
Teams Leaving the field: 12 Teams reaching objective: 11
Formation:

(1) Sellers/Stokes
(3) Seaver/Holt (2) Townes/Johnson
(5) Tucker/Goodell (4) Brumbaugh/White
(7) Murphy/Fulton (6) Derge/Knox
(9) Baker/Graveline (8) Weimer/Turner
(11) Mandell/Fiske (12) Koepfgen/Willis (10) West/Frank

Departure Time: 14:50 Return Time: 15:50
Altitude: 12,000 Bombs Dropped: 16
Enemy Aircraft Seen: Enemy Aircraft Encountered:
Type: Markings:
Region: Rounds Fired:

Remarks: Burst on northeast part of town. Visibility poor.

ty of men who proved themselves to be men in the war. That has been the greatest benefit I have had yet. My ideas about things have not been changed fundamentally as have those of others who I know here who took a complacent and superficial view of most things. But I have undoubtedly been broadened greatly. Such a thing as a 50% casualty list in 7 successive days is apt to cause a little thinking.

Elizabeth's letter told me something papa assumed I knew and said practically nothing about the trouble with Mrs. Crump this summer. Perhaps a letter of an earlier date will tell me more about it, I hope so. I have recognized for a long time what I think has been the chief cause of unhappiness in the Crump family. . . .

Love to all, Stull.

Friday. Oct 18, 1918.

Dear Stull,

. . . Gee! Stull, I wish you'd hurry up & lick the Germans & come home. But please lick 'em hard while you're there. . . . Mama & Papa are worried for fear you'll do some fool thing about not punishing the Germans etc & get yourself shot so you'd better hurry up & relieve their minds. . . .

Lots & lots of love, Elizabeth.

October 19, 1918.

Dearest Boy,

Oh! don't I wish I could have cheered you up on that blue Friday, Sept. 27th. My heart just ached to comfort you this afternoon when I got your letter — I believe it did help you to whine to me and I wish you always would. It makes me think I am just a little good in the world — . . . .

I have not had time to write to a soul this week — Every available minute has been spent on Influenza work. The number of cases steadily increases and yet people go on as usual in the crowded cars & shopping — etc. We are wearing masks at the Bureau which the girls made for the whole staff — 200 — Gladys helped me last night & the night before — Last night we made a record — completing 8 doz. — nearly 100 you see — I tell you I was proud — We have had five deaths at the Bureau & many serious cases — . . . .

Lots of love — Lois.

Sunday-20th

. . . I have been wondering what made you blue, Stull and hoping it was not a letter. You will probably receive it tho, in fact you must have by this time, Sept. 27th sounds like the time it should have arrived. Forget it, dear till you get home anyway & we'll talk it over then — . . . .

Everyone sends love to you Stull — especially —

"Me."

Monday Oct 21, 1918

Dear Lois,

Since I last wrote I have gotten two letters from you that of Sept 3, . . . and that of Sept 8 in which you enclosed the handkerchief.

. . . Things have been going remarkably quietly so far as our immediate unit is concerned. The rainy season has set in and the valley of the Meuse is the rainiest part of France. As a result I have only made one raid since Oct 10. It was a very tame affair but the last one on the 10th was a thriller. We had the hardest and best fight I have been in yet.

Altho the rain prevents personal excitement we get a lot of the impersonal variety by following the daily losses of the Germans and from the peace news. We are all getting a bit used to the later and are not in the feverish stunned state which we were in at first but it still occupies a good part of our conversation. . . .

I had a chance, which I eargerly grasped, to go on leave about Nov 1. So if nothing goes wrong I expect to have a great time — a couple of days at Paris en route and then a week at Nice and the vicinity. . . .

I have gotten letters the last few days from home telling me of the trouble your mother caused this summer. Also my father said he had a couple of talks with you but what was said he didn't say. I wish I knew more about everything and also that I could talk with you. As it is I don't know what to think — and probably wouldn't write them if I had any thoughts.

As you surmised I certainly do feel years older since my birthday. A war and being in the positions I have ages anyone even those who don't think. And as I claim to think once in a while the process has been just that more rapid. When I think of how young I was when I

came over I often wonder how you will like me and my ideas when I get back.

Love, Stull

N.Y. City, Oct. 22, 1918

My dear Stull,

As you know, I have not written often of late because I was working like hell on my Bar Exams. Took them this week, pretty dubious about my chances of passing them. . . .

Your last letter, telling your father — confessor of your new love, was certainly a page right out of the book of life. Not knowing your former love, or dormant love, of course I can't analyze cause & effect. But I think you hit it right, lonliness, distance, a pretty little radical.

What you said in your letter — whether to take life as a big Brody, with a small chance of great success and a great chance of utter failure, or to lead the settled "try-to-become-President" life — that's the whole problem of life. [*A man named Steve Brodie had "successfully" jumped from the Brooklyn Bridge around this time.*] I'm up against it as well as you. If I follow the law earnestly, and prattle about "demurrers," "*absque hoc's*" "*quare clausum fragit*" [*or frigim*], "burden of proof" as distinguished from "burden of going forth with the evidence," I will probably become a successful lawyer, join the Union League Club, and have a nice family of children.

But like you, my inclination runs to being an educated hobo, living with the ease of a Latin. I would like to camp awhile in the Rockies of Utah, then do a bit of stevedoring in the South Sea Islands, screw and be screwed, and see what tomorrow brings. Then at the age of thirty-eight, settle down.

However, it really can't be called a problem, for one can solve a problem, but Fate takes our hand in this. For example, no matter how much I wanted to live the Epicurean, I have parents who want to see me become President, and a girl who is the quintescense of sweetness and conservatism whom I want to make happy and comfortable. Ergo, to hell with the Rockies and the South Sea Islands; "demurrers" and "leave to file undertaking on appeal" It must be; Fate has so decreed.

I am a bit wary of these intellectual females; they're sparkling company, but I think they make miserable wives. To wit: — Last year at school I was in a predicament much like yours. There was a girl in one of my quiz sections, a black-eyed, thin lipped, tiny ankled Jewess who was a perfect marvel of Oriental beauty. And, God help us, though but eighteen, she had real Karl Marx, was an intimate friend of Hillquist [*Hillquit*], was a dues-paying member of the Socialist party, and though of a wealthy Philadelphia family, had worked in a 10¢ store to get the "point of view." No animal — male, female, feline, bar none, had the zest of that God-damn little Cleopatra. When Dean Woody puts her through the long job of registering in the law school, she says to his Holiness: "Dean Woodruff, why all this red-tape; the Law school seems as backward as the law." Woody, to her delight, exploded and lectured her. Davy Hoy, in his brow beating way says to her: "Left your permit home; just like these young girls with powder on their nose." Says this bewitching imp: "Just like crabbed old men with a chip on their shoulder." Do you wonder I fell? But, to revert to the point of being wary: I went out with the young lady numerous times; I loved her and she though[*t*] Shakespeare wasn't fit to be in the same room with me; she loved me, But, this is what I found. To be in the presence of that little intellectual X-ray was exhausting. I felt as though I was on trial all the while. And all her sparkle, and wit, and observations wasn't worth as much as Freida's squeeze of the arm. Human frailty; human bullshit; 120 pound cave-man stuff, eh? But whether frailty or bull-shit, — yet human. Stull, after you rack your brain all day, you don't want a woman to rack it for you evenings. As between one of these even charming intellectual monsters, and the "one on the left" in Ziegfeld's Follies, — I take the latter for a wife.

Now, having played with that idea, what next on the rapid panorama of life, is to undergo my scintellations?

# # #

. . . The big dope of the hour is, of course, Wilson's peace talk with Germany. I suppose you are anxious to know what the people here thought of it. What the people think is always hard to tell because the people don't think. The bulk of the people took the attitude, "Leave it to Wilson; he's a pretty clever duck, & never got us in Dutch yet." They are simply non-committal and awaiting the next step. But three facts stand out: (1) the bulk of the newspapers and audible opinion was decidedly against the whole business of talking with Germany; (2) The Republican party actively criticised Wilson's war diplomacy for the first time; (3) the diplomatic chasm between the Allies and the U.S. has become noticeable to more people and dangerous.

Noisy opinion is in harmony with what a big lawyer said in this office today: "I always stood for Wilson, and I'm a Democrat, but what in hell is he doing now when we've got the Germans on the hip; now, after they've murdered and plundered Europe, and killed our boys, now is that damn fool going to spoil the whole business?" This is the opinion of most people in America who hold any opinion. It is more easy to be vengeful than to have far-seeing charity. The American temperament responded to the moral plea of downing the Kaiser, and spreading "democracy" (meaning thereby the vote, with control in the hands of the hardshells), and would willingly sacrifice two million lives to over-throw the Kaiser; but the American people have decidedly not responded to Wilson's intellectual pacifistic appeal, the war to end the war. It's a strange thing, — parents willing to have their sons killed for the tom-foolery of patriotism and national boundaries, but not willing to lend an ear to Wilson's new diplomacy, which would save the sons of the future. Sentiment in this country would be overwhelmingly against a surrender of our armaments to a League; or of leaving Alcase-Lorraine to a plebecite. The eternal *quaere*: The reformer wants to save the people, but do the people want to be saved?

The Republicans spoke up dangerously. Senator Lodge, who for some unknown-to-God reason is regarded as a master mind in diplomacy; who would be up-to-date, if you set the clock back to 1890, the extent of whose ultra-radicalism is that he makes speeches against election bribery (generally Democratic elections in the South), who never smelt a labor union, — Lodge, the Republican Senate leader, assailed Wilson's notes the very day they were issued. Roosevelt accused Wilson of "nearly treacherous" diplomacy in not consulting the Allies. He called on the Senate to publicly repudiate Wilson's 14 points of the speech of Feb. 8 (?) last. Another Republican senator whose name has slipped me, introduced a resolution that it was the sentiment of the Senate that Wilson should no longer deal at all with Germany, and gave an interview in which he said that if Wilson violated the resolution, he ought to be "impeached." Taft, who formerly loyally supported Wilson, denounced the notes.

. . . Wilson gave a remarkable speech in N.Y. Sept. 27. If you didn't get it I will summarize it; from the summary you will say that I am unintentionally coloring it, but this is a true summary of it: The war was begun by "statesmen," but it has become a "peoples' war" and must be ended not by statesmen but by the people. The people have become suspicious of the "statesmen" who, they fear, still think in terms of national boundaries and trade. The League of Nations is an indispensible result of the war, — without which the war would have been fought in vain. . . .

That was a startling, epochal utterance; yet nary a chirp out of the present official Allied governments who he subtly indicted, and it went off the Americans like water off a duck; the people didn't know he had said anything big. Not a single paper, except the World & Post noted his challenge to the old order. Like that great letter to New Jersey Democrats, wherein he spoke of the search-light criticism which the American soldiers, now in the trenchs and "liberated for a few brief moments from the economic serfdom under which they formerly labored," would throw on the empty political maxims of the old parties, — only two newspapers in New York, of its twenty or more papers, mentioned that speech, to say nothing of quoting it, the Post and Call.

The press no longer follows public opinion; it makes it; it is owned by the wealthy few; the newspaper has become as much of a business venture run by corporations as has the carpet-tack business, and has no more individuality. Those few see to it that the press preaches the old doctrine: Vote straight, don't go on strike, aim to become president; and take as your motto: "Those of lowly fortunes not only are, but ought to be down and out."

However, Stull, if more young fellows like you continue to put dents in the German line, and fewer like me stay home and peep about it, it is possible that the Wilson-Henderson-Thomas-Italian Socialist alliance will be formed and the great truth become a reality. Intellectually, crabbing about the war aims and yet diligently fighting the Germans are perfectly consistent, for, the defeat of Germany is the absolute prerequisite of the realization of the Wilson ideal. When Wilson licks the Kaiser, he can take on Teddy and Clemenceau [*Georges "the Tiger" Clemenceau, 1841-1929, was a journalist and politician, serving as French premier from 1917-1920. As a negotiator of the Treaty of Versailles, he believed Wilson was too soft on Germany.*] next.

. . . Good-luck, Stull, I certainly wish you good-luck.

Till the next time, Bill.

Post-Script: To show you that I am not altogether an intellectual yellow-belly, just before I got this job, I tried to enlist as clerk in Air Service. Was conditionally accepted, with proviso that Local Board put me in limited

TRIP NUMBER: 23rd Date: October 23, 1918
Objective: Bois-De-La-Folie, Barracks and Woods
Leaders: Lieut. Seaver and Lieut. Stokes
Teams Leaving the field: 10 Teams reaching objective: 8
Formation:

(1) Seaver/Stokes
(3) Mandell/Fiske (2) MacWhirter/Holt
(5) Derge/Knox (4) West/Frank
(7) Tucker/Goodell (6) Brumbaugh/White
(9) Weimer [K]/Turner [K] (8) Baker/Graveline
(10) Sellers/Bunkley [W]

Departure Time: 14:10 Return Time: 16:00
Altitude: 13,000 Bombs Dropped: 16
Enemy Aircraft Seen: 15 Enemy Aircraft Encountered: 15
Type: Fokkers Markings: Black and white on wings and fuselages.
Region: Buzancy Rounds Fired: [Not specified]

Remarks: No bursts observed on account of combat. Bombs dropped on road between Thonorques and Sivery-les-Buzancy. Enemy Aircraft Artillery light and inaccurate. Enemy Aircraft attacked very aggressively some carrying four guns in front. One Allied plane went down in flames and one Enemy Aircraft went down out of control. Confirmation for Lieut. West and Lieut. Frank for one plane. Lieut. Weimer and Lieut. Turner down in flames in region of Bayonville. Lieut. Frank slightly wounded. Capt. Sellers and Lieut. Bunkley landed at Allied Drome with bullet hole in radiator.

service. Am taking up the matter with them now. May see you yet. Tried lately to get in Red Cross; nil doing because my mother and all my grandparents were "made in Germany," and the French gov't won't issue passports to us Boches. God, I'm a cruel Hun.

Brooklyn, N.Y., Oct. 25-1918.

Dear Boy: —

. . . Now, dear boy — I come to the unpleasant thing which happened last Summer — I wish it had not happened — but because it did, and because it was done by Lois's mother — it is right that you should know. — I shall read this part of my letter to papa & to Elizabeth to see if I have been inaccurate or exaggerated in any particular.

. . . Mrs. C. was very peculiar about her visitors — Mrs. Slauson & others visited her & she was at great pains to keep them from meeting or being introduced to me or Mrs. Graham or Elizabeth — I concluded it was because we knew all about the divorce case each [*of the Crumps*] was going to sue for & which was compromised out of court because Mr. C. refused to face the accusations in court that some man in Williamsbridge was Lela's father. . . . All this seems very silly gossip to one who is facing real things — but it is part of the picture — I have not yet found out whether Mrs Crump is simply insane like Mrs. MacKenzie — or intensely jealous of other women & girls or whether she is simply extremely malicious, wickedly trying to injure other girls so she can push her own on.

. . . Up to this time — I had made up my mind that Mrs Crump was an unhappy nagging woman, that she was making Enid and Lela both conceited and unkind, that the Dr., who had been up twice & was very kind, was very much hen-pecked & had a hard time, but it did not seem to concern us very much — I was sorry for Mrs C. & though[*t*] I would keep away from her in future — but none of us showed her in any way — any unpleasant feature — . . . [*Then*] Kendrick came rushing across the lake to tell me that Mrs Crump had called his mother (Mrs B.) [*Mrs. Brown*] in to tell her that on the evening before Ken & Eliz were in bed together under covers & that Enid saw it for herself & told Mrs C. — This was too shocking for me alone — so papa joined the investigation — Mrs B. was told by her younger son Waldo — that this statement was absolutely false — that facts were as [*illegible word*] wrote you above. Papa & Mrs Brown & I went to Mrs. C. — who faced us all & stuck to it that Enid told her this thing — & more over showed the most fiendish — the most malicious joy over the matter — (if it had been true, any good woman would have been sorry and would have come at once to the girl's mother). Then we called every one who had been present. Ken — Eliza. — Elma — Waldo — Enid. They all agreed in the one statement — what I told you first. Mrs C. tried to make Enid help her out saying "Why Enid, I understood you to say so — & so — & so." Enid said — No Mother — I did not say so. Then Mrs C. said she had misunderstood Enid — Mrs. Crump then was forced to withdraw her statement and to apologise — which she did. I find however that Mrs Crump has been carrying on this work for a long time.

. . . When Elizabeth understood what Mrs Crump had done — and how nasty Enid & Lela were — she said "Lois had nothing to do with this" and Paula wrote when she heard of it — that Lois was not like the rest of them. —

Lois certainly had nothing to do with this affair — but Papa thought I had better let her know exactly what had happened, so three or four days later, I asked her to come up to see me — I told her how Eliz & Paula felt about her — & told her that papa & I both thought as much of her as ever — I asked her if she knew what her mother accused E. of — & Lois said "it is true is it not, that they were, on the cot under covers — (this 3 or 4 days after her mother had withdrawn her statement & apologised) — I said — Lois, ask your own sister Enid. — . . . I went over the whole question with Lois — giving her any proofs — and finally asked her what she thought of it all — she said she was glad we had the talk — she could see my point of view. — I told her, her mother was either insane or very wicked — & I thought she must be insane for I could hardly believe that the mother of girls could be so wicked and that is my opinion still. — I dislike extremely to tell you all this — if there had been no friendship between you & Lois — we would have dropped them then and there & not said any thing to you —

If Mrs Crump is insane and it is in the family it is a pretty serious matter — Mr. Magie had a horrible life with his wife & son. — If Mrs C. is wicked — that is pretty bad too. However as it is, you ought to know. —

. . . On reading over what Lois said — I don't want you to think she was ugly. She was not — she was simply judicial in her manner — as if she were saying the best she could for her mother — but no time did she say her mother was wrong. — Dear Boy, God keep you safe.

Your loving Mother

Friday Oct. 25th '18

Dear Stull,

This sure has been a gala week for me. I received ten letters in three days — five of them being from you — Sept. 17, 27, 30 & Oct 4th then a card to show you had some new stationery — Oct. 3rd.

. . . I am enclosing some stuff which may make you laugh. (See "Rules For Influenza")

. . . Stull, your idea about roving around the globe with short stops in various places may be all right but how do you expect to travel? Perhaps you like to heave coal but the only things I could do would be to cook or act as Matron and honestly I'd much rather cook for you and make your bed. If you think I can't overcome inertia just watch me fly around the office some day. I know what you mean, dear, and I often feel the same way, but since I'm not an heiress we will have to be content with one month or so during the year, in which to rove —

. . . I'm following you up on my war map —

Good night honey, Lois.

RULES FOR INFLUENZA

Oh, shun the common drinking cup,
Avoid the kiss and hug,
For in them all there lurks that Hun,
The influenza bug.

Cough not, nor sneeze when in a crowd;
'Tis neither kind nor neat,
Because it scatters germs around.
So try to be discreet.

Lick not the thumb in turn o'er
The papers in your file,
And wear your health mask, though you look
Like time. Forget it. Smile.

Remember doorknobs harbor germs,
So wash before you eat.
Avoid the flying clouds of dust
While walking on the street.

Most anything you do — or don't —
Is apt to cause disease,
So don't do anything you do
Without precautions, please.

Dr. Waters. (Chemistry)

TRIP NUMBER: 24th Date: October 27, 1918
Objective: Brigneney
Leaders: Lieut. Seaver and Lieut. Stokes
Teams Leaving the field: 8 Teams reaching objective: 6
Formation:

(1) Seaver/Stokes
(3) Mandell/Fiske (Camera) (2) MacWhirter/Holt
(5) Derge/Knox (4) West/Frank
(7) Tucker/Goodell (6) Brumbaugh/White
(9) Koepfgen/Willis (8) Baker/Graveline
(10) Murphy/Fulton

Departure Time: 13:40 Return Time: 16:00
Altitude: 12,000 Bombs Dropped: 12
Enemy Aircraft Seen: 1 Enemy Aircraft Encountered:
Type: Biplane Scout Markings: Black and white stripes on fuselage.
Region: Rounds Fired:

Remarks: Burst observed in edge of woods immediately west of Brigneney.

Sunday Oct 27, 1918

Dear Folks,

. . . I learnt to-day that leaves have been called off which puts an end to my pipe dreams for a while at any rate.

Springer will get his because he got wounded yesterday — a clean bullet hole thru his shoulder which will probably mean three weeks or so in the hospital and then as long to recuperate somewhere in the south.

I have a lecture to get off my chest. I note that papa promises me a lecture on Bill Smith, pacificism, soft heartedness etc and that in his letter of Aug. 25 he speaks of the Germans as quitters, cowards, and that the world would be better off when the race is extinct. This is the first time I have known papa to go absolutely wrong on such a big question. Also it is typical of the view aparently according to the press of most of America. To me it is unreasonable, insane and horrible

being false to all the ideals and principles for which we are fighting and for which so many have already died and so many more will die. If that were our war platform I never would have gotten in the army under any circumstances.

America has aparently gone crazy with the exception of a small minority among whom thank goodness, is Wilson. We read of towns in which at a certain hour everybody faces east and says "No," of Daniels [*Josephus Daniels was Secretary of the Navy from 1913-1921*] **saying we must fight on German soil, of Senators saying similar barbaric things. The public seems to be seeing red and seeking a vengance not worth the life of the meanest buck private in the army. The ideals and principles for which we entered the war are lost sight of. Wilson has said over and over again that we are not fighting the German people — yet you want to exterminate them. Even in his latest note he shows that he is willing and anxious to do business with the German people; he says if we do business with the war rulers it must be surrender but we will negotiate with the people.**

The whole problem brought up by the various peace proposals in the last month is essentially simple. We stated that we were fighting for certain principles.

Germany accepted them *en toto*. So far so good. But Wilson answered very properly that we must be sure that their acceptance could be trusted and that we had found we couldn't trust their government that had carried on the war. Then followed several exchanges of notes on that point — the Germans seeking to show they had a new government which was controlled by the people. You know Wilson's last note (so far) in which he said that the changes made while assuring the people's control in future wars did not establish it now. In all this he has been absolutely right and sane. If we can establish in the world the principles and terms we think are just and worth fighting for[,] **why in the name of reason should we continue to fight even with the alluring prospect of fighting on German soil, of raping German women, losing more and more of our best manhood. The war-must-end-on-German-soil only smacks of vengance, hatred, lack of ideals and traitorism to our real cause. How could we hope to establish justice and lasting peace in the world if we acted that way — under a philosophy as anti social as that of the Junkers in their junkiest days.**

As for exterminating them the idea is preposterous and hardly mer-

its an intelligent man's notice. It is such an idea as I would expect from a man who was once cheated by a German grocer and who since has lived, partially demented, a hermit in the woods. How anyone who knows any history or has any reason at all can tolerate the thought for even a moment is beyond me.

As for the boche being quitters and cowards, I have found that idea prevalent where the most hatred is, i.e. among civilians and people who never fought them themselves. I never actually engaged in the fighting on the ground but I was in and around it and know how the fighters themselves think. And in the air I have fought and believe me the German air service is not composed of cowards. I have found the contrary to be the truth.

I feel bitterly on this whole subject because if the mad people should become numerous enough and prevent Wilson from putting through his program of justice (impartial justice dealt to Germany and the U.S., England France etc) it will result (1) all chance of political justice and lasting peace in the world will be lost for the present (2) the most altruistic international act i.e. our entry into the war on Wilson's principles would become transformed into one of hatred and vengance (3) Lives, of young, intelligent red-blooded, life loving men, that were given for one cause would be wasted, the cause unachieved, and perverted to uses to which they would never have given them (4) I could go on and enumerate horrible results but hate to even think of them.

It is lucky, I think, that I am not in the States at present. Hating unreason always, and this particular manifestation of it especially I would probably be ridden on a rail by some narrow-minded, loud-mouthed fools who would consider themselves true patriots and the act a proof of it.

These are essentially the views of all my friends here, not because they are afraid to die and therefore want peace. They are willing to die in the right cause but not otherwise.

Please, as a special favor to me, let Bill Smith read this letter or send him a copy of it. Please.

Love Stull.

October 28, 1918. Holt in the 1980 interview explained the circumstances of the unusual mission on this date, "Trip Number: 25th":

> **After we had these heavy casualties we got orders never to fly over the lines with less than five aircraft. I led one formation where people dropped out and I had to cancel the mission and return home. I was chagrined because it looked like I had trumped it up. We were supposed to meet several other flights but they were not at the appointed rendezvous area. I could not see them anyplace and I was furious.**[36]

Stokes and Seaver continued toward the target area while others in the formation turned back with mechanical trouble. They joined up with the 166th squadron but were hit by antiaircraft fire while 7 miles behind enemy lines. They crashed in a forest just inside Allied territory. Both received the Distinguished Service Cross.[37]

TRIP NUMBER: 25th Date: October 28, 1918
Objective: Damvillers
Leaders: Lieut. MacWhirter and Lieut. Holt
Teams Leaving the field: 10 Teams reaching objective: 1
Formation:

(1) MacWhirter/Holt
(3) Mandell/Fiske (2) Seaver/Stokes
(5) (4) Townes/Johnson
(7) Derge/Knox (6) Brumbaugh/Schultz
(9) Murphy/Fulton (8) Koepfgen/Faulk
(10)
(11) Sellers/Herman

Departure Time: 14:05	Return Time: 15:45
Altitude: 13,500	Bombs Dropped:
Enemy Aircraft Seen:	Enemy Aircraft Encountered:
Type:	Markings:
Region:	Rounds Fired:

Remarks: Ten left field, five reached lines, leader turned back with formation. One team followed 166th Squadron to objective where they dropped 1200 propaganda leaflets. Lieut. Seaver and Lieut. Stokes have not returned from this raid.

20 Aero Squadron, A.P.O. 703
Oct 28, 1918

Dear Lois,

The last I have gotten from you is your letter of Sept 30 written at Washington. . . .

You ask for exact information as to what I am doing out here but you seem to forget the censor. I am not supposed to tell anything at all but will this much. I am doing day bombing, a gentle little art which I hope to be able to describe in detail at some future date. Our object and intense desire is to have as little to do with boche aeroplanes as possible. Unfortunately we are frequently balked of our pacific wishes, in fact we have a fight on about two out of every three raids we make and sometimes oftener. Also we fight in formation except when they shoot everybody down but one and then he fights alone. The number of incidents I could tell you about fellows who have had bullets go thru their clothing, graze their heads, hit their guns and do other queer tricks are innumerable. Springer got wounded yesterday, a bullet through his shoulder — no damage done and a long leave to recuperate on assured.

Speaking of leaves — mine that was to be, isn't. All leaves have been called off temporarily and so all my castles on the blue Mediterranean proved to have been built on foundations of sand.

. . . I have been thinking over new places lately and a trip to Japan to visit . . . certainly seems inviting. What do you think of that? Also they have some lovely countries down in South America. How would you like to pitch your tent up near the source of the Amazon?

In my last letter I told you I received the silk handkerchief safely. It is safely stowed away in my trunk for special days and gala occassions.

. . . I have lips I wish I could use but needs must wait.

Love, Stull

Friday Nov. 1st [*1918*]

Dear Stull,

. . . Your letter of Oct 9th arrived night before last. I shall certainly not complain of the picture enclosed. It is a beauty.

. . . It makes me feel dreadful to think you dont get any mail. I wish I

TRIP NUMBER: 26th Date: October 30, 1918
Objective: Naucourt
Leaders: Lieut. Koepfgen and Lieut. Fiske
Teams Leaving the field: 10 Teams reaching objective: 10
Formation:

(1) Koepfgen/Fiske
(3) MacWhirter/Holt (2) Seaver/Stokes
(5) West/Frank (4) Townes/Johnson
(7) Mandell/ ? (6) Baker/Graveline
(9) Murphy/Fulton (8) Derge/Knox
(10) Sellers/Herman

Departure Time: 6:55 Return Time: 11:45
Altitude: 12,200 Bombs Dropped:
Enemy Aircraft Seen: 7 Enemy Aircraft Encountered:
Type: Biplane Scouts Markings:
Region: Buzancy and Ancreville Rounds Fired:

Remarks: Our machines fired on enemy troops. Three bursts in the northeast part of Naucourt and others on field and road. Two bursts were seen on town of Barricourt. E.A.A. and artillery light and inaccurate on us, but heavy and accurate on formation of five planes probably the 11th Squadron in region of Buzancy and Bayonville.

could do something but I'm afraid I can't except to keep writing so you'll get a lot when they do find you.

. . . I surely would love to go out west. In fact there is no place I'd rather go first — Tell Lt. Springer we will visit him, house party or no. We can run up to see Pope's ranch too. Mr. Pope has not returned yet.

You cannot imagine how glad I was to get those letters telling of your trips into Germany. That's the kind of a letter I have been waiting for for ever so long. I love the cool way in which you state that a shell burst near not doing much harm except for one little piece which put a hole thru a wing — It makes me shiver —

. . . Be good & come home to me soon —

Love — Lois.

TRIP NUMBER: 27th Date: October 30, 1918
Objective: Belleville
Leaders: Lt. Seaver and Lt. Stokes
Teams Leaving the field: 10 Teams reaching objective: 9
Formation:

(1) Koepfgen/Fiske
(3) Seaver/Stokes (2) MacWhirter/Holt
(5) Baker/Goodell (4) Townes/Johnson
(7) Tucker/Faulk (6) Potter/Wilmer
(9) Murphy/Fulton (8) Derge/Brodeur
(11) Weimer/Turner (10) Woolfolk/Graveline
(13) Sellers/Payne (14) Howard/Hicks (12) Edwards/Christian

Departure Time: 14:15 Return Time: 16:20
Altitude: 14,000 Bombs Dropped: 18
Enemy Aircraft Seen: 18 Enemy Aircraft Encountered: 18
Type: Fokkers and Seiman Schukert
Markings: Fokkers, black with white tails. Seiman, black and white stripped [*sic*].
Region: Region of Belleville Rounds Fired:

Confirmations Requested: Lieut. Seaver, Lieut. Derge, Lieut. Koepfgen, Lieut. Stokes, Lieut. Willis, and Lieut. Fiske.

Remarks: Six bursts in the center of the town and two in the woods west of town were observed. The Seimens were very aggressive, coming into the center of our formation while Fokkers attacked to the rear and sides. One Enemy Aircraft seen to go down in flames. Lieut. Mandell and Lieut. Fiske, Lieut. Tucker and Lieut. Faulk, Lieut. Seaver and Lieut. Stokes landed within our lines.

On *November 3, 1918, Holt flew what turned out to be his last mission. He provided many details of it in the 1980 interview:*

> **Our motor began missing a little, not bad, but a little, so that we fell behind our flight. When we crossed the lines the flight was about half a mile higher and half a mile in front**

TRIP NUMBER: 28th Date: October 31, 1918
Objective: Tailly
Leaders: Lieut. Seaver and Lieut. Stokes
Teams Leaving the field: 10 Teams reaching objective: 7
Formation:

(1) Seaver/Stokes
(3) MacWhirter/Holt (2) West/Frank
(5) Baker/Graveline (4) Townes/Johnson
(7) Brumbaugh/White (6) Derge/Knox
(9) Murphy/Fulton (8) Sellers/Herman
(10) Koepfgen/Willis

Departure Time: 7:55 Return Time: 9:30
Altitude: 15,500 Bombs Dropped: 14
Enemy Aircraft Seen: 4 Enemy Aircraft Encountered:
Type: [Not specified] Markings: .
Region: Region of Buzancy Rounds Fired:

Remarks: Bursts observed in center of town, two on edge and two on northwest part of town. Two bombs were dropped on Barricourt but no bursts were observed.

of us. We should have returned for home, but instead we travelled on alone . . . foolishly. I don't know from where or how — but suddenly we were surrounded by five German fighter planes! Needless to say, as soon as we saw the enemy fighters we dropped our bombs, turned around, and headed for home. The Germans did the usual; dive down, zoom up, and shoot. I was standing up and shooting at them and I shot off one of our rudder control wires! Fortunately, the other wire continued to hold up and do the trick.

The attacking German fighters took turns diving and zooming up, never getting closer to us than about 150-200 feet. Although I could see the smoke from their machine guns, and they were putting bullets through the fuselage, the enemy machines did not crowd and they only came one at a time. The motor was still missing and we just made it back

to an advanced American fighter field. We ran into some telephone wires about two feet off the ground and we flopped right over. The fuselage twisted off and was caught between the wings. The rescuers had to cut a hole in the wings to extricate me. I had a lame back, so I was put into an ambulance and taken to a hospital. I think that it was late the next day or night that I returned to the 20th Aero Squadron. I told our boys, "Don't worry, the war's over! The Germans are hanging back and aren't taking any chances." The next day we lost three aircraft![38]

The report of the November 5th mission is included here because it was the last raid made over enemy lines by the 20th Aero Squadron, and it was also the second worst day for the 20th Aero (next to September 26th 2nd

TRIP NUMBER: 29th — Date: November 3, 1918
Objective: Stenay
Leaders: Lieut. Koepfgen and Lieut. Stokes
Teams Leaving the field: 10 — Teams reaching objective: 9
Formation:

(1) Koepfgen/Stokes
(3) Baker/Graveline — (2) West/Frank
(5) Mandell/Fiske — (4) Townes/Johnson
(7) Derge and Knox — (6) Tucker/Faulk
(9) Sellers/Herman — (8) Brumbaugh/White
(10) MacWhirter/Holt

Departure Time: 8:15 — Return Time: 10:25
Altitude: 13,000 — Bombs Dropped: 18
Enemy Aircraft Seen: 1 — Enemy Aircraft Encountered:
Type: Type unknown — Markings:
Region: [*Unspecified*] — Rounds Fired:

Remarks: Enemy Aircraft Artillery and artillery light and accurate at Stenay. Twelve accurate burst[s] in region of Sivry-sur-Meuse coming from direction of Damvillers. Lieut. MacWhirter and Lieut. Holt forced to land at Bethelainville. Machine crashed, no injuries.

The DH-4 in which Holt and MacWhirter flew, after a combat mission in which the plane's control wires had been shot away, the fuselage ripped, and the leading edge of the stabilizer damaged heavily. *Alan D. Toelle, Bellevue, WA*

formation), with three airmen killed and three more captured. Holt and MacWhirter did not fly in the two missions in which the 20th Aero suffered the heaviest casualties. Looking back in 1980, Holt attributed his survival to his location in the formation: **"Often I flew as deputy flight leader [#2 in the formation]. That was the safest place to be; that is why I am here today."**[39]

The weather was bad after November 5th, and the 20th Aero Squadron flew no more combat missions. With the official proclamation of the Armistice on November 11th ending the fighting, the grim statistics could now be compiled and "survivor photographs" taken. Holt was a prominent figure in what was probably the 20th Aero's most famous survivor photo (p. xviii), showing on November 11th the surviving 7 of 28 original flying officers assigned to the 20th. Three additional flying officers of the 20th ultimately returned after the Armistice from a German POW camp where they had been imprisoned. Of the original 24 DH-4 airplanes assigned to the 20th, only one still remained on November 11th. It was over two decades after the Armistice, according to Holt's 1980 interview,

TRIP NUMBER: 32nd Date: November 5, 1918
Objective: Mouzon
Leaders: Lieut. Howard and Lieut. Fiske
Teams Leaving the field: 10 Teams reaching objective: 8
Formation:

(1) Howard/Fiske
(3) Mandell [K]/Fulton [P] (2) West [K]/Frank [K]
(5) Weber/Herman (4) Townes/Johnson
(7) Brumbaugh/White (6) Baker/Graveline
(9) Edwards [P]/Payne [P] (8) Koepfgen/Alexander
(10) Seaver/Stokes

Departure Time: 8:20 Return Time: 10:20
Altitude: 12,500 Bombs Dropped: 16
Enemy Aircraft Seen: 18 Enemy Aircraft Encountered: 18, from 9:20 to 9:45.
Type: Fokkers and Seiman Schukert
Markings: Fokkers, blue with white cocards [?], red noses, others black and white striped. Seimans were blue.
Region: Region of Mouzon to Stenay to Dun-sur-Meuse
Rounds Fired: 3500
Confirmations Requested: Four planes
Credited with Planes: Lieut. Baker, Sgt. Graveline one plane.
Lieut. Townes, Lieut. Johnson one plane.
Lieut. Seaver, Lieut. Stokes one plane.
Lieut. Koepfgen, Corp. Alexander one plane.

Remarks: Four combats. Planes seen to have gone down in flames. Enemy Aircrafts [*sic*] two, Allied one. Planes seen to crash. Enemy Aircraft one. Planes seen to go down out of control. Enemy Aircrafts [sic] one. Bursts were observed on R.R. tracks and yards. One fire was observed in the yards. One explosion was caused in warehouse in the southeast part of town. Enemy Aircraft Artillery and artillery light and inaccurate in region of objective. Three formations of six to eight each, most of them Fokkers coming from the direction of Montmedy, attacked very aggressively some of them having four guns mounted in front. One of our planes was forced down, smoke coming from his engine and the Enemy Aircraft (Fokker) following him down firing continuously causing our plane to burst into flames. Our observers brot Fokker down and saw him crash. Much activity in R.R. yards at Mouzon, Dun-sur-Meuse observed to be on fire. Lieut. Mandell and Lieut. Fulton missing. Lieut. West and Lieut. Frank missing, believed to have gone down in flames. Lieut. Edwards and Lieut. Payne missing. One of our planes was seen at a low altitude near Dun-sur-Meuse and is believed to have landed safely within our lines but later reports show they landed in Germany. Corp. Alexander was slightly wounded in this combat.

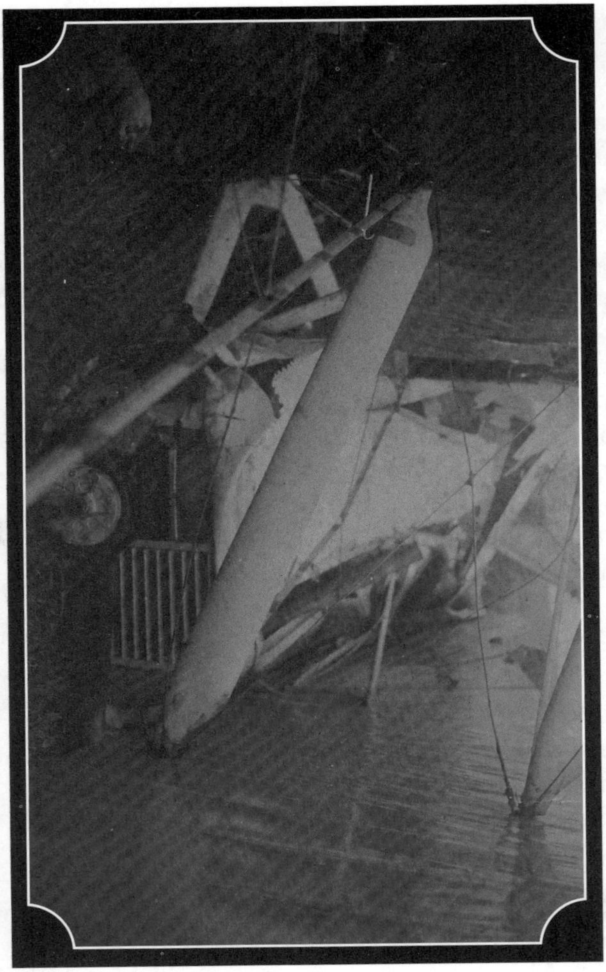

Holt and MacWhirter's DH-4 (#7) after they crashed at Bethelainville, on November 3, 1918, while returning from what turned out to be their final combat mission.
Holt Collection

when he was a participant in World War II, that he learned of one final incident concerning his service in the 20th Aero Squadron:

> **I never knew (or cared) that I had been awarded a Silver Star. In World War II, I ran into Gardner Fiske** [*who, like Holt, had been a 1st Lt. Flying Officer in the 20th*]**. He told me, and when I asked my General how to find out if that were true, he almost fainted at the innocence of professors. I cared about it then** [*in World War II*] **— as the ribbon helped me around H.**[*head*] **Q.**[*quarters*]**. Life is funny.** [40]

20 Aero Squadron, A.P.O. 703
Nov 10, 1918

Dear Folks,

. . . I suppose these are wild, delerious days in America. I see that on a rumor that the armistice was signed yesterday they had great doings in Wall St. and closed the exchange early. Over here, tho more immediately and perhaps more vitally effected, everyone seems to take it more calmly. Of course we have an endless stream of rumors; the Kaiser has been abdicated at least ten times the last one being yesterday; which we devour eagerly but never believe. Then too we hang about headquarters waiting for the scraps of official news. But it is amazing how ordinary and commonplace everything is. I know in reading of other crises in history I always imagined how tense, excited and extraordinary everybody must have been and felt. Sober reflection would tell me that such an assumption wasn't true but it was natural. Now in this greatest of all crises and one in which I am vitally and personally concerned, everything goes on as usual, three meals a day, a stomach ache if you eat too much and a headache if you read too much. I have reached greater emotional heights over a moving picture show.

If the armistice is signed, as I expect it will be, I will cable you so that you wont worry any longer. It will probably take four or six months after that before the actual peace is signed which means, of course, we will be kept here for possible emergencies and it will take a long time after that before we all get home again. I imagine that the aviators may be among the first.

This is my last sheet of writing paper and I had intended to write several of the many letters I owe.

Love to all, Stull

The Same Place
Nov 10, 1918.

Dear Lois,

I have no writing paper and rather than keep waiting for a chance to get some am going to write you a card-letter.

I have received two letters from you, the one of Oct 2 (it was a peach) and of Oct 12. We didn't realize over here (at least I didn't)

what a bad time you were having with the influenza. Dont let me hear of your getting it. Just because I am far away don't think you can run around getting sick and otherwise carrying on.

I had a close shave, it wasn't with a razor, myself about a week ago in an aeroplane smash. According to appearances I should have ended my young and brillant career but the devil looks after his own and I got off with nothing but a bump on the head and a sore back. It took them several minutes to get me out from the wreckage, I was pretty well pinned in.

I suppose you are having many a dance of glee over the war news these days. It does seem too good to believe, every little while I have to pinch myself mentally. After the first dazzling prospect we seem to be taking the developements very calmly here. At least life is as commonplace as ever, three meals a day, a stove that requires a stupendous amount of work to start, a stomach ache if you eat too much and all such ordinary things that somehow seem incongruous in such a crisis in history. But such is life. Probably when Eve gave Adam the apple he looked for worm holes in it and casually took a bite instead of the great mental struggles and deliberations which the crisis deserved.

Did you ever read "Ann Veronica" by Wells? You ought to. I just finished it.

As soon as I get some paper I'll make up for this with a letter.

Love, Stull

Paris, November 15, 1918

Dear Mr. Holt —

Can you really believe that it is all over? I can't. I'm feeling very breathless, quite gasp-y and a bit uncertain. To see Paris ablaze with lights, crowds of people thronging the Boulevardes, to know that these wonderful moonlit nights do not mean raids — its all too much to appreciate all at once. One can't realize all that it means. And it is insane to try to express one's feelings at this time, especially on paper. I wish you were here — there would be so much to talk about, wouldn't there?

I'm sorry you missed your leave and "crashed" at the same time. Were you hurt very much? Perhaps now you can have your Nice [*France*] and roses and blue Mediterranean — and nothing to do but enjoy it. I don't suppose you know anything about when you go home.

I'm to have two weeks of long hoped for canteen work up where the front used to be. I don't know yet just where I shall go. I expect I shall get off in a week or so — but shall hope that you get into Paris before I leave.

Last week I was at G.H.Q. and was muchly thrilled over a few minutes conversation with the C. in C. himself.

I enjoy my work tremendously and shall not think of going home for a long time yet. So, please, remember that I shall always be waiting to hear your tales of woe or otherwise whenever you are ready to talk or write to me. And shall look forward to some quiet supper parties in some out of way corner where we can talk, talk, talk over the coffee (I'll drink yours too, you know, unless you feel you need some to get re-acquainted on) and then some music, when you're able to get into Paris.

You can't imagine how much I've enjoyed Alan Seeger. It was very thoughtful of you.

The picture is great. Many thanks.

Marjorie Mallory

Saturday Nov 16, 1918

Dear, dear Lois,

This is my first letter since the Armistice — since I know that I am going back so I[']ll try and make it a good one even though my mind cant yet realize that the war is over and the strain is past. There was a time when it looked certain that I wouldn't last through (I'll tell you about it when I can) and I had made up my mind to meet that situation and as yet it isn't entirely unmade.

Another reason why this should be a good letter is that I have just gotten two fine ones from you, those of Sept 17 and Oct 19, with all those pictures. When I get home (I don't have to think "if" any more) I am going to make you read me that letter — it should make a good conversation. By the way the reason I was feeling down in the dumps on Sept 27 was not because of any letter I had received (I guess I haven't received it yet) but because the day before eleven men of my squadron had been killed, among them being some very good friends of mine. The mere fact that they were gone wasn't the bad feature, the

sickening part was that they were wasted[—]thrown away by enormous mistakes.

In a couple of days I expect to go on my long expected permission and my two best friends over here, Springer and Simpson, will be with me. Simy goes with me and Springer will meet us in Paris if he can sneak out of the hospital where he is convalescing. All the plans we have made so far are to go to the opera in Paris — what else we will do is for the future to decide.

The big question of the hour, one which everyone is discussing and about which everyone has a new rumor, is who is going to be in the army of occupation and who is going home. If the occupation were only going to last three or four months I would be glad to get the experience and to see the people and places. But my guess is that it will last over a year in which case I would rather be somewhere else. In any case where I go will be decided for me and I will go where I'm sent. But I have heard on good authority that we (our squadron) are to move in the immediate future to the rear which would mean that we would probably go home as soon as any getting there in three or four months. It would take another three or four months to demobilize us out of the army and then I wouldn't know what to do. It would be almost time to take one of those September vacations you spoke about.

It has gotten cold during the last week — a crisp, clear, cold that invites long walks in the afternoon and long talks about our little stoves in the evenings before bedtime. I haven't the apples nor the rest that you spoke about and which does make me homesick but I hope to have them all some day[.] [M]eanwhile I'm waiting. Which, when you think of it, isn't strange[;] what else could I do.

It[']s time for bed. Good night dearest girl xxx.

The next day, Sunday. How are you this morning. I saw a celebration last night made over some French soldiers who had been prisoners and have just gotten back. Just imagine if our soldiers will feel excited to get back to the States, how these men must feel after four years separated from their families as prisoners. Many a person is having the highest emotional time of his or her life. Don Malcom was just telling me of the greatest sight he saw in the celebrations — two old men, one about 75 and the other at least 90, had drunk the bottle of champagne they had saved since 1914 to celebrate victory with, and

were parading down the street one with a drum and the other with a huge flag.

I am enclosing a picture of Don, Springer and myself, taken during the great war. I wish I could thank you enough for the pictures you sent, I've almost worn them out already. Perhaps it wont be long now before I can substitute the real for the pictures. Here's hoping.

Lots of love, Stull.

P.S. Hereafter you had better address mail: — "20 Aero Squadron, Am. E.F." leaving out A.P.O. 703.

Nov 16, 1918

Dear Holt:

Is there now sufficient proof that we may be sure with whom we are dealing? The Mail and Herald have fits of momentary recovery from the shock of big events, order their minds (if such they have) a bit, and, reverting back to true form, suspect a trick. *Mon Dieu* [*my God*]!

Well, it is all over but the shouting, tho there has been much of that, but, peering into the near future with an eye most as keen even as yours, I see the bulk of the shouting degenerating into hollering when the President attempts to put into effect his various stated ideas of peace. The Allies are intoxicated by Germany's collapse; they stand in suspense with one foot on her neck, not knowing under just what conditions they had better let her up. You may be sure that any proposition which has the slightest appearance of a concession or mitigation in favor of the enemy will raise a hell of an uproar. I really fear for some of our internationist principles. Let us hope that Wilson attends the conference himself, for I believe only his presence in person can save us some of the most vital principles vitally involved in the war. More than ever must the peepul have their mind directed, for the great general idea is to try the Kaiser and a few of his cohorts as perpetrators of the war, and then put Germany in such a position that the present allies may live happily ever afterward, leaving untouched the underlying causes of the whole thing. It would be a farce for us to permit such a settlement, and go ahead ourselves to train a great army, and compete with England in naval construction. Daniels says our naval program will continue undiminished, he having announced before it contemplated the greatest navy in the world. England regards her naval supremacy as essential to her safety and to the welfare of a free world, as evidenced by a clipping enclosed. The President has some job ahead of him!

I am having a hell of a time. You recall my idea of the intelligence of the average man. I am now among a bunch of all sorts of officers, and, tho constantly alert, have not been able to find a single one who has the slightest conception of the real meaning of the war. I nearly go wild listening to the line to the effect that the Kaiser is the sole culprit and the remedy is to kill him and distrust all Germans from now till infinity. Not only that, but I have run into a lot of the "U.S.-won-the-war" gang. I know I am going to be unpopular the rest of my life.

Now that the fighting is over one naturally looks back on his own participation with a view to appraising it. I do not hesitate to say that I am well disgusted with what I accomplished, all in all, but I do not attribute the whole fault to myself. I hate to look back upon the amount of time spent and the result in what I did in the end. It is absurd.

It is not that I aspired to medals and distinction of that sort. I am not envious of the birds who are sporting the evidence of various kinds of citations. The great distinction has been bestowed upon me by fate, that of living it out. My great satisfaction will come in being a living and thinking individual during the period of unravelling. As for medals I wouldn't trade what I believe is a fairly good appreciation of the big things in the war, for all the medals extant.

I am still held here as unfit. It is maddening but there is absolutely nothing to do but wait. Surely in the next few days they will let me go. I shall hurry back and put in for a leave. Be sure and wait for me. You can, for the necessity for immediate leave is not what it used to be.

I write as tho there were no possibility of your having been brought down. I feel somehow that you and Don are alright, tho I have worried on that score. I have wired several times, and anxiously await an answer. I should surely feel lost if, when I return, I do not find you to enter upon one tremendous discussion. We may let Baker in at times.

When I go to Paris, I am going to tackle every elderly looking Y.M.C.A. Miss I see and ask her if her name isn't Mahony? or — what is her name anyway, that's alright; You are going home soon, where the other one waits — for her Q.M. Lt.

Yours, Lew W. Springer'
1st Lt ASUSA.

New York, Nov. 17, 1918.

My dear boy: —

. . . We are wondering what you are going to do, now that you have put the Kaiser out of business. We hope that, even if you have the opportunity, you will not become a regular or professional flyer. We hope that you can find some other way of making a living — less dangerous and less attraction. Do you expect to finish your college course? I think your leave of absence expires in 1919 — perhaps Jan. 1. I do not want to see you go back to Cornell, if you are to go to the smoke houses there. Besides, Ma Hennessy would not give you your old job if she saw you eat. Please give us a line on your future policy. We rather assume that you will be permitted — if not required — to remain in Europe for many months. Possibly to instruct in aviation or in the soldiers schools and colleges.

. . . Don't continue in the flying game any longer than you have to. Your anxious father

Byron W. Holt

Monday. Nov. 18th [*1918*]

Dear Stull,

I received your letter of Oct. 21st and hardly know how to answer it. I could sit here and write page after page like those I tore up after writing them at the lake the first part of Sept, but it wouldn't be satisfactory to you or to me so we shall have to wait till you get home when we can talk about our families' troubles —

You have probably heard of the peace celebrations in America. Nearly everyone went quite wild with joy, and the crowds which flocked downtown and paraded up and down Penn. Ave. were the best natured and most orderly I have ever been in. Gladys, one of the girls from B.S. and I went down at about 2:30 p.m. and stayed till 10:30 or so. Potomac Park blazed with bonfires, — one for each state in the Union, — around which were gathered the people from the respective states — It was a wonderful sight. The famous Marine Band kept things lively, the Camp Meigs movie truck gave us pictures fresh from the front of prisoners being captured & searched, tanks travelling over No Man's Land — etc. Great searchlights played on the Monument until an airplane went up, then they followed that around the heavens — What a sight! I have never seen anything which thrilled me more, possibly because it was Peace Night.

. . . Do you hear anything about how, when, & why you will be sent home? Last night's paper said they would not start bringing our gallant heroes home till after January 1st. All camps here are being emptied to receive men from France, the soldiers being mustered out, or discharged and sent back to industry — on request. The military part of my work has almost completely vanished during the past week and it feels sort of funny to be doing common, ordinary things again. . . .

With love, Lois.

Thursday Nov 21, 1918

Dear Lois,

Here I am in a most luxurious room, its best feature is the bathroom where I spend most of my time splashing in the water, in Paris en route to Nice. I expect to leave for Nice tomorrow night. As yet I am alone but I expect Springer and Simpson to blow in to-day. Paris looks different and in some ways I dont like the change. The streets are beginning to be lighted at night; Place de la Concorde is full of German guns big ones, little ones and others, a few tanks, part of a Zeppelin and smashed up aeroplanes; worst of all are the crowds. They spoil everything spoilable.

The day I left the squadron I got your letter of Oct 25 with the quotations from the War Risk's [*life insurance*] **mail. They brought many a laugh but some are truly pathetic. Think of the tradegy** [*tragedy*] **hinted at when that poor woman wrote that if she didn't get her allotment she would be forced to lead an "immortal" life. As as for the lady whose allotment number was four boys and two girls, she is out of luck.**

Don't worry too much about my ideas of roving around. First I only want to rove on holidays and vacations. What I want is to get in a more of less new country like parts of the West because of the people you always find there and because of the life. The life of the average business man is a very poor imitation of how a person should live. But I haven't any particularly wild ideas. I know there are certain facts in life that you have to reconcile yourself to and make compromises with to be happy. One of them is that you cant eat your pudding and have it too. Which is sad but true.

Speaking of eating reminds me that I'm hungry and must make a

raid on the dinning room. I wish you were going to Nice with me — perhaps you will some day.

Give my best to all the Popes and keep the very best for yourself because it is all yours.

So am I, [*Stull*]

The Holt papers contain no further letters from Holt to Lois Crump or to his family until mid-February, 1919, when he was on the way back to the United States. What happened to Holt during that three-month interval is not clear. When interviewed in 1980 he simply states: **"I was detached from the Squadron three or four days after the Armistice. I went to Nice and then took several months to return home."**[41]

Perhaps he spent most of the interval at, or near, some French port, waiting for space to sail home. In any case, his friends and family continued to write him as before.

672 East 219 St.
Nov. 23, 1918.

Dear Stull,

. . . I am very anxious to hear your views on peace, situation in Germany — etc. It seems wonderful to me that the war is really over and the boys will soon be coming home again. . . .

The boys in England are being sent back, but what of the boys in France? Will they really have to stay over till after the first of the year? . . .

Here's to your speedy return.

Au revoir, Lois.

Nov. 24, 1918.

Dearest Stull, —

Well, we have seen Bill Smith and we are his. I was just wondering whether I hadn't better write and ask you for his address, when the bell rang. I found a smiling young man who said his name was Smith. I said "Oh you're Stull's Bill Smith" and dragged him in.

We all liked him very much and, for some occult reason, felt very sorry for him. I don't know whether the boy is lonely or whether he was merely keeping himself away from his girl by staying here too late. At any rate, we, mama, Elizabeth, and I, immediately longed to mother him and sister him and give him something to eat. Some men always inspire women with those thoughts.

He is coming here for Thanksgiving dinner. I am very glad, for, with Elizabeth in Naugatuck, and you, the Lord only knows where, we would be a very small family. He gives our Thanksgiving an object. He was going from here to Mt. Vernon and he intimated that "she" lives there. What the dickens is she doing, letting him be lonesome at Thanksgiving time! Also he said that you took your love affairs sanely or with your head or some such thing. What he means you'll have to guess.

. . . Poor Bill Smith has courage to come out here again. For he was sat upon most strenuously by both mama and papa on the question of the treatment to be accorded Germany. Papa sat on him most politely and he seemed to enjoy it, for he stuck to his points every time. He looks as if he needed a little fun and a home where he could go into the kitchen and watch dinner cooking while he talked. Really the effect he made is weird, and I can't imagine why. He probably is perfectly happy and doesn't know what it is to be homesick. But he gets all the credit for it.

. . . Best love and kisses. Be a good boy.

Your loving sister, Paula.

Xiory Circourt, Meurthe-et-Moselle
Nov. 24, 1918 —

Dear Stull,

As you are doubtless aware, I wasn't able to get to Orly, or any other port. Orders came through the 19th for us to go to Mainz, and here we are at the first stop. I never did have any luck on vacations.

Denneson sent me on ahead to take charge of the moving, of which I made a wonderful mess, but that is gone by and things are settled down again — . . . .

Old Cockalorum, I'm sorry as I can be that this Paris stuff side slipped. It looks as if it is off for good. If you beat me home, and I hope you will, we'll attempt to redress in N.Y., at your expense —

Best to Springer, Simmie —

Wednesday, Nov. 24th [*1918*]

Dear Stull,

We had a pleasant surprise today — in the form of a half-holiday. . . .

-- -- -- -- -- -- --

<u>Thanksgiving</u>.

Today is the rainiest, dreariest, dullest, sweetest day we have seen in many a year. When I think of all the thousand things I have to be thankful for, I wonder if I deserve them all.

. . . Your letter of Oct 28 has ended its journey safely. What ever did I say to make you think I was working too hard? I wouldn't really enjoy my work if I weren't busy and if I didn't get tired sometimes.

. . . Well, our President leaves us next week to seek foreign lands. They are really not foreign any longer tho are they? When our boys have been there so long and have fought side by side with the people of those lands, have helped care for the motherless children of those lands and thus won the love and admiration of the world, they somehow seem nearer to us. I hope Congress will cease to argue it's silly old head off about the propriety of Wilson's visit abroad and apply itself to the task of backing him up and of watching the country entrusted to its care.

. . . I am sorry to hear Springer was wounded, but glad it wasn't very serious. Since he is from the West he is probably strong physically and will be well in no time. What do you think I'm most thankful for?

Best love, Lois

New York, Nov. 27, 1918.

My dear Stull and Mac.,

. . . The armistice was signed Nov. 4th [*with Austria*]. But on the preceeding Thursday, Oct. 31st., the United Press came out with great headlines, — "The War Over; Armistice Signed." It seems that the president of the United Press had gone to Europe personally to get a scoop on the Associated Press; in his eagerness he had cabled the above message four days ahead of time, hoping to have it confirmed by the rapid movement of events; he took a chance and lost. But the whole country believed it.

. . . The celebration here was one of the strangest experiences in mob psychology that I ever witnessed or heard about. First came the headlines. Then came the shrieks of the whistles of the harbor boats and the "L" trains; then the tolling of the bells. The news went like wildfire. I was up in City Hall Park at the time. Then came one of the queerest, wierdest most spontaneous methods of celebrating that one ever dreamed of. Somebody threw a roll of ticker tape out of a window of the Woolworth Bldg., then every body started throwing paper out of the windows, — ticker tape, carbo copies, ripped up newspapers, telegraph pads, — every bit of paper in the offices, except bank-books, was torn into bits and thrown out the windows. You will think I am trying to write like a newspaper reporter when I describe this scene, but the fact is that I never saw a snow storm so thick as was that paper storm; you simply couldn't see the tops of the buildings. Walking through the streets was like wading through piles of dead leaves in the Autumn. They say it cost the City about $15000 to clean up that storm in down town New York. . . . But the following Monday came the true news announced by the State Dep't, and then the celebration began all over again; this time redoubled.

. . . The elections came and went. The Republicans won the Senate by about two and the House by about ten. Like all our elections it pans out to have proved nothing. There really was an issue, Wilsons internationalism against Roosevelt and Lodges puny nationalism. But the people didn't know it; they felt the war was over and so they could vote their party ticket, which they did, and there being more Republicans than Democrats, the Republicans won. To show how little the election means, Taft, who bitterly assailed Wilson, is now the old time militant for the League to Enforce Peace. And a group of mid-western Republican Senators have combined to keep Penrose from becoming Chairman of the Committee on Finance, and Lodge from the Foreign Affairs Committe.

The labor trouble has started here. The dockers here who were working at the embarkation wharves have gone on strike because the Gov't has cut out the Sunday and overtime work on their jobs, — cutting down their pay. So have the carpenters working on the government warehouses. Gompers made a speech yesterday in which he said that Labor would fight to the last gasp before it would give up the high wages it had earned during the war. We are going to see some great times; I have been thinking of giving up cigarettes so as to be sure of living through them; our politics which have in the past been a mere matter of tweedle-dee and tweedle-dum are now going to be economic in their nature. Wall Street knows this, you see I am right down here in the district and I hear all the talk: "How far is this damn Bolshevikism going to spread?", "How much do these damn working men want?", "We just threw over the tyranny of autocracy and now we've got to throw over the tyranny of Labor." Apparently an effort is going to be made to police Russia with American soldiers and kill radicalism in Russia.

. . . Things go well with me. I passed the Bar Exams. and will be admitted in January. . . .

When you get to N.Y., drop over to 46 Cedar St., on your way home.

Good luck, Bill

N.Y. City, Nov. 29, 1918.

My dear Stull,

Your last was about Oct. 16; my last to you was about Nov. 21st.

. . .Your folks are quite typical on the war Stull, just like my folks. Going over their heads in Liberty bonds, giving up proposed expenditures for the Red Cross, Hooverizing with delight, religiously in the cause, — yet on the wrong track, thinking that there is something inherently fiendish in the Teutonic corpuscle, believing that the German Revolution is a fake, and urging punishment, But you should soft-peddle criticizing your folks, for, any family that has an only son in it is no judge of it. Your father is certainly a calm, brainy man, — but if you could see how nervous he was for your safety when I went over to see him last summer, you would understand his view; he is human.

I enclose a article on the "Reds" riot in Madison Square Garden; it was duplicated by practically every other paper in N.Y., — except the "Call." Read the article before you finish this paragraph. The article paints a picture resembling a Bolshevik invasion; mobs, shrieks, anarchy, broken heads, etc., etc., etc. If all this were true, it would be disgraceful enough for the World to speak so approvingly of the soldier raid on the Socialist meeting. A soldier semi-lynching of Socialists sounds of the Vaterland about 1913, good old Berlin But here are the N.Y. papers approving it in N.Y.

But the significant fact of this article is that it is practically false in toto, — there was no riot!! I was there; hence I ought to know fairly well whether I was "rioted' or not. The whole article is simply one step in the lying scheme to queer Radicalism, — whether in Russia or in America. Here is what happened at the meeting. 13000 people, mostly Socialist. Entirely tame speeches, no Emma Goldie [*Emma Goldman (1869-1940) was an anarchist Russian-American author who opposed the draft*] stuff, a jesting with the police who dotted the Hall every where to see that no red flags were displayed, a resolution of Congratulation and God-speed to the new Republic. Really exceedingly tame, — a few references to the war of the classes, but no suggestion that John D. be disfranchised. Then a speaker named Pankin, a Municipal Court Judge arose. Apparently he is the Socialists' darling because they cheered him three minutes, — the cheers of those hero-worships were inspiring. The first words he uttered (and he has a wonderful, profoundly stirring voice, such as I imagine Beecher must have had, or Webster) were: "The newspapers who are so bitterly railling at and bewailing the German Revolution should remember that our own country was born of a revolution." At this oratorical turn, the audience simply went wild; cheering, shrieking, stomping, a terrific din. Two young girls, maybe paper box "hands" or Porosknit underwear "hands" unfurled a red banner from a balcony. Now, Hizoner The Mayor, Hylan, has forbidden by proclamation the display of a red flag in public. The Bulls started for the girls, snatched the banner, arrested them, and marched them from the Hall. The audience parted to make an aisle for the police could get the girls out, not a person raised a finger, 12,000 simply stood still and "boo"-ed. I don't know if you ever heard 12,000 people "boo" in a resounding hall, with all their heart in it, believing that they were oppressed martyrs, but believe it, it is a spectacle never to be forgotten. In their hearts was the same feeling of the thousands in St. Petersburg in 1905, who marched unarmed to the castle gates behind their monk, Gregory, to be butchered by machine guns.[42] That "boo" had the devil in it. John D. wouldn't sleep for a month if he heard it. At that minute I was nearer a Socialist than I have ever been, though common sense tells me that the scheme won't work. The "boo" thundered on for four or five minutes. The police were beginning to pet their clubs, — when the band started some rag-time, human nature got working, everybody began to laugh, and the meeting procluded. I went outside and saw about forty drunken sailors and soldiers, quietly arguing with the cops and the cops quietly arguing with the drunks. And thus is all there was to the great Riot of the Reds, the military attack *en masse* on the pro-Germans.

# #

. . . Your folks made me very much to home, treated me like a king. Your Dad single-taxed me a bit, and I confessed to him that I was an awful ameteur at economics, but assured him that I made up for it in my profundity of English History (shades of Cheyney [*Edward P. Cheyney, 1861-1947, historian, wrote many books concerning the history of England*] lie quiet). Methinks you have boosted me to your pater as a young Ricardo [*David Ricardo (1772-1823) British economist*], because he was surprised that I wasn't up on the single-tax. I laid at rest the family fears that you smoked too much at college; kept my fingers crossed and disclosed no secrets.

The best from, Bill.

Sunday, Dec. 1st. [*1918*]

Dear Stull,

. . .I received your letter of Nov. 10 last night. Stull, will you will you, will you please be careful. You take great care not to mention why it was that they had to pull you from a mass of splinters which was once an airplane, which leads me to believe the smash might have been due to carelessness. Now that the war is over I'll have to begin to worry I suppose. It isn't the devil who looks after his own either. However, even tho I sound fussy, I'm so thankful that you wrote about it.

What would you think if, when you got home, you found me a toolmaker? Such might have been the case if I had heard Secretary [*of Commerce*] Redfield speak before I came down here. He predicts a much wider field for women in the future with which we all agree — and considers women much better fitted to do many of the things men are now doing and things which are or seem peculiar to them because men have always done them. We shook hands with our Secretary after his talk.

. . . I wonder if your mail is travellling after you O.K. or are you still in the same place. Somehow I can't keep myself from thinking you are following the boche somewhere in Germany —

Best love & wishes for a Merry Christmas & Happy New Year — because you know you'll be home pretty soon.

Lois.

New York, Dec. 2, 1918.

Dear Stull,

. . .You are due for a strange letter from home. Your father is about to lecture you on your amicable view toward the new Germany. Your parents do not take the view that we should march over Germany and humiliate and oppress her to satisfy any petty feelings of vengeance or vanity, but for Germany's own good; that while Germany had genuinely overthrown the crowned crowd, she has not confessed the downright horror of her causing the war or her acts during it. And believe me, Stull, there is something to be said for that view. . . So you are in for a letter on our views. Suffice it to say . . . that your folks, having put all their eggs in one basket, are apt to be overzealous. I think your recent letter, likening [*their view*] to that of a small mind who had been cheated by a German grocer was a bit strong and hurt your parents.

Woody Wilson gave his parting address today, his longest speech without saying anything, — which was probably his reason for making it. A real end-of-the-war speech would have made anything that he could say at Versailles a bit of ante-climax.

The president has of late had a great drop in popularity. And this is not solely the reaction of the war's-end, the feeling that we were not free to differ and criticise. That this is a real drop in popularity, witness, four old rank-line Democrats in this office knocking him with a will, and others tell me the same. The feeling is that while one man government was necessary during the war, now he should take the people a bit more into confidence; that it should not be his peace but America's peace. Here he is, trotting off to Europe, with a rubber-stamp delegation, about to do tremendous things, without so much as a chat with anyone outside his Cabinet, that much in-bred group. The president is now suffering from that which is a large part of his strength, a head-strong, exclusive egoism. Even "Old Faithful" David Lawrence goes back on him in the Post. Also, the president is up to his old tricks in his not reading well the public prejudices, — for example, at the very, very same time that he announces his going to Europe at the head of the peace delegation, he announces (1) that Creel is to be head of the news-service, and (2) that the Government had taken over the cable and telegraph service. You can see what a chance this gave the Republicans — "The Country Gagged — Secret Diplomacy" — and they word it effectively — of course it is all nonsense. We learn today that it was by Wilson's pressure that the British and French censorship had been completely let up during the Conference. But Wilson should have felt the pulse more keenly, and have said this earlier. Also Congress — just as after the Civil War — is beginning to assert itself; most plaintively begged a representative at the Peace Conference and didn't get it. He could as well have appointed a man like Borah, a Republican, a Liberal, and the best man in the Senate on the League of Nations. That delegation — Lansing, House, Bliss, and one White, whoever he is, is a pretty poor showing, — all except House. We have bigger timber he could have used, men like Brandeis or Walter Lippman.

Of course, for myself, I just as soon see Wilson go alone. He's on the right track. But he has committed a lot of political blunders that are hurting him. Political strength, which he now needs as a backing at the Conference, is not what his acts are, but what the populace thinks they are. . . .

Good luck, Bill.

Friday the 13th of Dec., [*1918*]

Dear Stull,

I do hope you have had the rumor that your squad. was to move to the rear confirmed. I am simply wild to get acquainted with you once again. I hope they have sense enough to send you to Camp Meade. Can't you whisper in the Col's ear or something?

Your letter of Nov. 21st arrove followed by that of the 16th. So I knew you were in Paris waiting for the rest of the trio before you told me you were going. Ain't it queer?

. . . Did you get to Brest in time to welcome your President when he landed? It would be just your luck to have been there, tho I don't really suppose you were.

I have been trying and trying to imagine how, when, where & why I'll see you first after you get back. It's lots of fun to invent ways of meeting etc. What would you do if I put out my hand, gave you a nod & said "How do you do"? Shake my hand & say "Howdy yourself" I suppose. . . .

Stull, what do you mean by a time when it looked certain you wouldn't last thru — and, as yet it isn't entirely unmade — ? Do you mean your accident was more serious than you represented it? Or did something else happen about which you never told me? I suppose you wont tell me about it till you get home so I can only hope you aren't and wont suffer from or with "it" —

. . . Best love X Lois — . . .

Tuesday Dec. 17th [*1918*]

Dearest Boy,

Life's a funny proposition after all —

I love you very much tonight — because I'm happy I guess. . . .

I started home, thru the woods as usual. It was long after dark but the moon was gorgeous — just wonderful, — (It is yet) and you seemed to be so near that I could almost feel your arm on mine — Do you wonder now why I'm happy?

. . . *Bon soir* — XXX Lois.

115 B'way, N.Y.
Dec. 20, 1918.

My dear boy: —

. . .You are certainly seeing things over there. You are entitled to see and forget after all that you have been thru in the last two years. We are wondering to what extent your nerves have been shaken by your experience. Also as to your mental attitude toward the ordinary affairs of life. I doubt if you yourself can as yet tell what the resultant will be.

. . . If you intend to return to Cornell, please write or cable promptly. I think your leave of absence ends Dec. 31, Perhaps you will study and teach in French or English universities. I suppose you will visit England before you return.

Hoping that you will have a happy holiday season,

Your loving father, Byron W. Holt

Sunday Dec. 29th [*1918*]

Dear Stull,

. . .The holidays are nearly over and it doesn't seem as tho they have been here. This was the queerest Christmas I have ever experienced and I can't say I want it repeated.

. . . We have been watching for the announcement of the sailing of 20th Aero Squad. but have seen no notice yet. . . .

Best love for the New Year. I hope it wont be very old before you get back home —

Love, Lois.

Carte Postale

[*New York postmark date is February 20, 1919*]

Expect to sail within a week. Have been expecting to sail for two months. Am at Bordeaux. Have been here for three weeks. Save me a date sometime in March. Also have the bands tuned up and the flags ready

Stull

Union Postale Universelle

Gibraltar

[*Postmark not clear; may be "13 Feb 19"*]

Sailed from Marsailles. Stopt here for coal and I am spending the day "doing" Gibraltar. It is one of the most unique and interesting places I have been in yet. The trip down the Spanish coast to here was wonderful.

Stull

Here, Now

[*March 12, 1919*], **Brooklyn, NY**

Dear Lois

Its 12:15 and everyone has gone to bed except me and I'm going soon.

. . . I told the folks here (just the family) that when you come up we were going to invest in a diamond. It was no great surprise to them, I guess, because they must have seen for a long time how I felt. Any sentiment that will stand the test of the subway trip from here to the Bronx must be the real thing. So they probably felt sure of me and, being my parents, couldn't conceive of your refusing. Parents are funny things. No matter how rational and well balanced they are, their judgment of their children is not a real judgment but an emotion. What a world it would be if everyone was as good as their folks thought them. There would be no reason for going to Heaven. I wonder how rational we will be!

I am going up to see your folks and I don't know whether you want to wait till you come up here before letting them know. In any case it

AIR SERVICE DEPOT

Garden City, L.I.N.Y.

March 7th. 1919

SPECIAL ORDERS)

No. 63)

Extract

** ** ** **

30 In compliance with authority from the Director of Military Aeronautics, by direction of the President ... the following officers are honorably discharged from the service of the United States....

** ** ** **

Extract

William Stull Holt ______ ______ 1st. Lt., A.S.A.

** ** ** **

By order of Liet. Colonel Gregg:

will probably not be such a surprise. Let me know immediately (that's put in to get a letter) what you prefer.

Mama wanted you to stay here for a couple of days but I told her you probably wouldn't take a long holiday. They all sent their love etc. but I don't think there is even room enough in one letter for the amount I want to send.

Good night, you dear. x
Stull

P.S. If this is a dull letter blame it on the late hour and my weariness. . . .

P.S. 2 I was going to add another postscript but I decided to save it until we have been married several years. What a woman you are!

P.S. 3 The next day. Mama and Paula want to enclose a note

E. 7 St. Brooklyn
March 13, 1919

Dear Lois: —

The first time you can get any chance to come north, I hope you will come to us, we all want you.

Yours affectionately, E.G. Holt

Dear Lois —

We will expect you early in the morning and we expect to keep you till you take the train for D.C.

It's about three years since I've seen you anyway. Please come, honey, and we'll have a wild time. I'll promise not to talk a word after 2:30 a.m.

Lovingly, Paula

Sunday, Mar. 16th [*1919*]

Dear Stull,

. . . Now for the question which demands immediate reply. — My family has been "notified" that you are the one and only man so you may say what you like and as much as you like when you go up to Wms Bdge.

It was very kind of your Mother to ask me to stay with you folks but much as I would like to accept the invitation I think I had better not this time, because I shall have only four or five days and since I haven't been home since Thanksgiving — I had better stay there. However, one day will be saved for Brooklyn. . . .

The more I think about it the gladder I am that it took me so long to decide, because I am absolutely sure now that I love you really truly, & rightly. It seems as tho I woke up all of a sudden last Monday night. Perhaps if I had not thought it all out — every little detail — and then decided that I really didn't know what I thought and it was better not to think, I would not have been so sure.

Intermission of hours

I am sure getting good practice these days. The only thing I want to know how to do will be the cooking. Perhaps Mother will allow me to experiment on the family for a while before I have to subject my own family (meaning you) to the trials of experimentation. I ought to be able do lots in two years. What an age it will be! But it is better than getting married now and then waiting ages for our own house don't you think so?

. . . Please remember me to everybody. Hope I'll see you in a few weeks — dearest boy.

Love, Lois

[*No date indicated, but probably June, 1919*]

The following letter is a pencil draft which bears numerous marks of correction. It is in Stull Holt's unmistakable handwriting and gives evidence of how hard it was for him to make this letter say what was in his heart and mind. We cannot know if this was the exact text which Marjorie Mallory received, but her brief, kind reply from Paris, dated July 6, 1919, leaves little doubt that she had received a letter from Holt containing thoughts and feelings similar to those which fill this sad, tormented outpouring.

Dear Marjorie:

This will be a surprise for you. You have probably already forgotten me except as one of the long procession that comes on the stage of your life, speaks a few lines and quickly passes on. I didn't say all my part so I am sneaking back on the stage to complete it.

First I must explain why I never even tried to find you and give you the promised airplane ride. When I got back from my leave on Dec. 3 I found orders there relieving me from duty and sending me back to this country. It rained all that day and all the next, making flying impossible so your trip faded into the land of might-have-been and I started for home.

Did you notice at the beginning of this letter that you are "Miss Mallory" no longer. It means that after a safe amount of time and space I have let down the bars which I kept up with such difficulty. I am sure that you must have felt that I loved you but I am surer that you had no idea of the great intensity of it. When I say "loved" I do not use the word loosely as is commonly done. All my life I have kept for it a separate and almost sacred meaning so that till this letter I had said it to only one other.

How could it have been otherwise. For over a year and a half I was starved, literally starved, for lack of contact with any girl of my own

kind, one who thought in the same terms I did, who saw beauty where I saw it, who felt and understood. — In this condition and brought by contact with the war down to fundamentals, I could have fallen in love with an average girl of my kind. When i did meet one so extraordinary as you are (this is no idle compliment. If I didn't believe it and trust to your ability to understand, do you think I would write this letter?) I straightaway fell down and worshiped.

But, as you know, I did all my worshiping from a distance, and altho my head was in the clouds I kept my feet on the ground. It wasn't always easy to do — there were several evenings in the Bois when I think I could have kissed you as I was burning to do. But if I had let myself go even ever so slightly I might have lost control of myself and spoilt everything. Because I realized that you had not been starved, and that there was no reason for you to have anything more than a benevolent and passing interest in me.

Besides it would hardly have been fair to the girl back here to whom I was engaged and with whom I was very much in love (I still am both). This may seem contradictory at first but it is a fact that you can love two people at once. It may not be advisable, it may not be proper but it is a fact.

So I worshiped at a distance and it was better so. I have two friends here (real men, both of them, Alan-Seeger-like men) to whom I have told much about "my girl in Paris," about the beautiful moments I had with her, and the fierce exultation I felt in loving her. And they always upbraid me for not writing [*to continue*] **the contact. But that cannot be. They would have me try to evade one of the laws of life, like the boy who cried for the moon. There are certain big laws or facts; such as death, birth, the laws of human limitation, the fact that you can't eat your pudding and have it too that most persons try to persuade themselves are not true. But an honestly intelligent person recognizes them as fact, reconciles himself to them and builds his happiness on a solid foundation. One such law is that human beings are much like the comb and the brush — they meet only to part. Friendships, close and intimate, are formed only to be ruthlessly torn asunder by some caprice of Fate. One of my closest friends moved out to Japan and we have gradually lost contact and drifted apart; another was killed in the war. I still have pangs when I think of them, but when I remember the law, the pangs die and leave only the pleasant memo-**

ries. So too with you, Marjorie. The weak regrets for what might have been are gone and there remains only the memory of those joyous moments we plucked from oblivion. "Out of the endless ore of deep desire we coined the utmost gold of passionate memory." You never guessed did you that you meant so much to

Stull Holt

Paris, July 6, 1919

My dear, I understand. It is a perfect memory for me, too — one which nothing can alter or destroy. It is ours forever.

Marjorie

Stull Holt and Lois Crump were married in February 1921. This photo was probably taken in March 1919, shortly after Holt arrived back in the United States. *Holt Collection*

Epilogue

STULL HOLT returned to Cornell University and graduated with the A.B. degree in 1920. On February 12, 1921, he and Lois Crump were married and lived in Washington, D.C. and Baltimore for most of the next two decades. Two daughters were born to them, Jocelyn and Enid. Holt received the Ph.D. degree from Johns Hopkins University in 1926, and then in 1930 became a member of the Johns Hopkins faculty in the Department of History.

He maintained contact with several of his friends who have appeared in these pages. William Dudley Smith practiced law after the war; his life had increasingly tragic overtones, marked at times by alcoholism, and he died in 1956.

Lew W. Springer resumed flying in the 1920's in his own plane, and died in 1928 when his plane crashed in Mexico. Lesley Byrd Simpson had many similarities of post-war careers with Holt. Both became university professors, participated in the Second World War, and remained in touch after World War II, when Simpson was on the faculty of the University of California at Berkeley and Holt was on the faculty of the University of Washington at Seattle.

Holt's move from Johns Hopkins University to the University of Washington came in 1940, when he accepted the position of Chair of the Department of History there. When World War II broke out, he volunteered for service and from 1942 to 1945 he was Commanding Officer (Lieutenant-Colonel) of the P.W. and X. Detachment of Military Intelligence Service in England. After the Second World War, he returned to the University of Washington and served on the faculty until his retirement in 1967.

Lois Crump Holt died in 1975, and shortly after that Holt was diagnosed with cancer. Suffering from the cancer, Holt took his own life in 1981, a few days after his 85th birthday. It was characteristic of Stull Holt that he told his family of his plans to take his life, and that he wrote his own obituary; it serves as the last entry in this volume:

> **W. Stull Holt died on October 13, 1981, from an overdose of sleeping pills taken to avoid the "slow and now miserable" process of death from the cancer discovered some four years ago.**
>
> **He was born in New York City on October 2, 1896, was educated in the public schools, received an A.B. from Cornell in 1920, an M.A. from George Washington University in 1923 while employed by what became a part of the Brookings Institution, and the Ph.D. degree from Johns Hopkins in 1926.**
>
> **After several years on the George Washington University faculty he was appointed to the Johns Hopkins faculty in 1930 where he served until 1940 when he became chairman of the department in the University of Washington. Before his retirement in 1967 he was active in university affairs, serving on many important committees and as an elected member of the Faculty Senate and of its Executive Committee. He was also active in various scholarly organizations, especially the American Historical Association, serving on**

committees as an elected member of its Council. In 1963-1964 he was appointed editor of the *American Historical Review* and executive secretary of the Association, the last person to hold those two positions of leadership simultaneously.

Professor Holt's main scholarly interests centered on American foreign relations and on American historiography. His best known book, first published in 1933, was *Treaties Defeated by the Senate*. It was widely regarded as the standard study for several generations. When he left Hopkins in 1940 some of his students presented him with a *Festschrift* entitled *Historiography and Urbanization.* When he retired in 1967 a new generation of his students sponsored the publication of some of his writings as *Historical Scholarship in the United States and Other Essays.* In 1974 he was coauthor of a book entitled *An American Faculty.*

Holt served in both World Wars. In 1917 he entered the French service, during which he was awarded a Croix de Guerre for action on the ground at Verdun. Later he received a pilot's license at a French Air Force school, entered the American army, served at the front in a Day Bombing Squadron, and received an American Silver Star. In World War II he again volunteered and served from June 1942 until after V.E. Day in May 1945 as commanding officer of an important intelligence unit in Europe. This work was closely integrated with a comparable British unit. He was awarded an O.B.E. by the British government as well as another American medal.

At home, Professor Holt was active in local politics, serving many years as precinct committeeman, as a delegate to county and state conventions, as chairman of a legislative district, as a Hubert Humphrey delegate to the 1968 convention in Chicago, and as a Jackson delegate to the National Convention in Miami in 1972. On both occasions, he was a member of the National Platform Committee.

Professor Holt always maintained that the best reward in his academic life was his association and later friendship with students, especially advanced graduate students.

End Notes

Prepared by Nancy Vesta

PART ONE

1. In April 1916, American Norman Prince, whose interest in aviation and love of a family vacation home in France, was inspired to create Escadrille Americaine. The volunteer flying corp of seven included two former members of the American Ambulance Field Service. Pressure from the neutral United States government encouraged the unit to change its name to "Lafayette Escadrille." Perhaps their most famous pilot was the French-born American ace Raoul Lufberry. Meirion Harries and Susie Harries, *The Last Days of Innocence: America at War, 1917–1918* (New York: Random House, 1997), 46–48; Hudson, James J., *Hostile Skies* (Syracuse, NY: Syracuse University Press, 1968), 233–234.
2. In April 1917, Robert Nivelle replaced Marshal Joseph Joffre as commander of the French, and then the Allied forces, at the western front. Using tactics successful at Verdun the previous year, Nivelle initiated an attack on the Hindenburg (Siegfried) line between Reims and Soissons. The Germans expected the attack. After only 5 days and approximately 600 yards, 130,000 Frenchmen were lost. Anthony Livesey, *The Historical Atlas of World War I* (New York: Henry Holt and Company, Inc, 1994), 122–123.

3. French desertions were rampant after Nivelle's offensive in April 1917. Over 20,000 people were arrested. In 1914, only 500 mutinies were reported. Neil Grant, *Chronicle of 20th Century Conflict* (New York: Smithmark Publishers, Inc., 1993), 96; Livesey, *Historical Atlas*, 123.
4. Grant, *Chronicle of Conflict*, 95.
5. For Spad VII and Spad XIII specifications and drawings, see Christopher Campbell, *Aces and Aircraft of World War I* (Poole, Dorset, England: Blandford Press, Ltd., 1981), 67, 135.
6. Goethals promised 3,000,000 tons in 18 months. U-boats were sinking an average of 600,000 tons a month. Harries and Harries, *Last Days*, 151; By the end of 1917, 8,000,000 tons were lost at sea, but the convoy system and Allied shipbuilding helped reverse the supply problems between the United States and Britain. Livesy, *Atlas*, 118.
7. Robert Ferrell, *Woodrow Wilson and World War I: 1917–1921* (New York: Harper and Row Publishers, Inc., 1985), 103.
8. The first battle of Ypres began on 31 July. Within weeks the British were bogged down into mud in which 40,000 missing presumably drowned. On November 4th, the objective, the area around Passchendaele, was finally secured in large part by the Canadian Corp. British losses were over 250,000 in the Ypres three-battle campaign. Livesy, *Atlas*, 128–129; Grant, *Chronicle of Conflict*, 100, 103.
9. Salonika, a sea port in Greek Macedonia, saw Franco-British troops arrive in 1915. With the Russians and Serbs, they launched an offensive against Bulgaria in mid-1916 that pushed the latter into retreat. On September 29, 1918, Bulgaria finally surrendered to the Allies after two weeks of Allied attacks north of Salonika. Grant, *Chronicle of Conflict*, 74, 88–90, 116. Livesy, *Atlas*, 86, 80–81, 174–175.
10. In late summer 1917, the Italians began to overpower the Austrian forces with whom they had been fighting along the Alps for 2 years. However, the Germans sent seven infantry divisions to support the exhausted eight remaining Austrian divisions. The Austro-German forces, lead by Otto von Bülow, overpowered the Italians in late October at Caporetto and forced them back to the Piave River. Two hundred and fifty thousand Italians were taken prisoner and an estimated 350,000 were killed. Livesy, *Atlas*, p. 132; Grant, *Chronicle of Conflict*, 102-103.
11. In April 1917 the 4th Australian Division briefly penetrated the Hindenburg Line at Bellecourt in the Allied offensive at Arras. Livesy, *Atlas*, 124–125.
12. Grant, *Chronicle of Conflict*, 97.
13. On March 16, 1917, Czar Nicholas abdicated after months of strikes, increased army desertions, and citizen disillusionment with the war began. Troops were ordered to stop riots that erupted, but they were ineffective and a provisional government was created by the end of the month. Grant, *Chronicle of Conflict*, 93.

14. By the end of World War I, 45% of all combantants, 15,800,000 were killed or maimed for life. Another 8,000,000 civilians were killed. For a list of casualties broken down by nation, see Susan Everett, *The Two World Wars, Vol 1–World War I* (CN: Bison, 1980); also available on-line: http://www.worldwar1.com/tlcrates.htm. See also, Michael E. Hanlon, *About The Great War* (El Sobrante, CA: THC Publishing, 1992); available on-line: http://www.world1.com/sfnum.htm for other World War I statistics.
15. For a brief biographical sketch of Raoul Lufberry, see Campbell, *Aces and Aircraft*, 69–70.

PART TWO

16. For brief biographical information on Edward Rickenbacker see Campbell, *Aces and Aircraft*, 133–134; for biographies, kill numbers, and other war-related information on American fighter pilots, including Frank Luke and Charles Biddle, see Hudson, *Hostile Skies*.
17. During the summer of 1917, the IWW held a growing number of strikes—many of them in industries of prime importance to the war effort: copper, lumber, and steel. Inflammatory language by IWW leaders, staged "accidents," and rumors of German funding all contributed to IWW's reputation as a radical group of anti-American saboteurs. In early September, the Department of Justice raided IWW offices, resulting in the arrest and conviction of some prominent IWW leaders, including the very vocal Bill Hayword. Harries and Harries, *Last Days*, 186–189, 288–289.
18. Charles Bairnsfather, 1888-1959, was a cartoonist and British officer who served in France. His cartoons of the front were enormously popular during World War I. For a selected sample of Bairnsfather cartoons, see Mike Iavarone, 1996, *Trenches on the Web—Bierhaus: Wartime Cartoons* [on-line]. Available: http://www.worldwar1.com/bier001.htm
19. Harries and Harries, *Last Days*, 88.
20. In September 1918, New York and other states were holding "slacker" raids, which found men eligible for the draft but who had not registered. The inspection of draft cards was conducted by blocking streets and subways, raiding hotels and restaurants, and then retaining the subjects for registration. For interesting stories on draft dodging techniques, see Harries and Harries, *Last Days*, 88–89, 292.
21. *Ibid*, 292.
22. Wilson was loathe to take over the railroad, but fractioned service created serious backlogs of necessary war supplies. *Ibid.*, 203. Ferrell, *Woodrow Wilson*, 104.
23. The Bolsheviks took over the Russian government late in 1917. Leon Trotsky, commissar for foreign affairs in December 1917, called for a peace treaty with Germany, but a deal could not be worked out and fighting resumed. However,

in March 1918, Russia and Germany signed the treaty of Brest-Litovsk despite Allied protests. Grant, *Chronicle of Conflict*, 104–108; For a summary of the October revolution and details of Kerensky's last Russian offensive, see Livesy, *Atlas*, 134–135.

24. On January 17, 1918, amdist a very cold winter, Harry Garfield, head of the Fuel Administration, issued a shut-down order for all factories in the northeastern United States because of a severe coal shortage. See Harries and Harries, *Last Days*, 202–204.
25. The first of Erich Ludendorff's three major offenses, operation MICHAEL, began on March 21on the Arras area of France. By the end of the month, the Germans had taken 40 miles of ground toward Amien and 80,000 prisoners. The Allies and Germans each incurred approximately 250,000 casualties. Grant, *Chronicle of Conflict*, 109; Livesy, *Atlas,*150.
26. One thousand two hundred DH-4s, with Liberty engines, were sent to the American Expeditionary Force. All of them were delivered after March 1918. See Hudson, *Hostile Skies*,14–18. While the engine was of superior American design, it did not fit well into the British designed de Havilland. American experts, using relatively unskilled auto workers, had a difficult time reproducing the British frame. See Harries and Harries, *Last Days*, 200.
27. In spring 1917, 846 acres on the Delaware River were set aside for the Hog Island shipyard. Fifty boats could be assembled while half as many were being worked at the docks. Though the operation cost over $2.5 million, only 107 steel, 67 wooden (for inland use), and 4 composite vessels were produced by the time the war was over. *Ibid,* 150–151; Ferrell, *Woodrow Wilson*, 100–102.
28. The United States mobilized 4,355,000 men (of which 126,000 were killed and 234,300 were wounded). Susan Everett, *The Two World Wars,* http://www.worldwar1.com/tlcrates.htm
29. The production of aircraft was woefully short of initial optimistic manufacturing promises. A critical public inspired investigations into the efficiency and possible corruption of the airplane industry. Charles Hughes provided a report to the U.S. Attorney General in October 1918 that put an end to corruption charges. Hudson, *Hostile Skies*, 9.
30. Ludendorff's third offenisive, OPERATION BLÜCHER-YORCK, was resisted by Allied forces in early June, depleting German reserves and lowering morale. Italy also managed to hold their position at Piave River. Livesy, *Atlas*, 158–161; Grant, *Chronicles of Conflict*, 110.

PART THREE

31. William Stull Holt, "William Stull Holt, 20th Aero Squadron, France, 1918," interview by Alan D. Toelle, *Cross & Cockade Journal*, vol. 21, no. 4, Winter 1980: 323–324.

32. Six hundred Allied planes supported John Pershing's attack at the St. Mihiel salient. The operation was overwhelmingly successful, providing an opportunity for the complete French recapture of Verdun and the end of the war. For a detailed account of the battle and the role of American air power, see Hudson, *Hostile Skies*, 175-193. For a general summary, see Livesey, *Atlas*, 168–169.
33. Interview, *Cross and Cockade*, 327.
34. After the Ludendorff's offensives failed in August, Germany could not mount another signficant attack. In September, Bulgaria surrendered leaving Austria without help at the Italian front, and Turkey was falling under Allenby's superior strategy in Palestine. The U-boat power that had dominated the Atlantic had been rendered impotent. Allies breached the Hindenburg line in early October. Livesey, *Atlas*, 166–176. Grant, *Chronicle of Conflict*, 111-118.
35. Interview, *Cross and Cockade*, 327.
36. *Ibid.*, 326.
37. Hudson, *Hostile Skies*, 187.
38. Interview, *Cross and Cockade,* 327-328.
39. *Ibid.,* 326.
40. *Ibid.*, 318.
41. *Ibid.*, 318.
42. In January 1905, an assembly of unarmed, peaceful strikers—lead by Father Gregory Gapon—assembled in front of the Czar's palace to complain about a company lock-out. Palace guards shot into the crowd, killing 1,500 and setting off a backlash that included strikes and police assassinations. Grant, *Chronicle of Conflict*, 25.

SELECTED ADDITIONAL READINGS

M. R. D. Foot and J. M. Langley, *M19: The British Secret Service that Fostered Escape and Evasion, 1939–1945, and its American Counterpart* (London: The Bodley Head, 1979).

C. G. Barth, *History of the Twentieth Aero Squadron: Frist Day Bombardment Group* (orig. pub. 1920) (reprinted by The Battery Press, Nashville, TN, 1990).

Arlen J. Hansen, *Gentlemen Volunteers: The Story of American Ambulance Drivers in the Great War, August 1914–September 1918* (New York: Arcade Publishing, 1996).

Thomas G. Miller, Jr., *History of the First Day Bombardment Group* (Pamphlet. West Roxbury, MA: World War I Publishers, Inc., no date).

SELECTED WRITINGS BY HISTORIAN W. STULL HOLT

Treaties Defeated by the Senate (Baltimore, MD: John Hopkins University Press, 1933).

Editor, *Historical Scholarship in the United States, 1876–1901: As Revealed in the Correspondence of Herbert B. Adams* (Baltimore, MD: John Hopkins University Press, 1938).

Historical Scholarship in the United States and Other Essays (Seattle: University of Washington Press, 1967).

Joint author, *An American Faculty* (New York: Vantage Press, 1974).

Appendix

Maps and Photos from Stull Holt's Album

1917-1918

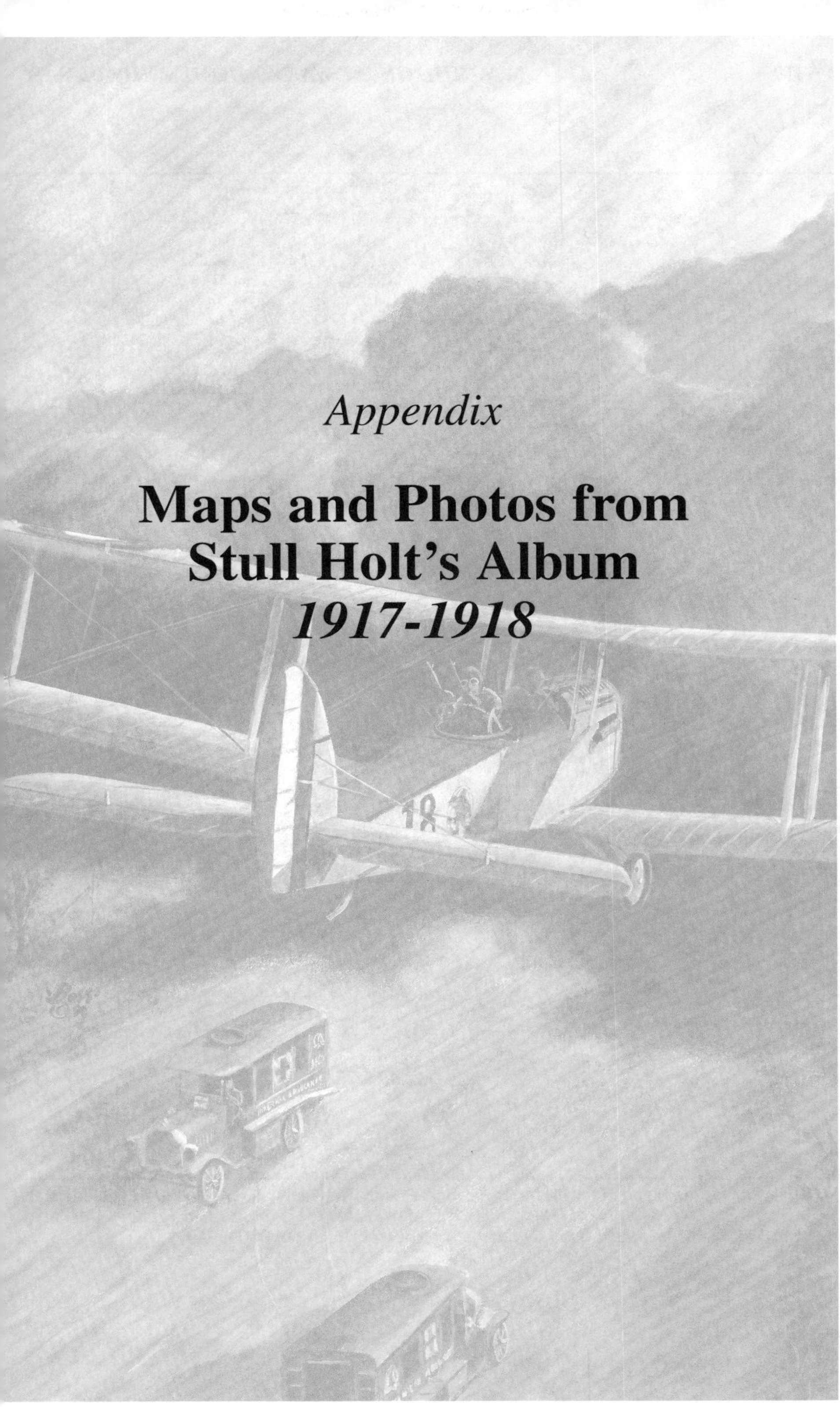

While driving ambulances in the area around Reims, May-July, 1917, Holt was stationed at Muizon, St. Thierry, Louvois. (Map adapted from *Michelin Motoring Atlas France*, 11th ed., 1997, 38, © Michelin, and used by permission, Authorization no. 9709461.)

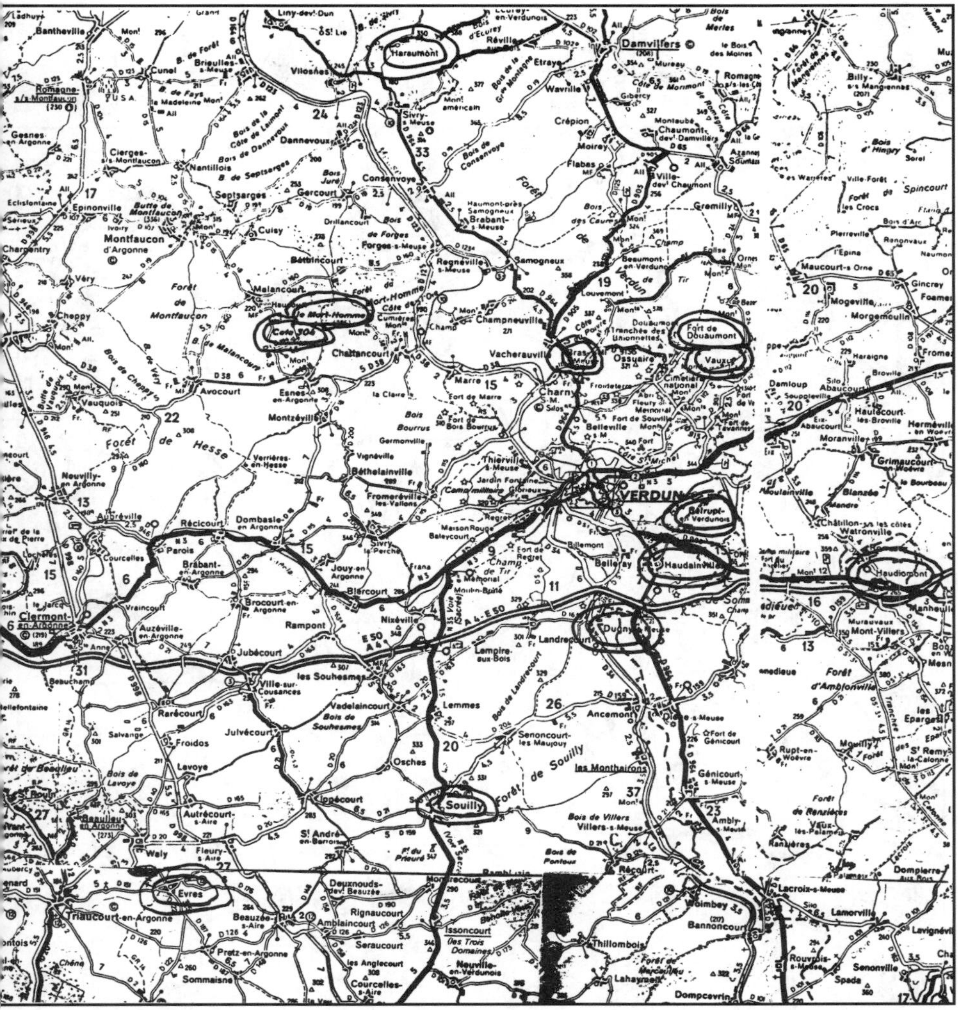

Places Holt mentioned when he drove in the Verdun sector, July and August 1917. (Map adapted from *Michelin Motoring Atlas France*, 11th ed., 1997, 39-40 © Michelin, used with permission, Authorization no. 9709461.)

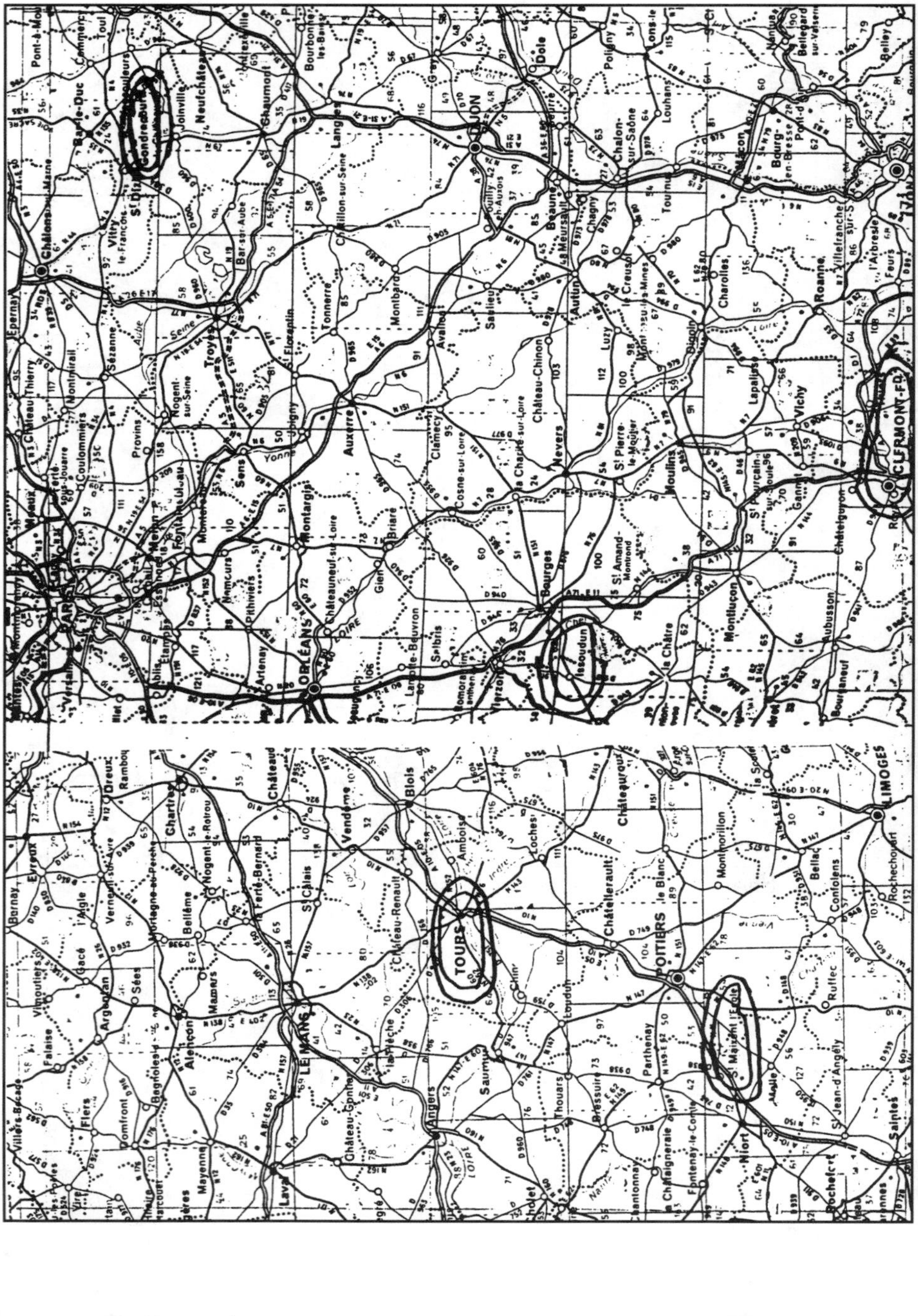

In the months from September 1917 until August 1918, Holt took pilot training at Tours and Issoudun, gunnery at Gondrecourt, and bombing at Clermont-Ferrand. In between sessions of training, he was stationed at St. Maixent. (Map adapted from *Michelin Motoring Atlas France*, 11th ed., 1997, "Route Planning," iv-v, © Michelin, used with permission, Authorization no. 9709461.)

Stull Holt writes: "Camp crew at the front." The man on the left wears a U.S. Army campaign hat; the man in the center obviously wears a captured German helmet.

German prisoners at Verdun, being led by a French *poilu* (infantryman).

German POWS.

From left to right: Lieutenants William Stull Holt, John Y. Stokes, Jr., "Stuffy" Greene, and Gardiner H. Fiske. Stokes and Fiske were observers, like Stull Holt.

Ground crew of the 20th Aero Squadron in front of DH-4s.

Observation balloon at Verdun — a French Cauquot, with observers in a basket underneath.

Right: A canal at Verdun near bank fortified with barbed wire to slow down the enemy.

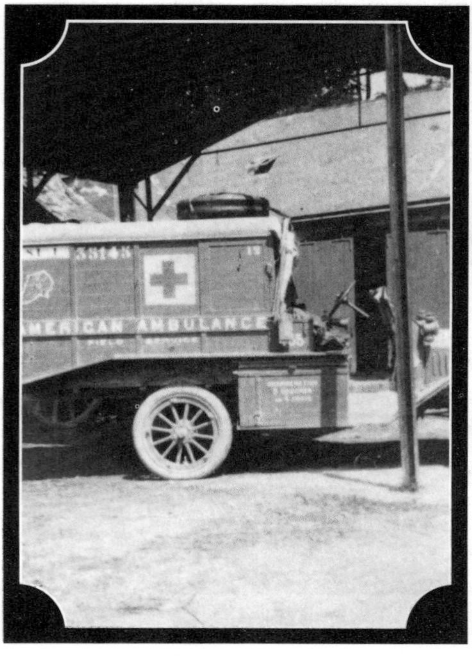

Ambulance of the AAFS.

Above and below: French casualties at Verdun.

Left: German helmet and bones at Verdun.

Brequet of the 96th Squadron.

DH-4.

Noticeable in this airborne shot of Brequets in loose formation are the masses of flying wire typical of the biplanes of the day.

Above: Logos of the early aviation squadron.

Left: Wrecked Caudron aircraft.

Index

by Lori L. Daniel

— A —

Action Front, 42
Adamite, 100
A Diversity of Creatures, 51
Agerter, Harry, 179
Aircraft
  Biplane, 246
    Scout, 264
  Breguet, 176-177, 215, 320
  Caudron, 95, 168, 171, 173, 321
  de Havilland DH-4, 215-217, 227, 230, 241-243, 273, 275, 317, 320
  Farman, 191
  Fokker, 233, 239, 249, 251, 260, 274
  Fokker D-VII, 216-217
  Lewis, 190
  Morane parisol, 168, 171
  Morane-Saulnier monoplane, 97
  Nieuport, 94-95, 97-99, 159, 167-168, 171, 173, 176, 178
  Siemens Schuckert D-IV, 217, 274
  Sopwith, 171
  Spad VII, 38
  Spad XIII, 38, 98-99, 171, 227
  Vickers, 190
  Zeppelin, 206, 283
Albany Law, 199
Alexander, Corporal, 274
Algerian, 100
Allies, xvii, 29, 49-50, 62, 64, 119, 204, 210-211, 216, 223, 232, 258-260, 267, 274, 280
Allied Chasse, 248-249, 251
Allied Drome, 260
Amazon River, 268
ambulance, xix, 4, 18, 23, 56, 58, 74, 115, 148, 318
Ambulance No. Ten, 1, 11, 164
America, xix-xxi, xxiii, 8, 16, 22, 36, 47-50, 65, 86, 102, 106, 110-111, 120, 128, 147, 153, 188, 192, 195, 200, 204, 219, 223, 258, 264-266, 276, 282, 288, 291
American, xix, 1-2, 9, 11-12, 14, 20, 31, 38-39, 42, 49-50, 54-57, 64, 75, 78-79, 81, 84, 91-92, 97-99, 116, 132, 134-135, 145, 147, 149, 152-153, 159-160, 167, 171, 174-175, 178, 186, 191, 195, 201, 204, 207-209, 211, 215-217, 219, 227, 229-230, 236, 246, 252, 258-259, 272, 288-289, 303
American *(continued)*, 229-230, 236, 246, 252, 258-259, 272, 288-289, 303
American Air Service, xix, xxi, xxiii, 95, 225, 230, 259
American Ambulance Field Service (AAFS), xvii, xix, xxiv, 1, 2, 4-5, 19, 48, 56-57, 227, 318
  Section One, xix, 115
American Aviation school, 91
American Expeditionary Force, 92, 105, 110, 114, 121
American Express Co., 164
American Federation of Labor, 223
American Historical Association, 303
American Historical Review, 303
An American Faculty (Holt), 303
Anderson, Mr., 192
André, Madamoiselle, 192, 198
Andrew, A. P., 53, 56, 59, 75, 79
Annanite, 100
Ann Veronica (Wells), 277
Arab, 44
Armistice, 273, 276, 278, 284, 286
Articles of War, 107
Associated Press, 286
A Tale of Two Cities (Dickens), 6, 144
Atlantic Ocean, xix, 115
Aunt Ethel, 86, 139
Austen, Miss, 82
Australia, 12
Australian, 79, 87
Austria, 286
Austrian, 77
  Army, 192

— B —

Bailey, Miss, 202
Bairnsfather cartoon, 104
Baker, Newton D. (Secretary of War), 181-182, 193, 239, 241, 249, 251, 253, 260, 264, 269-272, 274, 281
Baltimore and Ohio Railroad Company, 49
Bannon, Hal, 225
Baret, M., 102, 104, 113, 201
Barker, Mr., 168
Barleycorn, John, 14
Barth, Clarence G. (Lieutenant), 230
Bartlett, Gordon, 69-70, 73, 117
Baruch, Bernard M., 49
Bastille Day, 53, 209
Batcher, Mrs., 6
Beaumont, _____, 107
Beecher, Henry Ward, 289
Belgian, 242
Belgium, 156
Belmont, Elenor (Robson), 152
Bennett, William, 135
Biddle, Charles, 99
Blackstone Jr., 237
Blaine, James G., 130
Bliss, Tasker H., 292
Bobrikoff, Colonel, 91
Bolshevikism, 287
Borah, William, 292
Brace, _____, 90
Brandeis, Louis D., 292
Brennan, Mark, 76
Bretz, Professor, 200
Brewer, _____, 100
Bridgman, Jon, xii
Brieux, Eugene, 159
Britain, 171
British, 27, 60, 73, 211, 290-291, 303
  Army, 31, 252
    Second, 100, 201
  government, 303
  Labour Party, 193, 223
British de Havilland, 215
Brodeur, _____, 246, 248-249, 251, 270
Brodie, Steve, 256
Bronx River, 158
Brookings Institution, 302
Brown, 198
  Enid, 225
  Kendrick, xxi, 225, 234, 261
  Mrs., 225, 234, 261
  Waldo, 225, 261
Brown University, xxi
Brumbaugh, _____, 253, 260, 264, 267, 271-272, 274
Bryan, William Jennings, 193
Buchan, John, 140, 151, 164, 190
Bulgarian, 60
Bunkley, _____, 233, 239, 246, 248, 260
Burg
  Maclyn P., xi-xiii, 230
  Patricia, xi-xii
Buswell, Leslie, 1
Butler, Ed, 181

— C —

Cable, Boyd, 42
Cadbury, _____, 155, 160, 168, 182
Caesar, 201
California, 147, 187
  Berkeley, xxiii
  Los Angeles, 213
  Pasadena, xxiii
  San Francisco, 130
    Barbary Coast, 130
Call (NY), 259
Camp
  Devons, 134, 199
  Meade, 292
  Meigs, 282
  Mills, 151
Canadian, 163, 193, 199, 252

Carlyle, Thomas, 28
Carson, Edward (Sir), 193
Chaplin, Charlie, 177
Chatkoff, _____, 44
Chaucer, Geoffrey, 118
Cheyney, Edward P., 290
China, 189
Chinese, xix, 189-191
Christian, 225
Christian, _____, 231, 233, 241, 251, 270
Civil Service Exam, 158, 162
Civil War, 130, 246, 291
Clemenceau, "Georges the Tiger," 193, 259
Clubb, Jerry, xii
Cohalan, Judge, 120, 163
Cohen, Warren, xii
Coldefy, _____, 118, 121-123
Colliers, 171
Columbia Oval, 116
Columbia University Teachers' College, xx
Columbia War Hospital, 116
Conflans Railroad Yards, 231
Connecticut, xxi, 225
Cooper, _____, 239
Cornell University, xvii, xix-xxi, 1, 16-17, 36, 72, 100, 119, 133, 179, 282, 293, 301-302
Corry, Dr., 39
Coulter
  Jack, 7, 10, 78
  John, 8
Craig, Mr., 190
Crowder, General, 130, 211
Crump, xiii
  Curtis, 19, 86, 104, 118, 121-123, 195
  Dr., 226, 261
  Enid, 6, 44, 55, 86, 129, 143, 154, 156, 165, 174, 225-226, 234, 261-262
    see also Dolstad, Enid
  Lela, 51, 86, 114, 129, 156, 170, 226, 261-262
  Lois, xix-xx, xxiii, 1, 5, 9, 13, 15, 17, 21-22, 26, 30, 32, 34, 38-40, 45, 51, 53-55, 66-67, 69, 75, 79, 92, 99, 108, 110, 117, 122, 154, 168, 171, 174, 178, 184, 186, 212, 214, 219, 225-226, 234-235, 262, 284, 300
    see also Holt, Lois
  Mrs., 129, 225-226, 234-235, 254, 261-262
Czecho-Slavs, 192

— D —

D., John, 289
Daily Mail, 223, 280
Dallin, _____, 55, 76, 108
Damaged Goods (Brieux), 159
Daniels, Josephus, 50, 265, 280
d'Arc, Jean, 33
Darwin, _____, 162
Davidson, _____, 149, 155, 174, 176
Davis, Lieutenant, 167
Day, Red, 112, 163
de Blois, Duc, 146
de Medici, Catherine, 146-147
Democracy, 117
Democrat, 129-130, 135, 258, 287, 291
Denneson, _____, 285
Derge, _____, 246, 248-249, 251, 253, 260, 264, 267, 2690-272
Desmond's Daughter (Diver), 125
De Ville, _____, 42
Dickens, Charles, 45, 144
Dink, Hinkey, 130
Diver, Maud, 125
Dolstad
  Enid Holt, xiii
    see also Holt, Enid
Doyle, Arthur Conan (Sir), 91
Draft Board, 120, 129-133, 179, 211, 259
Draft Camp, 193
draft dodger, 206
du Barry, 12
Dudley, 127
Dumas, Alexandre, 126, 135, 146
Du Pont, _____, 200
Dutch, 142

— E —

Eastman, Max, 193
Eastman Gaines, 21
Edison, Thomas, 49
Edwards
  Brooke, 202, 218, 238
  Lieutenant, 231, 233, 239, 241, 246, 248, 251, 270, 274
Egypt, 112
Egyptian, 83
11th Squadron, 269
Elliot, _____, 53, 65
Emmet, _____, 49
Endler, Joe, 218, 231, 233, 238
Engine
  Anzani, 95, 101, 127, 135-136, 139, 141, 160
  B.M.W., 216-217
  Gnome monosoupape, 171
  Hispano-Suiza, 98-99
  LeRhone, 95, 140, 158, 160
  Liberty, 135, 215-217
  Mercedes, 216-217
  Rolls Royce "Eagle," 215
  Siemens Halske Sh IIIa, 217
England, 24, 36, 57, 102, 193, 206, 223, 237, 266, 280, 284, 290, 293, 302
  London, 145
English, 33, 38-39 41, 44, 49, 56, 78-79, 86-87, 90-91, 102, 118-119, 181, 185, 189-191, 203, 223, 293
Epicurean, 256
Era (Cornell University), 108
Estey, _____, 149
Europe, 1, 11, 13, 38, 49-50, 120, 193, 223, 236, 256, 282, 286, 291, 303
European, xxiii, 9

— F —

Faith (ship), 199
Fankevitch, General, 91
Fanny's First Play (Shaw), 160
Farman
  Henri, 191
  Maurice, 191
Farnham, _____, 108
Farnol, Jeffrey, 142
Faulk, _____, 231, 239, 241, 246, 248-249, 251, 267, 270, 272
Faust, Professor, 134
Fawcett, Margi, 181
Federation Aeronautique Internationale, 95
Field, Jr., Marshal, 50
First Corps Infantry School, 190
Fiske, Gardner H. (Lieutenant), xviii, 248-249, 251, 253, 260, 264, 267, 269-270, 272, 274-275, 316
Florida
  Miami, 303
Flyn, Jim, 60-61, 64, 71
Forbes, _____, 233, 239
Ford, Henry, 236
Foreign Legion, 2, 11
Fortan, _____, 71
France, xvii, xix, xxiii, 1-2, 4-6, 8, 18, 35-36, 41-42, 49, 84, 86-87, 89, 92, 100-102, 106, 108, 113, 115-117, 120, 124, 128-129, 134, 142-143, 147, 154, 156, 162, 166, 169-170, 174, 185, 188-189, 196, 198-199, 201, 204, 207-209, 211, 215-216, 219, 222, 226, 235, 240, 283-284
  Abberville, 233
  Aisne, 128
  Alsace, 56
  Alsace-Lorraine, 258
  Amanty, 190, 214, 220
  Ancreville, 246, 251, 269
  Bantheville, 248
  Bar-le-duc, 56, 78, 220
    Cafe de Rochelle, 56
  Barricourt, 269, 271
  Bayonville, 253, 260, 269
  Beauzee, 57
  Belleville, 270
  Belrupt, 60, 66-67
  Bethelainville, 272, 275

France *(continued)*
Beveaux, 66
Bois-de-la-Folie, 260
Bordeaux, 7, 189-190, 294
Bras, 61, 69, 72
Brest, 292
Brigneney, 264
Brimont, 32-33
Bullecourt, 79
Buzancy, 260, 269, 271
Cambrai, 185
Caporetto, 128
Carrier Sud, 73-75
Caserne Marceau, 60-61, 64, 71-72, 77
Cazaux, 98
Chalons, 34, 41-42, 44, 56, 59
Champagne, xix, 19, 196
Chartres, 149, 191
Chateaudun, 142, 148-149, 176
Hotel St. Louis, 148
Chaucenay, 56
Chaumont, 147, 190
Clermont, 155, 177, 179, 184, 186, 192, 200-201, 209, 218
Clermont-Ferrand, 139, 192, 314
Clery-la-Grand, 239
Clery-le-Petit, 251
Coiffe, 191
Conde, 56
Craonne, 21
Cunnel, 246
Damvillers, 249, 267, 272
Devant Dun, 249
Dijon, 190
Doulleon, 246
Dur-sur Meuse, 239, 274
Epernay, 19, 44, 52-53, 56
Esperance, 53
Evres, 57, 115
Flanders, 60, 64, 73
Fleville, 248
Fontennel, 245
Fort Douamont, 60-61
Fort Vaux, 60-61
Gondrecourt, 186, 189-191, 314
Goshen, 52
Haraumont, 61, 67, 69, 71-74
Haudainville, 60, 67
Hill 304, 74-75
Hill 344, 75
Ippecourt, 60
Issoudun, xix, 3, 95, 96-98, 110, 141, 151, 160, 164, 166, 173, 191, 314
Is-sur-Tille, 190
Le Mort Homme, 75
Louvois, 3, 45-47, 51, 65, 72, 312
Ludes, 52
Mairy, 56
Mainz, 285

France *(continued)*
Mareq, 248
Marne, 56
Marseille, 294
Mars-la-Tour, 233
Maulan, 214, 220-221, 243
Metz, 221, 234
Meurthe-et-Moselle, 285
Xiory Circourt, 285
Meuse, 255
Montmedy, 274
Mouzay, 241
Mouzon, 274
Muizon, 3, 9, 18-20, 29, 45, 58, 67, 312
Naucourt, 269
Neiully, 12, 79
Neufchateau, 190
Nice, 255, 277, 283, 284
Nilly Dun, 249
Orleans, 7, 55
Orly, 285
Paris, xxi, 3, 5, 7, 10, 15-17, 39, 55, 62, 68, 71, 74-76, 78-80, 83, 86, 90, 92-93, 122, 148, 151, 160, 163-164, 179-180, 185-186, 213, 218, 237-238, 255, 277-279, 281, 283, 285, 292, 297-299
Bois, 298
Folies Bergére, 13, 79, 90
Hotel de Calais, 78, 163
Hotel de Ville, 16, 29
Hotel Universe, 155
Maxims, 13
Municipal Theatre, 160
Notre Dame, 12
Olympia, 12-13, 91
Opera-Comique, 213
Petite Arch, 160
Rumplemayers, 13
Soldiers and Sailors Club, 163
Perthes, 56
Place de la Concorde, 283
Poitiers, 7, 55, 186, 189
Pontleroy, 141-142, 157
Prouilly, 20
Puy-du-Dome, 200, 209
Reims, 3, 9, 19, 28, 32, 45, 47, 312
Revigny, 78
Romagne, 246
Route National 44, 33
Rue Raynouard, 78
Rumont, 57
Salonika, 76
Sedan, 221
Sens, 149
Sillery, 51
Sivery-les-Buzancy, 260
Sivry-sur-Meuse, 272
Sogny, 56
Somme, 64
Souilly, 66-67, 76

France *(continued)*
St. Dizier, 56
Stenay, 272, 274
St. Fismes, 71, 77
St. Maixent, 186, 189-192, 314
St. Mihiel, 227, 229, 231
St. Thierry, 3, 32, 34, 312
Tailly, 271
Talon, 75
Thonorques, 260
Tours, xix, 3, 7, 55-56, 84-85, 92-96, 99-100, 112, 118, 126, 160, 164, 167, 171, 173-174, 179, 181, 185-186, 189, 191-192, 201, 220
Trigny, 20, 34
Vadlincourt, 60
Verdun, xix, 3-4, 56-61, 63, 66, 69, 77, 80, 93, 112, 127-128, 195, 221, 303, 313, 315
Versailles, 12, 83, 90, 291
Vierzone, 186
Vignevills, 227
Villers, 251
Vitry, 56
Vouziers, 221
Ypres, 100
Francis, 15, 203, 212
Francois I, 146
Frank, Lieutenant, 239, 241, 253, 260, 264, 269, 271-272, 274
French, xvii, xix, 2, 7-9, 11-13, 15, 17, 19-20, 22-27, 30, 32-35, 37, 39-44, 52-55, 57-58, 60-61, 64, 69-70, 72, 74-75, 77, 79-80, 86, 91, 95, 97-100, 103, 117-118, 126-127, 133, 142, 144-145, 155, 159, 163-164, 170, 178-179, 185, 188-189, 195, 198, 201, 203, 213, 215-216, 227, 229, 232, 236, 259-260, 279, 284, 291, 293, 303, 315
Air Force, 303
Army, 39, 41, 55, 64, 92, 100, 111
government, 4, 10, 87
Hussar unit, 12
plane, 22, 38-39, 94, 133, 139, 176
French Ambulance Service, 48
French Revolution, 12
Friends of France, 11
Fuller, Al, 167
Fulton, Lieutenant, 246, 248-249, 251, 253, 264, 267, 269-271, 274
Funston, Frederick (General), 150
Further Foolishness (Leacock), 64-65
Fusion-Independent, 135

— G —
Gamble, _____, 43-44, 53, 65, 71
Gatton, _____, 201
Gaul, 201
Gelfand, Larry, xii
General Electric Co., 35, 65, 129, 132
George Washington University, xxi, 302
Georgia
Atlanta, 130
German (Boche), xxi, 4, 11, 20, 25, 30, 32-35, 38-39, 44, 48-50, 52-53, 56-57, 62, 64, 67, 73-77, 80, 86, 90, 100, 102, 107, 111, 120, 128, 132, 137, 152, 160, 168, 179, 181, 185, 194, 206, 213-214, 216-217, 219, 224, 227, 229-230, 232, 238, 243, 245-246, 250, 252-255, 258-260, 264-266, 271-272, 281, 283, 289-291, 315
Air Service, 216
Jagdgeschwader I, 216
Jagdgeschwader II, 216, 219, 230-231
Jastas, 216-217
League, 134
Luftwaffe, 217
plane, 19, 20, 22, 26, 29, 45, 52, 88, 232, 240, 242, 245, 248, 252, 268
POW camp, 273
Revolution, 288-289
Germany, 1, 35, 49, 52, 86-87, 92, 102, 123, 128, 141, 160, 168, 171, 200, 204, 219, 223-224, 227, 232, 240, 251-252, 257-260, 265-266, 269, 274, 280, 284-285, 290-291
Berlin, 53, 223, 288
Kahrlsrue, 179
Kiel, 46
St. Petersburg, 289
Gertrude, 45
Gibraltar, 294
Gironde River (France), 7
Gladys, _____, 234, 254, 282
Globe, 77, 113
Goethals, Colonel, 49
Goldman, Emma, 288
Gompers, Sam, 49, 223, 287
Goodbody & Company, xx
Goodell, _____, 241, 249, 251, 253, 260, 264, 270
Gorrell, Colonel, 230
Gorrell Histories, 230
Graham, Mrs., 261
Graveline, Sergeant, 246, 248-249, 251, 253, 260, 264, 269-272, 274
Great Expectations (Dickens), 45
Greene, "Stuffy" (Lieutenant), 316
Gregory, Jim, xii

— H —
Hal, 162
Hall, J. N., 31, 247
Hamilton, _____, 128, 149
Hammond, Hays, 49
Hanna, 55, 67
Harden, Maximilian, 223
Harding, _____, 171
Harington, _____, 194
Harjes, H. H., 56
Harold, 60, 67
Harris, _____, 231, 233, 239
Harter, Les, 218
Harvard University, 191, 250
Heidelberg University, 76
Heligoland, 38
Henderson, _____, 193, 259
Hennessy, Ma, 282
Henry III, 146-147
Herman, _____, 267, 269, 271-272, 274
Heyward, 99, 104-105, 108, 113-116, 123, 172
Heywood, V. E. "Vinx," 9, 89-90, 117, 123, 126-127, 139, 141, 147-149, 151, 155, 166, 172, 177, 182
Hicks, Lieutenant, 231, 233, 239, 241, 246, 248-249, 251, 270
Higham, Robin, xii-xiii
Hillquit, Morris, 135, 193, 257
Historical Scholarship in the United States and Other Essays (Holt), 303
Historiography and Urbanization (Holt), 303
History of the French Revolution (Carlyle), 28
Hog Island, 193
Hollweg, Von Bethmann, 52
Holmes, Sherlock, 93
Holt, xiii
Byron W., xx, xxii, 5, 13, 108-109, 226, 234, 293
Elizabeth, xxi-xxii, 6, 54, 62, 73-74, 88, 172, 213, 225, 235, 247, 253-254, 261, 285
Enid, 301
Jerry, 74
Jocelyn, 301
see also Marchisio, Jocelyn
Lois, xiii, 301-302
see also Crump, Lois
Elizabeth G. (Kinsella), xx-xxii, 6, 16-17, 226, 295, 296
Paula, xx, xxii, 6, 14-15, 26, 46-47, 51-52, 54, 59, 66, 74, 78, 124, 143, 174, 180, 185, 194, 285, 295-296
see also Selover, Paula
William Stull (Lieutenant), xi-xiii, xvii-xxiii, 1-4, 8-10, 18, 29, 63, 94-99, 119,
Holt *(continued)*
William Stull (Lieutenant) *(continued)*, 127, 138-139, 173, 175, 203, 214, 230-231, 233, 235, 239, 241-243, 246, 248-249, 251, 253, 260, 264, 266-267, 269-273, 275, 297, 300-304, 312-316
Holt papers, xxiii-xxiv, 284
Home Pattern Co., 161
Hoover, Herbert, 49, 170, 205, 288
House, Edward M., 292
Howard, Sidney (Lieutenant), xviii, 231, 233, 239, 246, 248-249, 251, 270, 274
Hoy, Davy, 257
Hubbard, Mr., 202, 208, 210, 234
Hughes, Charles, 200
Humphrey, Hubert, 303
Hunter College, 234
Hylan, John F., 135, 139, 289

— I —
Illinois
Chicago, 130-131, 303
Indian, 134
Inglis, Ellis, 201
Ireland
Dublin, xx
Iriquois, 59
Irish, 57, 133
Italian, 47, 60, 77, 128, 201, 259
Italy, 90, 128
Italy at War (Powell), 62
Ithaca Daily News (NY), 108, 121
Ivy League, xvii
I.W.W. (Industrial Workers of the World) "Wobblies," 102, 104, 223

— J —
Janus Club, xxi
Japan, 268, 298
Jastas, 216-217
Jayne, Les, 36
Jew, 12, 160-161, 257
Jocelyn, Dorothy, 7-8
Joffre, General, 192
Johns Hopkins University, 301-303
Johnson, Lieutenant, 246, 248-249, 251, 253, 267, 269-272, 274
Jonas, Ray, xii
"Judge," 59
Junkers, 265

— K —
Kaiser, 36, 223, 236, 258-259, 276, 280-282
Kamai, Edward, xii
Kaplan, Harry, 154

Keopfgen, L. P. (First Lieutenant), xviii
Kerensky, Aleksandr, 88
Kipling, Rudyard, 51, 85
"Kiss for Cinderella," 93
Kitchener's Mob (Hal), 31
Kloski, Si, 184
Knight, Lieutenant, 135-136
Knight Templars, 12
Knox, _____, 253, 260, 264, 267, 269, 271-272
Koepfgen, Lieutenant, 231, 233, 239, 241, 246, 248-249, 251, 253, 264, 267, 269-272, 274
Kornilof, General, 88
Kreutzberg, _____, 67, 72, 77, 108
Kurtz, _____, 102
Kyaham, Omar, 52

— L —

Lafayette, Marquis de, 27, 200
Lafayette Escadrille, 2, 91
Lansing, Robert, 292
Latin, 256
La Touraine (ship), xix, 7-8
Lawrence, David, 291
Leach, _____, 233, 239
Leacock, Stephen, 65
League of Nations, 172, 193, 200, 224, 259, 292
League to Enforce Peace, 287
Leonard, _____, 239
Liberal, 193, 292
Liberator, 223
Liberty bond, 134, 141, 192, 229, 288
Liberty Loan, 120, 200, 236
Lippman, Walter E., 292
Literary Digest, 89
Lodge, Henry Cabot, 200, 224, 258, 287
Loire River (France), 147
London, Jack, 102, 122
Long, _____, 90
Long Island Railroad, 211
Louis III, 146
Louis XV, 12
Low, Seth, 159
Lufberry, Raoul, 91
Luigi, _____, 211
Luke, Frank, 99
Lunn, Doc, 35, 211-212

— M —

Macadoo, Secretary of Treasury, 200
Mach, General, 235
MacKenzie
  _____, 120
  Mrs., 261
MacTaggart, _____, 235
MacWhirter, Donald H. (Lieutenant), xviii, 202, 214, 218, 227, 230-231, 233, 238-239, 241-242, 244, 246, 248-249,
MacWhirter, Donald H. (Lieutenant) *(continued)*, 251, 260, 264, 267, 269-273, 275
Magie, Mr., 262
Malcolm, Don, 248, 279-281
Mallory, Marjorie, xxi, 278, 297, 299
Mandell, Lieutenant, 239, 241, 246, 248-249, 253, 260, 264, 267, 269, 272, 274
Marchisio, Jocelyn H. (Holt), xi, xiii
Marie Antoinette, 12
Married (Strindberg), 181
Marx, Karl, 257
Maryland
  Annapolis, xx-xxi, 180, 210
  Baltimore, 301
Massachusetts
  Worcester, 147
Matthews, Dick, 218, 239
McCabe, Mr., 109
McClures, 196
McCutcheon, George Barr, 155
McGuire, _____, 120
McKinney, _____, 149, 174, 176, 179
Medal
  Croix de Guerre, xix, 4, 55, 98, 107-108, 111-112, 124, 127-128, 137, 303
  Distinguished Service Cross, xviii, 267
  Silver Star, 275, 303
Mediterranean Sea, 268, 278
Meredith, Ted (Lieutenant), 167-168
Mexico, 10, 111, 301
Michel, John P., 135
Michigan, 236
Mingame, Miss, 7, 99
Minnesota, 236
Missouri, 133
  St. Louis, xxiii
Mitchell, Mayor, 106, 137
Montana, 143, 203, 207
Moody's Magazine, xx
Morrocan, 201
Muller, Charlie, 91, 168
Munford, Dr., 35
Murphy, _____, 246, 248-249, 251, 253, 264, 267, 269-271

— N —

Napoleon, 189
National Food Com., 127
National Platform Committee, 304
Navy League, 117
Ned, 42, 72, 77, 112, 163
Nelsons Short History of the War (Buchan), 164, 190
New Jersey, 66, 259
  Jersey City, 247
  Pagoda, 12
New Mexico, xxi, 148, 249
New Republic, 27, 44, 73, 206
New York, xxiii, 5, 8, 14, 44-47, 85, 90, 92, 104, 106-107, 117, 120, 130, 135, 139, 147, 159, 161-162, 170-171, 181, 189, 199, 208, 222-224, 229, 232, 236, 247, 250, 258-259, 282, 285-288, 290, 294
  Allentown, 48
  Barren Island, 68
  Brooklyn, xx, 46, 104, 107, 126, 132, 260, 294, 296
    Bronx, 146-147, 294
    Crescent Club, 104
  Brooklyn Bridge, 11, 256
  Flatbush, 150
  Fulton Ferry, 247
  Highland Lake, xix, xxi, 59, 76
  Ithaca, 5, 84, 108, 113, 118, 128, 193
  Lakewood, 66
  Naugatuck, 285
  New York City, 27, 36, 66, 211, 222, 234-236, 256, 288, 302
    Carnegie Hall, 208
    Bowery, 222-223
    Broadway, 211, 236
    Madison Square Garden, 288
    Wall Street, 13, 154, 156, 276, 287
    Woolworth Bldg., 211, 236, 287
  Schenectady, 35, 48, 65, 120, 129, 131-132, 192, 200, 212
  Schenectady County, 133
  South Amboy, 66, 247
  Staten Island, 66
New York Court of Appeals, 130
New York Herald, 90, 108-109, 115, 280
New York Post, 259, 291
New York State Bar Examiners, 235
New York State Military Census, 133
New York Sun, 119
New York Sunday Times, 22, 24
New York Times, 223, 236-237
New York Tribune, 102, 126, 171, 236
New York University, xx
  Law, 199
New York World, 259
96th Squadron, 320
Nivelle, Robert, 29, 192
Non-Partisan League, 130
Northcliffe, Alfred (Lord), 171
North Sea, 38
Norton-Harjes volunteer ambulance, 56, 69, 71, 73, 77
Norton, Richard, 52-53, 55-56

— O —

O'Brien, _____, 211
O'Connell, _____, 71-72, 76
Ohio, xx
Oklahoma, 134, 150
O'Leary, _____, 120
Oller, _____, 67, 75-76
166th Squadron, 267
Oriental, 237
Osbourne, Thomas, 224
Ostrander, Remmie, 194
Over the Top, 115

— P —

Palmerston, Lord, 237
Panama, 200
Pankin, _____, 289
Parks, Captain, 167-168, 201
Parrott, Lieutenant, 231, 233, 239
Patterson, _____, 9, 37, 39, 42, 71
Payne, Lieutenant, 231, 239, 241, 246, 248-249, 251, 270, 274
Peace Conference, 291-292
Pearl, _____, 28, 60, 73, 76, 79
Peary, Robert E., 52
Pennsylvania, 132
  Philadelphia, 257
Penrose, _____, 287
Perrault, Lieutenant, 177
Pershing, General, 36, 120, 150, 236
Pétain, Henri Phillipe, 29
Peyton, Major, 191
Philipoteaux, _____, 176
Pike, _____, 180
Plane News, 185
Plow, _____, 112
"Pollyana," 110
Pope, 169, 203, 207, 209, 225-226, 234, 284
  Darwin, 226
  Grandma, 245
  Mr., 143, 163, 170, 174-175, 184, 186-188, 269
  Mrs., 169, 180
Portuguese, 78
Potter, Willie, 239, 246, 248-249, 250-252, 270
Powell, Alexander E., 62
Pressly
  Cameron, xii
  Thomas J., xiii, xv
Preston, _____, 239
Princeton University, 8
Prison Reform, 224
Prohibition, National, 14
Prussia, 52
Prussian, 17, 87, 200
Puerto Rico, 236
Purdy, _____, 42, 53, 60, 67-68, 71, 74, 77, 108

— R —

Radical, 193, 223
Radicalism, 288
Ramsey, _____, 231, 239, 246
Reconstruction, 237
Red Cross, 5, 9, 17, 56, 151, 167, 170, 177, 200, 250, 260, 288
Redfield, Secretary of Commerce, 290
Reed
  John, 223
  Tom, 176, 201
Republican, 129-130, 135, 200, 257-258, 287, 291-292
Reviews Magazine, 161
R.F.C. (Royal Flying Corp), 169
Rhinelander, _____, 239
Ricardo, David, 290
Rice, _____, 61, 71, 73, 77, 89
Richards, Bill, 7-8
Richardson, _____, 239
Richthofen, Manfred von, 240
Rickenbacker
  Cord Meyer, 159
  Eddie, 99
Rob, 170
Rochambeau, 8
Rocky Mountains, 256
Roll of Honor, 169
Roman church, 200
Roosevelt, Theodore "Teddy," 50, 189, 200, 223-224, 258-259, 287
"Rules for Influenza," 263
Rusby, _____, 224
Russia, 85-88, 90, 115, 129, 140-141, 143, 153, 168, 223, 288
Russian, 19, 22, 44, 85, 90-91, 192, 289
  army, 85, 91
  Bolshevik, 87-88, 200, 219, 223, 288
Ryan, Dr., 7, 9

— S —

Salute to Adventures (Buchan), 151
Saturday Evening Post, 171, 196
Sayre, _____, 168, 181
Schultz, _____, 239, 267
Schurnan, Jack, 120
Schwab, _____, xii, 49, 211
Seaver, Arthur E. (Lieutenant), 218, 239, 241, 248-249, 251, 253, 260, 264, 267, 269-271, 274
Seeger, Alan, 51-52, 278
Sellers, Cecil G. (Captain), xviii, 231, 249, 251, 253, 260, 267, 269-272
Selover
  Newton P., xx, 6, 44, 66, 180, 210, 222
  Paula, 210, 22, 225, 247, 262
    see also Holt, Paula
Senegalese, 6
Shakespeare, William, 190, 257
Sharp, Ambassador, 16
Shaw, Bernard, 159-160
Sherman, General, 155, 236
Simpson, Lesley Byrd "Simy," xxiii, 155, 157, 160, 168, 171, 213, 229, 279, 283, 285, 301-302
Sing-Sing Prison, 224
Skotheim, Bob, xii
Skow, Judith, xii
Slauson, Mrs., 261
"Smilage Tickets," 236
Smith, William Dudley "Bill," xxi, 36, 45, 50, 65, 92, 108, 128, 142, 155, 181, 186-187, 194, 206, 212, 219, 224, 237, 259, 264, 266, 284-285, 288, 290, 301
Socialist, 57, 87, 102, 107, 128, 135, 193, 222-223, 236-237, 257, 259, 288-289
South Africa, 232
South America, 12, 206, 222, 232, 268
South Sea Islands, 256
Spanish, 222, 294
Spanish American War, 102, 141
Spatz, Carl "Tooey" (Major), 181
Spenser, Edmund, 118
Spony, _____, 44, 79
Spoon River Anthology (Masters), 79
Springer
  Frank, (Dr.), xxi
  Lew Wallace, xxi, xxiii, 148, 154-155, 157, 159-160, 168, 171, 174-175, 180, 184, 190-192, 229, 248-249, 264, 268-269, 279-281, 283, 285-286, 301
Sterritt, _____, 157, 159
Steve, 44, 59-61, 65, 72, 99, 163
Stevenson
  McRae, 190, 196, 218
  Robert Louis, 190, 196
Stocky, 59, 67, 71, 73, 77-78
Stokes, John Y. (Lieutenant), xviii, 218, 267, 239, 241, 249, 251, 253, 260, 264, 267, 269-272, 274, 316
Stout, _____, 42, 72-73, 108
Strater, _____, 60-61, 71
Strauch, Harry, 201
Strindberg, August, 181
Sunday, William Ashley "Billy," 14, 17, 21, 44-45, 47, 170
Sunflower University Press, xii-xiii
Swann, Paul, 131
Swiss, 82
Switzerland, 117

— T —

Taft, William Howard, 50, 258, 287

Tapley, _____, 71
Taylor, Everette A., 218, 239
Tennyson, Alfred (Lord), 195
Texas, 236
The Definite Object (Farnol), 142
The Diary and Letters of Alan Seeger, 197
The Forty Five (Dumas), 135, 146
The Green Mantle (Buchan), 140
The Light that Lies (McCutcheon), 155
The Mutiny of the Elsinore (London), 102
The People of the Abyss (London), 122
Theosophy, 225
"The Tales of Hoffman" (Hoffman), 213
The Valley of Fear (Doyle), 91
Thomas, _____, 193, 259
Tiddle, Captain, 191
Toelle, Alan D., xii
Townes, Lieutenant, 233, 239, 241, 246, 248-249, 251, 253, 267, 269-272, 274
Townsend, _____, 120
Treaties Defeated by the Senate (Holt), 303
Treaty of Versailles, 259
Tucker, _____, 231, 239, 241, 246, 248-249, 251, 253, 260, 264, 270, 272
Turner, _____, 248-249, 251, 253, 260, 270
Turoc, 201
Tuttle, _____, 134
20th Aero Squadron, xii, xviii-xix, 215-217, 227-230, 243, 268, 272-273, 275-276, 280, 293, 317
  1st Day Bombardment Group, xix, 214, 219, 228-229, 231, 303

— U —

Ukraine, 168
Union, 282
Union League Club, 256
United Press, 286
United States, xvii, xix, xxiii, 1, 6, 9, 11-15, 24, 27, 35, 37-38, 46, 48, 56, 62, 85, 87, 102-103, 113, 124, 131-132, 134, 160, 168, 189-190, 215, 219, 223, 225, 235-236, 258, 266, 279, 281, 284, 300
  Air Force, 181
  Army, 75, 92-93, 100, 167, 171, 199, 211, 225, 252, 303, 315
  Aviation Corps, 113
  Congress, 49, 206, 286, 291
United States *(continued)*
  Congress *(continued)*
    House, 287
    Senate, 287
  Council of National Defense, 49
  Federal Court, 134
  Marine Band, 282
  National Guard, 48
  Navy, 65, 199, 265
  Signal Corps, 210
  State Department, 287
  War Department, 129, 212
University of California (Berkeley), xxiii, 302
University of Washington (Seattle), xi-xii, 302
U.S. Envelope Co., 148
Utah, 256

— V —

Vanderbilt, _____, 50
Van Loon, 193
Very pistol, 201, 204
Vesta, Nancy, xiii
Vickers machine gun, 99
Vietnamese, 100
Virginibus Puerisque (Robert Louis), 190, 196
von Richtofen, Manfred, 216

— W —

Wait, _____, 199
War Insurance Board, 206
War Risk Life Insurance, 283
War Work Report, 194
Washington
  Seattle, 151
  Snohomish, xii
Washington, D.C., 16, 35, 49, 131, 148, 158, 162-163, 169-170, 174-175, 177, 180, 182-184, 198, 204, 206, 222, 229, 233, 246, 268, 296, 301
  Bureau of Standards, xx, 169, 177, 184, 192, 244, 250, 254
  Committee on Public Information, 206
  Council of National Defence, 204
  Department of Justice, 206
  Enemy Property, 206
  Food Administration, 204
    Communications Division, 205
    Enforcement Division, 205
    Mail Division, 205
    Statistical Division, 205
  Foreign Trades Board, 204
  Fuel Administration, 204
  Mt. Vernon, 285
  National Archives, 230
  Office of Air Force History, 230
  Potomac Park, 282
Washington, D.C. *(continued)*
  Rock Creek Park, 246
  War Industries Board, 204
Washington, George, 166
Waters
  Dr., 263
  Stacy, xii
Weanie, 56
Weber, _____, 274
Webster, Daniel, 289
Weimer, _____, 246, 248-249, 251, 253, 260, 270
Wells, H. G., 172, 277
West, Lieutenant, 253, 260, 264, 269, 271-272, 274
Whalen, E. E., 5
White
  Henry, 292
  Jim, 21, 55, 71-72, 192, 253, 260, 264, 271-272, 274
Willard, Daniel, 49
Williams, R. Norris (Second Lieutenant), 119, 190
Williams, Carol A., xiii
Willis, _____, 246, 248-249, 253, 264, 271
Wilmer, _____, 233, 239, 246, 248-249, 250-251, 270
Wilmington, _____, 100
Wilson
  A. H., 172, 176
  Woodrow, 12, 27, 49-50, 106, 133, 159, 188, 193, 199-200, 219, 224, 236-237, 245, 249, 252, 257-259, 265-266, 280-281, 286-287, 291
Wilson War, 193
Wiser, _____, 231, 233, 239
Woman Suffrage, 138-139
Woodruff, Dean "Woody," 28, 44, 182, 257
Woods, Major General, 102
Woolfolk, _____, 246, 248-249, 251, 270
World War I, xi-xiii, xvii, xxiii, 97, 214, 303
World War II, 181, 275, 301-303
Wright Brothers, 52
Wurster, _____, 12

— Y —

YMCA, xxi, 83, 85, 124, 142-143, 152, 163, 166-167, 170, 181, 188, 190, 236, 281
Young
  Fran, 234
  Suzanne, xii

— Z —

Ziegfeld's Follies, 257